D1213267

The Dutch Barrier
1705–1719

Δ = *Barrier Fortress*

THE SOUTHERN NETHERLANDS IN 1715

The Dutch Barrier
1705–1719

By the late

RODERICK GEIKIE

AND

ISABEL A. MONTGOMERY

With a Memoir of Roderick Geikie by

G. M. TREVELYAN

and a General Introduction by

P. GEYL

GREENWOOD PRESS, PUBLISHERS
NEW YORK 1968

First Published 1930

Reprinted with the permission of
Cambridge University Press

First Greenwood reprinting, 1968

LIBRARY OF CONGRESS catalogue card number: 69-10096

PRINTED IN THE UNITED STATES OF AMERICA

CONTENTS

Biographical Note *page* xi

General Introduction *page* xiii

Editor's Introduction *page* xviii

PART ONE

THE DUTCH BARRIER FROM 1705–1709

By Roderick Geikie, edited by I. A. Montgomery

Chapter I

The disputes relative to the Provisional Government of the Spanish Netherlands *page* 3

Origin of Anglo-Dutch Treaty for the guarantee of the Hanoverian Succession, in 1706, *p.* 3; dispute between the Dutch and Goes after Ramillies, *p.* 5; Marlborough's visit to The Hague and rapprochement with the Dutch, June, *p.* 8; the Emperor offers Marlborough the government of the Spanish Netherlands, *p.* 13; indignation of the Dutch: Marlborough refuses the offer, *p.* 18; Provisional "Condominium" of the Maritime Powers, July, *pp.* 24–32; relations between Marlborough and the Emperor, *p.* 32.

Chapter II

The Barrier Treaty in 1706 *page* 38

Relation of the government of the Spanish Netherlands to the Barrier Treaty, *p.* 38; the Dutch raise objections to the guarantee of the Protestant Succession, *p.* 39; the Succession Treaty made reciprocal by the inclusion of the Dutch Barrier claim, 2nd–16th July, *p.* 43; attempt to define the Dutch demands, 17th August, *p.* 49; the Dutch vindicate their claim, *p.* 54; the English reject the Resolution, *p.* 56; effect of French peace proposals of July and August upon the Barrier Treaty, *p.* 58; Buys and Godolphin dispute methods of negotiation with France, *p.* 62; effect upon the Dutch position with regard to the Barrier Treaty, *p.* 69; the preliminaries of November 1706, *p.* 70; fruitless conferences on the Barrier between Marlborough, Sinzendorf and Heinsius, *p.* 74; Dutch conception, *p.* 75; Austrian view, *p.* 76; fatal indecision of Marlborough, *p.* 78; Heinsius hopes to come to an agreement with England, *p.* 80; Charles confirms the offer of the Patent, fury of the Dutch, *p.* 83; deadlock in Anglo-Dutch negotiations over Ostend, January 1707, *p.* 87; review of the Dutch position at the end of 1706, *p.* 87.

Appendices

RODERICK GEIKIE

THOSE who knew Roderick Geikie, only son of Sir Archibald Geikie, are less numerous than they were. But it is safe to say that all of them vividly remember him, even if it were only as he appeared on the amateur stage. He was one of the unforgettable experiences of life.

It was my privilege to know him, a little at Harrow and more at Cambridge. The stage did not then claim so much time and thought at school and college as it does to-day, but wherever Geikie went he made the drama a feature of the common life, not by advertisement or imposition of his will, but because he was so great an actor. I first remember him as a French soldier in a little French scene we were acting on Harrow Speech day: I remember feeling dimly that greatness had come among us—great art though in a form so friendly and unpretentious. More will recall him at Cambridge in *Our Bitterest Foe* at the A.D.C. with the late Reginald Balfour and the present Lord Lytton, and in 1894 his "tender, grave, Hellenic speech" as Iphigenia in Tauris.

It may seem strange by some standards that a man so modest, sane and tenderly considerate of all others should have been so great an artist. And more remarkable still that so great an artist should have been so fine and patient a scholar as the work now published shows him to have been.

He and I were contemporaries and friends, and were rivals in the History Tripos. We both took the Queen Anne Wars as a special period and often talked about them together. Between us we visited all the "great four" battlefields. He visited Ramillies, Oudenarde and Malplaquet, and I plumped for Blenheim, and sure enough it was Blenheim in the Tripos papers! He followed up the subject and won a King's Fellowship with the dissertation now first presented to the public, on the Dutch Barrier Treaty, the hinge of European diplomacy for that generation. I was a less faithful subject of Queen Anne, but now that after many years I am returning to her allegiance,

I am at once struck by the very remarkable qualities of Geikie's work, and the great value his researches will be to all future students of the period. Thirty years ago people did not publish historical dissertations and theses as much as they do now. It has lain long in the King's Library, but the King's authorities are most willing that it should now be published. They, too, would fain have some memorial of one of the most gifted and sweet-natured of the sons of their College. It is part of the pathos and tragedy of life that there is no way of recalling his dramatic power as this will perpetuate his scholarly gifts.

It is a fortunate coincidence that just at the time when the publication of Geikie's work becomes both practicable and specially desirable, we have in Mrs Montgomery a scholar competent both to edit his work and to complete it with her own. The two works together carry the story of the Barrier disputes down to their final settlement.

G. M. TREVELYAN

GENERAL INTRODUCTION

I HAVE no doubt that historians, especially in England and the Netherlands, will welcome the present publication. The diplomatic history of the War of the Spanish Succession has received little attention in both these countries which took so active a part in it. Especially the Dutch side of the story has been woefully neglected, in spite of the industry of certain German historians who for works of a more general nature did some research in the Dutch archives, but who could not, in the absence of all preparatory studies, see things in their proper perspective. In the following theses the curious system known as the Barrier, which was throughout the war the principal aim of Dutch diplomacy, has been made the subject of a searching examination based on Dutch no less than on English documents. By throwing light on unfamiliar aspects, this work should enable historians to obtain a more satisfactory view of the whole of the period.

The Barrier Treaties were an attempt to deal with the problem of the Southern Netherlands. The Southern Netherlands did constitute a problem. They were those ten provinces of Charles V's seventeen, which, situated south of the rivers, had been unable in the revolt against Spain to maintain themselves against the armies of Philip II. Their more fortunate fellow countrymen of the Seven United Provinces had not only kept the Spaniards out, they had in the later stages of the Eighty Years' War pushed forward across the rivers and by annexing the Northern parts of Flanders and Brabant as well as an isolated district of Limburg, they had robbed the Southern provinces of their natural frontier towards the North, so that the character they presented after the peace of Münster was that of a truncated territory very difficult to defend against the attacks of its neighbours. This situation was aggravated not a little by the fact that the Southern provinces, having remained under the subjection of Spain, could develop no active national sentiment to animate them for their own defence even if their distant master had allowed them to exert themselves for that purpose; by the middle of the seventeenth century moreover, Spain had herself entered upon the last stage of an incurable decay. At the same time France, in the first flush of renewed vigour, was resuming old ambitions and in the first decades of Louis XIV's reign succeeded in detaching large slices from the helpless Netherlands: Artois, Walloon Flanders, parts of Flemish Flanders, half of Hainaut. Had Spain been left to her own resources, no doubt Louis XIV would have realised the French national programme of northward expansion.

But in these circumstances the Dutch came to the rescue of their one-time fellow-subjects of the Southern provinces. They were not inspired by feelings of racial or linguistic community, they were inspired, as the North-German powers and England were when they joined in the great struggle, by considerations of their own safety. It was clear to them that the Southern Netherlands in the possession of France meant the end of their own independence. In the course of a series of wars they interfered ever more deeply in the defence of Spain's threatened dependency and in the end, as sketched in the ensuing pages, elaborated a system which was the nearest approach to annexation without actually infringing upon the rights of sovereign possession vested in the Hapsburg dynasty, which to that conservative age were sacred.

It is interesting to see how the Dutch, under the stress of international circumstances, came to propound a solution that would in a certain sense have repaired the split of the Netherlands from which the critical situation in that corner of Europe had arisen. How vicious a system was the Barrier as they devised it becomes however very clear in the account given hereafter. Far from being a real reunion it was a subjection all the more hateful because accompanied by economic exploitation. When after the disasters of the Revolutionary and Napoleonic era the danger resulting to Europe from the division of the Netherlands was realised even more keenly, the Barrier tradition was still invoked by the statesmen responsible for the establishment of the Kingdom of William of Orange, but he himself no less than they had come to see that only on a basis of equality could the Netherlands be expected to present a united front to France. The evil memories left behind by the Barrier system and the closure of the Scheldt had something to do with the failure of that great experiment, although no doubt the principal causes were the religious cleavage that had resulted from the split in the sixteenth century and the denationalisation of the Flemish middle-class during the twenty years' annexation to France.

In another respect it is interesting to trace the line of development in which the episode treated in this volume has its place. England had from the days of Elizabeth realised the danger of the shores opposite her own being in the control of a great power. This had made her a more or less consistent supporter of Dutch independence in its early and uncertain stages, just as afterwards it caused her to resist the attempt of vigorous France to take the place of enfeebled Spain in the Southern Netherlands. But England never wanted the Dutch state that rose from the revolt against Philip II, to become itself a power of the first rank, and under Charles I and Charles II she strenuously opposed any plans, such as cropped up from time to time (especially in 1632 and between 1662 and 1667), for the reunion to the Northern Republic of the whole or part of the Southern provinces. In spite of the intimate association into which the overwhelming menace of France had forced the two Maritime Powers, this jealousy, the sources of which were largely economic, will be seen to persist in the period treated by Mr Geikie and Mrs Montgomery. It explains the reluctance with which the Whigs assented to the Townshend Treaty and the bitterness with which the Tories assailed it. And yet at that time the commercial and imperial development of England had—as we can see now—little to fear from Holland any more, and the dangers that threatened England in the next century came from the weakness rather than from the strength of the political system in the Netherlands. This explains the fact that in 1814 English statesmen were undismayed by the prospect of Holland acquiring that "noble territory" which to Swift seemed "the only advantage they wanted...to undersell us in every market of the world". And yet again in 1830 the recollection of the competition that English industry and commerce had suffered from Ghent and Antwerp strengthened by the Dutch colonial market, as well as the likelihood of easier economic dealings with two small kingdoms, helped to reconcile them to the undoing of their own handiwork. Whether earlier Netherlands unity was remembered in 1914 who shall say?

The conclusion of the Townshend Treaty and its repudiation constitute a far from edifying chapter in the diplomatic history of either Holland or England. The crudity with which the Dutch used the diplomatic situation in order to squeeze concessions out of their unwilling ally and the blind faith with which they proceeded to sacrifice their last chance of a separate agreement with France to the pledge they had obtained, hardly give a high opinion of their political tact or perspicacity. On the other hand the careful treachery with which the Tory Government made their private arrangement with the common enemy so as to withhold from the Dutch the price that had been promised them for refraining from doing so, and their unscrupulous appeal to the national dislike and contempt of foreigners in order to obtain the necessary support against the country's allies, do not constitute a pretty spectacle. It is small wonder to find an English envoy at the Hague, more than thirty years later, reporting that Mr Buys, then, in his extreme old age, Secretary to the States of Holland, still distrusted the English: "deep in his memory is engraved the recollection of the events preceding the peace of Utrecht".[1]

But more profitable than to discuss the merits or the ethics of the actions of Dutch or English statesmen will be a consideration of the question how it was possible for England to free herself from the pledge given to the States General and to dictate to her indignant allies a peace of her own designing. If the Dutch had seemed to be dictating to England when they forced her to consent to the Townshend Treaty, it was only at the price of surrendering their own judgment on the larger issue of peace or war. The reckless obstinacy with which the Whigs pursued the extreme war aim that Louis XIV could not grant offered to the Dutch an opportunity of which they ought

[1] J. R. Trevor to Lord Harrington, 5 July 1746, F. St. P., Holland, P.R.O.

to have realised the precarious character more clearly than, judging by their attitude at Geertruidenberg in 1710, they did. There was nothing precarious about the superiority of England in the negotiations of Utrecht. As soon as with the Tories a sense of the realities of the political and military situation returned to the counsels of England, the immense disparity in power and in position between the Maritime Powers was bound to assert itself. It was not merely that Holland was beginning to feel the strain after a generation of wars on a large scale, nor that in any case she was, compared with England, intrinsically a weak state. It was more in particular that the smallness of her resources had compelled the Republic to concentrate on the land war, and on the war nearest home, in the Southern Netherlands. Her backwardness in fulfilling her engagements for naval contributions, her failure to keep up her contingents in Spain, the very shortcomings for which the Tory House of Commons so mercilessly reproached her, made it impossible for Holland to prevent England from making with France and Spain the arrangements that suited her concerning the Mediterranean and America. The negotiations of Utrecht afford a striking instance of the importance of sea power in international relations and of the freedom of movement which the possession of sea power and her detachment from the continent impart to the foreign policy of England. It is not the least of the reasons why the treatises that are here presented to the public are worth studying.

P. GEYL

LONDON

7 *June* 1930

EDITOR'S INTRODUCTION

THE second part of this book was originally a thesis for the Ph.D. of London University. While I was engaged on my researches on the subject of the Barrier Treaties, I came across the MS. of Mr Geikie's work. As it was still unpublished, my thesis included some preliminary chapters on the period covered by Mr Geikie and now dealt with in Part I. When, through the kindness of Professor Trevelyan, I was given the opportunity of incorporating the two MSS. into one book, certain alterations were necessary and my own thesis was considerably shortened in order to avoid repetition.

My warmest thanks are due to Professor Geyl for his generous assistance and many valuable suggestions, to Dr Japikse and the officials at the Rijksarchief, by whose aid I was enabled speedily to find the necessary Dutch material for my researches, and to my husband for his help in reading the proofs.

In 1715, the signature of the Barrier Treaty between the Emperor and the Maritime Powers completed the treaties by which the War of the Spanish Succession was concluded. The Barrier Treaty dealt with the security of the Southern Netherlands, a problem older than that of the Spanish Succession.

The conception of a "Barrier" arose in the seventeenth century,[1] when it became necessary to maintain a line of fortresses along the French frontier for the defence of the Southern Netherlands. The decline of Spain deprived the inhabitants of those provinces of any adequate assistance from their overlord, and they found a protector in their Protestant neighbours, the United Provinces.

The Dutch, no longer threatened by Spain, found in the rising power of France a new threat to their independence. For this reason, the preservation of the Southern Netherlands became of the utmost importance, as it was a guarantee of their

[1] Willequet, "Histoire du Système de la Barrière" (*Annales des Universités de la Belgique*, vol. VI, 1848).

own integrity. At first, the States confined their assistance to troops and money, but from this arose the idea of undertaking the defence of the Barrier or key fortresses themselves. The Dutch aim was to obtain a recognition of their right to garrison these fortresses. Experience taught them what strongholds to demand. The thin line of fortresses from the Meuse to the coast which was arranged at Nymwegen (1678) proved inadequate. After an effort to obtain more at the Congress of Courtrai (1684), the peace of Ryswick marked a further gain on the part of the United Provinces. "Mixed" garrisons (garrisons of troops of the King of Spain and the Dutch) were to be permitted to garrison Mons, Charleroi, Namur, Luxemburg, Nieuwport and Oudenarde.

With the conclusion of this treaty closed the first stage of the history of the Barrier. When the problem was next discussed, the Dutch advanced far greater claims. At the same time the probable partition of the Spanish Inheritance made conditions very different from those in which the conception of the Barrier had arisen. If the new overlord of the Spanish Netherlands were the Archduke Charles, the Hapsburgs' power would seem to make Dutch assistance unnecessary. Amid the alarms occasioned by the capture of the Barrier fortresses by French troops on February 6, 1701, this fact passed unnoticed and the Dutch were more than ever determined to gain an adequate Barrier. The first expression of their claims was made during the negotiations which were carried on at the Hague from February–August 1701, between the French Ambassador, d'Avaux, the Dutch and Stanhope, the English Plenipotentiary on whose admission to the discussions the Dutch insisted.[1] On March 22, an important conference was held in which the Maritime Powers referred to the abrogation of the Partition Treaty of 1700 by Louis XIV's recognition of the will of Charles II and demanded reasonable satisfaction for the Emperor. The States General demanded the evacuation of the Spanish Netherlands by Louis and the cession to the Dutch of Venloo, Roermond, Stevensweert, Luxemburg, Namur, Charleroi, Mons, Dendermonde and St Donas. Further they

[1] Legrelle, *Guerre de Succession en Espagne*, vol. IV, p. 117.

stipulated that they should be given power to appoint such troops as they thought fit to those garrisons, to nominate the governors and all military officials, and to repair and maintain the garrisons (Articles III–VII). Finally they declared the Spanish Netherlands to be inalienable (Art. VIII) and asked for the confirmation of the privileges granted them by the Treaty of Münster (1648). This document was accompanied by one signed by Stanhope, in which the same terms were stipulated, with, in addition, a claim that English troops should be permitted to garrison Ostend and Nieuwport.

Although the d'Avaux negotiations came to nothing and war was declared in September 1701, the enunciation of the claims of the Maritime Powers in the Spanish Netherlands is of great importance in the development of the Barrier principle.

In the first place, it expressed the Dutch determination to obtain much more extensive powers in the Southern Netherlands, whether according to the March proposals, or to those advanced by the Regents of Amsterdam, that the Dutch should be given Spanish Guelderland, Damme and Dendermonde.[1]

Secondly, the English claim to garrison Ostend and Nieuwport revealed not only the intention to assist in the preservation of the Southern Netherlands, but also an incipient jealousy of the United Provinces. It should not be forgotten that the Maritime Powers were rivals for the trade of the Southern Netherlands and that the towns important in a military sense were also important commercially.

Finally, although these claims were advanced for the protection of the Southern Netherlands, they were not calculated to appeal to their future overlord,[2] who would in all probability be able to undertake their defence alone, and who would accordingly resent such limitations on his sovereignty.

These divergent interests proved a stumbling-block to the conclusion of the Grand Alliance; accordingly those articles which concerned the Barrier were worded with a vagueness which, while concealing all dissensions, left the way open for future disputes. By the 5th Article the Allies pledged themselves

[1] Legrelle, IV, p. 140.
[2] Cf. p. xix.

to "make all possible efforts to retake and conquer the Spanish Low Countries, to make them serve as a dyke, rampart and Barrier, to separate France and the United Provinces" and by the 9th Article, when peace was made "to find adequate means of making the States secure by the afore-mentioned Barrier".[1]

It is with the definition of the Dutch Barrier and with the problems arising from this definition that we are concerned. The foregoing sketch of its history during the seventeenth century has been made in order to show that the statesmen employed on this task continued to work along lines already laid down for them, in dealing with the problem of the Southern Netherlands after the readjustment of the Spanish inheritance. In the process of definition, one important distinction may be noted, between the Treaties of 1709 and 1713 and that of 1715. The two former, since they were made between the Maritime Powers only, represented their designs in the Southern Netherlands; the third Treaty, between the Maritime Powers and the Emperor, contained the actual concessions granted by the Sovereign. The concessions of 1715 fell far short of Dutch hopes after the treaty of 1709, and even of the modified pledges given by the Tories in the Treaty of 1713.

ISABEL A. MONTGOMERY

EDINBURGH
17 *June* 1930

[1] Translated from the Grand Alliance. The original in French is printed in *Select Documents for Queen Anne's Reign*. (Edited by G. M. Trevelyan.)

PART ONE

THE DUTCH BARRIER

FROM 1705–9

BY

RODERICK GEIKIE

EDITED BY

I. A. MONTGOMERY

CHAPTER I

The disputes relative to the Provisional Government of the Spanish Netherlands

I

THE problem of the Dutch Barrier dates from the Grand Alliance (September 1701), but it was not until May 1706 that a treaty was discussed. So long as the Spanish Netherlands remained in the hands of Louis XIV, who had captured them in 1701, the settlement of Dutch rights in them was of necessity relegated to the future. The battle of Ramillies (1706), by bringing the provinces of Brabant and Flanders into the power of the Allies, at once brought the settlement to the fore. The hostility of Austria, the determination of the Dutch and the power of England prevented a final settlement in that year, but two events occurred which were to influence its development. In the first place, a provisional agreement was made between the Maritime Powers for the government of the newly conquered provinces; secondly, the idea of a mutual guarantee was accepted by the English and the Dutch as a fundamental principle of the treaty and the "Barrier and Succession Treaty" took that definitive shape which it was to assume when finally concluded in 1709.

The conception of a treaty for the guarantee of the Protestant Succession in the house of Hanover, arose out of the Regency Bill, carried in December 1705 by Lord Somers, in opposition to Lord Haversham's motion for inviting the Electress Sophia over to England. Their opposition to the Tory proposal, a proposal which at first sight seemed favourable to the interests of the Hanoverian Court, appeared to the Whigs to need justification in that quarter. The Earl of Halifax, a statesman who combined with steady adherence to the Whig interest, great talents and a captivating personality, was chosen to explain matters to the Elector.[1] It was considered necessary to obtain a guarantee from abroad for the Protestant Succession, and both from geographical position and from community of religion and political interests, the Dutch Republic was marked out as the guarantor. Later in the summer the Dutch raised the objection that it was an unheard of thing for one country to guarantee the internal constitution of another, but this objection missed the real point. What the Dutch were really asked to do, was not to guarantee an internal constitution, but to render assistance, if, on account of that constitution, England was attacked from without.[2] The recognition by Louis of the Old Pretender, as James III of England, in September 1701, was the event, which more than any other, brought England into the Alliance against France. To that recognition, the Regency Bill was the direct rejoinder. But England was not yet strong enough, unaided to throw down the gauntlet to France. She did not in 1705 hold the same position among European nations that she gained after the Peace of Utrecht; and even after the latter date, the events of 1716 showed that the danger she sought to avert was no imaginary one. Beyond this, there was still in 1705 the menace of a separate government north of the Tweed. It is interesting to note how, in the following year, as the prospects of accomplishing the union brightened, the importance attached to the Dutch guarantee of the Protestant Succession became less keenly felt.[3]

This important negotiation was entrusted to the first diplomatist of Europe, the Duke of Marlborough. He and Halifax started together for The Hague and arrived there on the 14th/25th April 1706. On the 8th of May the Duke presented to the States a memorial in which they were requested to consider whether it was not the occasion for them to enter into a

[1] Letter of Lord Somers, 12/23 April 1706, to Elector of Hanover, taken by Halifax. Campbell, *Lives of the Chancellors*, IV, 189.

[2] This point is well put in Stephen Poyntz, *The Barrier Treaty vindicated*, p. 223.

[3] Thus Godolphin wrote to Marlborough on the 18/29 Oct. 1706: "I hope you may soon conclude the Treaty and the guaranty of the succession which will be of less importance to us every day if they go on as well as they have begun in Scotland. The letters to-day from thence give great hope of carrying the Union". Coxe Papers, British Museum.

treaty with Her Majesty, to guarantee the Protestant Succession of England, as being a matter of the greatest consequence for the peace, not of England only, but of all Europe.[1] The reception given to this proposal was surprisingly cordial.

The Deputies (Halifax wrote home) gave him all imaginable assurances of their willingness and readiness to enter upon such a Treaty, to show their inclinations to comply with everything that the Queen desires of them, and that may be for the good and safety of England.[2]

Similarly, Marlborough informed Godolphin that the Deputies had expressed themselves in the most obliging terms imaginable to the Queen.[3] Having been so far successful, Marlborough left The Hague to join the army on the evening of the 9th of May. During the next two months there followed such a rapid succession of startling developments in the fate of the Spanish Netherlands, that the Guarantee Treaty was relegated temporarily to the background.

No battle in the War of the Spanish Succession—unless, perhaps, the relief of Turin four months later—was so immediately productive of results as that of Ramillies. The defeat of the hitherto invincible French arms at Blenheim was, perhaps, more of an overwhelming surprise, but its great consequences were only gradually realised. On the other hand, within a week of the great cavalry charge by the tomb of Ottomond, Marlborough and the Dutch Deputies, already in possession of Louvain, were granting the "Joyeuse Entrée" to Brussels and Brabant.[4] Six days later the estates of Flanders were similarly at their discretion. This torrent of success brought at once into relief the mutual antagonism of Dutch and Imperial interests in the Netherlands. Who should provisionally administer these conquests? The King in whose name they were made, or the Maritime Powers who had made them? That was the great

[1] Memorial printed in Marlborough's *Despatches*, edited by Sir George Murray, II, 491.

[2] Halifax to Harley, 11 May. Record Office.

[3] Marlborough to Godolphin, 9 May; Godolphin to Marlborough, 9/20 May. Coxe Papers.

[4] Gachard, *Documents Inédits concernant l'histoire de la Belgique*, III, 223 (and note). Grant to Brabant, 26 May; to Flanders, 1 June 1706.

question. But this was not all. The difficulty involved far deeper and more permanent issues than the settlement of a satisfactory *modus vivendi* which might continue till the final peace. The Dutch realised that beyond the temporary dispute there lay the permanent question of their Barrier right, which had been so vaguely worded in the Grand Alliance. The time seemed to have arrived when the spoil, for which they had fought for five years, was to be grasped. Should they show weakness at this critical moment, their due reward might be lost to them for ever.

Marlborough, pleased no doubt with his reception at The Hague, sided with the Dutch. The conquests were indeed to be ultimately delivered up to Charles, but for the time being measures were to be taken in the name of the Maritime Powers.[1] To stimulate defection from the Bourbons, he, with the consent of the four Dutch Field Deputies, gave an assurance to the Provinces of Brabant and Flanders that His Catholic Majesty would maintain them in the entire enjoyment of all their ancient rights and privileges. This promise was made in the name of the Queen and the States.[2]

Meanwhile the news of the battle of Ramillies and of the surrender of Louvain brought Count Goes, who held the double post of Imperial Envoy to the Dutch and Spanish Commissioner for Guelderland, upon the scene of action at The Hague. The struggle which was about to ensue between the Dutch Deputies and the Hapsburg Minister had already been enacted on a small scale after the capture of Limburg in the autumn of 1703. On that occasion a compromise had been effected, by which the military power continued in the hands of a governor appointed by the States, while the civil administration of the province was to belong to Charles.[3] At that time the Archduke had nominated Count Sinzendorf as his commissioner, but the employment of this statesman elsewhere had made it necessary to find a substitute for him in the Netherlands. Accordingly, on the 19th of

[1] Marlborough to Heinsius, 25 May, in Vreede, *Correspondence Diplomatique et Militaire de Marlborough, Heinsius et Hop*.

[2] Gachard, *Documents Inédits*, III, 223.

[3] Gachard, *Histoire de la Belgique au commencement du XVIIIme Siècle*, p. 120.

October 1705, the commission was given to Count Goes. He was instructed "to receive into his master's protection and service all towns which should in the future be conquered or submit".[1]

Acting on these instructions, Goes, on the 26th of May, presented a Memorandum to the States, which stated that he had received orders to repair at once to any place, where either a voluntary or forced submission took place and, in his master's name, administer the oath of allegiance. As, therefore, Louvain had just surrendered, and other towns would no doubt follow, he was preparing to execute His Majesty's orders, and requested their High Mightinesses to give him all possible facilities for doing so. This referred to the administration of the provinces. As regards "Military Rights", he expressed himself as authorised to come to an understanding with the Dutch.[2] Having handed in this document, and given out that he was going to Brussels, Goes then paid a visit under the strictest secrecy to the Elector Palatine, the Emperor's brother-in-law, at Dusseldorf, to whom he was directed to refer in cases of difficulty and with whom, moreover, it was necessary for him to come to an understanding as the Elector had also been designated as Imperial Commissioner in the Netherlands.[3]

In the meantime the Dutch had authorised their Deputies with the army to take provisionally, in concert with Marlborough, all measures they should judge necessary for the public affairs. They were re-enforced by the Treasurer, Hop, who was to superintend the financial department, and were expressly reminded "not to depart from the principle that the right of possession belonged to the Republic before all others".[4] Goes, on his return from Dusseldorf, found no answer from the States to his Memorandum. Realising that things were not going so

[1] Copy of Patent of 19 Oct. 1705 to Count Goes in the Archives at Blenheim Palace.

[2] Goes to Marlborough, 27 May, enclosing copy of Memorandum. Archives at Blenheim Palace.

[3] Stanhope to Harley, 4 June, "Count Goes parted two days hence in a very silent manner to Brussels". Record Office. Stanhope to Harley, 8 June, "I told you in my last Count de Goes was gone to Brussels, as everybody then believed; but he is since returned hither having, it is said, been only to Dusseldorf". Coxe, *Marlborough*, I, 435–6.

[4] Secret resolutions of the States General, 3 and 5 June, cited by Gachard, *Histoire de la Belgique*, pp. 324, 325.

smoothly for his master's interests as he had anticipated, and that in the face of opposition he was powerless, he applied to Marlborough for assistance.

Hop (he wrote) starts to-morrow for Brussels. If my information is correct, he goes there to sequestrate the revenues until an agreement has been come to with England on what they are to be employed. I do not fail to insinuate my wish that they would take the right course from the beginning with the people of the Netherlands; I am not the only person who thinks this not the right one, but as their High Mightinesses have taken it, I cannot prevent its being pursued. I wait for your answer and help with impatience. With instructions such as mine I would I were in a condition to execute them.[1]

Conscious that he was cutting a poor figure in the dispute at The Hague, Goes announced his intention of going to Brussels to protect the interests of the King of Spain. He received an answer, almost in threatening terms, that he had better not provoke the government of the Republic against him.[2] An appeal for the support of the Imperial pretensions was also made in England through the Austrian Envoy, Count Gallas, but the answer was not encouraging. The ministers asked indignantly whether they believed at the Imperial Court that the cabinets of the Sea Powers wished to defraud Charles III of even a portion of his inheritance.[3]

These growing dissensions made it highly necessary for Marlborough to intervene, and it so happened that he had decided to pay a short visit to The Hague to settle with the States the plan of campaign and the disposition of the troops to be followed through the summer—a question which various circumstances combined to make one of great delicacy. He arrived at The Hague on the evening of Wednesday, the 9th of June.[4] There seemed to the Dutch no doubt as to the frame of mind in which he came. Four days previously he had written to Heinsius,

[1] Goes to Marlborough, 3 June 1706. Archives at Blenheim Palace.

[2] Goes to Emperor, 10 June, cited by Klopp, *Fall des Hauses Stuart*, XII, 86.

[3] Noorden, *Europäische Geschichte im XVIII. Jahrhundert*, II, 343.

[4] Marlborough to Harley, 10 June. Murray. Stanhope to Harley, 11 June. Record Office.

I think it absolutely necessary that I come to The Hague for a day or two, to settle with you the operations of the campaign, and to take the best measures we can to prevent the Comte de Goes and the Elector Palatine destroying what the Deputies and I have done in the name of England and Holland, which has put this country (the Southern Netherlands) in so good humour, that they are generally on our side. The hand of God is so visible with us that if we can hinder the Court of Vienna from troubling the country only this summer I should hope that this campaign would be the best that was ever made in this country.[1]

The three important interviews between Marlborough and Heinsius, Marlborough and Goes, and Goes and Heinsius, which took place on the 10th of June, the day following Marlborough's arrival, mark an epoch not only in the diplomacy of that year but of the whole war. It was a day of triumph for the Dutch. An understanding was arrived at by Marlborough both with Heinsius and Goes, which, had it not been upset by an event a fortnight later, might have successfully established the footing on which the campaign of that year should be conducted. Beyond this, two important principles affecting the whole course of the war were laid down.

The first question for Marlborough and Heinsius to decide was to fix the towns against which the allies should next direct their arms. The Ministry in England were very anxious that it should be Dunkirk. Godolphin plied Marlborough with letters on the subject. As it was a base for French privateers, the capture of this town was of vital importance to England but of comparatively little to the Dutch. Marlborough realised, therefore, that the proposal would raise in the minds of the Dutch the suspicion that the English were fighting for their own interest only. Moreover, the undertaking was for the moment strategically impossible. He fully realised the importance to England of capturing the place, but this, he wrote, "was not to be thought of till we are masters of Nieuwport and Ypres".[2] It was also very necessary to secure Ostend, which would serve as the most direct channel for military communications between

[1] Marlborough to Heinsius, 5 June. Vreede.

[2] Godolphin to Marlborough, 31 May/11 June. Coxe, *Marlborough*, I, 430. Marlborough to Godolphin, 14 and 21 June. *Ibidem*.

England and the Netherlands. His plan of campaign was therefore to take Nieuwport first and Ostend next. Here again a delicate question arose. The Dutch had not forgotten that in the negotiations that took place at The Hague with d'Avaux preparatory to the formation of the Grand Alliance and the declaration of war, England had stipulated for the right to place garrisons in these two towns. William III had at the time expressed his fears to Heinsius that the demand might cause great dissatisfaction in the United Provinces.[1] The memory of it still lived. It was therefore necessary for Marlborough, if he wished to secure the harmony in which the two Maritime Powers had worked together since the beginning of May, to explain himself on this point. He did so by protesting that Her Majesty claimed nothing in the Spanish Netherlands.[2] Marlborough repeated this declaration later in the day to Goes and a few days afterwards wrote a letter to Godolphin which affords further evidence of his sincerity on this point. The latter had urged as a further reason for attacking Dunkirk that they had better take anything that would be of advantage to the British while they could, as whenever peace came he did not expect that any great advantages would be stipulated in it for England,

I see by yours (Marlborough replied) that you do not expect any great advantages for England, when the treaty of peace is once begun. I ask your pardon on being of another opinion, for I think you may expect everything that is for the good and safety of England. I do not mean by that any places in this country, for I am persuaded that it is much more for Her Majesty's service and England, not to be master of any towns in this country, since it would create a jealousy both at home and abroad. I know this should not be the language of a general but I do it as a faithful subject.[3]

Heinsius was delighted with Marlborough's declaration. It had, he said to Goes, entirely destroyed any idea that might

[1] William to Heinsius, 18 March 1701 (Grovestins, VIII, 56), cited by H. Reynald. The demand was made in the penultimatum of 22 March 1701 to France. Legrelle, *Succession d'Espagne*, IV, 117–20.

[2] Hop, in a later interview with the Duke on the subject of the Patent, reminded him of his promise, referring presumably to this occasion. Cp. article on Gispert Cuper's Diary by H. Reynald in the second volume of the *Revue Historique*, 1876. Cuper was one of the four field deputies and evidently an exceptionally broad-minded man.

[3] Marlborough to Godolphin, 21 June. Coxe, I, 430.

have remained with the Dutch as to the previous coveting by the English of Nieuwport and Ostend.[1]

What passed between the English General and the Pensionary relative to the government of the Low Countries can, in the absence of any direct account of the interview, be gathered from the fact that on the strength of it the States, on the 19th of June, threw off their previous hesitation and reserve and drew up first a "Décret Organique", in which they practically arrogated to themselves the supreme power in the conquered provinces, and, secondly, delivered to Count Goes a reply to his Memorandum, in which they informed him that by the Grand Alliance the Spanish Netherlands, although restored to the King of Spain, were at the same time to constitute a Barrier for the States; that it was therefore impossible to permit His Majesty to take possession of the provinces until a convention on the subject had been made as had been done at Limburg[2]; that in the meantime, while all acts were done in the name of Charles, the States General and Great Britain would see that the ancient constitution of the provinces was preserved; and that for the rest, they would be quite prepared to communicate to him the affairs of the country and come to an agreement with him about them.[3]

After his successful interview with Heinsius, Marlborough repaired to Count Goes, who was still waiting for an answer to his appeal, of the 3rd of June, for assistance. It was no light ordeal he had before him. It was easy enough to come to an understanding with the Dutch by talking ill of the Hapsburgs, or with the Imperial Envoy by expatiating on the greed of the Dutch. But how to please both parties and at the same time maintain anything like a consistent policy was a task which a less skilful diplomatist than Marlborough might well have despaired of accomplishing. The general drift of the Duke's advice to Goes might be summed up in the word "Wait". The conversation between the two is important not only in reference to the question of the Southern Netherlands but also to the

[1] Goes to Emperor, 10 June, quoted by Klopp, XII, 88.
[2] Cf. p. 6.
[3] Resolution of 19 June cited by Gachard, *Histoire de la Belgique*, p. 326.

views of the party predominant at that time in England with respect to the ultimate aims of the war. Concerning the Southern Netherlands Marlborough answered that he had found the minds of the secret Deputies so prejudiced that at last he had had to give in. It was impossible to devise a convention about their contributions of troops, with the States of Brabant and Flanders alone, without the assistance of an Imperial Minister. Goes denied that this right belonged to these States; he would use the powers given him to prevent it. Marlborough, dissuading him, bade him wait, and said that he himself would guard the interests of Charles III. "But what shall I report to the Imperial Court", asked Goes?

Write merely (he answered) to the Emperor and the King of Spain, that the Netherlands are for His Catholic Majesty, that the Queen makes no pretention to any part of them nor to any place in the Spanish Monarchy, that she herself will not allow the States General to claim anything in them and that the delay that I ask of you at present is only in order to content the people here, and perhaps even for His Catholic Majesty's great advantage; as I imagine you could not with any self respect, bring the States of Brabant and Flanders to do the things which will be asked of them, although in themselves these things may be just, equitable and reasonable.

Goes asked Marlborough further, whether he agreed with the view that France should be brought back to the limits of the Treaty of the Pyrenees. Marlborough replied that Goes had better discuss that matter with Heinsius. At the end of the campaign he himself would make an effort to unite them firmly on this point and he hoped for success, especially if peace were restored in Hungary. "Should the latter take place", said Marlborough, "I hope to engage the Republic in the re-conquest of the whole Spanish Monarchy."[1]

Goes went to the Pensionary and communicated to him the interview. How much he communicated of it is uncertain, but that he should have gone at all was probably far from Marlborough's intention. But Goes' actions were often weak and

[1] This description of Marlborough's interview with Goes is taken verbatim from the passage in Klopp, XII, 87–8, quoting Goes' despatch of the 8th (this is the date given there) of June. As Marlborough was at The Hague from the 9–11th of June only, this must be the 10th.

ill-considered; he was a diplomat of very different calibre from the Pensionary and the English Duke. Heinsius gathered from the Austrian, that in stating that the Queen demanded nothing in the Spanish Netherlands, Marlborough had at the same time expressed the hope that the Republic would desire as little. A time might come when this hope would fit in very inconveniently with the Dutch plans about their Barrier. Against this, however, was to be put the knowledge, which he also got from Goes, that Marlborough had extended the Queen's intention to lay claim to nothing, to cover the whole Spanish Monarchy, a declaration which the Pensionary received with "particular satisfaction".

Such were the results of the three interviews on the 10th of June. A friendly understanding had been established between Marlborough and the Dutch, the Imperial claims had been relegated to the future, and the two important principles had been laid down in the pledge that had been given that England claimed no part of the Spanish Monarchy as a reward for her assistance and that she would endeavour to recover the whole of that Monarchy for King Charles. It is in the circumstances hardly surprising to find Stanhope writing, "the States seem to have so entire a confidence in the Duke that they will readily consent to everything he proposes without the least scruple or jealousy", and the Duke himself informing the Duchess that he had "all the reason imaginable to be satisfied with declarations these people have made".[1] A fortnight later a bomb had shattered this harmony, leaving an atmosphere of mistrust on one side and disappointment on the other which never afterwards wholly disappeared.

II

The "Entente" between Marlborough and the Dutch reduced the Emperor to a position of absolute helplessness. The remedy that offered itself to him was to sow dissension between the Maritime Powers. With this end in view, he offered Marlborough the government of the Low Countries. It would be

[1] Stanhope to Harley, 11 June. Record Office. Marlborough to Duchess, 10 June. Coxe, I, 432.

difficult to exaggerate the influence of this incident upon the whole course of the war; it fixed for the future the attitude of the Emperor and Dutch towards one another, and the attitude of the most important personality in the war towards both. The opposition raised by the Dutch to the offer placed Marlborough in a most difficult position. Three courses were open to him: to accept the offer openly—that meant the secession of the Dutch; to refuse it definitely—that meant almost a declaration of hostility towards the Emperor and would probably lead to the appointment of someone else as governor, which would only have rendered the situation more impossible; to temporise—Marlborough's public policy combined with his private wishes to decide him in favour of this course. It is quite certain that he keenly desired the lucrative appointment, and it is equally clear that the first outburst of Dutch resentment did not cause him to abandon the hope that both parties might soon be reconciled by the settlement of the Barrier question, and that he might be enabled to assume the governorship. It is almost impossible to decide when, if ever, Marlborough abandoned the secret hope and desire of at last grasping the golden prize. The point is one of great interest, for a definite settlement of it would go far to provide a clue for determining the proportion of self-interest in all his other actions, the real motives of which were as unfathomable to his contemporaries as they have been since to posterity.[1] But from our present point of view—that of international diplomacy—the solution of that difficulty is the less essential in that there is no uncertainty as to his public professions on the subject, which were the objective factors that regulated the conduct of the two Powers principally concerned. The third way seemed the only one that was capable of maintaining the alliance. But, from the moment that he adopted it, Marlborough was forced to adopt with it a "double front" policy towards the Emperor and the States which to the last he was never able to throw off. He embarked upon the hopeless task of supporting equally the Imperial and Dutch pretensions in the Netherlands, while these grew yearly more irreconcilable. He became henceforth the confidential agent of the Emperor,

[1] See special note on this point in Appendix A.

while still forced by circumstances to court the assistance of the States. It was a position which could only be rendered tenable by putting off as long as possible inevitable decisions. The effort was fore-doomed to failure from the first; that the Duke kept it up with success for three years is an astonishing proof of his diplomatic skill. But the process was disastrous for the Duke himself. It schooled him in that temporising indecision which produced at last the inglorious end of a glorious career.

The whole incident has been so grossly misrepresented by Coxe, the chief English authority on the subject, that it is desirable to examine in some detail the circumstances in which the Emperor decided to send Marlborough the Patent. Charles had left with the Emperor a blank Patent for the government of the Southern Netherlands to be filled up by the latter, and Joseph had already decided to fill it up with the Elector Palatine's name, when the disquieting despatch arrived, in which Goes gave a full account of his interviews with Marlborough and Heinsius. It so happened also that at the same time Wratislaw, the Imperial Chancellor, who had been absent in Hungary, returned to Vienna. The inclination described by Goes, of the Dutch to "choose Marlborough for their stadtholder"[1] rendered some action necessary at once. Whether or not the English had only their own interests at heart, and not those of the Hapsburgs, the latter had early realised that only in England could they find an active protector from Dutch covetousness. A month after the battle of Blenheim Wratislaw had written a letter to Leopold pointing out the advantages to be gained from keeping the Duke of Marlborough firmly attached to the Imperial interests.[2] Further than this, there is in the Archives at Blenheim a letter from Wratislaw to Marlborough which almost dispels any doubt that the two had at some time previously to the summer of 1706—probably in the autumn of 1705, when the Duke was at Vienna—discussed the question of the government of the Netherlands and come to an

[1] Klopp, XII, 89. If Goes used these words, they are an exaggeration due no doubt to his state of alarm.

[2] Wratislaw to Leopold, 12 Sept. 1704, quoted by Landau in his *Geschichte Kaiser Karl VI als König von Spanien*, p. 532.

understanding that, if the opportunity occurred, it should be offered to him. After the receipt of Goes' despatch Wratislaw represented strongly to the Emperor that in the circumstances the Elector Palatine was not suitable for the appointment and that Marlborough was the only man who could curb the greed and ambition of the States. He experienced some difficulty in getting the Emperor to consent to alter his decision, owing to what he styled "the blind complaisance certain persons have for the Elector Palatine". But at last, supported by the Duke of Moles, who was about to leave to assume the post of Imperial Ambassador at the Court of Barcelona, he carried his point. Marlborough was nominated as "Representant" rather than "Governor"—a distinction made to mollify the Elector—and Goes was joined with him to act for the Duke in his absence, and especially, as being a Catholic, to take charge of religious matters.[1] The Elector Palatine and Count Goes were favoured with many explanations. To the former it was represented that the decision was necessary for the good of the common cause, and that the appointment could only be for a short time, as neither Marlborough's foreign services nor his religion would allow him to remain in such a post. Goes was told that while it had been ascertained that the English commander was not averse to such a "Representance", it was to prevent the feared dismemberment of the Spanish Netherlands that such a remarkable step had been taken. In return the Imperial Court expected from Marlborough a prompt transference of part of the revenues of these provinces to the Hapsburg sovereign and likewise the admission that the Imperial Court was supreme in the Southern Netherlands. Care had been taken to restrict the authority of the English Duke as much as possible—the military affairs indeed were to be left to his judgment—but on questions of foreign policy a Junta, composed of well-disposed inhabitants devoted to the Austrian House, should advise Marlborough. The civil administration should be carried on by Charles III and exclusively through persons in the King's confidence. Finally, the head of the House of Hapsburg contemplated Marlborough's appointment as provisional only. Yet Coxe

[1] Wratislaw to Marlborough, 16 June 1706. Blenheim Archives.

describes this offer as being made in "a transport of joy and gratitude", and as being a "spontaneous and unexpected proof of favour and confidence".[1] Marlborough received the commission on the evening of the 27th of June, and it is clear from his letters that he did not anticipate that any difficulties would be raised to his accepting it. It was however advisable to have a clear understanding with the Dutch on the subject, and for this purpose it would be very instructive to see what the attitude of an influential Dutch statesman would be when informed unofficially of the news. Hop was at Brussels at the time. Marlborough's first action was therefore to write and request him to come to the camp as he had a piece of news of the greatest consequence to communicate to him.[2] In the next place it was necessary to sound the all important Pensionary on the subject. He communicated the news to him in strict confidence, adding

> I will do nothing in this matter, but what you shall think best for the public good;...though I must do nothing till I hear from Her Majesty, yet your thoughts are what shall govern me; for I do assure you, if they would give me this country for my life, I would not take it, if it were not liked by the States.[3]

There remained only one more step to be taken, namely, to obtain the Queen's definite consent to this continental commission; but here again he anticipated no difficulty. With confidence in the result, he declared to Godolphin that he would, with all the submission in the world, be pleased in this matter with what the Queen should think was for her interest.[4] Two days later, having in the meantime received further particulars with regard to the commission from Goes, he wrote to thank the Austrian Ministers. He kept back his answer to the Emperor himself until he could give a definite decision. To Prince Salm, however, he expressed his gratitude, assuring him that he would neglect nothing in his endeavour to render himself worthy of this great favour, and that, so far as in him lay, all

[1] Coxe, I, 437.
[2] Marlborough to Hop, 28 June. Murray.
[3] Marlborough to Heinsius, 28 June. Vreede.
[4] Marlborough to Godolphin, 28 June. Coxe, I, 438.

the revenues of the country would be employed in the maintenance of a strong body of troops for the service of His Catholic Majesty. Special letters of thanks were also sent to Wratislaw and Moles, for their share in obtaining for him the Patent, in which letters he expressed the hope that from the manner in which the appointment had been made the Elector Palatine could hardly take it ill.[1]

Then the process of disillusionment began. Hop appeared on the 1st of July, and the interview between them opened Marlborough's eyes to the possibility of the coming storm. Hop, in describing the interview afterwards to the four Dutch Deputies, said that he found the Duke much troubled and undecided what to do. He asked Hop for his opinion. The latter replied openly that "there was no disguising the fact that it was a very delicate business and one that might cause misunderstanding"; he pointed out that the Queen had declared at the time of the formation of the Grand Alliance, that she claimed nothing in the Spanish Netherlands, that the Duke had both made this Treaty himself, and had, moreover, only a few days before, made a declaration to the same effect not merely to the Deputies with the army but also in a conference at The Hague. He feared that the acceptance of the offer would certainly be considered a breach of the declaration.[2] His words seem to have made a great impression on Marlborough, who at once wrote home describing Hop's uneasiness at the offer and added that if he found Heinsius of the same frame of mind, he must ask to be excused; "for", said he, "the advantage and honour I might have by this Commission is very insignificant, in comparison to the fatal consequences that might be, if it should cause a jealousy between the two nations".[3] Soon after there arrived a letter from the Pensionary, dated the 30th of June, which still further showed the feeling of the Dutch. The letter was conciliatory, even friendly, in tone but there was no doubt as to its meaning. Heinsius explained that Goes had imparted the news privately to him and went on,

[1] Marlborough to Salm, to Moles, to Wratislaw, 30 June. Murray.

[2] Quotation from Cuper's Diary given by H. Reynald in *Revue Historique*, II (1876), 507.

[3] Marlborough to Godolphin, 1 July. Coxe, I, 439.

Your Grace knows what need there is of delicacy in the handling of affairs at this juncture, if one is to remove umbrage and jealousy, and also what harm such umbrage and jealousy can do to the common cause, and to England and this State in particular...I beg you to consider whether the States, who think it a settled principle that by the Grand Alliance King Charles cannot enter into possession of the Spanish Netherlands before an agreement has been come to about our promised Barrier and Surety, will not be surprised when they hear that His Majesty as also the Emperor, wish to regulate the possession of these territories, in the name of the said King, not only before the formation of any agreement as to our Barrier and Surety but even without having previously consulted them in any manner whatsoever.[1]

The next letters from The Hague dispelled any lingering hopes the Duke might have had. On the 2nd of July the States General was summoned to hear the Imperial letter read. It must have been a dramatic scene. The announcement was received in "astonishment and silence", more eloquent than words. The Pensionary was disconcerted because the news had been read in the full assembly before he had come to any decision upon it. Goes, in his hurry to carry out Marlborough's wishes, had handed the document, not, as usual, to him, but direct to the President of the Week. Heinsius, wholly unprepared therefore, was unable to answer the questions that poured in upon him. Then the torrent of abuse began. The Southern Netherlands, the Deputies declared, had been won back by the arms of the Republic. Neither the Emperor nor the King of Spain had the right to take such steps in the reconquered territory without their consent; the Grand Alliance, the stronghold of their Barrier claims, had been defied. Marlborough would have been the next victim, had not Heinsius been able to hold up before them the Duke's letter, in which he had declared that if he were given the country for his life he would not take it, if it were not liked by the States.[2] Finally two Resolutions were drawn up. The first instructed Vryberg, their ambassador at London, to put all possible

[1] Heinsius to Marlborough, 30 June 1706. Vreede.

[2] Klopp, XII, 92, 93, quoting from Goes to Emperor, 6 July; Goes to Marlborough, 9 July. Coxe Papers. Heinsius to Marlborough, 3 July. Vreede.

pressure on the English Ministers to prevent their returning an answer to the Emperor's letter, without previously consulting the States; the second directed Hop to return to the Duke, to inform him how agreeable to them had been his declaration that he would not act against their wishes; to show him of what consequence to the Republic the step taken by the Emperor would be, if adhered to; what difficulties and jealousies it would create, which might spoil the harmony and destroy mutual trust existing between the two nations; and to dissuade him therefore from accepting the commission, by pointing out that this refusal would win for him as much glory as it would give satisfaction to the States.[1]

After the sitting of the States General, Heinsius had sent for Goes and overwhelmed him with reproaches because of his not having communicated the letter to him previously. Goes pleaded in defence that Marlborough had enjoined him to communicate directly with the States General. Thereupon the Pensionary's indignation fell upon the latter. "He was", the Austrian reported, "so beside himself as I have never seen him, though I have had frequent opportunities for observation."[2] After the interview, Heinsius wrote to Marlborough a second letter in which he said that he could not change the opinions expressed in his first, and that the action of the Emperor still appeared to him as incomprehensible.

I was right (he continued) when I stated in my last that the States would be extremely surprised when they heard about it; for when the letter written by the Emperor to them on this subject, was read in the Assembly there was a general astonishment at his procedure, and if I had not used the permission your Grace gave me in your last letter, to communicate the declarations contained in it, with which they were very well pleased, the result might have been extremely bad.[3]

Slingelandt, the Secretary of the Council of State, declared "that jealousy itself could not regard such a refusal but as the

[1] Resolutions of 2 July, cited by Gachard, *Histoire de la Belgique*, pp. 332–3.
[2] Goes to Emperor, 6 July, cited by Klopp, XII, 93.
[3] Heinsius to Marlborough, 3 July. Vreede.

mark of a magnanimity, of which History furnishes no example".[1] Goes, in the meantime, washed his hands of the whole business. "For my part", he wrote a few days later, "as the new disposition destroys my power, I am in inaction while they (the Field Deputies) are acting at Brussels, but as this is now the business of your Highness, I do not give myself any trouble about it."[2]

Marlborough bowed before the storm. Even before the receipt of these last letters he had, in answer to Heinsius' first letter of 30 June, repeated in stronger terms his previous declaration and assured him, that if the States wished it, he would willingly excuse himself from accepting the commission.[3] Accordingly he now wrote to Godolphin:

> Though the appointments of this Government are threescore thousand pounds a year, I shall with pleasure excuse myself, since I am convinced it is for Her Majesty's service, unless the States should make it their request which at present they are very far from doing; for they have told me that they think it not reasonable that the King of Spain should have possession of the Low Countries till they had assurances of what barrier they should have for their security.[4]

He wrote also to Vienna regretting his inability to accept the commission; but to this point we shall return later. On the 8th, Hop arrived with the Resolution of the 2nd of July, and the final scene in this tragi-comedy took place. Marlborough protested to him that he considered this affair as finished and that he would think no more about it. Up to that moment he had had no answer from the Queen, but should this answer not conform with the intentions of the States, he said he would throw himself at the feet of his sovereign and entreat for permission to disobey her. He added that he had the misfortune to have no son, and that his present riches and reputation were sufficient for him. Henceforth, therefore, his unique object would be to labour for the public good by maintaining the mutual confidence between England and the Dutch

[1] Slingelandt to Marlborough, 3 July, in the Archives at Blenheim.
[2] Goes to Marlborough, 9 July. Coxe Papers.
[3] Marlborough to Heinsius, 3 July 1706. Vreede.
[4] Marlborough to Godolphin, 6 July. Coxe, I, 440.

Republic.[1] It would have been impossible to express himself in stronger terms; small wonder that the Dutch declared themselves completely satisfied.[2] Immediately after this, news arrived from England that made the necessity of refusal even more mortifying to the Duke. Godolphin had communicated the proposal to Somers and Sunderland who both strongly approved. "They seemed to think", wrote the Treasurer, "that there was no reason for the Dutch not to like it just as well as we do, and both concluded with myself that it was one of the rightest thoughts that ever came from the Emperor's counsel." The matter was therefore left to the Duke to do as he should judge best for the Queen's service and the common cause.[3] On the 7th, Gallas and Vryberg presented their respective documents on the subject, the latter "being mighty apprehensive lest the English should make any step towards accepting the offer". Both envoys were informed of the answer previously given to Marlborough.[4] Notwithstanding Vryberg's demeanour the English Ministry was quite unprepared for the opposition raised by the Dutch and on the receipt of Marlborough's letter requesting to be allowed to resign the commission, Godolphin's indignation knew no bounds. "It is amazing", he exclaimed, "that after so much done for their advantage and even for their safety, the States can have been capable of such a behaviour." But he too recognised that there was no alternative but to acquiesce.[5]

Such was in outline the story of the offer and refusal of the ill-starred "Patent", so far as it came immediately before the Dutch. It is far from easy to pass judgment upon their action

[1] Hop to the Greffier Fagel, 9 July, quoted by Gachard, *Histoire de la Belgique*, p. 333; Cuper's Diary quoted by H. Reynald in "Négociations entre la France, l'Angleterre et la Hollande" printed in the *Publications de l'Académie des Sciences Morales et Politiques*, CIX, 508–9.

[2] Heinsius to Marlborough, 14 July. Vreede.

[3] Godolphin to Marlborough, 24 June/5 July. Coxe, I, 438.

[4] Godolphin to Marlborough, 7 July (N.S.). Coxe Papers. "Pour ce que regarde le Gouvernement des Pays Bas Espagnols par interim, la reine a remis cette affaire au Duc de Marlborough pourque L.H.P. puissent être pleinement convaincues combien elle a leur intérêt à cœur"(?). Harley to Vryberg, 9 July (N.S.). In the Letter Book to Stanhope. Record Office.

[5] Godolphin to Marlborough, 4/15 July. Coxe, I, 440.

in the incident. It is clear that such violent opposition on their part was as unexpected as it was galling. Marlborough yielded and he was statesman enough to yield with a good grace. But even a less grasping man might well have been pained at the ingratitude of a people for whom he had done, and apparently was willing in the future to continue to do, so much. His reproaches later in the year when the news of the confirmation of the Patent by Charles caused a fresh ebullition, showed how bitter the sacrifice had been to him. And the remark which escaped him two years later, that if there was need of a governor for the Netherlands he could not see why he should be less acceptable to the Dutch than another, proved that the wound had not yet wholly healed.[1] Unfortunately he had committed himself to a policy of temporising[2] and still hoped to gain the prize. For this indecision he paid the fullest penalty in the long suspense unrequited even at the end—the "Tantalus-torments" as Landau has well called them—which for years he was destined to endure. The result was that his relations with the Dutch never quite regained their old footing of confidence, nor was the friendship between him and Heinsius ever quite so close. Marlborough had given in with scarcely a murmur, but he never forgave. Goslinga thought—not from any feelings of friendship, but from the point of view of Dutch interests—that a fatal mistake had been made in thus alienating a man who would have been more acceptable and less dangerous as governor than anyone else.[3] The Dutch Field Deputy went so far as to attribute the ill-success of the campaign of 1707—the worst blot on the Duke's military reputation and one that has never been sufficiently explained—solely to his spite and resentment against the Dutch. That is no doubt only one of the many misrepresentations in which the *Mémoires* abound, but it is true that this double course which Marlborough now adopted in his dealings with the United Provinces and Austria, led directly to that determined opposition with which three years later he withstood the Barrier Treaty.

This is one side of the picture: the Dutch case was made in

[1] Cf. p. 93, *note* 2. [2] Cf. p. 14.

[3] Goslinga, *Mémoires*, pp. 8–9.

a letter to the Imperial Court, which is printed on a later page.[1] For the present we must turn to the arrangement for the government of the Southern Netherlands, to which the Dutch gave their attention as soon as they heard of the refusal of the Patent by Marlborough. A temporary constitution for the conquered provinces under a Condominium of the Maritime Powers had been traced out, and almost concluded before their relations were disturbed by the offer of the Patent.

Mention has already been made of the instructions which the States General, in order to counteract, or rather anticipate—any action on the part of Count Goes, had sent to their four Field Deputies on the 3rd and 5th of June.[2] Acting on these instructions, the Deputies had received deputations from the Estates of Brabant and Flanders and tendered, as their advice to the States, the suggestion that a Council of State should be established at Brussels similar to that which had existed there before the death of Charles II.[3] The States adopted the proposal and on the 19th of June passed the "Décret Organique" to which reference has been made in dealing with the events of the 10th of June.[4] In this important document the States laid down that the Grand Alliance showed both on what basis and to what end the war was conducted; that among the articles of that Treaty it had been provided that the Spanish Netherlands should be recovered from France, "principally to serve as a barrier for the States"; that these Netherlands were indeed to be given back to King Charles, but not until a convention had been made regarding the rights of the States in them, as had been done in the case of Limburg. Some of these provinces, continued the Resolution, had now been recovered, and it was impossible to leave them without a provisional government. To show that it was intended to restore them to the King of Spain, reserving always the Dutch Barrier right, the provisional government should from the moment of its formation do everything in the name of King Charles and should in particular maintain both the authority and prerogatives of the King on the one hand,

[1] Cf. pp. 29–30. [2] Cf. p. 7, *note* 4.

[3] Letter of the four Field Deputies to the Greffier Fagel, 12 June. Gachard, *Histoire de la Belgique*, p. 325.

[4] Cf. p. 10.

and the rights and privileges of the inhabitants on the other. Meanwhile, the revenues of the country should be employed with economy for its defence, safety and usefulness, as should be judged best by common consent. Accordingly,

for the maintenance and better direction of the Barrier and Surety of the State, according to the project enclosed with the letter of the Deputies with the army, the Council at Brussels shall be re-established by the States in concert with England, and be composed of such persons as these Powers shall judge most useful and capable.

The Deputies were therefore instructed in concert with the Duke of Marlborough to establish the provisional government on the above basis. Finally, one remarkable provision was added. The Deputies were further to proclaim abroad that

their High Mightinesses have absolutely the intention of maintaining the said country in their form of Government under Charles III...in the expectation that this country recognising the deliverance and protection which the States have procured for them, will do its best for the preservation of its own and the common safety.[1]

With this resolution and the corresponding one of the same date to Count Goes, the Dutch, trusting in the support of Marlborough, threw down the gauntlet to the Imperial House.

In drawing up this document the Dutch had overshot the mark in one fundamental point for which they were soon to be taken to task. The Resolution was communicated, in Dutch, to the Deputies at Brussels and to Marlborough. The latter, anxious that some settlement should be arrived at on the subject of the provisional government as soon as possible, sent his copy to the Deputies, saying it would be useful to them and asking them to return him a copy translated into French.[2] He would have acted rather differently had he then known the contents of the Resolution.

The Deputies drew up a scheme establishing the Council of State and submitted it to the Duke on the 23rd of June. The scheme contained the names of the proposed members of the

[1] Resolution of the States General, 19 June 1706. A copy of it exists in the volume of Alexander Stanhope's Correspondence for 1706 in the Record Office.

[2] Marlborough to Field Deputies at Brussels, 24 June. Murray, II, 626.

Council, the instructions to be given them and the oath of allegiance they should be required to give. The Deputies laid particular stress upon impressing upon the Council their dependence upon the Maritime Powers, for fear that, otherwise, they might on the first occasion take the side of anyone who should exhibit a mandate from the King of Spain and thus exclude the Maritime Powers from the direction of affairs.[1] Marlborough approved of the scheme in its entirety but took occasion to impress upon them the care that should be taken not to give any umbrage to the "well-intentioned" among the inhabitants while providing for the future security of the Dutch Barrier.[2] The scheme was then submitted to the States who also approved, subject to the final and formal consent of the Duke.[3] This consent Hop was authorised to obtain. It was with this second object also in view, that the latter paid the visit to the Duke on the 8th of July which has been described already, in so far as it related to the attempt to obtain from him a final and definite refusal of the "Patent". Hop brought with him to the camp a translation of the "Décret Organique" of the 19th of June, from which Marlborough for the first time realised its contents. Smarting already under the pain of the great sacrifice forced upon him by Dutch ingratitude, he now discovered that the same people had authorised the establishment of the Council of State entirely on their own initiative, without any reference to the Queen, and that they had wound up by declaring their intention—as if they alone had a voice in the matter—to maintain the provisional government, and by asserting that they had been the instrument by which the Netherlands had been delivered and protected. After such statements, the provision that England should share in the control and appointments to the Council of State was nothing but the insulting largesse of a superior power. If the Condominium was to be a reality, the final initiative control must be equally with the two nations. Marlborough had just a few days previously cautioned the Field

[1] Field Deputies to Marlborough, 23 June, in the Rijksarchief, cited by Gachard, *Histoire de la Belgique*, p. 327.

[2] Marlborough to Field Deputies, 26 June. Murray.

[3] Secret Resolution of States General, 3 July, cited by Gachard, *ibid.* p. 338.

Deputies to be careful not to offend the "well-intentioned" and now he found himself asked to consent to an arrangement which when known, would not leave a single "well-intentioned" person throughout the country. The Duke was indignant, but Hop attempted to justify the Dutch attitude. The Resolution, he said, was based on the Treaty of the Grand Alliance in which England had not stipulated for anything in the Spanish Netherlands, whereas the Republic had obtained the insertion of important claims concerning her Barrier. From this he argued that the affairs of the Netherlands might, pending a final settlement, with justice be conducted solely under the name of the States and not in conjunction with England, although of course the States had no intention of doing anything without England's consent. This novel claim Marlborough rejected at once; he replied that if he put his signature to such an arrangement without the express order of the Queen he would never dare to set foot in England again.[1] Not content with this declaration he sent a protest at once to Heinsius, pointing out that from the very beginning of the campaign everything had been done in the name of both Sea Powers, to which system he attributed their extraordinary success. "It has always seemed to me", he continued, "that the States had nothing in view beyond a good Barrier and reasonable surety for their country. I pray you therefore with all submission to their High Mightinesses to reflect seriously whether such a step can be the real way to succeed in that object."[2]

Two days afterwards Hop broached the subject again but he

[1] Hop to Greffier Fagel, 9 July, cited by Gachard, *Histoire de la Belgique*, p. 339.

[2] Marlborough to Heinsius, 10 July. Vreede. In the translation of this letter given in Coxe, *Marlborough*, I, 442, there is a serious mistake which makes nonsense of the fourth paragraph, as it stands. For the words, "which is perhaps", the words "whether it can be" should be read. The strength of Marlborough's feeling as regards the Dutch Resolution of 19 June is abundantly shown in the two letters which he wrote almost immediately afterwards to Godolphin, and in which he expressed the hope that the Treasurer would find some way of not "letting the Dutch play the fool", as he called it. He felt his own position after the Patent incident an invidious one, and thought therefore that the complaints against their conduct would come better from other sources. With great emphasis does he impress upon his English friend that the great towns in the S. Netherlands would sooner be under any nation than the Dutch.

found Marlborough immovable. On the 13th of July, therefore, the States instructed him no longer to insist upon the Resolution of the 19th of June but to arrange with the Duke for the organisation of the Council of State in the manner that should seem to him best for the preservation of harmony between the two nations.[1] Even on the receipt of these instructions, Hop with the tenacity characteristic of his race, kept them back for a time; when at last he communicated them, the Duke approved of everything that had been done by the Deputies at Brussels and Hop could write that the understanding between them was complete.[2]

Three days later, on the 21st of July, an "Acte d'Établissement", creating a Council of State to regulate the public affairs of the Provinces of Brabant, Flanders and Mechlin, was drawn up by Marlborough and the Deputies in the name of the Queen and States, to replace the Resolution of the 19th of June. The Republic had to share with England the initiatory power, but her interests were not neglected. In the first section of the Act the Dutch Barrier claim was fully recognised; the fourth and fifth forbade the Council to obey any orders from without, except with the previous consent of the two Maritime Powers, or to take any important resolutions without their concurrence; by the sixth the revenues of the country were apportioned principally to its defence; and the seventh declared that this system should remain in force until the two powers should agree to another arrangement with King Charles.[3] Possessed already by this the letter of the constitution, of an equal share of the supreme power, the Dutch element in the Condominium in actual practice became supreme. So long as Marlborough remained on the spot his personality and position would leave him the dominant factor, but neither of his successors, Stepney, nor Cadogan, were the men to maintain this ascendancy. In February 1707 the four Dutch Deputies were replaced by a permanent commission of two, Renswoude and Van den Berg.

[1] Secret Resolutions of 13 July, cited by Gachard, *Histoire de la Belgique*, p. 340.

[2] Hop to Greffier, 18 July. Gachard, *Histoire de la Belgique*, p. 341.

[3] The "Acte d'Établissement" is given in full in Gachard, *Documents Inédits*, III, 237.

The former was soon entirely subordinate to his more active comrade who became, as it were, Viceroy of the Netherlands and ruled them with the uncompromising spirit of a characteristic Dutchman. The United Provinces had planted her foot firmly on the conquered prize. Henceforth she had but to choose her portion and to throw round it the impregnable rampart of an English guarantee.

There remained one thing more for the States to do before the thorny question of the government of the Netherlands could be removed from their list of current diplomacy. The "Acte d'Établissement" had been the objective result of an (outwardly) complete understanding with England in the matter; some attempt must be made to come to a similar understanding, for the future, with the Emperor. The task of framing the despatch which should attempt this Herculean labour was entrusted to Hop. The Imperial letter informing the States of the "Patent" offered to Marlborough still remained unanswered. The Duke and Heinsius desired the Dutch Treasurer to prepare a reply to this which might be sent to Vienna as the expression of both parties in the Condominium. Hop prepared a draft accordingly, which, when approved by Heinsius, was submitted to Marlborough who observed in returning it that he was far from claiming to make any correction in it. The draft was translated into Latin by the Field Deputy Cuper and despatched to the Emperor on the 12th of August reaching Vienna on the 24th.[1] This dignified and moderate remonstrance sums up, most clearly and logically, the whole Dutch attitude with regard to their Barrier. The letter recapitulated the claim to a Barrier, which the Dutch grounded upon the Treaty of the Grand Alliance, and laid stress upon the reciprocal agreement of the States to surrender the Netherlands to Charles, and of Charles to settle with them their Barrier. These two parts of the agreement were, they maintained, inseparable.

[1] Hop to Marlborough, 1 Aug. Blenheim Archives. Marlborough to Hop, 4 Aug. Murray. Stepney to Harley, 25 Aug. Stepney Papers, British Museum. The letter of the States is printed in French in Vreede, p. 73, and there is a copy of the document in Latin in Vryberg's Correspondence, British Museum Add. MSS. 5131. The enigmatical footnotes in Vreede are Heinsius' corrections of the draft.

It is for this reason, Sire, (the letter continued) that we do not believe that anyone can or wishes to claim, or exact, from us that we should give up the said Provinces either wholly or in part, and let His Majesty the King take possession of them and their Government, before we have come to an agreement as to what is due to us, in virtue of the Treaty, as regards our Barrier and Surety.

It went on to describe how shadowy and insecure had been the Barrier promised them in the previous wars; how those responsible for the maintenance of the fortresses had left these without provisions or defence, till the neglect had culminated in the disastrous treachery of February 1701. It was these memories which had forced the States to view with such dread the prospect of this all-important country passing into the hands of a foreign ruler before their safety had been secured, and had induced them to dissuade the Duke from accepting the Patent. Finally the assurance was given that by the Council of State which had been re-established all the rights and prerogatives of King Charles III would in the meantime be safely guarded.

Had it not been for Marlborough's good advice, this letter would have been absolutely ignored by the Austrian Court. As it was, the reception given to it was little better than rejection. After three weeks delay an evasive reply was sent to Bruyninx the Dutch Envoy, to the effect that the letter had been forwarded to the King of Spain, and that till his pleasure could be known, no declaration from the Emperor could be given upon it.[1] Six weeks later, Wratislaw wrote to Charles that in the circumstances it was hopeless to resist the Dutch refusal to admit a Spanish governor. "One must", he confessed, "accept the lesser evil and content oneself with their promise to devote the revenue to the raising of troops and the continuation of the war."[2]

Hop's despatch had failed to produce the desired reconciliation. Its failure to do so was perhaps a foregone conclusion. The Emperor had been thwarted by what he considered a petty republic, and he had not that which Marlborough had to such

[1] Stepney to Harley, 15 Sept. 1706. Stepney Papers, British Museum.

[2] Wratislaw to Charles, 31 Oct. 1706, in the selections from their correspondence, edited by Arneth, and printed in the *Archiv für oesterreichische Geschichtsquellen*, Vienna, XVI, 1856.

a conspicuous degree, the art of yielding with a good grace. Nor was this despatch a solitary fancied insult which he saw himself called upon to swallow; it had been heralded by a long expostulation from the same quarter on the Münster election,[1] and was followed shortly by an angry remonstrance at the bigoted folly which dissipated upon an unnecessary war with the Hungarians those Imperial forces which should have been concentrated against France. To add to the friction, the States' two Envoys, Rechteren and Bruyninx, were unpopular for their plain speaking at an arbitrary court, where, as Stepney complained, "no man of principle could serve either with ease or reputation".[2] The provocation was, however, not all on one side. With success the Republic became defiant.

Both nations (observed the same pungent critic later in the year) are equally incapable of bearing prosperity with moderation. Since

[1] It is fortunately unnecessary in this connection to do more than refer to the long wrangle between the States who supported the Bishop of Paderborn and the Emperor who supported the Bishop of Osnabrück for the See of Münster. The chief importance of the dispute for our present purpose, is that it brought the English to the side of the States against the Emperor.

[2] Stepney to Cardonnel, 21 Aug. As to the Hungarian war Stepney to Harley (Private), 4 Sept., "A letter has been sent to Mr Bruyninx for the Emperor wherein the States General complain heavily that our congress (with the Hungarians) was dissolved so abruptly. They have likewise answered Prince Racotsky's letter in very obliging terms. But I don't see what effect either of these letters can have, since the Court seems resolved to proceed after their own methods, without having the least regard to any remonstrances which shall be made in favour of the Hungarians". The state of the tension which the relations between the Imperial Court and the Dutch had now reached is further disclosed in the following curious passage in a letter from Harley to Stepney, 27 Aug./7 Sept. (Stepney Papers), "I understand the States have sent positive orders to their Plenipo^{ty} to return, and a very strong letter to the Emperor on the subject of breaking off the negotiation with the Hungarians. It is very plain that there is a faction among them which would be very glad to drive matters to extremity with the Emperor, and at the same time either embroil the Queen at your Court, or have some handle to complain of our conduct in order to have a better colour of setting on foot their negotiation for a peace with France. It is too true that the Emperor's Ministers give great occasion to be angry and their pride is equal to their impotence. Some of their Ministers—not Wratislaw, for that would have been no wonder—have written a very impertinent letter, which has fallen into Dutch hands, that there are but two powers in Europe, the House of Austria and the House of Bourbon, and that all the rest must attach themselves to one of those two, and a great deal other such peddling politics; and those in Holland are justly provoked at the arrogance of a Court which is scarce 'magni nominis umbra'".

the victory of Ramillies I have perceived the Dutch are apt to assume much to themselves, and have abated a great deal of that deference which they used to show to the (Imperial) Court.[1]

The change did not escape Count Goes, who through the summer watched with dismay the control of affairs passing more and more into the hands of the Maritime Powers. "England and the United Provinces", he lamented, "will settle our affairs between themselves and present the decision to us with the words: 'Eat, Bird, or die.'"[2]

III

We have endeavoured to describe the relations of the States, firstly with Marlborough, and secondly with the Emperor, as to the government of the Netherlands; we must now turn to the third combination and trace the arrangement on the subject made between the Duke and the Hapsburgs.

Marlborough's first letter of thanks to Vienna on the 30th of June was written in the full hope that he would be able to accept the Patent, but between it and the date of his next communication, arrived the letters from Heinsius, from which he gathered that in all probability this would be impossible. On the 7th of July he sent a copy of the Pensionary's letter of the 3rd in the strictest confidence to the Prince of Salm, deploring the jealousy which had been shown by the Dutch and expressing the fear that he would be obliged under the circumstances, to decline the commission. He was waiting for the answer from England before replying to the Emperor.[3] Four days later that reply arrived, and during that period his last decisive interview with Hop had taken place. On the 12th he wrote to the Emperor, professing unspeakable gratitude, but informing him that although the Queen had indeed sanctioned his acceptance of the commission, he could not in the interests of the common cause, take advantage of it yet. In the meantime, he would do his utmost to maintain the authority of the Imperial House in

[1] Stepney to Harley from the Court at Cambron, 24 Oct. 1706. British Museum.

[2] Gallas despatch of 5 Oct. 1706, cited by Klopp, XII, 222.

[3] Marlborough to Salm, 7 July. Murray.

the Netherlands.[1] The Imperial Ministers recognised with keen regret on the receipt of Marlborough's letter of the 7th, that they would probably be unable to carry their point. Objections from the States had indeed been expected.

> I never doubted such a result, (wrote Wratislaw to the Duke) knowing on what principles of avarice or parsimony these gentlemen wish to take absolute possession of all that the arms of the allies place within their grasp; that was one of the strongest reasons for which I urged that the government should be conferred on you.[2]

What very much surprised the Imperial Court was the pretension on which the Dutch actually based their objections, namely, that the Spanish Netherlands should not be restored to Charles till the Barrier question was settled.

> It is certain (observed the same statesman) that the Grand Alliance gives the Dutch no authority for such a pretension, and you will remember that during the presence of the King of Spain at The Hague, they, after a long wrangle, yielded the point and allowed Count Sinzendorf to receive the homage of the Province of Limburg, in the name of the King of Spain. I cannot therefore see how they can refuse at the present time to allow the same arrangement for the rest of the Netherlands.[3]

The Limburg incident was thus twisted by the Austrians to support a contention exactly contrary to the interpretation put upon it by the Dutch. The former were in a difficult position. On the one hand, they had had no intention of making a decision as regards the Barrier for some time to come, fearing no doubt that the Dutch—of whom Marlborough truly remarked that "when they had misfortunes they were desirous of peace upon any terms, and when blessed by God by success were for turning it to their own advantage, without any consideration how it might be liked by their friends and allies"[4]—would, when once their Barrier had been granted to them, insist upon making peace. On the other hand, they fully realised that it was necessary to come to some arrangement before peace

[1] Marlborough to Emperor, 12 July. Murray.
[2] Wratislaw to Marlborough, 14 July. Blenheim Archives.
[3] Wratislaw to Marlborough, 27 July. Blenheim Archives.
[4] Marlborough to Godolphin, 14 July 1706. Coxe, I, 443.

negotiations began, lest during these the French, in order to sow dissension, might endeavour to detach the Dutch from the Alliance by advantageous offers.[1] Then Marlborough's letter of the 12th arrived. The allegiance of Marlborough was the Austrians' main support in this difficulty and they caught eagerly at the word "yet" with which he had qualified his inability to accept the Patent. The Court was in the greatest state of indecision and could only write and ask the Duke for further advice in case he found himself compelled to refuse the offer altogether. They pointed out that the Dutch could not be allowed permanently to act as they were doing now, and that England must intervene somehow or the impertinence of the Dutch would become unbearable. Absolute reliance was therefore placed upon the Duke. Gallas was to be given no instructions whatever for the present and Goes was told to refer himself in all things to the English commander. At the same time, the envoy at The Hague was directed to make another effort to obtain the consent of the Dutch to the Patent and to explain to them that things could not possibly continue on their present footing.[2] This was the Austrians' last card and it failed. They had now no hope for assistance unless from Marlborough and England; but the Duke could only tell them to wait. They were unable to carry their point as to the government of the Netherlands and had perforce to accept the Condominium instead. Nor was this all. They had the mortification of learning at the same time how far short of the other this second alternative was, since they were powerless to intervene, although the Netherlands might become disaffected through tactless administration.

Marlborough's batch of replies by the next post brought the Austrian councillors but little assistance. He rightly impressed upon them that it would be absolutely fatal to the Alliance at the present moment if things came to an open rupture. His advice was therefore to defer action till the end of the campaign. He took the opportunity, however, further to ingratiate himself with the Imperial party. He had already sent them a copy of

[1] Salm to Marlborough, 24 July 1706. Coxe Papers. Stepney to Cardonnel, 25 Aug. Stepney Papers, British Museum.

[2] Wratislaw to Marlborough, 4 Aug. Coxe, I, 444. Salm to Marlborough, Sinzendorf to Marlborough. Coxe Papers. Emperor to Goes, 4 Aug. Blenheim Archives.

the "Acte d'Établissement" and assured them that so far as he was able, the Council of State should be employed in the Imperial interest, and this arrangement had been accepted at Vienna as a second best to his acceptance of the commission.[1] But complaints of the Dutch harshness in the Netherlands were so plentiful that it was necessary for him to dissociate himself from these proceedings. He declared that he was far from approving all the steps that were taken at Brussels, but that though he there insinuated his disapproval, the state of tension prevented him often from daring to insist. He added, as a further explanation, that he had not the time to give his due share of supervision to the Condominium and that he had therefore requested the Queen to entrust that duty to some other official, who should remain at Brussels.[2]

Shortly before the arrival of Marlborough's letters of the 21st, the Remonstrance of the States against the Patent reached Vienna to complicate the position. The effect of this document was to shift the point of discussion there from the government of the Netherlands—in which matter the Austrians themselves had begun to realise that it lay beyond them to alter the existing arrangement—to the Dutch Barrier claim. The Remonstrance did not come as a surprise, for Marlborough had carefully prepared the way for it. When on the 1st of August Hop sent him the draft for his approval, he had a copy made for transmission to Vienna. The original draft he returned to Hop with the assurance that he had no correction to suggest; the copy he sent on the 6th of August to Wratislaw with the explanation that he was far from approving all their arguments and that in less delicate circumstances he would not have scrupled to say so.

He was glad, he continued, to send on the copy beforehand in order that the Court might receive the letter, when it arrived,

[1] Marlborough to Salm, 31 July. Murray. Salm to Marlborough, 25 Aug. Coxe Papers.

[2] Marlborough to Salm, Wratislaw and Sinzendorf, 21 Aug. Murray. The fact that the correspondence with the Court of Vienna throughout this summer had to be carried on practically in triplicate, adds a good deal to the complexity of this subject. Fortunately for the historian, this Cerberus of Austrian politics was soon to come to an end. Salm was to be relegated to the oblivion which his incompetence deserved, Sinzendorf constantly employed at The Hague, and Wratislaw left to manage affairs at headquarters.

without prejudice, and reflect seriously upon the disastrous consequences which a misunderstanding between the allies must have, at a moment when the complete failure on the Rhine had given them such cause for complaint. Marlborough's representations had their effect.[1] Hop's letter was accepted and "many things overlooked", though it dealt with a subject which the Court had not "thought of a nature to be taken into discussion".[2] The Barrier question presented two points of difficulty to the Emperor. The first was the period of the war at which it should be granted, the second was how much should be granted. The refusal of the Dutch to admit a foreign governor till their Barrier was settled had at once raised the first point, and, as pointed out above, had placed the Court in a considerable dilemma.[3] The spirited Remonstrance of the 12th of August made the whole question so far a matter of urgency that it became necessary also to consider the second point with regard to which the Emperor took the usual step and consulted Marlborough.

The meaning of the Dutch, (he wrote) if I rightly comprehend it, is not to deliver up the Government of the Spanish Netherlands before the settlement of a firm Barrier for the security of their commonwealth, which, though they have frequently made public professions of, yet the explanation of their bound or Barrier is still left in the dark, to be determined by future agreements. I have given my brother, the King of Spain, an account of this affair, but as it is the common concern of my August House, and consequently affects me, I desire you in confidence to explain to me with all sincerity what you think the States General mean by that demand....I hope if they should endeavour to wrest the Treaty of 1701 to a wrong sense, the Queen will adjust the whole business according to the rule of equity and with so just a balance that the whole Netherlands will have reason to rejoice.[4]

This letter was enclosed in one from Wratislaw in which he informed the Duke that an Imperial Minister would be sent to

[1] Marlborough to Wratislaw, 6 Aug. Murray. The reference concerning the Rhine is to the inactivity and incompetence which the Prince of Baden had again shown there in 1706, after having by the same faults ruined the proposed campaign on the Maas in the previous summer.

[2] Salm to Marlborough, 4 Sept.; Sinzendorf to Marlborough, 8 Sept. Coxe Papers.

[3] Cf. above, pp. 11 and 33.

[4] Emperor to Marlborough, 8 Sept. Blenheim Archives.

the army to discuss the situation with him at the close of the campaign. The letters reached Marlborough at a time when the united efforts of the English Ministry were being employed, hitherto without result, in the task of inducing the Dutch to explain themselves upon the all-important point on which Joseph had requested to be enlightened. "As to the pretensions of the States," wrote Marlborough in his reply to Wratislaw, "you may imagine that it is quite impossible for me to inform you of their extent when I venture to assure you that they don't know themselves." "But this very circumstance" made it imperative for the interests of the whole Alliance to set the doubt at rest at the earliest opportunity. With regard to the Emperor's request that the Queen should arbitrate between him and the States, the Duke explained that the Queen had already entered into the negotiation by a treaty which Lord Halifax had set on foot at The Hague for the guarantee of the English Succession and Dutch Barrier. He concluded with the hope that the minister who was to be sent to discuss affairs with him from Vienna might be fully instructed, and that, if the Emperor considered the occasion favourable to treat of the Barrier question, the minister might accompany the Duke for that purpose to The Hague.[1] Soon afterwards Marlborough learnt with pleasure that the minister chosen was Count Sinzendorf, over whom he had considerable influence.[2] Sinzendorf left Vienna on the 5th of October and reached the camp at the end of that month.

At this point we must break off and pass to the consideration of the long and eventful negotiation, first at The Hague and then in London, through which the Barrier Treaty had passed, when on the 9th of November 1706 Marlborough and Sinzendorf arrived at The Hague, with the fond hope of concluding it.

[1] Marlborough to Wratislaw, 22 Sept. Murray.

[2] On the subject of the selection of Sinzendorf, Stepney has the following remarks, "I don't wonder that Count Sinzendorf has an itch of giving you a visit. The poor man has domestic cares, which render his life here very grievous to him and makes him catch at anything; sometimes he wishes himself in Spain; sometimes is for attending one of our Brides (either for the King of Spain or Prince of Portugal) and would be something either in the Netherlands or at the General Peace merely to get out of the way; for he loses ground here and is in danger of being removed from his office, if he lays not hold of something else in time. He has many distractions and few friends" (Stepney to Cardonnel, 15 Sept. Stepney Papers).

CHAPTER II

The Barrier Treaty in 1706

I

It has been necessary to follow closely the complex diplomacy which centered round the question of the government of the Spanish Netherlands, for the compromise arrived at in that matter was, as it were, the foundation on which the scheme of a mutual Succession and Barrier Treaty was erected. It would be impossible to realise the full bearings of the latter Treaty without taking into careful account the atmosphere of Dutch hopes and fears, secret suspicions of England and open disagreements with the Empire, in which it came into being and passed the first phases of its existence.

When once the all-important and pressing question of the control of the conquered provinces had been decided by Marlborough's refusal of the Patent, and by the establishment of the Council of State under the Condominium, the Dutch were free to discuss the terms of the Treaty by which they should enjoy their Barrier rights in time of peace. We have followed in the last chapter the course of the negotiations for the temporary government of the Netherlands; we must now trace the growth of the other thread, which we may call the origin and gradual definition of the idea of a treaty for the mutual guarantee of the English Succession and Dutch Barrier.

The Memorandum drawn up by Marlborough on the 8th of May, in which the Dutch were invited to join with England in a treaty to guarantee the English Succession in the Protestant House of Hanover was, as has been stated above,[1] favourably received by the States. A week later Stanhope presented to the Deputies a draft of a treaty which Halifax had prepared on the basis of this Memorandum and his general instructions. The Deputies affected to receive this draft also with great cordiality

[1] See p. 5.

and promised to refer the matter to the States General and then to the different provinces, but in an interview with Halifax, Buys, the Pensionary of Amsterdam, expressed some misgivings on one—and that the most important—of the clauses.[1] The draft consisted of seven articles. The first confirmed the previous treaties of friendship between the Queen and the States; by the second the States were to bind themselves to guarantee the succession to the English throne in the Protestant line as established by the Act of Settlement in 1701 and the Regency Bill in December 1705; the third and fourth articles provided for the armed assistance which the two countries should give one another if either should be attacked in consequence of their part in the Treaty. In the fifth article it was suggested that other Princes of the Grand Alliance be invited also to become guarantors. The sixth article provided for the recognition by Louis of Anne as Queen and of the Protestant succession. Time, it was stated, had shown the results of the omission in the Peace of Ryswick, of a clause for the succession as apart from the recognition of the actual reigning sovereign. All efforts were therefore to be made by the Queen and the States at the eventual peace conferences, to compel Louis to recognise the Hanoverian Succession. No negotiation for peace should be entered into until this recognition had been agreed to. The seventh clause was of a purely temporary nature.[2] It was to the sixth clause that Buys raised his objections.

I have given my reasons for it, (wrote Halifax on the 18th, already on his way to Hanover) and I think, convinced those that spoke with me that it is of that consequence for settling the future and lasting quiet of England that they ought not to make any difficulty in obtaining that for England which is the chief, if not the only particular advantage we are to have at the conclusion of the war.

On the whole he considered that the affair was in a "good way" and his optimism found an echo in the replies sent to him and Stanhope by Harley as Secretary of State.

Halifax arrived at Hanover on the 1st of June and remained there for three weeks. His mission was completely successful.

[1] Stanhope to Harley, 14 May; Halifax to Harley, 18 May. Record Office.
[2] Draft of the Treaty in Lamberty, IV, 77, etc.

He acquainted the Court with the negotiations which had been begun and communicated to them the acts on which they were based, explaining why the Houses had preferred such an establishment to the motion of "Invitation". The Elector assured Halifax that he had never approved of this latter proposal and declared himself as extremely gratified with the care for his interests which had been taken in England. He expressed implicit confidence in the English Ministers. As regards the actual negotiation of the Treaty, he objected strongly to appearing in it as a principal party, and preferred to place himself entirely in the hands of the Queen. Delighted with the results of his embassy, Halifax left the electoral Court towards the end of June and on the 30th of that month arrived again at The Hague.[1]

During his absence at Hanover, the Guarantee Treaty had made no progress. Harley had constantly pressed Stanhope for further news, but the latter, when he approached the Deputies on the subject was put off with one excuse or another. "Something there is", he wrote on the 29th of June, "that they are unwilling to speak out as long as they can avoid it; but in a little time they will be forced to speak plainer."[2] To clear this matter up Halifax waited on Heinsius on the 2nd of July, the second morning following his return, when he found that it was still the sixth article that caused the difficulty. It was thought too much to insist on the Succession as a preliminary to the treaty of peace.

> They imagined (he wrote soon afterwards to his friend Somers) the peace was to be made like that at Ryswick; that we were to use their intervention, that the Queen was to be treated with, only as an ally to them, and to be acknowledged last when the treaty was signed. I confess this way of discourse did a little provoke me.[3]

Halifax answered that in the last war the owning of the King's title was a great ground of the war; which was not the present case, as it was the Spanish Monarchy that was now the matter

[1] Letters from Halifax to Harley, June 1706. Record Office.
[2] Stanhope to Harley, 29 June. Record Office.
[3] Halifax to Somers. Letter written in July and enclosed in a letter, one from the camp at Helchin dated 26 July. Hardwicke State Papers, II, 468.

in dispute; moreover, the owning of the Queen's title and the Protestant Succession would not involve the conclusion of anything to the prejudice of France, and that the French King, having formerly owned King William, ought not in reason to make any difficulty about the Queen and the Succession.[1] Driven from his objections on this point, the Pensionary next observed that if England and the States did all this for the Elector of Hanover, why did he not appear in the Treaty and why did he not do more to assist the common cause? Halifax replied that as to the first it was only a becoming modesty that kept him out of the Treaty and made him leave the regulation of that to the Queen. As regards services rendered to the common cause, he enumerated the many good offices the Elector had performed for the Allies in recent years; he pointed out that the troops supplied by him were more complete and given at a cheaper rate than those of any other prince, and added that indeed the interest of the family was so bound up with the success of the war that their assistance could not be doubted, and that if any further proofs of their affection were wanted, these had only to be specified and explained to the Queen for her to join with the States in obtaining them. But Heinsius had a third subtle objection to urge. He suggested that the Treaty should "go further and extend to be a general guarantee between the Allies for securing and maintaining the peace". In this Heinsius raised an issue in which the interests of England and the Dutch were exactly antagonistic. To have carried this point would have made the Dutch practically masters of the situation.

[1] All through this negotiation the English laid great stress on having the Queen and Protestant Succession recognised as a preliminary before the actual conferences for any final peace-treaty began. There is an interesting passage in Somers' answer to the letter from Halifax referred to in the previous note. "I have always had a great dread", he wrote, "of the beginning a treaty with France. I am in some degree versed in treaties of the last age. The French as soon as it is once entered into will transact with particular plenipotentiaries, and are more busy in showing them their respective interests than in convincing the several commissions; I could enumerate instances of this kind from the Treaty of Vervins downwards. You can judge if there be any danger of this sort from the state of things in Holland. This seems to me the difference that is of moment, between a preliminary article and an article of the treaty" (undated letter, Hardwick State Papers, vol. II).

The Republic, the least trustworthy link in the chain against France, would be the determining factor in settling how much—or rather how little—should be asked from Louis; and England, to preserve the guarantee of her all-important Protestant Succession, would have found herself bound to force the other allies to rest satisfied with a scanty satisfaction from the fallen enemy.[1]

Halifax was too good a politician not to perceive the full meaning of the suggestion. He replied that the proposed general guarantee was a very wise and necessary consideration, but that perhaps it would not be proper to insert it in this place. Such a general treaty, he pointed out, must be general and reciprocal, whereas there were some of the allies, particularly Savoy, that were not of sufficient importance to be asked to come into the Treaty for securing the Succession.

Whenever it shall be thought fit (he said) to begin the other negotiation, it shall be made a separate and distinct treaty, and perhaps some caution should be used as to the time of setting it on foot lest some umbrage be taken that we are looking too fast after a peace.[2]

Halifax seemed to have won on all points. He fancied he had cured the Dutch of their reluctance to include the recognition of the Queen as one of the preliminaries, and wrote to Marlborough that he thought he had satisfied the Pensionary as to all the objections he had made. Heinsius requested him to remain on at The Hague[3] till the treaty could be referred to the Estates of the Province of Holland which were to meet in a day or two. He consented. All the English claims had been allowed;

[1] There was all the difference in the world between this suggestion of Heinsius and the proposal made by the English in September and October that the two Sea Powers should settle peace preliminaries to be offered to France. The Dutch wanted to bind the preliminaries to a previously settled Barrier Treaty; the English to bind the Barrier Treaty to previously settled preliminaries. The important difference involved in these two suggestions was that in each case the country making the proposal would be predominant in fixing the terms of the preliminaries.

[2] Halifax to Heinsius, 3 July. Heinsius Archives at the Rijksarchief at The Hague; Halifax to Marlborough, 3 July, in the Archives at Blenheim. The former letter is undated but the latter fixes the date conclusively.

[3] Halifax had promised Marlborough to pay him a visit at the camp on the way home to England.

the all-powerful Province had only to give its consent to what the Deputies had agreed and the Treaty would become an accomplished fact. Such was the prospect that Halifax could hold out to himself as the result of this, the first of the three decisive days in the course of the negotiations for the Guarantee Treaty at The Hague in the summer of 1706.

The second phase of the negotiations lasted from the 3rd to the 16th of July. This was perhaps the most momentous period for the Dutch in the diplomacy of the whole of this momentous year. It was during these few days, while Halifax was waiting for the meeting of the States of Holland, that Goes communicated to the astonished Deputies the news of the Imperial Patent for the Duke of Marlborough; that the tidings arrived from the latter that he had definitely refused the offer, but on the other hand had entirely rejected the "Décret Organique" of the 19th of June; and that in its place the Condominium of the two Maritime Powers was practically established. These events could not but exert a very decided influence on the course of the Guarantee Treaty. Just at the moment that the antagonism of the English Duke had shattered their hopes of an exclusive control of the conquered Netherlands, the States began to realise that the importance which England attached to the Protestant Succession gave to the Dutch guarantee of it a marketable value. What more natural than that they should recompense themselves for enforced self-denial on one side by securing additional advantages on the other? If the constitution completed on the 21st of July seemed to offer less security for their future frontier towns than that of the 19th of June, this disadvantage could be neutralised by the insertion of their Barrier right in the Guarantee Treaty.

The opposition which Halifax had met with on the 2nd of July surprised and pained Marlborough, who from the camp was following the course of the proposed treaty, and remembered the good dispositions which he had found in The Hague in May. The objections of the Dutch were all the more mortifying after his refusal of the Patent.

I must beg of you (he wrote to Heinsius) that you will use your interest in making the treaty for the succession to succeed whilst you have Lord Halifax; for should he at his return to England report that you make difficulties it would do great hurt, their hearts in England being much set upon it; and I see no consequences to you but that of making a compliment to the Queen and England.[1]

To Portland he expressed himself even more strongly:

Your Lordship must give me leave to tell you that the difficulties about the Treaty for the succession cannot be taken very kindly with us, and I daresay, if it could have been foreseen in England, it would never have been proposed.[2]

There was, however, worse obstruction to follow.

On the 16th of July the States of Holland met to discuss the Succession Treaty. They came together, after the excitement of the last fortnight, in a tumultuous disorderly frame of mind that boded little good for the success of the Treaty. The Deputies were sworn to secrecy, so that Halifax could only learn at second hand what happened at the meeting. At first the whole question of the guarantee was treated there as a joke. Had anyone ever heard, it was asked, of one State guaranteeing the internal constitution of another? Then it was urged that they had been drawn into a burdensome war on just such an excuse, namely the guarantee of the succession of Spain which should have been partitioned.[3] But finally, as Halifax gathered, it had been agreed that the Queen should be acknowledged as a preliminary and her Ministers received as such at the negotiations, and that the Succession also should be settled and acknowledged in the Treaty; but in return for this, as a security to them, the Queen was to promise that their Barrier should be settled and specified according to the right given to the Dutch by the ninth article of the Grand Alliance. On this head, however, all was as yet vague and uncertain. Some wished to have the demand made in general terms, others were for specifying the particular towns wanted.

After they have turned it several ways, (wrote the Englishman) I believe it will end in desiring the Queen to be guarantee to them that at the conclusion of the peace they shall have such a Barrier given them as they shall think sufficient for their safety and security.

[1] Marlborough to Heinsius, 15 July. Vreede.
[2] Marlborough to Portland, 21 July. Murray.
[3] Lamberty, IV, 311.

Halifax had no difficulty in at once accepting this new demand for a reciprocal treaty, as he considered the demands made by each of the two parties to be mutually advantageous.

> If the Queen (said he) is pleased to give them this Covenant, as an equivalent for their being Guarantees for the Succession, I hope the thing is done, and I cannot doubt but this will be approved; the terms are equally reasonable on both sides, for securing the succession is truly their interest and their Barrier is our security.[1]

Brilliant but impetuous, over-sanguine in success and petulant in opposition, Halifax again considered the negotiation as good as over. On the 17th of July the States of Holland broke up for a short interval and on the same day, in order to pay his promised visit to Marlborough at the camp, Halifax left The Hague expecting to return no more thither.[2] In due course Stanhope, on whom it was thought in England (after the last despatch from Halifax) that the duty of concluding the treaty would fall, received an intimation from Harley that the Queen agreed to the principle of a reciprocal treaty of Barrier and Succession as points mutually advantageous to both.[3]

Thus the 16th of July marks the end of the second period of this negotiation. In this period the Treaty had passed from the one-sided condition in which it was first brought on the "tapis", and had become the peculiar reciprocal undertaking which it was henceforth to remain. There remained still to be decided the definition of the Dutch Barrier demand. That was attempted in the third period. There was a curious irony in the change which the advantages to be gained from this Treaty underwent. Originated by England for her own profit, the gain in it had already become mutual; henceforth while the Union with Scotland and the growing supremacy of England in the Alliance made a foreign guarantee of her succession less vital to her, the Dutch, by playing off France and England against one another, were enabled so to extend their Barrier claims that it became

[1] Halifax to Harley, 16 July. Record Office. Also printed in the Appendix to Somerville's *Queen Anne* among extracts from the Hardwicke Papers.

[2] Stanhope to Harley, 20 July. Record Office.

[3] Harley to Stanhope, 16/27 July. Record Office.

possible to contend—in language warped by partisan hostility—that

> a reasonable person in China, ignorant of European politics, would, on reading the final treaty of 1709, have conceived the States to be some vast powerful commonwealth like that of Rome, and Her Majesty to be a petty prince whom they could depose at pleasure.[1]

Halifax had in his official despatch to Harley accepted the principle of the mutual guarantee, but on his journey to Marlborough he wrote a confidential letter to Somers, the head of his political party, which, with the latter's reply, is exceedingly interesting as showing the point of view from which the uncompromising Whigs regarded the Barrier question. Subordinating all their diplomacy to their one central aim, the preservation of the Protestant Succession, they courted abroad the Power which could most assist them in this endeavour, and was at the same time most predisposed to a premature and dangerous peace. Halifax realised quite clearly that the Dutch Barrier claim would create jealousy in Vienna but he deliberately chose to befriend the Dutch. The passages in the two letters bearing on this point are so instructive that we give them in full in the note below.[2] These letters show that the Whigs were

[1] Introductory remarks to Swift's *Barrier Treaty*.

[2] "There will be some nicety", wrote Halifax, "in expressing this (the Barrier); for if it be worded in general terms it will be very uncertain; and if they name the particular places which shall be put into their hands it will be very hard to agree upon them and may give offence to some other of the Allies. In my opinion they should word this as strong and as particularly as they pleased; for I think it is our interest that their barrier should be as good as we can get for them; and if they insist upon too much, it will be the greater tie upon them, not to make peace till it is procured for them. Perhaps this alone is better than all the rest; for if they are thus drawn in, at their own desire, to oblige themselves not to run too fast into a peace, it were the most desirable part of the treaty. My Lord, I must beg your thoughts upon this with speed; for the whole affair will turn upon this." This letter written on his way to Marlborough was enclosed in one written on his arrival, from the camp at Helchin, in which he observed that the Duke, who had received him very kindly, agreed with him in his thoughts as to what would make things easy. After a few appreciative remarks about the Duke, he concludes, "I cannot say so much for some others; the evil spirit takes place again amongst them and had they been left to model the government of the Spanish Netherlands according to their own fancies they would make them more uneasy than they are". To this letter Somers answered, "I am of your Lordship's opinion as to penning the 6th article concerning the barrier. The stronger the better if they and we mean the same thing by that word; but

willing to favour the Dutch as the Power whose guarantee of the Protestant Succession would be extremely useful to them. But the reason of this usefulness lay in the fact that the Dutch had it in their power to offer the most effective opposition to the aggression of France, the champion of Roman Catholicism in England. This opposition could best be rendered effectively by a strong Barrier; but this Barrier must be in its essence a military one, and against France. It was for this reason that the Dutch desire, which soon began to manifest itself, of establishing what would in reality approximate to a complete civil rule over the Spanish Netherlands and upon the inner part of them rather than along the French frontier, was viewed with suspicion, as being a departure from the real purpose of the Barrier. That desire was the "evil spirit" alluded to by Somers in the letter quoted in the previous note. This "evil spirit" had indeed gone further than either Halifax or Somers at this time imagined and the Dutch Deputies were secretly discussing with French emissaries the possibility of an amicable arrangement with Louis by which the whole Spanish Netherlands should be handed over in return for peace, to the tender mercies of the States General. It was just such an understanding that the Whigs laboured to prevent. The Whig attitude in this matter was very much that of the Duke of Marlborough, at that time all powerful in English diplomacy. But the years were coming when the breach would widen between him and his colleagues; the one paralysed by his cosmopolitanism, if not unmindful of the bait wherewith the Hapsburgs sought to lure him to their service; the others forced to purchase with increased robberies from the Imperial domains the continuance of Dutch assistance in a war with which their political existence seemed bound up, and the preservation of that mutual guarantee, which, from a national defence, passed, under its later conditions, into little more than a party buttress.

Three days after the arrival of Halifax at the Helchin camp,

I am not so clear as to that point in my own thoughts since I understood they were so forward in modelling the Government of the Spanish Netherlands; and since you tell me the evil spirit takes place again amongst them. Your Lordship who knows how this article is worded, sees through this doubt of mine".

Marlborough wrote to ask if it was necessary that the Earl should return to The Hague, as otherwise he would go direct by Ostend to London. Heinsius replied that, as the Estates of Holland would be meeting in a week for a further discussion of the Treaty, the presence of the English statesman would be very useful.[1] Halifax accordingly started from the camp on the 3rd of August taking with him, probably, Marlborough's letter to the Pensionary, in which he stated that he had learnt from Harley that the Queen was willing there should be a clause for the security of the Barrier in the Treaty for the Succession, so that the only difficulty would be in taking care that the clause be so worded that Austria should have no reason to take it ill.[2] The Duke had no doubt explained to Halifax the necessity for safeguarding the interests of the House of Hapsburg. Halifax arrived on the 9th at The Hague to find an interminable series of meetings, discussions, and disputes which soon exhausted his patience.[3] The English Ministers at home were pressing for an explanation of the Barrier claim, but Halifax to his surprise found that there was not yet unanimity in the States of Holland as to whether there should be a treaty at all. The matter had been referred to the several towns in the Province and all but Leyden had approved it.

> The deputy of that city (he wrote to Marlborough) continued obstinate to oppose it but his reasons and arguments were such as made me suspect he was set on by some body that would stop the treaty, and not acted and governed by his own principles. He was willing to guarantee the Protestant Succession, but was against particularising the House of Hanover, which is incomprehensible.[4]

This "humour and perverseness", as he called it, irritated Halifax. He informed Harley that he had done his best to satisfy the obstructing Deputy but without avail.[5] He reasoned

[1] Marlborough to Heinsius, 26 July; Heinsius to Marlborough, 28 July. Vreede.

[2] Marlborough to Heinsius, 3 Aug. Vreede.

[3] Portland wrote of him to Marlborough, "La longueur et les manières de ce Gouvernement et de ces delibérations à quoy il n'est pas accoutumé ont un peu épuisé sa patience". Portland to Marlborough, 25 Aug. Blenheim Archives.

[4] Halifax to Marlborough, 11 Aug. Blenheim Archives.

[5] Halifax to Harley, 10 Aug. Record Office.

with the Deputy for two days, his consent being by the Dutch constitution necessary, before he could feel hopeful of success.[1] But even when the requisite unanimity had been obtained, there remained the question of the definition of the Barrier claim. Here again difficulties occurred.

Just as between the 2nd and the 16th of July extraneous events connected with the government of the Low Countries had exerted a strong influence indirectly on the Succession Treaty, so now between the latter date and the 17th of August, the third decisive day in this negotiation, another external incident of great importance occurred. A definite set of peace proposals had arrived from France, among which it was stipulated that the Dutch should have the whole Spanish Netherlands handed over to them to deal with as they pleased.[2] The hopes excited by this offer made the Dutch very unwilling to lessen their chances of acquiring the whole by specifying in the Guarantee Treaty a part of the whole as sufficient for their needs. Halifax as yet knew nothing of the French proposals which were, of course, completely antagonistic to the Whig programme; he saw only the objective result of the offer, which was an unaccountable unwillingness on the part of the Dutch to come to an understanding with him. At last, on the 17th of August, the final resolution was taken, and on the 7th/18th Halifax was summoned to hear the imposing document read over to him by the Pensionary and Buys. "'Tis long," he wrote to Marlborough, "'twas in Dutch and though the Pensionary put it into French, I did not understand all of it very clearly, but I think it is agreeable to what your Grace approved. I am now preparing to embark as soon as I can."[3] A few days later he was on his way and after a tedious passage arrived in London on the 18th/29th of August, bringing with him the Resolution of the States of Holland as the outcome of his four months' embassy at The Hague.

This Resolution contained all the germs of the future Barrier treaties. The first five articles of the original project handed to

[1] Halifax to Elector of Hanover, 12 Aug. Macpherson, *Original Papers*.

[2] Hannequin arrived with these pleasing proposals on 23 July. We shall return to this point later. See pp. 60–61.

[3] Halifax to Marlborough, 18 Aug. Blenheim Archives.

the Deputies in May were incorporated, but the all-important sixth appeared in a mangled form, which showed how over sanguine Halifax had been when he thought on the 2nd of July that he had conquered the Dutch objections to it. The article now merely stated that no formal negotiation for peace could be entered upon by the King of France and his allies, except in conjunction with the Queen and her Ministers, thus the recognition of the Queen and the Succession, as a preliminary to be accepted by France, had been bodily struck out, and all that remained in its place was an assurance that the Dutch would, when it came to the final treaty of peace, "make all efforts imaginable to induce the King of France in a special Article to recognise the Hanoverian Succession". They had in fact gone back to the system of Ryswick.

So much for the English claims. On the other side of the bargain the provisions were more liberal. First, the English were to help the Dutch to recover all the Spanish Netherlands, and to conquer as many other towns as possible; they were further to bind themselves to obtain that in the final treaty

> all the Spanish Netherlands and what shall be found necessary in addition, whether conquered or unconquered towns, shall serve as Barrier for the States, and for this purpose, their High Mightinesses shall have the right to maintain garrisons in all such towns, etc., of the Spanish Netherlands, and in all other towns without exception which may be added for the strengthening of the Barrier, according as they may judge necessary.

Secondly, in the Barrier towns, the States were to have the right of placing as many troops as they pleased, of provisioning them, and supplying them with arms, of placing in them commanders obedient to no one but the States, and of fixing a sum, which should be found by the various provinces of the Spanish Netherlands, and delivered up to the States for the maintenance of these garrisons.

Thirdly, the Queen was to bind herself to obtain that all the provisions relating to the Barrier contained in the Guarantee Treaty, should be inserted in the Convention which was to be made between the King of Spain and the House of Hapsburg, in accordance with the 9th Article of the Grand Alliance, and should also promise to guarantee this Convention. Thus did the Dutch protect themselves beforehand against the certain hostility of Vienna.

Fourthly, this protection was extended to cover opposition from any quarter by a further provision that no treaty of peace should be concluded without the insertion in it of everything here stipulated as to the Succession and Barrier; and that, when it had been concluded, the two Maritime Powers should guarantee against all, both the whole Treaty, and especially the provisions for the Succession and Barrier.

Lastly, the States were to have the right of placing their garrisons there and then in the towns already conquered, of similarly garrisoning each successive town that should be taken and of maintaining this military occupation until the conclusion of the Convention mentioned above. Thus did the States intend to render their rights still more secure by maintaining an unbroken continuity of actual possession.[1]

The Dutch were delighted with their Resolution. "They seemed to think", wrote Stanhope, "that they have put the matter on so good a foot, as that everything therein will be approved, so that there will be nothing more to be done but to conclude the Treaty immediately." A copy was sent to Marlborough in case of any possible objections, but they were confident that there would be nothing of the kind.[2] The opinion of Halifax, when he had mastered the document, was widely different. "The Dutch demands for their Barrier", he complained to the Elector of Hanover, in a letter written soon after his return to London and explaining how the Treaty stood,

> are so extravagant, that I doubt whether they will be consented to, as they have projected them. I represented this very amply to the Ministers in Holland and it appears to me that they have made this proposal concerning a Barrier altogether like merchants. They know very well that their demands are exorbitant, but they hope to obtain a better bargain by lowering a great deal of their pretensions. The Pensionary is so convinced of this, that he entreated me to send him

[1] Resolution of the States General, 17 Aug. 1706, in the Hanover Papers of the Stowe MSS. at the British Museum.

[2] Stanhope to Harley, 20 Aug. Record Office.

in writing, the objections which I made to them. I will not fail to do so.[1]

II

From the time that Halifax left The Hague in August up to Marlborough's arrival there in November, the centre of gravity of the negotiation for the Barrier Treaty was transferred from that capital to London. During this period the negotiation was developed in two important respects which we may call "internal" and "external" respectively. In the first place, a long step in advance was made in the process of rendering the actual terms of the Treaty more definite; and in the second place—and this is a point of the greatest importance—the Treaty was brought into definite connection with the general negotiation on the subject of the future peace. Leaving the consideration of this second point for the next section, we will confine ourselves for the moment to the "internal" development of the Treaty, and trace the efforts of the English Ministry to obtain from the Dutch a definite statement of what they meant by their Barrier. The Resolution of the 17th of August had indeed included a certain explanation of their claims, but this was of so vague and comprehensive a character as to be practically useless.

Before the end of August Heinsius had gathered that the English Ministers were pleased with the Resolution.[2] There was no ground, however, for that belief; all that had really happened had been that Harley, before he had ever seen the Resolution, had made some characteristically vague and empty statements, expressing his satisfaction that Halifax had made "so great progress in the Treaty".[3] As a whole month passed with no news from England the optimism of the Pensionary began to be shaken. This long silence, Halifax explained, in a letter to the Elector of Hanover, had been caused by the unwillingness of the English Ministers to declare themselves

[1] Halifax to Elector, 23 Aug./3 Sept. Macpherson, *Original Papers*. The packet boat which carried this letter was lost, but a copy of it was sent later on, 20 Sept./1 Oct.

[2] Heinsius to Marlborough, 28 Aug. Vreede.

[3] Harley to Stanhope, 13/24 Aug. Record Office.

openly against the extravagant hopes of the Dutch, already so disposed to listen to terms of peace, until the news of the result of the campaign in Italy was known. It is a striking fact to what an extent, all through the war, the various branches of it were interconnected and what an immediate and profound influence a military event in one corner of Europe exerted upon diplomacy in another. The brilliant forced march by Eugene right across the plains of Lombardy, which culminated in the relief of Turin, came in a measure to compensate for the failure of the Imperial arms to achieve anything of note during the earlier part of the year, a failure which had played no inconsiderable part in inclining the Dutch towards peace. The Ministry could now with safety begin a paternal lecture to the Dutch on their greediness.[1] The actual letter from Halifax, however, which broke the long silence, took Heinsius by surprise. After stating that it was the common opinion that the matter of the Barrier had been too strongly expressed in the Resolution and that a treaty so worded would in effect give up the entire Spanish Netherlands to the Dutch, the writer continued:

How proper this is, if it was my business, I must judge, but as it is not I leave it to others. I entered into this matter not by commission but as a volunteer out of a desire to serve both the United Provinces and England in points that were for their mutual security. I was sorry to see so many difficulties started in a matter I thought so plain; I wish I knew how to remove those that remain. I have still the same zeal and the same inclination to promote our Succession and your Barrier, but it is not my business to meddle any more nor has it been my business to find expedients in these cases.[2]

An explanation arrived a few days later through Portland, that this letter, which seemed to put a stop to all negotiation, was written in a moment of pique at a statement reported to emanate from Vryberg to the effect that the Dutch had made extravagant demands merely in order to baffle Halifax and

[1] "The surprise turn which the affairs of Italy have taken will redress everything. But before that happened, the Dutch were so disposed to listen to terms of peace that it was no wise proper to declare ourselves openly against their extravagant hopes." Halifax to Elector, 20 Sept./1 Oct. Macpherson, *Original Papers*.

[2] Halifax to Heinsius, 20 Sept./1 Oct. Heinsius Archives at The Hague.

prevent him personally from concluding negotiations. It appeared that the statement was very probably an invention; moreover, that Halifax should have written as he did at a moment so critical makes his letter doubly inexcusable.[1] The historian, however, must be grateful, for it called forth from Heinsius a comprehensive and able vindication of the claims that the United Provinces had made on the 17th of August.

The Grand Pensionary began by remarking that it was unnecessary for him to dwell upon the Dutch need of, or right to, their Barrier, as both points were freely conceded by the English.

> The question is therefore (he continued) merely the foot upon which we should have it (the Barrier). It must be effective or it is useless. We know that Spain will not be in a condition to render us secure by herself, and we have learnt by disastrous experience that the troops of that country, together with the Dutch troops which we kept in the Netherlands before this war, did not guarantee us from the seizure of that country and our Barrier. The reason is obviously because we were not masters there either of the troops or of the fortresses in which they were stationed. It is clear, therefore, that the mere country cannot serve us as a Barrier, and that, for the security which is our right, it is not just that we should repose upon others like the Spaniards. We should keep troops in the country for its defence, and place them where they are required for this purpose. As it is not yet known which places will be the most convenient, since they have not yet been captured, nor, consequently, how many troops will be necessary, it seems just that the States should choose and fill with the necessary forces such places as they may deem indispensable for the preservation of the Barrier. Next it is necessary that these places be fortified and that the troops continue under the command of the States, as indeed our Resolution stipulates, unless we are to run the same risk as previously when we came within an ace of losing all the country which God has graciously preserved to us.

The Pensionary went on to say that for thus undertaking the defence of the country it was only right that the States should be reimbursed from the revenues of the Netherlands, and that Charles would remain sovereign in the matters of police, finance, justice and religion. The fear that the States would choose too many places he endeavoured to dispose of, by the assurance that

[1] Halifax to Portland, 24 Sept./5 Oct. apologising for his last letter; and Heinsius to Portland on the subject, 9 Oct. Heinsius Archives.

the Dutch would never expose themselves to such expense beyond what was absolutely necessary.[1]

Halifax was still unconvinced, but in the temporary absence of the chief Ministers from town, he did not dare to frame a reply on his own responsibility. He contented himself for the present, therefore, in sending a copy of the Pensionary's letter to Marlborough, observing that it would be neither safe nor honourable to promise the Dutch all, in the confidence they would be reasonable in their choice, and asking whether there were any great objection to naming the towns and places which they should have, though the greatest part of them were yet in the enemy's hands.[2] Four days later with the sanction of the Ministry he returned an official reply to the Pensionary.[3] In this, the last and ablest of all his despatches throughout the negotiation, Halifax completely answered the arguments of Heinsius. He concurred in much the Pensionary had said, both as to the necessity of a sufficient Barrier for the Dutch, and their right to control it themselves and to be indemnified for doing so. He allowed further that he should be content to have the general words of the 5th and 9th Articles of the Grand Alliance extended as far as their safety should demand, even though the proper notion of a Barrier was thus exceeded. He pointed out, however, that the Resolution of the 17th of August extended much further than all this. He declared that no confidence in the moderation in which the choice would be used could justify the grant, to a nation, of such an indefinite power as the clause of the proposed treaty which delivered up to the Dutch all the Spanish Netherlands and all the towns, forts and places without exception that they should judge fit to select.

You are pleased to say (he continued) that some of the places being yet in the enemies' hands, you could neither judge which would be most convenient nor know what troops would be necessary nor what sum of money required for maintaining them. But except these particulars are agreed on, what use is there of this Treaty, unless to explain the general words of the Grand Alliance by more general and uncertain terms in this.

[1] Heinsius to Halifax, 8 Oct.; copy in the Blenheim Archives.
[2] Halifax to Marlborough, 4/15 Oct. Blenheim Archives.
[3] Halifax to Heinsius, 8/19 Oct. Vreede.

He requested the Pensionary, therefore, to change the form of the Resolution, name the places required, settle what number of troops were necessary and what contribution should be paid by the Spanish Netherlands, and expressed the hope that these points might be agreed upon with the Duke of Marlborough.

In their approval of Halifax's letter of the 8th/19th of October, the English Ministry had definitely rejected the interpretation of the Barrier contained in the Resolution of the 17th of August. It remained to be seen whether the Dutch would consent to the changes proposed by Halifax, and if so, whether the list of places which they should propose could be accepted. Marlborough, on whom the negotiation would soon devolve, cordially approved of the demand that the towns should be specified. He had already pointed out the necessity of insisting upon this course to Wratislaw.[1] But the prospects of agreement did not appear hopeful. It is clear that he had quite expected a successful result to Halifax's negotiation in the summer, but the recent conduct of the Dutch had destroyed these hopes. "They cannot agree among themselves", he wrote, late in September, "concerning their Barrier, but the most reasonable are extravagant."[2] Similar apprehensions were felt by the Ministers in London.[3] There was, however, a further and stronger reason for the Duke's pessimism. The Dutch demands were such as would necessitate his acting the part of a very candid friend. An incident now occurred which showed how little underlying friendship there was between the two Sea Powers to stand this candour on his part. The new ground for friction was furnished by the recall of Stepney from Vienna to act as English representative at Brussels. Marlborough had written to Godolphin to suggest that, as this appointment would certainly be regarded with dislike in the Republic, he should speak to Vryberg about it and say that the appointment was

[1] Marlborough to Wratislaw, 22 Sept. Murray.

[2] Marlborough to Godolphin, 26 Sept. Coxe, I, 485.

[3] Halifax to Stepney, 22 Oct./2 Nov. 1706, "I apprehend you will meet with great difficulties in assigning the places. The Dutch will affect to have some that are rather a Barrier against the Spanish Netherlands than against France". Stepney Papers, British Museum. Godolphin was rather more sanguine.

necessary to prevent time being lost, through Marlborough's absence, in settling the Barrier with King Charles.[1] On the 28th of September, therefore, Godolphin wrote to Heinsius, that as the Duke was too much occupied to give the necessary attention to the administration at Brussels, the Queen had sent for Stepney from Vienna to attend to that service and, in the absence of Stanhope, to act at The Hague.[2] This letter arrived while the Dutch were still waiting for the long expected news from England about their Barrier Treaty. In their suspense and anxiety at the silence of Halifax, this new proposal awakened all their old suspicions. They saw in Stepney's appointment a return to the dreaded system of placing a foreign governor in the Netherlands. This second "Patent" seemed, like the first, a direct menace to their Barrier right. The Pensionary wrote at once both to Marlborough and Godolphin urgently requesting that, if Stepney arrived at The Hague first, he might remain there till Marlborough came, or that, if he went direct to Brussels, he should not be allowed to take up his duties at the latter place until the matter had been talked over with the Duke.[3] Marlborough replied that the assurance which the States had received that the Queen desired nothing in the Spanish Netherlands should have made such jealousy at Stepney's appointment impossible.[4] Heinsius gained this point inasmuch as Stepney had not yet entered upon his duties at Brussels when he accompanied Marlborough to The Hague.[5] This recrudescence of Dutch suspicion and opposition to that factor in the Condominium which alone had kept the people of the Southern Netherlands from open revolt against the Allies,[6] pained and discouraged the Duke. Heinsius might indeed, in his despair of making any further progress with Halifax, look

[1] Marlborough to Godolphin, 9 Sept. Coxe, I, 454.
[2] Godolphin to Heinsius, 17/28 Sept. Vreede.
[3] Heinsius to Godolphin, 8 Oct.; Heinsius to Marlborough, 9 Oct. Vreede.
[4] Marlborough to Slingelandt, 10 Oct. Murray.
[5] "I will take care he shall not go to Brussels till I go, and afterwards I shall bring him with me to the Hague; so that everything may be adjusted." Marlborough to Heinsius, 12 Oct. Vreede.
[6] "It is certain," wrote Marlborough to Harley on 21 Oct., "as they have managed it, nothing but the Queen's authority and good offices can keep these people in any tolerable measures with the Dutch."

forward impatiently and hopefully to Marlborough's arrival at The Hague.[1] The English General could not share these feelings, and to confirm his fears came a warning even from Slingelandt, whom he considered the most favourably disposed of all the Dutch statesmen, "that the Spanish Netherlands and the Barrier question would become a stumbling block to the two nations unless they worked together to remove all subject for jealousy which seemed to exist already on both sides".[2] Slingelandt should have added a third cause for jealousy—the French overtures.

The Pensionary tells me (wrote Marlborough a week before he started on his journey to The Hague) I must stay to finish the Treaty of Succession and their Barrier, which, should I stay the whole winter, I am very confident would not be brought to perfection. For they are of so many minds, and all so very extravagant concerning their Barrier that I despair of doing any good till they are more reasonable, which they will not be till they see that they have it not in their power to dispose of the Low Countries at their will and pleasure, in which the French flatter them.[3]

The significance of these last remarks will be brought out in the next section.

III

The sentence quoted at the conclusion of the preceding section gives the key-note to the present section which treats of the effect of "French flattery" upon the Barrier negotiations. This influence was the chief cause of the bringing of the Treaty from its isolated position into definite connection with the general peace negotiations. The tenacity of the Dutch and their reluctance to define the Barrier they desired was attributable to

[1] "C'est votre Altesse qui doit finir cette affaire." Heinsius to Marlborough, 25 Sept. "On ne nous a pas envoyé les remarques qu'on pourrait avoir sur le sujet du Traité de la Succession et de la Barrière; mais il paraît qu'on s'en remettra tout-à-fait à votre Altesse." Heinsius to Marlborough, 16 Oct. "Tout se rapporte à cette heure à votre arrivée ici." Heinsius to Marlborough, 20 Oct. Vreede.

[2] Slingelandt to Marlborough, 6 Oct. Blenheim Archives. Marlborough sent this letter on to Godolphin, observing, "It has always been and is still my opinion that Mr Slingelandt is the best inclined for carrying on the war of any at the Hague. This opinion makes me send you the enclosed letter that you may see how the humour runs in that place". Coxe, I, 489.

[3] Marlborough to Godolphin, 29 Oct. Coxe, I, 492.

the offer which they had received from France in July, of the whole Southern Netherlands, as part of a general set of proposals for peace. So long as there was any possibility of these proposals being accepted the Dutch were naturally unwilling to forgo their chance of the whole Southern Netherlands by committing themselves to any less comprehensive estimate of their wants. Thus the French offers served materially to retard the "internal" definition-process of the Barrier Treaty, with which we have been concerned in the foregoing section. Even more important was the effect the proposals exerted upon the "external" environment of the Treaty. In the summer of 1706 the Barrier Treaty had been negotiated between the two Powers on its own merits. It had indeed been subordinated to the general "entente" between the two Maritime Powers manifested in the provisional Condominium; but it was not dependent upon any other co-ordinate thread of negotiation between the two Powers. This isolation of the Barrier Treaty was now to cease. The general "entente" to which reference has just been made had a double significance. To the Dutch, it meant that the English were at one with them in their claim to immediate and effective occupation of the conquered provinces; to the English, it meant the presumption that the Dutch were at one with them on the fundamental policy of the war, both as to the end for which they fought and the conditions which they would accept for peace. But the eagerness with which the States in July and August received these French overtures at once destroyed the English interpretation of this underlying "entente". It, therefore, became necessary for the Ministry to have a surety for the good behaviour of the Republic. The negotiation for the Barrier became bound indissolubly to a co-ordinate negotiation for determining preliminaries of peace. Just as the Dutch had insisted upon making the Succession and Barrier mutual and reciprocal, so in turn the English were soon to make their consent to the Barrier Treaty and Dutch adherence to concerted peace preliminaries similarly mutual and reciprocal conditions.

Ever since the beginning of the war France courted the Dutch as the member most likely to secede from the Alliance.

Louis saw with delight the growing breach between them and the Emperor and thought in July that the time had come for making a determined effort. The proposals which Hennequin delivered to Heinsius and Buys on the 23rd of July[1] were fully intended by Louis to bring about a "défection avantageuse" of the Dutch.[2] The principal conditions proposed were, that Anne should be recognised, no reference being made to the Succession—a proposal that England would not accept; that the Archduke Charles should have all the Spanish Monarchy with the exception of some provinces in the north of Spain, and of Milan—a proposal that the Hapsburgs would not accept; and, thirdly, that the States should have the power to settle the Spanish Netherlands, especially as regards their Barrier, just as they pleased—a proposal which the Dutch would be only too glad to accept.[3] But this last offer was in reality only that of a "fraudulent bankrupt who tried to hide his own debts by an endeavour to pawn other peoples' possessions". The Dutch knew that so long as the Barrier question had not been settled and recognised by the other two principals of the Alliance, the "sum of French offers was but smoke and powder".[4] What Louis gave he might—as experience had shown—at any moment take away again unless the States could find a guarantor of the gift with whom France would also have to reckon. England was to render the all-important service, and this made her the arbiter of these peace negotiations. The Dutch might coax and they might threaten; but they were powerless to insist. Both parties understood the situation perfectly. On the 27th of July, therefore, Heinsius laid the proposals before Marlborough.[5] This action

[1] A second and very similar set of proposals reached Heinsius about the same time. They were sent from Maximilian Emmanuel to Marlborough and forwarded by him. Vreede, pp. 61, 238; Legrelle, IV, 382 ff.

[2] "Louis en un mot souhaitait d'amener les Hollandais à une défection avantageuse, analogue à celle du 30 Jan. 1648, du 11 Août 1678, et de l'été de 1696." Legrelle, IV, 382.

[3] A few days after the first overtures Hennequin explained to Heinsius that Louis, in addition to acknowledging the Queen, "would take no interest in the steps that should be taken in England with regard to the succession", a stipulation which was still very far from recognising the Protestant Succession. Heinsius to Marlborough, 18 Aug. Vreede.

[4] Noorden, II, 426, 427.

[5] Heinsius to Marlborough, 27 July 1706. Vreede.

disappointed the French. It was hoped that the Dutch would have made further advances without the participation of England. "The subordination and dependence of the Republic upon the English will always traverse the effect of the Pensionary's good intentions"; so wrote the French War Minister to Hennequin, instructing him at the same time to say that, if the fortune of France improved, she would not consider herself bound by these offers.[1]

The Dutch were keenly anxious that the offers should not be refused. "I must tell you as a man of honour", wrote Buys to Marlborough, "that it is time to listen to such propositions."[2] But this was mere bluff. Heinsius was more diplomatic but not less importunate. The proposals, he thought, offered the basis for a possible plan. Should they not enter into a regular and open conference on the subject?

> We are not certain (he wrote on the 25th of August) that France will always continue these same offers. If fortune changes they may also change. Affairs in Spain are not well established; those in Italy are in a bad way; those in Hungary also; those in the Empire in a state of absolute inactivity; and for us, your Grace knows the condition of our finances. If we once let slip a good chance there is no means of recovering it.[3]

The modifications of the French offers which he proposed were: (1) that the following towns from French territory should be added to strengthen the Barrier in the Netherlands: Ypres, Menin, Tournai, Condé and Maubeuge.[4] (2) That Naples and Sicily, and not Milan, should be given to Philip, and that the recognition of the Queen and the Dutch Barrier should be regulated by the Treaty which the two Maritime Powers were about to make. In reply, Marlborough begged Heinsius to take no step till the Ministers had expressed their opinion. He believed that the latter would advise deferring action till the end of the campaign; for, on the one hand, if France prospered,

[1] D'Avaux to Hennequin, 8 Aug. 1706. Vreede, p. 246. Chamillart to Hennequin, 8 Aug. 1706. Legrelle, IV, 387.

[2] Buys to Marlborough, 31 Aug. 1706. Blenheim Archives.

[3] Heinsius to Marlborough, 25 Aug. Vreede.

[4] This proposal is interesting since the demand for the French places was clear and definite, very different from the vagueness of the Resolution of 17 Aug.

she would not hold to her offers; and, on the other, if Charles should gain possession of Spain, neither the English nor the Emperor would consent to the dismembering of any part of the Monarchy. At the same time he wrote to Godolphin to prepare him for the impending avalanche of Dutch peace arguments and to urge the necessity for caution in the present state of tension.[1]

The direction of this negotiation now passed from the hands of Marlborough and Heinsius to those of Godolphin and Buys.

Buys led off with a letter written on the 27th of August. He first explained the nature of the French offers, laying emphasis on their statement that the offers would only hold if the negotiation was proceeded with at once. He allowed that the proposals needed a good deal of amending, but held that the right course was to enter into negotiations at once and rectify them as far as possible. He proposed a plan—which followed closely that suggested by Heinsius—and intimated that the Allies ought to be very grateful to the Sea Powers if the latter succeeded in bringing things to the issue he proposed.[2]

Godolphin replied on the 3rd/14th of September. Following a classification made by Buys he divided his letter into a discussion as to (i) the "Time" at which the negotiations should be entered upon; (ii) the "Details" each Ally should insist upon. The first, he declared, should be the end of the campaign, for the same reasons which Marlborough had anticipated. He differed also widely from Buys in his estimate of the satisfaction which should be granted to the several Allies. (1) Savoy and

[1] Marlborough to Heinsius, 21 Aug., 28 Aug. Vreede. Marlborough to Godolphin, 21 Aug. Coxe, I, 483.

[2] Draft of letter from Buys to Godolphin, 27 Aug. 1706, in the volume of secret peace negotiations during the war in the Rijksarchief at The Hague. Buys' amended proposals were:

(i) That Austria should regain all she had lost.

(ii) That Portugal and Savoy should be reasonably satisfied according to their treaties.

(iii) That not only Anne but the Protestant Succession should be recognised by Louis.

(iv) "Que la Barrière dans les Pays Bas augmentée de Ypres, Menin Tournai, Condé, Maubeuge, fût réglée au gré de L. H. P. aussi bien que le traité de commerce."

(v) That Philip should have Naples and Sicily.

Portugal and Prussia, he thought, should have the "full effect" of their treaties, not merely a reasonable satisfaction for them. (2) With regard to the Spanish Monarchy, he repeated that no good Englishman could advise the dismembering of it. This view he supported by the somewhat sophistical argument that Philip would certainly continue to be recognised by Louis, and that there was not much to choose between being titular King of Spain and actual King of Naples and Sicily. Moreover—and there was more foundation in this argument—Philip in possession of the latter places would be a menace to English and Dutch trade in the Levant, and would so intimidate Savoy as to drive him to make his peace with France. (3) England, for her own part, he observed, could not submit to the indignity of treating with France, while the Pretender remained in France, and, among other things not specified in the French proposals, she would insist on the razure of Dunkirk. (4) As for the Dutch, he was willing that they should have a treaty of commerce to their satisfaction and "procure an addition to the dominions of King Charles in the Low Countries for a barrier to the full extent of what they should judge necessary for their future security".[1] But it was not in his remarks either as to the time or the details of the peace negotiations that the chief importance of Godolphin's letter lay. The passage with the real significance was the introductory sentence.

I must put you in mind (he wrote) that the strict security for preserving those conditions the allies shall obtain from France, is the preserving of the alliance, particularly between the States and England, for a joint and mutual warrant of maintaining the particulars of such a treaty, and the sooner this was set on foot it would be so much the better, and not an improbable way to procure more reasonable terms from France.[2]

The question of peace was to be carried a step further from the reach of the French and the way to it barred by a preliminary treaty to be initiated and maintained by the Maritime Powers.

[1] The difference between this proposal and the corresponding one of Buys is significant. Buys had proposed that the Barrier should be "réglée au gré de L. H. P."; Godolphin was willing that "an addition to be obtained to the dominions of King Charles" should serve as Barrier.

[2] Godolphin to Buys, 3/14 Sept., in the volume of secret negotiations referred to above. Rijksarchief, The Hague.

Buys replied on the 28th of September. His letter, which remains a masterpiece of diplomatic juggling, followed the same classification as Godolphin's. His reply to the latter's suggestion as to a preliminary guarantee was obvious. Affecting the greatest cordiality of agreement in the idea, he hastened to show Godolphin that such a preliminary guarantee was already in existence in the Resolution of the 9th of August, which had provided, among other things, that the Barrier and Succession Treaty should be inserted bodily in the final treaty of peace and that the two parties in the earlier Treaty should guarantee the later and general one against all comers. All diligence should, therefore, be shown in bringing this Barrier Treaty to a conclusion. Having thus answered—and apparently gained on—the first point, Buys went on to pervert, in the most subtle manner, Godolphin's idea of an initiation, by the two Maritime Powers, of a negotiation affecting all the other Allies. He did so in further reviewing the questions of (i) "Time", and (ii) "Details". (i) He pointed out that there was no such time as an ubiquitous "end of the campaign", as in Italy and Spain the armies fought all through the winter; but for the sake of argument he would assume Godolphin meant the end of October, the date at which the Netherlands campaign would ordinarily close. He pointed out that it was already near the end of September and, therefore, high time for the English and Dutch to communicate their thoughts to one another and prepare the enemy for their acceptance.

My Lord (he observed), we make here a great distinction between regular negotiations in form and informal "pourparlers." Now as the former cannot be begun except in concert with the Allies (which will be a lengthy business), we have always thought that this would not prevent England and the States (who have alone borne almost the whole burden of the war) from arranging matters informally so as to bring them to a reasonable footing and be able to enter afterwards upon the formal negotiation with more success: it is, of course, understood that England and the States in these "pourparlers" should guard not only their own interests but also those of their allies, conformably to their treaties. This procedure, my Lord, we have come to the conclusion is not only permissible but even absolutely necessary, in view of the number of our allies and the diversity of their pretensions and interests.

There should be no particular time, Buys continued, for starting such an informal negotiation, which should on the contrary take place whenever the enemy made a good offer, and the present was therefore an excellent opportunity. This ingenious plan amounted in fact, as Noorden has pointed out, to the abandonment of the whole groundwork of the peace to the discretion of England and the States, while the several allies would draw up their individual bills of damages from the war and would have to make out their own case for the particular compensations which they demanded.[1] But this was not all. Buys proceeded to confer upon the Maritime Powers the further right of adjudicating upon these special claims. (ii) Turning to the question of details, he agreed with Godolphin's amendment that England and the States were bound to guarantee to the Allies the full effect of their treaties. But, said he, we would indeed be miserable if we had to carry on the war till each of the Allies were satisfied in all their pretensions. Not only had these pretensions often no foundation, but they frequently included territories claimed by another of the Allies. He instanced Milan which Savoy and the Alliance generally wished should belong to Charles but which the Emperor would claim as an Imperial fief. His logical conclusion was therefore that (the preliminaries having already been drawn up by England and the United Provinces) the two Maritime Powers, who had almost alone supported the war, should appoint themselves interpreters of each special claim.[2] The scheme proposed in his letter would have given the Dutch the three things which, above all, they desired: (*a*) peace—for they would be careful to draw up preliminaries acceptable to France and "interpret" away any additional claims at the final conference which might prove a stumbling block; (*b*) a free hand to arrange their Barrier as they pleased—for the French had offered this and the Austrians were to be kept effectually from interfering until it was too late to object; (*c*) a guarantee for this comprehensive Barrier from their strong ally across the Channel—for the Resolution of the

[1] Noorden, II, 431.

[2] Draft of letter from Buys to Godolphin, 28 Sept. 1706 Rijksarchief. The letter is endorsed with a statement to the effect that it was approved of both by Heinsius and the Burgomasters of Amsterdam.

17th of August specified no less. The only drawback to these dreams lay in the fact that the Dutch had of themselves no power to realise them. They could only wait in the anxious hope of a favourable reply from London.

Godolphin had first to meet the argument that, as regards a preliminary, there was already the proposed Barrier Treaty. This proposal involved both a positive and a negative disadvantage to the English. The first lay in the fact that the Resolution of the 17th of August was unacceptable in its present form and, moreover, contained no security for what the other Allies should receive at the peace—the very reason for which the preliminaries were desired. The negative disadvantage lay in the fact that by accepting the Dutch suggestion the English would throw away their control over the Republic. The Dutch would have gained their Barrier Treaty unimpeded by any ulterior conditions, and, though on the one hand England would not by this arrangement be bound to any special (and disadvantageous) terms of peace, as she would have been by the proposal made by Heinsius to Halifax on the 2nd of July, yet on the other her one strong hold upon the Dutch would have passed from her hands, by which she could bind them to maintain the war. The remedy came apparently from a suggestion made by Marlborough. Godolphin had sent to the Duke a copy of his letter to Buys of the 3rd/14th of September and in doing so observed, "If the very first point be agreed to that before any formal step be made towards peace both England and Holland shall engage to warrant whatsoever shall be concluded upon that occasion I shall not doubt but the rest shall follow to our satisfaction".[1] Marlborough replied, "I am very much of your opinion that before any step be made towards peace, we ought to have a treaty with the United Provinces for the guarantee of any treaty of peace we may hereafter make with France; and that there be room left for the Allies to come into it".[2] The remedy lay in these last words; for by admitting the other Allies into the preliminaries it became inevitable that the terms should be such as all the Allies would, and the French

[1] Godolphin to Marlborough, 2/13 Sept. Coxe, I, 483.
[2] Marlborough to Godolphin, 20 Sept. Coxe, I, 483.

would not, accept; this disposed of the chance of an immediate peace. And further, the rejection of the French offers, when coupled with the interference of the other Allies in the preliminaries, completely wrecked the Dutch hope of regulating the Barrier as they pleased. The refusal of the English to accept the Resolution of the 17th of August demolished their third aspiration, that of an English guarantee to this comprehensive Barrier, and thus formed the "coup-de-grâce" to their disillusionment. The letter which conveyed this sentence of execution to the Dutch hopes was dated the 23rd of September/4th of October. Replying firstly to the proposal of Buys with regard to the sufficiency of the Barrier Treaty as a preliminary, Godolphin expressed his pleasure that the Dutch had "approved of the proposition of making a preliminary treaty among the Allies for maintaining the peace that shall be made", and he hoped that Marlborough would settle that business with them when he came to The Hague.

But, (he continued) I question whether this can properly be done in the treaty for the guarantee of our Succession and your Barrier; for it would not be convenient to ask some of our Allies to guarantee the Succession of the House of Hanover, who are too considerable to be left out of the Treaty for the guarantee of the peace.

The reason was puerile, the principle vital.

Then, as to the Barrier-Treaty itself, (Godolphin continued) I have seen that project of a treaty which my Lord Halifax brought over, and I believe there must be alterations made in it before it can be agreed to. I think that part which relates to your Barrier is so worded that it may be interpreted to extend farther than perhaps you yourselves mean it should.

Not satisfied with having thus pierced through Buys' political "aes triplex" the Treasurer continued his onslaught, following in his turn the old division into "Time" and "Details". As to the "Time" of beginning the transactions, he observed that this was not so material as the manner of managing them. If due firmness was shown, the sooner they were begun the better, but particular care should be taken to show equal concern for all the Allies, lest France should see a weak point in the Allies' defence and take advantage of it. Then as regards the proposal that England and the Dutch should be "interpreters" of each individual treaty, he expressed his agreement to the proposal, but added, "Would you make use of this authority to lessen any advantage that the Allies might have from the success of their arms?" He concluded by advising that, to dishearten France, the Maritime Powers should agree to listen to no proposals until they had settled their state of war for another year.[1]

In his reply of the 15th of October, Buys asked that Marlborough might be authorised to concert a plan with the States to serve as an answer to France. He was of the opinion that while drawing up preliminaries in the sense required it was unnecessary to settle whether they should insist on all demands, or give way on certain points.[2] As to the Barrier Treaty, he complained that Godolphin had not specified his objections to the Resolution of the 17th of August. The arrival, a week later, of Halifax's letter of 8th/19th of October set all doubts at rest on that head.

The refusal of the Dutch to treat apart from the English, and the decision of the English ministry which had put an end to the negotiations were the cause of great disappointment to Louis. He attributed his ill-success to the suspicion that he wanted to sow dissension among the Allies. He wrote therefore to Rouillé on the 14th of October that he would attempt to secure an open conference. On the 21st Maximilian Emmanuel informed Marlborough and the States that the King continued in his pacific intentions and suggested a conference.[3] The States were still to choose a Barrier according to their pleasure.[4] Marlborough at once communicated the new proposals to London, The Hague and Vienna. He warned Godolphin that in their present state of feeling the Queen should be very careful in the answer she gave to the States.[5] To the English Ministry the new French proposals appeared to afford an admirable opportunity of applying the principle they had just laid down with regard to negotiations

[1] Godolphin to Buys, 23 Sept./4 Oct. Rijksarchief. Slight modifications cause the original to differ from Draft in Coxe, I, 486.

[2] Vreede, p. 160.

[3] Lamberty, IV, 302, 305.

[4] Such was the assurance given by Sersanders, the intermediary employed, to Cuper.

[5] Marlborough to Godolphin, 24 Oct. 1706. Coxe, II, 491.

for peace. The instructions communicated to the Duke by Sir Charles Hedges were to the effect that the States should

first of all agree with the Queen on a scheme for an honourable peace, as such a method would be more effectual for the end desired than the Conferences proposed by the Elector of Bavaria in the name of France. Should the States approve, the Queen would be willing to enter upon the adjustment of particulars between herself and them. As to the matter immediately under consideration, the Queen could only see in the present proposals from France an attempt to sow dissension among the allies; the Duke should therefore concert with the States that their replies to the proposals might be uniform and suitable.[1]

It was the unanimous opinion of the English Ministers that their instructions were so reasonable that the States could hardly refuse to abide by them.[2] Thus were the Dutch debarred from availing themselves of the second French "ouverture", by the application of the principle started to debar them from accepting the first.

The diplomatic duel with England was over. Not only had the Dutch Republic failed to gain any advantage, but it was left in a much worse position than before. The contest had brought the Dutch no nearer to peace, while it had left their Barrier Treaty bound to a galling condition. They had been made the victim of a system by which, to use a mathematical phrase, the Barrier Treaty had become a "function" of concerted preliminaries of peace. They had had to bow to England's determination never to grant the Treaty until the Republic had first been bound over not to make a separate peace.[3] Before a month

[1] Instructions from Sir Charles Hedges, 21 Oct./1 Nov. enclosed in letter of that date from Godolphin to Marlborough. Coxe, I, 493.

[2] Godolphin to Marlborough, 22 Oct./2 Nov. Coxe Papers.

[3] This account from p.60 follows Noorden, II, 433, etc., in attributing the rejection of French overtures to anxiety to obtain the Barrier from England. In P. Geyl, *Nederland's Staatkunde in de Spaansche Successieoorlog*, another explanation is given, which, in the light of Dutch policy in 1709–12 would appear more rational. Professor Geyl suggests, pp. 14–18, that the Dutch remained in the Coalition because they could not permit England to obtain privileges in the American Colonies and the Mediterranean from which they would be excluded, as in the concentration of their efforts on the war in the S. Netherlands they had already allowed their naval contribution as well as their participation in the war in Spain to fall far behind Great Britain. [Editor's note].

was over, the States were to feel the incubus of that determination; during the two years which followed it was the chief reason why no progress was made in the Barrier Treaty; it was exemplified in the "Preliminaries of May" and it was their power to throw off the dead weight that obtained for the Dutch such favourable terms in the final treaty of October 1709.

IV

We have now reached by another road, that of the Anglo-Dutch negotiations, the point at which we broke off in dealing with the correspondence between Marlborough and the Court of Vienna, relative to the government of the Spanish Netherlands. The triangular conferences at The Hague were the destination to which both roads led. Owing to an unusually fine autumn, the campaign was prolonged beyond the usual time, but at the beginning of November, Marlborough began to prepare for his journey to The Hague. On the 19th of October, while still at the camp of Cambron, he was joined by Stepney, who came north to take up his duties at Brussels. Stepney had long been desirous of leaving Vienna and the opportunity occurred when the rupture of negotiations with the Hungarians made his presence at the Austrian capital less absolutely necessary. On the 27th of October Marlborough went with him on a flying visit to Brussels. On his way there, he met Sinzendorf, and on the 5th of November the three started together for The Hague. On the evening of the 8th they slept at Rotterdam, and the next morning arrived at the Dutch capital.[1] While at Brussels Sinzendorf had communicated his instructions to Marlborough. They dealt with the subjects of the Peace and the Barrier. On the former point, these instructions provided for preliminary agreement, much as the English proposal to the Dutch had done, but went much further in the direction of community of action. All the Powers were to give their guarantee for the Peace before a verbal or written communication on the subject took place with any emissary of the French King. As to the Barrier, Sinzendorf was to listen to

[1] Marlborough, despatches and letters of various dates. Murray and Coxe Papers.

the Dutch proposals and "although the best expedient to content them would be to give them Spanish Guelderland, he was to take no final resolution, but to say that the decision should be made by the King of Spain". In all matters he was to be guided by the Duke of Marlborough.[1] On the whole, the Duke was pleased with these instructions and thought that if the Dutch were reasonable, a conclusion was possible. At the same time, being desirous that no facility for this end might be wanting, he would have preferred Sinzendorf to have had full powers. He asked Salm that these might be sent and said he would act as if they had been.

The immediate pressing question at The Hague was that of the preliminaries for the Peace. Buys had prepared a set, with the approval of Heinsius, and this after considerable pruning was submitted by the Duke for approval in London.[2]

The terms were widely different from those offered by France in the summer, which the Duke had hoped to amend into acceptance. In particular these terms were to pledge the States to obtain from Louis and Philip the whole Spanish Monarchy. The conditions insisted upon were, shortly: (1) for the Empire, the basis of the Treaty of Westphalia. (2) For Charles, the whole Spanish Monarchy as possessed by Charles II, with the two following exceptions: (*a*) that the States were to have a Barrier from the Spanish King; (*b*) that to the Spanish Netherlands as defined by the Peace of Ryswick should be added Furnes, Ypres, Lille, Tournai, Valenciennes, Condé, Maubeuge and Menin (already recaptured by the Allies), all under conditions as to which the States General should agree with the King. (3) The recognition of Anne and the Succession in the House of Hanover. (4) That

[1] These instructions, and the information contained in the following pages, are largely derived from the account of Sinzendorf's embassy, given in the *Mémoires* of M. de la Torre, his private Secretary on this occasion (vol. IV, pp. 286–350).

[2] The volume of secret peace negotiations, at the Rijksarchief previously referred to, contains the original drafts of the preliminaries. Buys prepared them on 5 Nov.; Heinsius approved them on the 6 Nov.: Marlborough asked to have the essentials extracted. A new set was prepared, but Marlborough shortened this down again and of the result two copies were made, one being kept by Heinsius and the other sent home by Marlborough on the 12th.

Louis would send the Pretender out of his kingdom immediately after the conclusion of peace. (5) A favourable treaty of commerce for England. (6) For Portugal the full effect of his treaties with the Allies. (7) The recognition, as such, of the King of Prussia, and the satisfaction of his other claims. (8) That "the King of France shall agree that the Spanish Netherlands augmented as above shall remain for ever united to the monarchy of Spain and that they shall serve as a Barrier for the States General, conformably to the project, contained in the Resolution of the States of Holland of the 17th of August 1706". (9) A favourable treaty of commerce for the States General. (10) For Savoy the full effect of his treaties. (11) That during the negotiation, the Allies shall have power to extend these articles and make other demands as they may think proper.[1]

On the 9th/20th of November Marlborough was informed that the English approved of the preliminaries provided every one of the articles was strictly kept.[2] For the sake of secrecy these preliminaries had been discussed by Marlborough and certain of the Deputies without any reference to the States General. Now that they were approved, Heinsius was to lay them before the States, but as a matter of fact this was never done.[3]

It would appear that in drawing up and approving these preliminaries, Sinzendorf was never consulted. There is no mention of his name in the correspondence relating to them, nor are they alluded to in the account in Torre's *Mémoires* of the Austrian's embassy, in which however the

[1] The 2nd and 8th articles mark a further stage in the definition process of the French portion of the Barrier Treaty. Furnes, Lille and Valenciennes have been added to the five towns claimed by Heinsius and Buys in August. The distinction between the part of the Barrier that is to come from French Territory and from Spanish is clearly marked. In the first case the acquisition is definite, while in the second all is still vague.

[2] Godolphin to Marlborough, 9/20 Nov. Coxe Papers.

[3] Marlborough to Hedges, 12 Nov., sending the preliminaries home; 23 Nov. acknowledging the news of their approval in London. It is probable, cf. p. 102, that the preliminaries remained as a project and were not communicated to the States General because the English and the Dutch could not agree upon them. Nevertheless, the fact that the Barrier claim was recognised by England in clause 8 must be considered a gain on the part of the Dutch, despite the fact that Sinzendorf was not consulted. [Editor's note.]

remarkable statement appears that in the matter of peace "Marlborough acted with great skill in concealing behind an impenetrable veil the intentions of the English", and this too at a time when he was affecting to have a complete understanding with the Austrian Envoy. But in the meantime, the latter had been busily engaged in discussing the question of peace with Heinsius. The general outcome of his conferences with the Pensionary was a belief on Sinzendorf's part that if a negotiation for peace took place, the basis of Westphalia, with the exclusion of the Electors of Bavaria and Cologne, might be demanded by the Emperor: while Charles might insist upon the whole Spanish Monarchy, not at present specifying on what footing the Monarchy should be restored, but with the probability that, if the war continued favourable, the basis of the Peace of the Pyrenees might be obtained. The importance of this result was two-fold. It was the basis which, in the spring of 1709, the Court of Vienna took as that on which the peace negotiations should be resumed at The Hague. It would, moreover, have a considerable effect upon the attitude of the Imperialists towards the Barrier question. The desire of the Hapsburgs was that the Dutch security should not interfere with the integrity of the Spanish Netherlands. It made therefore all the difference to this point whether the boundary line dividing France from the Spanish Netherlands should be that of the Peace of the Pyrenees—as Sinzendorf proposed—or that of the "status quo ante bellum", as in the preliminaries which the Sea Powers had just laid down. In the first case all the towns in the dispute would have to be considered as Spanish; in the latter, the majority of them would be French.

The question of the preliminaries being settled, the answers from Marlborough and the States to the Elector of Bavaria could be taken in hand. This matter Marlborough had discussed with Sinzendorf on their way to The Hague and the replies were concerted by them together. Again the States bowed to the inevitable, and on the 19th and 20th of November, the two uncompromising answers were sent which Legrelle has characterised as "chefs d'œuvre de tartuferie" and which the Elector transmitted to Louis as the "deplorable result" of their combined efforts.[1] Marlborough determined to make most of this example of firmness on the part of the Allies. All the various envoys were called together to hear the letters read by the Greffier Fagel, and copies were sent with all expedition to Vienna and Barcelona.[2]

There remained the great question of the Barrier. On account of their Barrier, the States had been obliged to prepare for a new campaign with exhausted finances and under the impression that further military success would hardly increase the country's gain.[3] They had given in on the preliminaries, they had counterfeited a bellicose enthusiasm in rejecting the offers of the Elector. What was to be their reward? It seemed at last as if the time for a final settlement had come. Representatives of all the three powers concerned were present. Moreover, not only had the Dutch a claim on England's consideration for the way in which they had yielded over the preliminaries; they had practically been told by the English that they had only to formulate their Barrier demand for the latter to be accepted. The conferences which were now to take place between the three Ministers, and after the departure of Marlborough and Sinzendorf, between Heinsius and Stepney, mark the close of what may be called the first epoch of the Barrier Treaty. During these conferences all mists as to the respective interpretations of the term "Barrier" melted away and the rival pretensions stood out sharp and clear in all their hopeless irreconcilability.

On the very day of his arrival at The Hague, an interview with Heinsius confirmed Marlborough in the fear that he would not be able to bring the Barrier Treaty to a conclusion there. He foresaw that the Dutch would ask far more than he would dare on his own responsibility to grant.[4] The hopes which the French offers had inspired in the Republic died hard. On the other hand, Heinsius had now realised that it was impossible to adhere any longer to the previous vague and comprehensive

[1] Legrelle, IV, 414, 415. The letters to Maximilian Emmanuel are given in Lamberty.

[2] Goes' despatch, 24 Nov. Klopp, XII, 234.

[3] But see on this point p. 69. [Editor's note.]

[4] Marlborough to Godolphin, 9 Nov. Coxe Papers.

expressions of their Barrier claim. There was no mistaking the meaning of the long letter from Halifax. He yielded to the inevitable and informed the Duke that the States would formulate their demands.[1] In this all-important undertaking the Pensionary took the expert advice of the Field Deputies now returned from the camp. On the 15th of November they met to consider (1) what towns should compose the Barrier; (2) how many troops each should receive; (3) who should pay these troops.[2] A few days later the Pensionary presented Marlborough and Sinzendorf with the result.

The fundamental principle on which the Dutch grounded their claim was that, by the terms of the Grand Alliance, they were to have a Barrier to defend themselves, and that in so doing they would, at the same time, be defending the Spanish Netherlands for the King of Spain, who had shown himself incapable of protecting his own dominions. From this fundamental principle three logical conclusions followed: (1) the Dutch must have a strong line of connected fortresses along the French and Spanish frontier; (2) the Dutch must have absolute command and control of the troops in these fortresses; (3) as the Dutch were conferring a benefit upon Spain in thus protecting the Netherlands, it was only right that the King should contribute to the expense of their garrisons. This principle and its conclusions was now put into practice in the Dutch demands presented to Marlborough and Sinzendorf. (i) The towns specified were, taking them in order from south to north, Thionville, Luxembourg, Namur, Charleroi and Mons; Maubeuge, Valenciennes, Condé, Tournai, Lille, Menin, Ypres and Furnes; Nieuwport, Ostend and Dendermonde.[3] These towns may be classed in three groups. The middle set, from Maubeuge to Furnes, represented those which were to come from French territory. These towns were the same as had been specified in the recent preliminaries as the Barrier fortresses which Louis was to surrender. A glance at the map will show both what a strong line along the French frontier they formed,

[1] Heinsius to Portland, 9 Nov. 1706. Heinsius Archives, The Hague.
[2] Cuper's Diary cited by Legrelle, IV, 414.
[3] The list is taken from Torre, *Mémoires*, IV, 339.

and also the significance of the additional garrison towns now demanded out of the Spanish Netherlands. The first set, from Thionville to Mons, was to round off the line on the southern side; and, of the last set, Nieuwport and Ostend were to continue the line northwards to the sea—an all-important consideration both for trade and defence—while the remaining town, Dendermonde, was to be the central point and secure communication for the Barrier fortresses with the Republic. The system might be compared to a huge anchor, the curve of which ran in a long unbroken line of ports from Ostend to Thionville, while the central shaft was represented by the direct line of communication through Dendermonde to the mother country. (ii) As to the command of the troops, this was, of course, to be in Dutch hands. (iii) In the matter of payment the Spanish Netherlands should contribute a sum sufficient to maintain forty, or at least thirty battalions.[1]

Such were the Dutch demands, to which both in principle, logical conclusions and applications, Sinzendorf's scheme was diametrically opposed. The Austrian's fundamental principle was that the King of Spain should undertake the defence of the Spanish Netherlands and that *ipso facto* his troops would be the security that the Dutch needed; any other Barrier in addition would therefore be really unnecessary. From this principle three logical conclusions followed as before. (i) That if in virtue of the Grand Alliance (which said nothing about Barrier towns being carved out of the Spanish Netherlands) the Dutch were to have an additional Barrier, the latter should come out of French Territory and should, moreover, be carefully selected so as to admit of no possibility of usurpations from the Spanish Netherlands—a condition which could only be attained by these places being isolated and not contiguous. (ii) As to the garrisons of the Barrier fortresses, it followed naturally that, as the fortresses would form part of the Spanish Netherlands, these garrisons should be Spanish troops under Spanish command—under which command also any troops the Dutch might choose to add would naturally come. In short, the arrangement existing before February 1701 should be maintained. (iii) In the

[1] The Field Deputies had suggested forty-two battalions.

matter of payment, Spain would support her own contingent, necessary for the defence of these fortresses. If the Dutch chose to add to the garrisons, this should be, of course, at the expense of the States. Sinzendorf proceeded to apply this principle, with its conclusions, in a definite statement, just as the Dutch had done. The project which he handed to Marlborough provided that: (i) the following places should be given to the Dutch for their Barrier: Gravelines, St Omer, Aire, Arras, Cambray, Bouchain, Valenciennes, Condé, Maubeuge, Charlemont and Givet. Such was the meaningless assortment of scattered towns in place of the Dutch project of two connected lines from Ostend to Thionville, with Dendermonde as a central base. Surrounded by an enemy's country, the towns proposed by Sinzendorf would be so isolated as to be valueless; absolutely cut off, by the intervening Netherlands, from any connection with the mother country, they would depend on the benevolence of the Spanish King for their very existence. (ii) In the remaining garrisons should be Spanish troops, under Spanish command. (iii) The King of Spain would provide twenty battalions for this purpose, and for any additional troops the Dutch should pay. Thus, not only were the States not to have anything out of the Spanish Netherlands (as they existed in 1701), either in places or money, for their defence: they would, on the contrary, probably have to pay a sum, and were to see the Spanish Netherlands enlarged in order that a system might be consolidated which had been shown to be no defence whatsoever to the Dutch.

Sinzendorf did not delude himself into thinking that the Dutch would like this arrangement, which practically set them up as a target for the first French shots in any war. He had talked the question over with Marlborough and suggested that the latter should endeavour to obtain the Dutch consent to his scheme by using the following arguments, which again correspond with the three "conclusions" on which the scheme was drawn up: (i) Marlborough was to point out that the Grand Alliance referred to a Barrier against France, and that it was quite impossible to interpret that Treaty to mean that the

Barrier should come out of the Spanish Netherlands. The Dutch therefore should not ask for places which might cause a jealousy among the Allies. (ii) He was to insist again upon the old fallacy at Vienna that the Barrier in the hands of Spain was as secure as in those of the States; and that the disaster of February 1701 was a very extraordinary event which would never occur again. (iii) That the States in their proposals had intended to have both the revenues and the military command in the places designated by them, powers which when taken together amounted to absolute sovereignty, an obvious infringement of the rights of His Catholic Majesty.

It is very unlikely that the Duke, who evidently kept very much in the background during these conferences, ever executed this little commission, given to him by Sinzendorf. After giving the vague promise to the Count that he would induce the Queen to do nothing that would be contrary to the interests of King Charles, and thanking the Imperial Court for sending Sinzendorf, who had been a "great solace" to him, he left for London on the 24th of November. Sinzendorf certainly was under the impression that Marlborough was in complete agreement with him as regards the Barrier. He himself repeated to the Dutch the admonitions which he had requested Marlborough to give them, and on the 25th of November started for Vienna, arriving there on the 23rd of December, to find all his proceedings at The Hague fully approved by the Emperor. He had come north "ad audiendum" so that he could have concluded nothing; he had laid bare to Marlborough the absurdity of the Imperial pretensions in the Netherlands; and he had succeeded in cementing the bond of hatred between the States and the Hapsburgs.

Marlborough's conduct in these conferences upon the Barrier question was even less satisfactory than that of Sinzendorf who, in reality, did little more than obey instructions. Not only does Marlborough seem to have most carefully avoided committing himself to either party; but one also looks in vain for any indication that he really made an effort to bring the two disputants together. In temporising he had no longer the same excuses that it had been possible to urge in his defence as regards his conduct, when offered the "Patent". A course of duplicity was, in the critical circumstances of that incident, perhaps the only way of avoiding irrevocable misunderstandings with the Emperor, and at the same time, of keeping the Dutch true to their allegiance. In November, however, the circumstances were different. The moment was one at which the hopes of the Allies stood perhaps higher than at any other time during the war. They had in the previous months been blessed with a series of striking successes which, if anything could, should have put them on good terms with one another. Again, there was not now the danger of misunderstanding by a far distant court, to prevent the Duke from taking a decided line. Representatives of all the three allied Powers concerned in the Barrier question were on the spot. Thirdly, Marlborough was no longer shackled, as he had been in the previous instance, by any delicacy in his own position. He was free to use to its fullest extent his great personal influence, and enhance its value by the additional glamour of a disinterested public spirit. It is not, of course, to be denied that, even when undertaken in such favourable circumstances, the task of making the Dutch and Austrians agree over the Barrier would have been exceedingly difficult, perhaps impossible. But it certainly should have been attempted, and Marlborough was the only man in Europe who could do so with any prospect of success. The Duke, however, endangered the good relations of the Allies to avoid committing himself to either party and to maintain the abnormal position which his duplicity in the matter of the Patent had given him, as confidential supporter both of the Dutch and the Hapsburgs. He still believed that matters would right themselves somehow when the war had been brought to a successful termination. But the opportunity of patching up the quarrel between the States and the Emperor, once lost, never returned. The blots in Marlborough's public life were faults of omission rather than commission. In omitting to make a supreme effort to restore harmony in the Alliance before it was too late, he made his first great and irretrievable mistake.

V

The effect of these triangular conferences between Marlborough, Sinzendorf and Heinsius upon the history of the Barrier Treaty was far-reaching and permanent. The enforced inclusion of Sinzendorf and the consequent failure of negotiations had convinced Heinsius that he must strain every nerve to come to an advantageous agreement with England as regards the Barrier Treaty, and with her help, compel the Hapsburgs to accept the project. The success of this plan therefore depended upon the reception of the Dutch project by the English. Of their demands the line of French fortresses had already been conceded to them in the preliminaries. Difficulty therefore could only occur in one or both of the two sets of the flanking buttresses of that line. Now these two buttresses represented a very different value to the States, and they had intimated as much to the Duke and Sinzendorf. Thionville and Luxemburg were isolated towns far away both from the Netherlands and from the other fortresses named; they lay, moreover, on a side from which the Dutch were not so liable to be attacked. Mons stood behind the long row of great frontier fortresses forming a second line of defence in itself. This position, while it rendered the town very valuable, made it a luxury rather than a necessity. Charleroi on the Sambre would strengthen a security which, on the other hand, might seem to be adequately given by Maubeuge and Namur. It was otherwise with Nieuwport, Ostend, and Dendermonde, all of which the Dutch considered as quite indispensable. By the possession of Nieuwport and Ostend, the gates of the Netherlands, the Dutch could prevent the French entering them along the coast, and become at the same time guardians of the maritime trade in the Channel. Dendermonde was perhaps the most necessary of all; for it secured the safety of communication between the Republic and the Barrier, on which the value of the latter so largely depended. With the irony of fate, it was just against two of these three places, Dendermonde and Ostend, that England's objections were raised most strongly.

Marlborough had assured Sinzendorf that the English would

oppose the demand of Dendermonde, because that town could only serve as a Barrier against Spain, and of Ostend, because it was necessary to keep the latter place open for freedom of trade.[1] On his departure for London, he left definite instructions with Stepney, who had recently received powers to continue the negotiation, on no account to yield on either of these two points. It would seem as if the Duke when he left for London still believed that Dutch obstinacy as to the two towns might be overcome, for he told Stepney to address all communications to him, doubtless, in the hope, that he might have the credit of concluding the long debated treaty. From the outset, however, Stepney met with the most determined opposition. He went about among the Dutch Deputies, hoping that inter-provincial jealousies might induce some of them to support the English pretension. He succeeded in finding that Wellandt, Deputy for Utrecht, thought the demand of the Dutch unreasonable, and confronted Heinsius with this expression of opinion. Heinsius explained that Utrecht was an inland province and therefore not concerned with the question. On the other hand, the Provinces of Holland and even more that of Zealand, would not hear of abandoning either of the towns, and General Fragell, the commander of Dutch Flanders, was equally vehement.[2] Stepney had several conferences with the Pensionary and on both sides the same arguments were worn threadbare. The Pensionary urged that no objection had been made by the English when, on the surrender of Ostend in the summer, General Spaar had occupied it with his troops. Stepney replied that this was merely a temporary arrangement, very different from a solemn and permanent treaty. Then Heinsius observed that Spain was so weak that in her hands the town would not be safe from French attacks or intrigues; to this Stepney answered that the Dutch were to have Nieuwport, which was sufficient to prevent them. "Why does England raise these objections?" then asked Heinsius. The Englishman, endeavouring to conceal any interested motives, replied that it was to prevent the susceptibilities of the inhabitants of Flanders from being wounded. Heinsius

[1] Torre, *Mémoires*, IV, 340.
[2] Stepney to Marlborough, 3 Dec., 7 Dec. 1706. British Museum.

explained that in the first place the Dutch claimed only the military garrison of the town, and that trade would therefore not be affected; secondly that as regards England—for he was convinced that it was her fears for her own commerce that prompted this opposition—by the 13th Article of the Treaty of Munster, Spain was bound to impose upon goods coming into Ostend the same dues as the Dutch charged on goods entering the Netherlands by the Scheldt. England could not therefore secure any differential treatment even if the Dutch did not have Ostend.[1]

As he made no progress whatever, the British Minister wrote home on the 10th of December suggesting that the English should give way. Marlborough's reply was that they had quite made up their minds not to do so.[2] All advance therefore was impossible. "There we stick," wrote Stepney, "and I don't perceive any disposition on either side to give way."[3] Feelings could find expression only in increased bitterness on both sides. The Dutch "began to have strange notions that the English must needs have at bottom some national interest of trade prejudicial to theirs".[4] "I don't express an opinion", wrote Slingelandt, "as to whether we have as much reason to insist upon Ostend and Dendermonde as many people think, but I confess that I see no solid reason on England's part to refuse us these places, especially if, as is to be feared, this refusal might have prejudicial consequences".[5] Similarly, Heinsius expressed his apprehensions of coming evil from English opposition.[6] On the other side, Harley inveighed against Dutch ingratitude and declared that their pretensions "would reasonably stir up a suspicion that they were not started with any good intention".[7] Matters had reached this state of

[1] Stepney to Marlborough, 3 Dec., 7 Dec., 10 Dec., 17 Dec. Drafts in the Stepney Papers; copies in the Coxe Papers.

[2] Marlborough to Stepney, 6/17 Dec. Murray.

[3] Private letter from Stepney to Harley, 28 Dec., written before the latter had received Marlborough's permission to correspond with the Secretary on the subject of the Barrier. Stepney Papers.

[4] Stepney to Cardonnel, 28 Dec. Stepney Papers.

[5] Slingelandt to Marlborough, 28 Dec. Blenheim Archives.

[6] Heinsius to Marlborough, 28 Dec. Vreede.

[7] Harley to Stepney, 24 Dec., 4 Jan. Stepney Papers. At the same time Harley had already begun his malicious insinuations against his colleagues. It was, he told Vryberg, the leaders of the Whig party, Sunderland and

friction and mutual distrust when the news came that Charles had confirmed the Patent offered to Marlborough in the summer. At once the smouldering fire of discontent burst forth with all its old fury.

Charles had not entered with any cordiality into the project of making Marlborough governor of the Netherlands. The Duke had written to him, at the same time as to the Imperial authorities, to express his thanks for the offer and to say that he could not "yet" avail himself of it.[1] As a matter of fact, at that time Charles had never made the offer and was in reality opposed to it. Stanhope had thought the battle of Ramillies a good opportunity for pressing the Duke's claims, but he had met with a refusal on the grounds of religion and the previous promise given to the Elector Palatine,[2] in September. It was only when he had already heard that Marlborough could not accept the Patent, that Charles, on the advice of Moles, confirmed the appointment. Marlborough's refusal was understood at Barcelona to mean that he would really carry on the governorship under another name. The Archduke, therefore, sent to him, together with his decree of nomination, three Patents; one for him alone, the second for him and Quiros, and the third for the formation of a council of persons attached to the King's service, with Quiros at their head.[3] Marlborough was to use whichever one of these the circumstances might permit, and one of the specified purposes for which they were to be used was the settlement of the Barrier with the States.[4]

Halifax, who, to pay court to the English nation, subjected the Dutch Barrier claim to scathing censure (Vryberg to Heinsius, 17 Dec., quoted by Noorden, II, 560). It seems that Heinsius had already that opinion of Halifax. To the latter, Stepney wrote: "As far as I can gather from his discourse, he (the Pensionary) fancies your Lordship is the main obstacle in England why we do not consent to those towns (Ostend and Dendermonde) as well as others" (17 Dec. 1706).

[1] Marlborough to Charles, 16 July 1706. Murray.

[2] James Stanhope to Marlborough from Tarragona, 3 July 1706. Coxe Papers.

[3] Lichtenstein to Emperor, 4 Oct. 1706, cited by Landau, p. 535. The gist of the first two Patents is given in Coxe, I, 446–7. The third is mentioned in the account of the Blenheim Archives in the Hist. MSS. Comm., 15th Report, vol. VIII (Appendix) as forming part of the letter from Charles to Marlborough on 8 Oct. 1706, from Valencia.

[4] Marlborough to Charles, Lichtenstein, 17/28 Jan. 1707. Murray.

Again Dutch opposition made all three proposals impracticable. The Patents were taken, the first two by Count Lescheraine, and the third by Zinzerling. The former, apparently, "behaved in the matter with great prudence", but Zinzerling was much too free in imparting the object of his commission. On the 21st of December, Stepney wrote to Marlborough that the Dutch had got wind of the matter. "They were already flying out in indecent expressions against the Imperial Court, and the King of Spain, for persisting in this nomination after the States General had peremptorily declared by letter in both places that things were not yet ripe enough in the Spanish Netherlands for such a determination."[1] Stepney very much regretted that both Envoys had not had the discretion to go round by Ostend instead of coming to The Hague, where Lescheraine had already arrived and Zinzerling was shortly expected. On the 3rd of January the storm burst. Zinzerling had communicated the news by letter from Dusseldorf to Count Goes, and it is quite likely that the latter was the channel through which the news officially reached the Pensionary.

The States General were at once in an uproar. Goes assured Heinsius that Lescheraine was only bringing a confirmation by the King of Spain of the offer the Emperor had previously made, and that Charles had not known at the time of sending the commission that Marlborough had already refused it.[2] This assurance calmed the States somewhat, but it was not enough. Heinsius attacked Stepney vigorously on the subject. "Mon Dieu", he exclaimed to the British Minister, "est-il possible qu'on voudrait faire ce pas sans notre participation." Stepney expressed his surprise at this unreasonable jealousy and remarked that the States General in their letter to the Emperor,

[1] Stepney to Marlborough, 21 Dec. 1706. Stepney Papers, British Museum. After a passage quoted in the text Stepney continued: "I am in duty bound to discover to your Grace an intrigue which I am persuaded you would hardly have suspected, which is that you may chance in time to have a competitor in Prince Eugene, if you do not take particular care of securing your interest with the King of Spain". Cardonnel had a little more information to add confidentially on this point. "His Grace", he wrote to Stepney on 14/25 Dec., "approves of your keeping yourself passive in relation to Eugene, though between you and I, he thinks the Prince's person more useful in Italy."

[2] Heinsius to Marlborough, 4 Jan. 1707. Heinsius Archives, The Hague.

objected only that the Barrier was not yet settled, which he had orders to treat of when they would come to reasonable methods. Heinsius answered abruptly that there was no thought of proceeding to that Treaty so long as there was any possibility of the Duke's accepting the said Patent. "All that I could do", wrote Stepney, "was to desire them to forbear that clamour and censure till your Grace thought fit to explain your own mind."[1] The post that brought this letter brought also remonstrances from the Pensionary and Slingelandt. Marlborough was deeply hurt.

I must confess (he replied) that it gives me great pain to see what little consideration is had for the services I have rendered to the States and for the zeal that I have shown on all occasions for the good and interest of your Republic; beyond that, I flattered myself that the promises I made after the battle of Ramillies would have gained for me a little more credit and confidence with those in whose eyes I have, without vanity, a right to some little merit. However, to quiet everyone on this subject, I pray you to renew my promise to all those whom you may think fit, that I have no desire whatsoever to take upon myself the government of the Netherlands and you will kindly do me the honour to believe that I would never be false to my word, even to get the whole country.[2]

Very different was his answer to the Court of Barcelona, the key-note of which was still "not yet". He was in a difficult position. On the one hand, it was obviously impossible for him to accept; on the other, the report about Eugene made it necessary to send a very guarded refusal. He explained to Lichtenstein that the unreasoning jealousy of the Dutch still prevented him from availing himself of the offer, but he appears,

[1] Stepney to Marlborough, 4 Jan. 1707. Coxe Papers, and (partially) in Coxe, *Marlborough*, I, 447.

[2] Marlborough to Heinsius, 27 Dec./7 Jan. 1707. Murray and Vreede. Cf. letter of same date to Slingelandt (in Murray) in which the Duke observes "I confess this hard usage, if I had less zeal for the public, would determine me to retire, and live quietly with those who seem to have a better opinion of my conduct and probity". Cardonnel, in his enthusiasm for his chief, was not quite so measured in his language. "Nothing in the world", he ejaculated, "would make me desirous his Grace should take the Government upon him but the obstinacy and ingratitude of the Dutch, whom I take for the most part of them to be the mere scum of the earth." Cardonnel to Stepney, 27 Dec., 7 Jan. 1707. The Private Secretary's correspondence at this period savours a good deal of "John Bull".

from an expression in a letter to Stanhope, to have considered that it needed only the settlement of the Barrier question to render acceptance possible. In the meantime, the King of Spain's anxiety for his Netherlands must be dispelled by the vague assurance that the Duke would use his favours in concert with Quiros, in the manner most conducive to the royal interest.[1]

The resuscitation of the "Patent" was not likely to improve the prospects of an understanding between London and The Hague on the subject of the Barrier. It is a significant fact that Marlborough now informed Stepney through Cardonnel that he should in the future direct his correspondence in the matter to the Secretary of State.[2]

Heinsius endeavoured to answer Marlborough's reproaches as to Dutch ingratitude by laying stress upon the fact that the Barrier was for the Dutch the sole object of war; but this explanation was not accompanied by any suggestion that might remove the "impasse" which the negotiation on that head had reached.[3] On the contrary, he advanced a new ground of opposition. The Dutch, he informed Stepney, had acquired a right to a Barrier by the Treaty of the Grand Alliance and therefore ought not to be controlled in their choice by England or by any other of the Allies, who had acquired no such rights by that Alliance. Stepney turned to Buys, but only to find that he "had picked up some more arguments to fortify the

[1] Marlborough to Stanhope and to Charles, 23 Dec., 3 Jan. 1707; to Charles and to Lichtenstein, 17/28 Jan. 1707. Murray. In the letter to Stanhope, Marlborough, after expressing his indebtedness in this matter to Stanhope's friendship, observes: "The unreasonable jealousies in Holland will not permit me to exert that authority with which H.M. is pleased to invest me till the business of the Barrier is settled, wherein I find no less difficulty". In his letter to Lichtenstein there is the following significant remark: "A mon arrivée en Hollande je travaillerai à lui (Charles) obtenir un bon établissement des revenus du pays; cependant il serait bon que V. A. m'envoyât au plustôt un petit mot de lettre là-dessus de la part de S. M. pour m'autoriser à y employer mes soins avec d'autant plus de succès". It looks very much as if this remark was intended as a delicately veiled attempt to ascertain how far his continued "not yet" had satisfied the King, and was not altogether unconnected with the anxiety which Stepney's story as to Eugene might have inspired; cf. the note on the general question of Marlborough and the Patent, Appendix A.

[2] Cardonnel to Stepney, 27 Dec./7 Jan. 1707. Stepney Papers.

[3] Heinsius to Marlborough, 18 Jan. Blenheim Archives.

opposition", the chief of which was that it was possible that the French could never be brought to give up or raze Dunkirk and that therefore Nieuwport alone would not be a sufficient defence. This was hardly a reason which would commend itself to the English.[1] It was even suggested as a last resource, that Buys should go over to London himself to overcome opposition, but Marlborough wrote that this was quite useless unless he came with powers to desist from the demand of Ostend.[2] So the weary wrangle dragged on, till in March Harley gave it up as hopeless.[3] Two months later, at the opening of the campaign, Marlborough could only declare that the decision of the Queen not to give up Ostend to the Dutch was irrevocable.[4]

Such were the results of the conferences at The Hague, which brought the first period of the history of the Barrier Treaty to a close. Heinsius was bitterly disappointed, and poured out his grief in a long letter to the Earl of Portland, reviewing the whole course of the negotiation.

The letter was so moderate in tone and in policy that it might have been written officially to a jealous ally instead of in confidence to a fellow countryman and intimate friend.

When England, (wrote the Pensionary) began to speak of the guarantee of the Succession, she appeared to be fully as eager for our Barrier as we ourselves could have been, and my Lord Duke adopted a similar attitude. But as soon as we had shown them the Resolution of the States of Holland—the contents of which you know—it was said that the terms on which we desired the Barrier were too general, and that we should specify the towns. We thought this wrong; nevertheless it was done. When we yielded, they at once raised objections to Ostend, Dendermonde and Mons, urging that these places were not frontier towns, and therefore could not be of

[1] Stepney to Harley, 18 Jan. Record Office.

[2] Cardonnel to Stepney. Stepney Papers. The corner giving the date has been torn away but the letter acknowledges one from Stepney of 18 Jan., so that its date can be fixed fairly accurately. The letter produced another characteristic effusion from Cardonnel. "His Grace", he wrote, "is indifferent whether M. Buys comes over or not; but if he has no power and inclination to leave Ostend out of the Barrier, he had as good stay away. I take him to be very positive, self-interested, conceited, and not over much our friend."

[3] Harley to Stepney, 4/15 March 1707. Record Office.

[4] Goes' despatch, 17 May 1707, cited by Noorden, II, 561.

use for the Barrier. This greatly surprised me, for before this they had agreed not only to Dendermonde, but also to Antwerp. Observe that they have changed their front; I should be very glad of some explanation of their conduct. I wonder if it is because they are no longer so desirous of the guarantee mentioned above—they show no eagerness for it at the present moment—or if the reason is a different one. To return to our Barrier, I must tell you that the principle to which they hold at present, namely, that of making the Barrier to consist of frontier towns and forts only (whether taken from the Spanish Netherlands or from the towns which the enemy may consent to add to the Netherlands) might easily prove our ruin. For if we cannot have communication between our own frontier and this other one, we shall be cut off from the latter whenever the enemy succeeds in taking any one of the Barrier towns. Dendermonde must serve for securing this communication, as also Mons. As to Ostend, which is the principal stumbling block, we think that nothing is more necessary than that town for the Barrier: for if the Spaniards are to guard it, is there anything more easy than to take it? Even if it were found impossible to corrupt a commander, the town would always be exposed to the sea. If the town were kept sufficiently supplied and fortified, time might possibly allow of coming to its assistance; but of all this there can be no surety if it remains in the hands of the Spanish. On the contrary, there will be everything to fear—more so from this town than from any other in the Barrier. Our plight is evil indeed, when our friends whom Nature herself has pointed out as our support, are more jealous of us than are our enemies; from the latter we have everything to fear, and yet they now offer us the Barrier for our disposal—a thing which hitherto they have never consented to do. We Dutch have interests in common with the other Allies and we have interests of our own; the former for the preservation of the liberty of Europe; the latter, for our defence. Those are the only reasons for which we have joined the war. We know how open we are to the whole of Europe, and that if we lose an effective Barrier we lose everything.[1]

But if for the Dutch the year had ended in the gloom of disillusionment as regards the Barrier, it had begun with a period of unexampled success and the balance was still on the right side. Much had already been gained and there was hope also that the rest could not be long delayed. Keen-sighted politicians had begun to realise that it lay in the hands of the Maritime Powers to fix the duration of the war, for they alone

[1] Heinsius to Portland, 3 Dec. 1706. Heinsius Archives.

had nearly attained, or might at any moment attain, their objects in it. Charles might call himself Lord of a long list of kingdoms and lands, both in the old world and in the new, but of all these possessions only Catalonia and Sardinia were actually in his possession. There had indeed been conquests, but he had benefited but little from them. Malta and Gibraltar, the keys to the Mediterranean, were in English hands and were not likely to leave them; while Minorca was soon to follow. The Netherlands had passed not to their sovereign but to the Condominium, and Milan his brother had wrung from him by a secret abdication.[1] Nor had the Emperor been more fortunate. He had indeed robbed Charles of Milan, but had no other gain to set against widespread defection at home. A few months more and he would indeed be master of Naples and Sicily, but those conquests cost him more than they could possibly repay by loosing the bonds of selfish ambition, and alienating his allies. On the other hand, the States had already advanced far towards the attainment of their object in the war and England might at any moment attain hers. She had entered the war to win the security of her trade and the recognition of her Succession. The first, her conquests had already made but a question of time; the latter was a demand which, unlike the dispossession of Philip, it would cost Louis merely the pang of wounded honour to grant.[2] The future lay, then, with the two Maritime Powers. For the moment they shared the power, which success had given them, unequally. The Dutch had, in the preliminaries, indentured themselves for service under England and then had been refused the Barrier, which they claimed as wages. But the help rendered to them by their ally in the critical months of June and July had left them self-supporting. They could afford to wait for payment, and would not on the day of Settlement forget to charge full interest.

[1] This point is well put by Landau, pp. 529, etc.

[2] There is in the Stepney Papers a masterly letter on this subject written by Stepney on 4 Sept. to Harley. It contains several predictions which were abundantly justified by the event.

CHAPTER III

The Interregnum from January 1707 *to December* 1708

I

THE history of the Barrier and Succession Treaty under the Whig Dispensation is like a drama in two acts between which a long interval is supposed to elapse. After the interval the old characters reappear upon the scene, but in that lapse of time their fortunes have completely changed. So it was with the Barrier Treaty. The first act of that drama was the diplomatic struggle in 1706 which ended with the discomfiture of the Dutch. The period from January 1707 to December 1708 was the entr'acte during which the drama indeed made no apparent progress, but the relative positions of the principal characters underwent nevertheless a gradual and complete transformation. The second act took place between January 1709 and January 1710 and resulted in the triumph of the Dutch.

Between the beginning of 1707 and the end of 1708 the Barrier question apparently stood still. The Dutch were ever desirous of bringing it to a conclusion, while the Emperor and England—which at that time meant Marlborough—were intent upon delay. To the Emperor the results of Sinzendorf's embassy to The Hague made it apparent that anything was better than conclusion on the Dutch terms. Wratislaw expressed the feelings of the Viennese Court in a letter to the Duke of Marlborough.

> The affair of the Barrier (he observed) is embarrassing. The Dutch are too exorbitant in their pretensions. If an immediate arrangement be attempted we have nothing reasonable to expect and the evil will be irremediable. If it is deferred the Netherlands will be ruined and the embarrassment will be increased at the General Peace. As for my part I had rather defer it than settle it at this rate.[1]

[1] Wratislaw to Marlborough, 2 April 1707. Coxe Papers.

Marlborough agreed entirely with this point of view and observed in reply: "There will be embarrassment and difficulty in whatever way the question be handled".[1] In the meantime the deadlock arrived at between England and the States continued unaltered. The States refused to give up Ostend; the Ministry refused to grant it or indeed to consider the Barrier question at all without special provisions for securing the Dutch state of war for the following year. They were determined to abide by the preliminaries of November 1706.[2] An additional obstacle to arriving at an understanding was the absence of any accredited British representative at The Hague. Stepney, who held that post, was at Brussels throughout the summer of 1707 till he came home in the autumn to die. The place which he had so ably filled was left vacant for some time, and when Cadogan was appointed his headquarters remained at Brussels. Heinsius several times drew Marlborough's attention to this state of things, and repeated his apprehensions of bad results if the Barrier question were not speedily settled. But his representations produced no result.

Meanwhile Charles at Barcelona was chafing at the inactivity in the Netherlands which continued to be forced upon him. Ever since the establishment of the Condominium, the arbitrary conduct of the Dutch had caused widespread disaffection in the conquered provinces. This made the King's position of impotence only more galling, as he wished to impress upon the inhabitants that their only escape from punishment for such disloyalty lay in the clemency of the King.[3] He made two

[1] Marlborough to Wratislaw, 19 April 1707. Murray.

[2] But there was a difficulty here. "The Dutch", wrote Marlborough, "should be told of the firm resolution of England not to think of peace except on the Preliminaries agreed to last winter. This may be difficult; for, as the Preliminaries were never brought in form to the States, so you may be sure they will pretend they know nothing of them" (to Godolphin, 11 Aug. 1707). Coxe, II, 122.

[3] Wagner, *Historia Josephi*, p. 266. This interesting work, written by one who apparently was the confidential confessor of the priest-ridden Emperor, is of course on a lower level, from the point of view of historical evidence, than the actual official letters of the period. At the same time the information in the book, where I have been able to test it, has proved so generally accurate (despite a woeful absence of dates) that I have not hesitated to make use of it as a provisional substitute for many of the Austrian Official dispatches which I have not had an opportunity of consulting.

efforts to assert his power, but the Dutch defeated both. In the summer of 1707 he appointed Quiros, the strongest and most faithful agent he ever had in the Netherlands, governor of Limburg, with power to exact homage from his subjects in the Low Countries.[1] Marlborough thought "nothing could be more reasonable", but he reckoned without his host. An effective remonstrance soon arrived from the Pensionary. "I cannot understand the Commission," he wrote, "for as long as we have not given back the Low Countries to the King, such an authorisation cannot take place." He took the occasion to refer again to the Barrier and to press for a conclusion, but vague promises were all he received in reply.[2] Baffled in this attempt, Charles, the next year, took a more decided step and renewed the offer of the "Patent" to Marlborough, this time for life. He again advised secrecy and expressed his approval of Marlborough's "prudent dissimulation" in the matter so far, "although", he added, "I don't doubt but that you will never allow the Netherlands, under the pretext of that pretended Barrier, to suffer any diminution either in their area or as regards my royal authority in them, which authority I wish to place in your hands".[3] This was the counterpart from Barcelona of Sinzendorf's mission from Vienna in 1706. The Dutch would not find one brother more tractable than the other. Marlborough replied that he would sacrifice everything that was dear to him

[1] Speaking of Quiros, Noorden observes, "He was as much at home at the Hague as at Brussels, a partisan formerly of the House of Bourbon, but since the outbreak of the war the sworn servant of the Archduke, active and tough, suited to play the part of Austrian influential agent owing to his friendly footing in Holland and his close and varied relations with the Spanish Netherlands.... Quiros took every opportunity of revealing how unnatural and disadvantageous the present condition of affairs was, and of preparing the ground for the speedy acceptance of the Spanish King. In order to be able to meet machinations of this kind, the Dutch Republic required to be reliably backed up by the English Government" (Noorden, III, 468). Quiros had the entire confidence also of Marlborough, and his death in January 1709 was a sad blow to Hapsburg interests in the Netherlands.

[2] Marlborough to Quiros, 30 July 1707. Murray. Heinsius to Marlborough, 20 Aug. Blenheim Archives. Marlborough to Heinsius, 25 Aug. Murray. Marlborough to Godolphin, 12 Sept. 1707. Coxe, II, 147.

[3] Charles to Marlborough, 5 Aug. 1708, in the Archives at Brussels, quoted by Gachard, p. 337. The letter is partly given in Coxe, II, 315; the most interesting passage is there omitted.

to render himself worthy of such a favour, and his letter on the subject to Godolphin showed that he still considered his assumption of the Government as only postponed.[1] In December 1708 the news of this offer reached The Hague only to add to the suspicion with which the Dutch had begun to view the Duke's procrastinating treatment of the Barrier question.[2] Ill-feeling meanwhile was growing steadily in the conquered provinces.

The burdens and hardships of the war were renewed from year to year; there were compulsory quarterings of troops, demands in the way of taxes, harsh commands and contemptuous conceit on the part of the Dutch Administrators. On the top of all this lay the well-known opposition between the Hapsburg claims of sovereignty and the Condominium of the Sea Powers. Farther, there were rumours of the intentions of the Protestant Republic with regard to military,

[1] He wrote to Godolphin: "This must be known to nobody but the Queen; for *should it be known before the peace* it would create inconveniences in Holland, and I beg to assure the Queen that it is not compliment, but real duty, that when the peace happens, if she shall not think it for her honour and interest that I accept of this great offer, I will decline it with all the submission imaginable" (Marlborough to Godolphin, 7 Sept. 1708). Godolphin replied, "I am very well pleased to hear that Charles has renewed the patent to you in the manner you speak of and must also agree with you that unless the secret of it be better kept than those things use to be, it cannot fail of doing a great deal of mischief not only with the States, but also in other places; so I think too much care cannot be taken to keep it quiet" (1/12 Sept. 1708. Coxe Papers).

[2] The letter from Field Deputy Pesters which brought the news is a curiosity. He describes the interview with Marlborough thus: "J'eus l'occasion de lui insinuer qu'on faisait une attention très particulière aux ménagements qu'il avait pour la Cour de Vienne, et en particulier pour ce qui regarde le roi Charles par rapport aux Pays Bas. Surquoi je le vis étudiant toujours son air, un peu décontenancé—du moins il me parut comme cela. Il s'écria 'Mon Dieu, qu'est-ce que j'ai à attendre du roi Charles? Il m'a donné à différentes reprises le gouvernement des P. B. J'en ai la patente', me montrant sa cassette; et puis se reprenant, dit; 'Non je l'ai laissé en Angleterre; mais quand j'ai su que cela déplaisait à votre République j'y ai renoncé, et je renonce pour jamais. Non, en vérité, Pesters' (comme il me nomme quand il veut me parler sérieusement), 'si l'on m'offrait en Hollande la charge de Stadholder, sur mon dieu et sur ma damnation, je ne l'accepterais pas; on se trompe beaucoup sur mon sujet; je sais de quoi on me soupçonne, mais je ne songe qu'après avoir contribué tout mon possible pour avoir une bonne et durable paix, de me retirer chez moi. Cependant', ajouta-t-il, 's'il fallait un Gouverneur pour les P. B. je ne sais pourquoi je serais moins agréable à la République qu'un autre, mais je vous assure que je n'y songe pas'". Pesters added in a postscript, "M. de Renswoude m'a dit de savoir de science certaine que le duc a reçu dernièrement une nouvelle patente pour toute sa vie" (H. Pesters to Heinsius, 17 Dec. 1708. Heinsius Archives).

financial and territorial dominion. All these circumstances exerted a most disastrous effect upon the disposition and behaviour of Official, Landowners, and Bourgeois of the conquered Provinces.[1]

So things drifted on in their unsatisfactory transitional condition; the members of the Condominium themselves were not on good terms, but they united to check the Hapsburgs.

II

From this apparent stagnation we turn now to the underlying process of transformation. Why was it that at the opening of the year 1709 the Dutch found themselves in a position in which not only did they no longer need to wait for the settlement of the Barrier Treaty, but which enabled them, before the year was out, to conclude it almost on their own terms? The reason was twofold: (1) ministerial changes in England, and (2) failure in the war on the Continent.

The winter of 1706–7 was the high-water mark in the career of that statesman who, from the outbreak of the war to his dismissal from office, held an ascendancy in the politics of Europe to which no other Englishman perhaps has ever attained. Marlborough had returned to London in December 1706 to find increased honours heaped upon his person and posterity, and enthusiastic speeches delivered for the maintenance of the cause which his countrymen saw personified in him.[2] From this point his credit gradually fell and for its fall he was himself largely responsible. Marlborough's character might be summed up in the phrase 'μηδὲν ἄγαν' and his policy as one of non-committal. Both his actions, and the motives which inspired them, were one inextricable maze of balancing calculations. In motive he was a patriot, a coalitionist—if we may use the word—and a self-seeker. That he had the interests of his country at heart there is little doubt; that he sincerely desired the success of the Alliance from the point of view of broad-minded statesmanship is hardly less certain; that he accepted with pleasure the aggrandisement which he gained from the war, while he made preparations for every possible change of

[1] Noorden, III, 471.
[2] Torcy to Hennequin, 5 Dec. 1706. Vreede, p. 182.

fortune, 'is incontestable. In the hour of success these three aims did not clash; in the hour of failure they did, and then the third consideration was apt to outweigh the others. Marlborough's diplomacy was the objective product of those aims. Conspicuous as an example of lifelong devotion as a husband, and capable of noble private friendships, he had, as a politician, carried to a unique perfection the power of self-control and the art of concealing his inward feelings. With an extraordinary personal fascination he combined a polished urbanity of expression, even under the greatest provocation, which rendered him equally irresistible and inscrutable.[1] It was these qualities, added to his consummate skill as a general, that marked him out as the leader of the Alliance. That position, once gained, he kept by his military genius and by maintaining, in diplomacy, a policy of non-committal. It was necessary for him to be all things to all men. Some such policy was indeed inevitable if all the Allies were to be kept in line in their simultaneous march towards the goal. Now while the war made a steady progress this policy was attended with excellent results. Bold decisions could be taken without producing difficulties, and, where he temporised, this would be put down as wise moderation in the hour of victory. But even at the zenith of his power the Duke began slowly, perhaps unconsciously, to lay the train for his downfall. He left The Hague in November 1706 taking with him the impression that both Heinsius and Sinzendorf believed him the champion of their respective causes, but in reality having started upon a hopeless enterprise with no possibility of retreat. Marlborough's policy rested for its success upon two conditions. He must keep control of the forces working under him, and the result of the war must fulfil anticipations. He bestrode the Alliance like a Colossus and those were the two conditions on which his position rested. But the two years 1707 and 1708 undermined both those conditions. During that period he began to lose his undisputed ascendancy at home, and the unexpected resistance offered by France, while it protracted the war, reduced the chances of obtaining, at the

[1] For a striking portrait of Marlborough by a Dutch contemporary see Goslinga, *Mémoires*, p. 42.

peace, those terms, the prospect of which had kept the Allies in concert under his guiding hand. It was then that Marlborough fell. It was then that the difference appeared between him and his great predecessor at the head of the Alliance. It was then, when it was most disastrous to temporise, that the temptation to do so became irresistible. What had appeared wise moderation now became fatal indecision. As difficulties multiplied he drifted more irresolutely, more helplessly. From trying to please all, he ceased to be acceptable to any. He, who had been the mainstay of the war, looked on while the decision of the terms of its conclusion passed from his hands. He, who had promised all things to the States and the Emperor, saw another receive the thanks of the Dutch for the conclusion of their Barrier Treaty, and another appointed governor of the Netherlands. He who had proudly declared he "would never be the slave of either party in England", became in turn the slave of both. But Marlborough had been so great in the noontide of his career that he was great even at its fall. A time-serving age did not spare him when once he had lost his power. But his detractors, while they heaped their insults upon him, still marvelled, like the Greeks of old who stood round the corpse of the fallen Hector, at the "wondrous beauty" of the man.

The two causes which undermined Marlborough's position were just the two which strengthened that of the Dutch. The changes in the Ministry of England, which began with the replacing of Hedges by Sunderland in December 1706, gathered impetus from the dismissal of Harley in February 1708, and culminated in the appointment of Somers as Lord President and the triumph of the Whig Junta, were all to the advantage of the Dutch. A body had been called to power which had a self-supporting solidarity and hardly needed the help of Marlborough; which lay under no obligation to the Hapsburgs, and was, above all, desirous of promoting the guarantee of the Protestant Succession and thus, by implication, of settling the Barrier.

In the second place the Dutch gained immensely by the fact that though two years had passed, things stood very much where they were as regards the reduction of France and

Spain. The various campaigns of 1707 and 1708 had not produced striking successes like those of 1706 to stir the enthusiasm of a lukewarm member of the Alliance, while they had so far exhausted the resources of France that Louis was willing to grant greater concessions than before. The campaign of 1707 in the Netherlands had been a failure all the more galling after the successes of the preceding year.[1] Disaster elsewhere served further to dispirit the Dutch. The defeat of Galway and Las Minas at Almanza discouraged them before the campaign began, and the news of the failure at Toulon depressed them at its close. In the south the strength of the Allies had been diverted from the central aim by the selfish reduction of Naples and Sicily, while in the east the Emperor had been engaged in a long wrangle with Charles of Sweden who remained a standing menace at Alt Ranstädt. The year 1708 on the whole did not atone for these disasters. The victory of Oudenarde was indeed followed by the reduction of Lille, Ghent and Bruges, which completed the successes of a wonderful campaign, but there had been a heavy leeway to make up and the central victory itself had been in a sense rather defensive than offensive. Moreover, while it improved the prospects of the Allies, it was welcomed by the Dutch not so much for the promise it gave of a prosperous campaign, as from the hope that it would soon compel Louis to renew his former peace offers which had ceased with the defeat at Almanza.

> They will endeavour (Marlborough wrote of them a fortnight later) to make use equally of good success and ill success towards their aim, which is peace; on the other side we must continue our efforts as zealously to keep them on, as long as we can, in the expectation of further advantages by doing so.[2]

The Allies had disputed their respective claims in the hour of success; it was not likely that failure would strengthen the

[1] The cause of the failure of the 1707 campaign in the Netherlands would in itself form an interesting subject for investigation. Goslinga complains that the army had been marched up and down by Marlborough over the country in an aimless way and only by good luck had escaped from several dangerous predicaments. This view is borne out by some rather striking letters from a Col. Cranston to Harley in the Portland Papers, *Hist. MSS. Comm. Rept.* xv, App. 4.

[2] Marlborough to Godolphin, 23 July 1708. Coxe, II, 270.

bond between them. The Court of Barcelona, supported chiefly by foreign aid and paralysed by racial jealousies, had missed the one opportunity of consolidating the seeming conquests of 1706 and had lost ground ever since. The Emperor, finding a French indemnity so elusive, had taken one out at the expense of his nearest ally. In Germany bankrupt princes were protesting that arrears of payment and the designs of the King of Sweden had made the recall of their troops inevitable. In England there were those, in the secret confidence of the court, to whisper that the country might not be so solidly behind the uncompromising Junta as was commonly believed. The early promise of Blenheim and Ramillies, Barcelona and Turin, had been darkened with clouds of mutual suspicion, while pretensions grew yearly further removed from the possibility of realisation. Such were the conditions which in 1709 warned the Dutch that the time had come when they must and could exact their payment. Hitherto the diplomatic skill of Marlborough had rendered promises sufficient to keep the States firm to their allegiance. But now, to the fear that these promises, indefinitely postponed, might eventually fail to be realised, was added the urgency of a fallen foe, crippled with debt and stricken with famine. The Dutch were arbiters of the situation and could name their own terms. They would have from England a guarantee for the Barrier they chose or make peace with France.

CHAPTER IV

The Barrier Question in 1709

I

THE Whig Junta had not been in power a month before the Dutch realised that a new era had begun and that a great statesman favourably disposed to them had attained to the post of Lord President, from which to dispute the supremacy which the Duke of Marlborough had held hitherto over the counsels of his country. Ever since December 1706, Heinsius had complained bitterly of the lukewarm interest that England had taken in the Barrier Treaty. That reproach could not be urged against the new Ministry. On the 21st of December 1708 Vryberg wrote to assure the Pensionary that they were ready to do all in their power to bring the matter to a conclusion.[1] Three weeks later, still better news arrived. Vryberg reported a long conversation on the subject with Somers, who had insisted upon the desirability of concluding the Treaty before peace negotiations were commenced; both, as he said, to prevent disputes on the subject with King Charles—a point of great advantage for the Dutch—and, as Vryberg gathered, to prevent interference on the part of the French—a matter of no less importance to the English. Somers recognised the advantage of the Barrier in giving security as well to England as to the States and was quite agreed that it should be made amply sufficient. There was in fact only one point in dispute—Ostend. Here again Somers took the initiative and suggested compromise. He pointed out that the overwhelming importance of this place was due to trade jealousy. The English were quite determined, he said, that the Dutch should never have it, but, on the other hand, there was no idea on their part to make any special stipulations on the subject with King Charles to the prejudice of the Dutch. He recommended that the two nations should draw up regulations

[1] Vryberg to Heinsius, 21 Dec. 1708, cited by Noorden, III, 479.

concerning trade, satisfactory to both, whereupon the importance of the place would disappear. Further, he again insisted that, if the French could be compelled to raze Dunkirk, Dutch security would be less dependent upon the possession of the much disputed town.[1] Not long after, Portland also reported similar assurances from the Lord President. On the 8th of February Vryberg had a conversation with Godolphin which showed that the latter was not less favourably disposed. Vryberg complained to him of the little progress that had been made during the last two years in the Barrier Treaty. Godolphin answered,

Have we not conceded to the State all the places the State herself demands; and not only that, but agreed to make and keep the places on the Barrier in such a condition of defence as best to provide for the security of the State, with the exception only of Ostend? This is the only place which England cannot give up in her Policy and this we have told you now for two years, both at the Hague and here; neither I nor any other of the Ministers can give in on this point; I know perfectly well all the arguments that are reciprocally alleged for and against, but I will not risk my head in the matter.[2]

The conclusion to be derived from all these interviews was that, so long as Ostend was not demanded, the English were both ready and anxious to conclude the Barrier Treaty at the earliest opportunity.

The communications of the Whig leaders to Marlborough at this time disclose a similar desire. The Duke was to be the means for accomplishing this result. On the same day that Vryberg had acquainted his government with the first indications of the new spirit at London, Godolphin set out in a letter to Marlborough the programme of the Junta.

Somers and I (he wrote) seem entirely to agree that the chief motive at this time with the States for pushing the war, is because no other way appears of coming at peace in such a manner as will be pleasing in any degree to England, but that in the bottom the States have the same kindness for peace and perhaps more than ever; and considering that the King of France may in all probability incline to leave that matter very much in the disposition of the States, that there may be no room for nor pretence for mistaking

[1] Vryberg to Heinsius, 15 Jan. 1709. Heinsius Archives.

[2] Vryberg to Heinsius, 8 Feb. 1709. Heinsius Archives.

the opinion of England, we have resolved some heads relating to this business.[1]

These heads were: (1) Restitution of Monarchy of Spain to King Charles III. (2) Due satisfaction to just pretensions of the Emperor, the King of Prussia, the Duke of Savoy and rest of the Allies. (3) Favourable treaty of commerce with the States General and a sufficient Barrier for their satisfaction and security. Marlborough received these communications while at Ghent on his way to The Hague after the protracted campaign of 1708. Anticipating that he would be pressed most on the subject of the Barrier, he requested Somers and Godolphin to explain themselves more on that head.[2] The answer was that the Dutch must not expect Ostend, but might be made easy in all other "particulars relating to that matter which themselves could reasonably desire".[3] This letter was ice-bound at Harwich for weeks, and Marlborough had not received it when in the second week in January he reached The Hague. As he had expected, the Dutch fell at once upon the question of the Barrier. He excused himself on the ground of having no instructions, and fancied that he had persuaded them to let the matter stand over till the middle of February, when he expected to be again at The Hague for a few days, after a stay at Brussels.[4] The other question he discussed with the Deputies was that of peace. A fresh set of French proposals had arrived, still suggesting a partition of the Spanish Monarchy. These Marlborough transmitted home.[5] The proposals were at once rejected by the Junta as running counter to one of their two central objects, namely the restitution of the whole Spanish Monarchy. The reply to Marlborough produced a further definition of the Whig policy.

Somers is desirous (wrote Godolphin) that some preliminaries should be settled with the Pensionary and others, as things agreed between England and the States, as a foundation to them, without

[1] Godolphin to Marlborough, 10/21 Dec. 1708; the Heads of Proposals followed by the next post, 14/25 Dec. Coxe Papers.
[2] Marlborough to Godolphin, 3 Jan. 1709. Blenheim Archives.
[3] Godolphin to Marlborough, 28 Dec./8 Jan. 1709. Coxe Papers.
[4] Marlborough to Godolphin, 23 Jan. Coxe Papers.
[5] Marlborough to Godolphin, 16 Jan. 1709. Coxe, III, 386, 387.

which no step ought to be made to peace, not so much as these negotiations, or "pour-parlers" as M. Buys used to name them, continued. His reason for this is, that except this method can be taken, it will always be in the power of the States to say to the Queen, "This we think sufficient". We hope you will be of our opinion, but if not, we must sit still; and then he added that it would be but a sorry excuse for you or me to make to the Queen of England, that the States forced us to do it.[1]

This letter settled the lines on which the Barrier question should be treated in 1709. It was the old system adopted in 1706, of first making sure of the Dutch by binding them to preliminaries, without which peace should not be accepted. The preliminaries of November 1706 had never been communicated by the Deputies, who framed them with Marlborough, to the States General,[2] and were accordingly not binding upon either party. A new chain must be forged with which to bind the Dutch. Designed in the letter just quoted, the chain was completed in the addresses of the Houses of Parliament, presented to the Queen on the 3rd/14th of March. On the 2nd Halifax moved in the House of Lords that no peace should be considered honourable without: (1) The restitution of the whole Spanish Monarchy. (2) A Barrier for the Dutch and Savoy. (3) The recognition by Louis of the Protestant Succession and the removal of the Pretender from France.

To this address, which passed unanimously in the Lords, Boyle, in the Commons, added the further condition that the harbour of Dunkirk should be destroyed, and the motion passed unanimously. The effects of this address were far reaching. It was the watchword of the Whig chiefs throughout the year, the unbending conditions from which they never departed. The immediate effect was a "rapprochement" with the Dutch. Halifax had spoken of them in the highest terms in his motion, and, ever ready to curry favour with the future dynasty of England, sent a copy of the address to the Elector of Hanover, expressing at the same time a hope that it would be the means of again setting on foot the negotiation for the Succession and Barrier Treaty, in which he had three years ago played so large

[1] Godolphin to Marlborough, 27 Jan./7 Feb. Coxe Papers.

[2] Cf. p. 72 *note* 3 and p. 91 *note* 2.

a part, but without success owing to the impractical demands of the Dutch.[1]

The difference between the new Whig policy and that of Marlborough lay not so much in substance as in treatment. Marlborough had procrastinated; the Whigs were impatient to conclude. That there might be no delay, it was suggested that, if the preliminaries could not be arranged in the States before Marlborough came back to England, either Cadogan should be instructed, or, better still, that someone be sent out from England. But Marlborough pursued his old method of delay, beyond which a desire for shirking responsibility now began to be increasingly apparent. He wrote that he thought the question both of the preliminaries and of the Barrier could wait till he came back to England, and that it might create jealousies if someone were sent over. If any decided step towards peace were made, it should, he said, be communicated by the Dutch to England. Both the Peace and Barrier negotiations should be transacted in England, so as to prevent disputes which might arise from falling singly on him.[2] He had now to learn that his methods were obsolete. Returning to The Hague from Brussels in the middle of February, he for a second time brushed the Barrier question aside as if he had no powers.[3] But the time had gone by for such a solution of the difficulty. At a moment when facts had become known which rendered Marlborough's conduct not above suspicion,[4] a succession of letters had arrived from England showing that the Dutch objects might be gained without the Duke's assistance. The encouragement which Heinsius had received from the reports of Vryberg and Portland had inspired hopes which brooked no delay. The Pensionary had been much disappointed by Marlborough's answers at The Hague in January, and had written to Portland that the Dutch had resolved, if Marlborough were not more accommodating on his return to the capital in February, to send Buys to London. The proposal roused the liveliest alarm among the Whigs

[1] Halifax to Elector, 4/15 March. Macpherson, *Original Papers*.
[2] Marlborough to Godolphin, 4 Feb. Blenheim Archives. 17 Feb. Coxe Papers.
[3] Heinsius to Portland, 12 March. Heinsius Archives.
[4] Godolphin to Marlborough, 4/15 Feb. Coxe Papers.

because Buys' connection in England had hitherto been with Harley, who, as Portland reminded Heinsius, was not only out of the Ministry but the subject of universal mistrust. To parry the blow, the Whigs reiterated the assurances of their good intentions, and as a proof hinted at the possibility of sending over someone with special instructions to conclude the Treaty. The letter informing Marlborough of all this reached him at Brussels after his second visit to The Hague and contained renewed expressions by Godolphin as to the necessity of concluding the Treaty at once.[1] The Dutch "coup" had been parried by the Whigs, but at the price of assurances on their part which rendered further delay impossible. To satisfy Heinsius, Marlborough informed him that Cadogan, who was to remain behind in Brussels, would be fully instructed, and on the 25th of February/8th of March he himself embarked at Ostend for England. Heinsius did not for a moment believe that Cadogan would be more fully instructed than Marlborough. He therefore pressed for the sending over of the promised Plenipotentiary from England.[2] The Duke's prevarication had given great dissatisfaction at The Hague; and it was not approved in London. Sunderland met Vryberg on the 26th of February and enquired why the Barrier Treaty was hanging fire. Vryberg answered that it was not the fault of the Dutch for, when at The Hague, Marlborough had referred the matter to England. "I cannot imagine", Sunderland replied, "what reasons my Lord Duke can have for doing so"; meaning, as Vryberg explained, for not avowing that he was authorised. It seemed to the Dutchman as if Sunderland was not well satisfied with the Duke over this matter. The State Secretary had added:

I am of opinion it would be better for both the nations to arrange and conclude a reciprocal treaty with regard to the Barrier and the Succession, and the condition of a future peace between England and the States, than if our generals lay encamped upon the plains of Paris.[3]

[1] See Pesters' statement that Renswoude knew positively that Marlborough had been offered the Patent for life. Above, p. 93 *note* 2.

[2] Heinsius to Portland, 12 March. Heinsius Archives.

[3] Sunderland's chief faults appeared to the Dutch as his chief virtues. Vryberg wrote of him in this same letter: "You know the open heartedness

Thus the inopportune obstruction of Marlborough led to the promise that England would send a Minister to The Hague: this would itself be a great gain to the Dutch. Their position was now strengthened by a piece of unexpected indiscretion on the part of the French. Marlborough had only been in London a day or two when the publication there of the news that Rouillé had crossed the frontier openly with offers of peace, produced a small panic and further precipitated the Anglo-Dutch negotiations.

To France, already exhausted, the fall of Lille in December 1708 was a heavy blow and, although a great effort was to be made for its recapture in the following spring, the thoughts of Louis turned longingly towards peace. Two events furthered this disposition. On the 6th of January began a severe frost which lasted for three months, killed the vines and froze the seed-corn in the earth. On the top of this calamity came a definite statement of what the Dutch would accept as the basis for negotiation. In December Heinsius learnt through Petkum that the French were willing to treat on the basis of certain proposals brought by Hennequin in March 1707. Philip was to have all the Italian possessions of Spain, except Milan, which was now excluded, and the Barrier was to be discussed with good faith on both sides. Above all, the negotiation was to be strictly secret. Heinsius had communicated the whole matter to Marlborough, and it was these proposals, referred home by Marlborough on the 16th of January, which caused such alarm among the Whigs.[1] Marlborough had agreed with Heinsius that the offer should not be straightway refused and had recommended Petkum as the intermediary. But this negotiation proved abortive, and the real peace negotiations are to be dated from a reply made by Van der Dussen on the 15th of January to Bergeyck who came from Philip with promises of favourable treatment of the Dutch by his master as King of Spain. Van der Dussen's answer was: "You will please know that unless

and thoroughgoingness of my Lord Sunderland, who does not hesitate even to gainsay his father-in-law's opinions when he thinks they are not right" (Vryberg to Heinsius, 26 Feb. Heinsius Archives).

[1] See above, p. 101 *note* 5.

the former offers of Spain, the Indies, the Milanese, the Spanish Netherlands, 'which had been added', as also a favourable treaty of commerce, are repeated, we cannot treat with confidence of the other preliminaries".[1] This answer only indicated a minimum, but, as it left Naples and Sicily to Philip, Louis caught at the opportunity and Rouillé was dispatched with voluminous instructions to conduct the affair. On the day after that on which Marlborough took ship at Ostend for England, Rouillé passed through Brussels on his way to Antwerp.[2]

There is no doubt that the Dutch were the gainers by this manœuvre. Marlborough had not known either of Rouillé's coming or what proposals the Frenchman brought. He declared frankly in London that, in not letting him know, Heinsius had deceived him.[3] This was literally, but not substantially true. He had known of all the negotiations up to the choice and arrival of the French agent. It had been his wish to know all along how the negotiation stood, but not to take part directly in a course of action for which he alleged he had no powers.[4] From London the Duke continued to write that, as he was obliged to show the Pensionary's letters to the other Ministers, Heinsius should, if he had anything for his correspondent's ears only, send it on a separate fly-sheet.[5] What most annoyed the Duke was, not that the Pensionary had failed to inform him of the nomination of Rouillé as French peace agent, but that the negotiation had become public property. It was this publicity that proved so advantageous to the Dutch. Rouillé made no secret either of his journey or of its object. One of his retinue went so far as to say that "his master had the peace in his pocket and was sure of Holland".[6] There were also other French agents wandering about the Netherlands. Albemarle, military governor at Brussels, who had not yet been instructed in these latest developments of Dutch diplomacy, was mystified. "Peace-gentlemen", he wrote

[1] Quoted in Legrelle, IV, 466, and Torcy, *Mémoires*, I, 186.
[2] Legrelle, IV, 470.
[3] Hoffman Report of 29 March from London, quoted by Klopp, XIII, 220.
[4] Heinsius to Portland, 12 March. Heinsius Archives.
[5] Marlborough to Heinsius, 12/23 March. Heinsius Archives.
[6] Cadogan to Heinsius, 12 March. Heinsius Archives.

to Heinsius, "are trotting about this neighbourhood in fine style." He wanted to arrest them all; but Field Deputy Pesters assured him they had passports. So he contented himself with leaving the Pensionary to deal with them.[1] Heinsius' view was one of alarm. "Is it possible", he wrote to Marlborough, "that the French should behave with so little discretion?"[2] But the situation was much more awkward for the Englishman. The news created great alarm in London and, as day after day passed with no letters from The Hague, the Duke was for the moment disconcerted. There was nothing for it but to confess the negotiation to the Imperial Court. "The proceeding of France", he wrote to Heinsius on the 8th/19th, "by making public the business of Rouillé is so very extravagant that I think you should lose no time in acquainting Prince Eugene with what you think proper, to prevent his being jealous."[3] Heinsius agreed; he had indeed already informed Heems, the Austrian resident at The Hague.[4] To Wratislaw Marlborough expressed his conviction that Rouillé's move was evidently intended to sow jealousy among the Allies, and, a few days later, he wrote that the intrigues of the French agents in Holland forced him to hasten his return to the continent.[5] To Hoffman, the Austrian resident in London, he said that he hoped to delay the negotiation until the beginning of the campaign, so that if the campaign were once in progress he would find ways and means to advance the matter and compel France to grant better terms.[6]

While the Duke thus strove to lull suspicion at Vienna, the general alarm of the Whigs took the form of a desire to anticipate any French hopes of Dutch defection by hastening on the negotiations with the Republic. Portland made the best of the opportunity to advocate the request made by Heinsius that an English Plenipotentiary might be sent over at once. He went to Somers and Godolphin and represented to them very fully that things could not stand as they did, that the jealousies on

1 Albemarle to Heinsius, 11 March. Heinsius Archives.
2 Heinsius to Marlborough, 12 March. Heinsius Archives.
3 Marlborough to Heinsius, 8/19 March. Heinsius Archives.
4 Heinsius to Marlborough, 26 March. Heinsius Archives.
5 Marlborough to Wratislaw, 11/22 March. Murray.
6 Hoffman Report, 29 March, quoted by Klopp, XIII, 220.

account of these pourparlers in the States increased in England and would soon grow into unkind distrusts, that, on the other side, the not putting an end to the affair of the Barrier would have an ill effect in the Republic, and that no right step could be taken while no proper person was upon the place to transact things on the part of England, so that, notwithstanding the best intention and disposition on both sides, things were like to take a wrong turn.[1] He began to hope that Ostend might become a possibility. "They have advanced me no strong reasons against it," he explained to Heinsius, "and the address of the two Houses shows that Parliament thinks the Guarantee Treaty necessary without mentioning any restriction."[2] In accordance with Portland's representations and a second address presented by Parliament, on the 13th/24th of March, Marlborough was appointed with full powers for the embassy. The choice could have fallen upon no other. The Duke possessed an unrivalled knowledge of the Dutch character and constitution; moreover, to have passed over the chief commander of the Maritime Powers would have been impossible.[3] Portland, however, who was no friend of the Duke, was not entirely satisfied with the appointment. He imagined that Marlborough would avoid, as much as possible, both listening to other people's sentiment on the peace, and giving his own, "so as not to burn his fingers". "There are jealousies here as well as elsewhere," wrote the Dutchman, "and he knows that many are watching him."[4] But to Heinsius, the Duke seemed better than Cadogan. The Pensionary had been sceptical as to the so-called full powers given to the latter, whom, he (quite rightly) thought, would not dare to take any steps beyond those the Duke's approval of which might be regarded as certain. On the 21st of March/1st of April Marlborough's instructions were drawn up on the basis of the addresses of the Houses presented to the Queen on the 3rd/14th of March. In these instructions, reference was made to the alarm caused by the appearance of Rouillé and the opinion

[1] Portland to Heinsius, 14/25 March. Heinsius Archives.
[2] Portland to Heinsius, 15/26 March. Heinsius Archives.
[3] Noorden, III, 481.
[4] Portland to Heinsius, 11/22 March. Heinsius Archives.

expressed "that no negotiation for peace should be concluded with France until the preliminaries are adjusted between England and the States". The conditions for these preliminaries were: (1) That no peace could be safe or honourable unless the whole Spanish Monarchy be restored to the House of Austria. (2) That the French King be obliged to acknowledge the Queen's title and the Protestant Succession. (3) That the Pretender be removed from France. (4) That the harbour of Dunkirk be destroyed. So much for England's demands. Marlborough was likewise

> to announce the Queen's desire that other preliminaries should be required for the security and interest of the States, particularly a Barrier, for which a Treaty had been so long pending, and of which the Queen was willing to become a guarantee, not doubting but the States would in like manner guarantee the Protestant Succession.[1]

These instructions marked the first stage in the development of the Barrier question in 1709. The Guarantee Treaty had passed from the future to the present and become one of the fundamental points in the general negotiation.

We have now reached the point in Marlborough's career when the seeds of disintegration, sown in the winter of 1706/1707, began to appear upon the surface. If that winter had been the real turning point, it was only in the summer of 1709 that Europe began to realise that the turn had been taken. The Duke had lost ground ever since the beginning of the year, and now the negotiations at The Hague were to bring into vivid relief the incompatibility of his private promises with his official position. The prospect of a speedy settlement had now brought the day of reckoning which was to show how irreconcilable were the assurances which he had given to the several Allies; the unexpected delay of that settlement was to plunge him further into hopeless irresolution. As the agent of the Whig Ministry, Marlborough bore instructions to hasten the conclusion of the Barrier Treaty which it was vital to his interests to delay, and, when the Dutch demands became known, to conclude it on terms which were certain to displease the Court of Vienna, and hardly less certain to call down at no

[1] Draft of the instructions contained in Coxe, II, 394, 395.

distant date the wrath of his own fickle country upon those who should sign it. He came, moreover, with unbending conditions of peace, of which he had in confidence expressed his disapproval to the Dutch, with the sure knowledge that, if the negotiation failed, it would soon be laid to his charge that he had wilfully prolonged the war.

Marlborough reached The Hague on the 9th of April, the day after that on which Eugene arrived with full powers from Vienna. The latter had returned to the Austrian capital, after the campaign of 1708, on the 30th of January 1709.[1] Almost immediately afterwards a letter arrived from Marlborough, written by him three days after his conference with the Deputies at The Hague on the subject of peace. It produced a great effect in Vienna. The Duke explained that matters had reached a critical point at which it was necessary for each one of the Allies to put forth his utmost strength in preparation for the ensuing campaign. "I should not hide from your Imperial Majesty", he continued, "that we perceive that the prospect of a speedy peace is one of the principal motives in inducing the States at the present moment to make all possible efforts, in the hope that this campaign will be the last."[2]

This letter sounded as if the day of settlement were at last approaching. The Emperor must take care that his share of the booty should not slip through his fingers. It was therefore determined to send Eugene to the scene of negotiations to defend Imperial rights and explain the Imperial conditions of peace. In the conferences which took place at Vienna with the object of framing the Prince's instructions, the basis taken was that arrived at by Sinzendorf at The Hague in 1706. That is to say, the whole Spanish Monarchy was to be restored to Charles, if possible on the footing of the Peace of the Pyrenees; while for the Empire the condition demanded was the Peace of Westphalia with the exclusion of the Electors of Bavaria and Cologne. The Dutch came in for a special share of attention from the Imperial Council. In the first meeting it was laid down that if it became necessary to leave something to the Duke of Anjou, who must

[1] Wratislaw to Marlborough, 2 Feb. 1709. Blenheim Archives.
[2] Marlborough to the Emperor, 19 Jan. 1709.

at all costs be excluded from Naples and Sicily, which were regarded as the gates of Vienna, the less dangerous position of the Spanish Netherlands should be named. This provision was included, "not indeed with the intention of really ceding them to the Duke, but only in order to distress the Dutch and so thereby to stir them up more, to go hand in hand with the Allies in the re-conquest of the Spanish Monarchy".[1] In later conferences the question of the Barrier was taken into consideration and the two former principles were again insisted upon; firstly, that the Barrier should be essentially one against France and that the towns taken from Louis to form this Barrier should be added to the Spanish Netherlands, the Dutch being only allowed military rights in them; secondly, that this arrangement should involve no expense to the Spanish Netherlands. It was further laid down that any place in the Spanish Netherlands desired by the Dutch should be a matter of discussion solely between the Dutch and King Charles, who looked to England for support in the preservation of the integrity of his rights.[2] The latter provision was, it will at once be seen, the direct negation of the fundamental principles of the Barrier negotiations, which were that the Dutch should first settle their Barrier with England, and that the English should side with the Dutch, and not with the Hapsburgs, in the negotiation. Eugene had already started north when the news of Rouillé's expedition reached Vienna. The Emperor was naturally indignant at this proof of separate negotiations, and some difficulty was found in believing Marlborough's assurances that he had not known beforehand of the Frenchman's coming.[3] All that could be done, however, was to instruct Heems to insist strongly that Naples and Sicily must not go to Philip,[4] and to wait for news from Eugene of the reception of the sweeping pretensions he carried with him.

[1] Conference Protocol, 27 Feb. 1709. *Feldzüge des Prinzen Eugen von Savoyen*. Published by the Ministry of War. Vienna, 1876.

[2] Conference Protocol, 13 March 1709. *Feldzüge des Prinzen Eugen von Savoyen*. Published by the Ministry of War. Vienna, 1876.

[3] "Il est presque incroyable que vous n'ayez pas eu une préalable connaissance de l'arrivée de M. Rouillé." Wratislaw to Marlborough, 13 April Blenheim Archives.

[4] Imperial Rescript of 4 April to Heems, cited by Klopp, XIII, 219.

II

The month of April 1709 marks a distinct advance in the diplomatic position of the States. From this date begins the period of Dutch ascendancy in the peace negotiations, which culminated in the Barrier Treaty of the 29th of October 1709, and only came to an end with the fall of the Whig Ministry in the summer of 1710. By the term "ascendancy" we mean the power which during that period the Dutch possessed of so playing off England and France against one another as to be able to obtain from each practically what terms they pleased. During the month of April Dutch diplomacy, subordinated as ever to their one central object of the Barrier, was directed into two separate channels, corresponding with the two classes of Barrier towns. There were the towns which had been possessed by France at the time of the death of Charles II and the handing over of which therefore needed Louis' consent: and there were also the towns to be obtained from the Spanish Netherlands, which were to be extracted from Charles III by the help of an English guarantee. In the first case it was necessary to coquet with France in such a way that the Dutch might obtain more than their proportionate share of what she was willing to give at the peace. It might, or it might not, be possible in the end to secure Naples and Sicily for Philip, but at all events the door of hope must not be closed to Louis by any definite refusal to treat on that head. Renswoude expressed the situation exactly when he wrote to Heinsius, "I think the French will be reasonable if we treat the matter with decision, and do not pull the strings too tight in favour of the Allies".[1] In the second case, the Dutch policy was to obtain as much as possible from England at as small a cost as might be, and for this purpose to withdraw from the awkward obligation to reconquer the whole Spanish Monarchy, in the hope, however slight, of that condition being after all removed.

The preliminaries of November 1706, and the Dutch Barrier demand of that same month, apportioned to the States a goodly

[1] Renswoude to Heinsius from Brussels, 25 March 1709. Heinsius Archives.

list of French fortresses. The consent of Louis to this spoliation had not, however, been received. It was the attempt to obtain this consent that formed the principal staple of negotiation between the Dutch and Rouillé in April 1709. Rouillé's initial instructions of the 5th of March stated that Louis was quite willing that Upper Guelderland should be given to the States and that he had no objection to the Archduke Charles introducing Dutch garrisons into any towns of the Spanish Netherlands he pleased, while Van der Dussen's expression, "what has been added", Louis interpreted by saying that he would give Ypres and Menin. The first two points caused no difficulty, but the two Dutch Deputies, Buys and Van der Dussen, appointed to treat with the Frenchman, dismissed the offer of Ypres and Menin at once as quite insufficient. They required also Furnes, Tournai, Condé and Maubeuge. At the same time they hinted that Lille might be given back to France.[1] The second set of instructions, sent to Rouillé on the 26th of March, added Furnes, but refused the other places. Louis explained that the Dutch did not need a strong Barrier of French towns on the side of the Sambre and Meuse, for they could have Ath, Mons, Charleroi and Namur, out of the Spanish Netherlands. On the other hand, Landrecy and Quesnoy were quite insufficient to prevent an enemy from invading France by the Sambre; to prevent which, Louis must therefore keep Tournai, Condé, and Maubeuge.[2] The Dutch being still intractable, Louis next found himself obliged to offer Condé and Maubeuge, but he still refused Tournai.[3] These third offers the Dutch treated with the contempt of statesmen "swollen with the pride of success". Adding insult to injury, they now blandly informed Rouillé that they had never had the least intention of giving up Lille, and had only hinted the contrary at the first conference because the town was at that time not in a state of defence.[4] Louis bowed to the inevitable and his letter of the 29th of April which Torcy brought with him to The Hague gave up the remaining towns

[1] For Rouillé's instructions of 5 March see Legrelle, IV, 468, 469; account of the first Conference, pp. 472, 473.

[2] Louis to Rouillé, 26 March 1709. Legrelle, IV, 475.

[3] Louis to Rouillé, 15 April. Legrelle, IV, 482.

[4] Rouillé to Louis, 22 April. Legrelle, IV, 485.

of Tournai and Lille. The States had waived their demand made in 1706 for Valenciennes, but had now obtained Louis' consent to deliver up all the other towns then specified. "The hour of revenge for 1672 had come in full earnest."[1]

The Dutch could not hope that the negotiation for securing the other part of their Barrier would be such a one-sided business, but they were determined to purchase that security from England as cheaply as possible. A few days after his arrival at The Hague, Marlborough communicated his instructions privately to the Pensionary. Heinsius expressed surprise at such sweeping conditions and feared that France could never be brought to agree to them.[2] It was as if the Maritime Powers were both applying for two-thirds of a fixed whole. Marlborough replied that he could not depart from any of the four points, and expatiated upon the misery of France.[3] Heinsius promised that he would do his best to obtain compliance with the English wishes, but—to put off the evil day—suggested that the Duke should at the first conference avoid speaking about anything except what concerned the Succession and Barrier, "by which", he urged, "we shall gain time and know the answer France will make by this last courier". Eugene concurred in the suggestion and Marlborough consented.[4] But Godolphin, who had not

[1] Legrelle, IV, 486.

[2] Marlborough to Boyle, 12 April 1709. Murray.

[3] It is very important to realise what an exaggerated view was generally held in England at this time as to the condition to which France had been reduced. Marlborough, writing to Heinsius on the subject of Rouillé's visit, observed, "If the French be told honestly and plainly what we will have, they will consent to it, for they are at this time necessitated to submit to whatever we will have". Countless other instances of this exaggeration might be given (cf. d'Hermitage's letters especially). There was one interesting exception. Cowper, the Chancellor, in his *Diary* for the 19/30 April, wrote: "During the remaining transactions of the intended peace which was laid in all its steps before the whole Cabinet, the Ld Treasurer, Ld President Somers, and all the other Lords did ever seem confident of a peace. My own distrust was so remarkable that I was once perfectly chid by the Ld Treasurer (never so much in any other case) for saying such orders would be proper if the French King signed the Preliminary Treaty. He resented by making a question of it, and said there would be no doubt etc. For my own part nothing, seeing so great men believe it, could ever incline me to think France reduced so low as to accept such conditions" (Cowper's *Diary* edited by Hawtry, Roxburgh Club, 1833). With the Whig leaders the wish was father to the thought.

[4] Marlborough to Godolphin, 12 April. Coxe Papers.

come under the influence of Heinsius' friendly assurances, saw through the design.

> The longer you defer exposing the matter of your instructions, (he wrote) the greater difficulty you will find in having them complied with, when at last you make your proposals. I see no use to us of gaining time, as you say Prince Eugene expressed it, till the return of M. Rouillé's Courier. It only gives the people in Holland more time to swallow the pleasing thoughts of a peace, to increase the too just jealousies of the Allies, and at best to make them careless and negligent in their preparations.[1]

Buys in the meantime used the delay to make a final effort to persuade Marlborough to omit the demand for the restitution of the whole Spanish Monarchy—an attempt which, although unsuccessful, when reported to London only heightened the anxiety there.[2] Marlborough presented his instructions formally on the 23rd of April and from that moment further resistance became hopeless.[3] The English commander placed implicit confidence in the sincerity and candour of the Pensionary, and the event showed that the confidence was not misplaced.[4] Though evidently more interested in their Barrier than in anything else, the Dutch presented the English demands along with their own as irrevocable decisions. "They are carried away by the torrent," lamented Torcy, "and prefer agreeing with the English to contradicting them."[5]

But the Dutch were now to exact the full penalty for their enforced complaisance. It has been stated above, that when Marlborough returned to England at the end of February he left instructions with Cadogan to continue the Barrier negotiation with the two Dutch Commissioners, Van den Bergh and Renswoude, at Brussels.[6] Only one conference took place, and it was prematurely interrupted. In this one interview Renswoude ascertained that England would not object to the Dutch receiving Spanish Guelderland, and retaining their garrisons in

[1] Godolphin to Marlborough, 4/15 April. Coxe Papers.

[2] Marlborough to Boyle, 16 April. Murray. Boyle to Marlborough, 12/23 April, in Sommerville's *Queen Anne*.

[3] Petkum to Torcy, 24 April. Legrelle, IV, 491. Coxe, II, 399.

[4] Marlborough to Boyle, 23 April 1709. Murray.

[5] Torcy to Louis, 16 May. *Mémoires*, II, 95.

[6] See above, p. 104.

Huy and Liège, but wished that Namur, Charleroi, and Mons should be left to Charles.[1] Not long after the interview, under the influence of the excitement caused in London by the news of Rouillé's arrival on the scene, Cadogan had been ordered to The Hague to watch the peace negotiations there and to assure the Pensionary of the Queen's desire to bring the Barrier Treaty to a speedy conclusion.[2] But this assurance had taken the unwelcome form of a request that Heinsius would have a list of the Dutch demands prepared for transmission to London. To the Pensionary it appeared a mere waste of time. He had expected Cadogan to come "with powers to finish and not to begin the affair".[3] He had therefore laid the matter on one side and resolved to wait for Marlborough. The Duke arrived on the 9th and repeated Cadogan's request. Heinsius was annoyed at what he suspected to be another attempt in London to mutilate the Dutch demands; but as Marlborough insisted, he had to give way.[4] On the 16th, however, Marlborough had still heard nothing. The silence was ominous. "I attribute it", he wrote, "to the extravagant demands of some of them and I cannot help apprehending we shall have a great deal of trouble and difficulty in that matter."[5] He was not disappointed. On the 19th he learnt from the Deputies the interest that they meant to charge for their two years' waiting. Returning that evening from a short excursion to admire the beauties of Amsterdam, Eugene found the Duke, as he informed the Emperor, "in great distress"; what they had both tried to put off as long as possible had at last happened.[6] The Deputies had presented the Duke with a list of the places they now required. "It encloses what might be thought a great Kingdom", Marlborough complained, as he sent the list home to Godolphin, "but the time is so critical that I dare not be of any opinion." There was still the hope that, before he received the formal document, he might induce the States to abate their pretensions.

1 Renswoude to Heinsius, 19 March, from Brussels. Heinsius Archives.
2 Marlborough to Heinsius, 8/19 March. Heinsius Archives.
3 Heinsius to Portland, 2 April. Heinsius Archives.
4 Heinsius to Portland, 29 April. Heinsius Archives.
5 Marlborough to Boyle, 16 April. Murray.
6 Eugene to the Emperor, 19 April 1709. *Feldzüge des Prinzen Eugen.*

But he realised only too fully the strength of the Dutch position. A few days later he received, as the final expression of their demands, the "Project" of the Barrier Treaty.[1] The terms of the Project are inserted here, as it is interesting to watch how they were subsequently modified in the English Counter Project and in the final Treaty.

1. The difference between the list of towns now claimed and those claimed in 1706 are instructive. These differences consist both in omissions and additions. The omissions are, firstly, Luxemburg and Thionville, the demand for which had never been very strong, whereas the places were of the utmost importance to the Empire, as guarding an approach to it from France; secondly, Charleroi and Mons, the latter of which had been specifically opposed by England, and which had become less necessary owing to the other places from the Spanish Netherlands which were now demanded for the first time; thirdly, Ypres, Furnes, and Maubeuge. The omission of these three places is significant. Rouillé had already been instructed to give them up. It would therefore appear as almost certain that the States, knowing they were sure of them, left them out that the list might not appear to the English too grasping, intending to bring them in at the final conclusion of the Barrier Treaty. The places now claimed for the first time—Hal, Lier, the Castle of Ghent, Fort Perle, St Donas, Damme, and Knocke—are still more significant. The demand for them shows that the States had now abandoned any conception of their Barrier as a line, however strong, of frontier forts, and intended to clench in their grasp the whole Spanish Netherlands. The list of places claimed, all of which the Dutch might fortify and in which they were to have the sole right of garrison, was such as to give them an ascendancy throughout the Low Countries. The sea coast was dominated by Nieuwport, Knocke, and Ostend; Bruges and its canal by Damme and Fort Donas; the Scheldt by Fort Perle at its mouth, and farther up by

[1] Marlborough to Godolphin, 19 April 1709. Coxe, II, 398. The Barrier Treaty itself may be found in Appendix E. In Swift's treatise on *The Barrier Treaty*, and in the *Journal of the House of Commons*, 13/24 Feb. 1712, XVII, the differences between the Counter Project and the final form are also noted.

Dendermonde and the Castle of Ghent; Lier and Hal guarded the plain of Brabant, and Namur the Meuse: while Menin, Lille, Condé, Tournai and Valenciennes protected the States from France (Art. VI).

2. Even more sweeping were the provisions which, in case of apparent attack on any side, enabled the States to throw any troops they might think requisite into all the towns in the Spanish Netherlands (Art. VII). To import munitions and what was necessary for the upkeep of the fortresses free of duty (Arts. VIII and XI) and to appoint such commanders, etc. as they saw fit (Art. IX).

3. Towards the maintenance of these Barrier fortresses a sum of 3,500,000 livres was to be raised from the Spanish Netherlands (Art. XII).

4. Not only were the States to be allowed to enter forthwith into these places and to enjoy the revenues, but King Charles III, the legitimate sovereign of the Low Countries, was not to be allowed to take possession of any part of them till the final convention with the State provided for by the 9th Article of the Grand Alliance (Art. XVI).

5. The 52nd Article of the Treaty of Münster provided that the Upper Quarter of Guelders (which belonged by right to the Spanish Monarchy) should only be exchanged for an equivalent.[1] But this project proposed that the States should enter into possession of that territory without any equivalent, as the Spanish King would soon receive from other quarters much greater gratification than this equivalent could give him[2] (separate article).

6. In return the Dutch promised the English to use every effort to oblige the French King to acknowledge Anne and the Protestant Succession and bound themselves only to treat of and make peace conjointly with their ally (Art. XXI).

7. Finally, the States were to receive these privileges on the understanding that the ecclesiastical and civil rights of Charles III should be reserved to him (Art. X).

[1] Dumont, *Corps Diplom.* tome VI, Part I, p. 431: "le Haut Quartier de Gueldre sera eschangé moyennant l'équivalence".

[2] For the history of Upper or Spanish Guelderland, see Appendix B.

The great inequality in this bargain would strike the most casual observer. It roused the anger of every member of the Alliance—particularly, at a later date, of England. The Tory parliament that sat in judgment on this "most extraordinary piece of diplomacy", as Swift called it, forgot that it expressed only a part of the compensation England claimed from France, but everything that the States could possibly hope to get. Even that does not wholly express the truth. Much of what England—the best rewarded of all the Allies in the war—obtained at the Peace of Utrecht was rendered possible by what she gained through this Barrier Treaty, the allegiance of the Dutch at a critical moment.

Marlborough knew that the Dutch demands would prove anything but acceptable when they became known at the Courts of Berlin and Barcelona. The King of Prussia was in actual possession of the town of Guelders,[1] and determined not to give it up until various monetary claims which he made upon the Court of Spain had been satisfied. The proposed appropriation of the whole district by the States would be sure therefore to infuriate the short-tempered monarch, and imperil the consent Marlborough had with difficulty just obtained from an augmentation of Prussian troops for the next campaign. Marlborough did not go so far as to tell him that he had had the Dutch proposals before him, but suggested that, as the States had begun to talk about their Barrier, the King should instruct the Prussian Envoy at The Hague as to his claims to Upper Guelders, adding that he would himself do his best to support them.[2] He received an answer from the King, thanking him for his good counsel and stating that he had ordered his Ambassador at The Hague to keep placing the matter of Guelders continuously on the "tapis"—instructions which the "long winded, incompetent" Schmettau obeyed most fully.[3]

With King Charles III the case was even more difficult. If the Project robbed Prussia of a town, it practically robbed Spain

[1] His troops had taken it on 12 Dec. 1703.

[2] Marlborough to King of Prussia, 26 April 1709. Murray, IV, 490.

[3] Frederick to Marlborough, undated, but endorsed May 1709. Blenheim Archives.

of the whole Netherlands. To the Duke of Moles, Marlborough wrote that there was every hope of the Dutch remaining firm to the Alliance, but that in the circumstances the Queen could no longer put off the question of the Barrier. He therefore advised Charles to send some authorised person of weight to discuss the matter with him. For himself, he said, he would do nothing without the concurrence of Eugene and Sinzendorf (who was shortly expected from Vienna). He endeavoured to place the matter in the most favourable light possible by observing

We will endeavour that the places which France shall be obliged to yield, in addition to everything that belonged to the late King of Spain, shall be delivered up to His Majesty, and that he may have the authority and civil government throughout this territory not less in the towns garrisoned by the States than in the others.[1]

Having thus warned the parties interested of the impending disaster to their pretensions, Marlborough prepared to return home to discuss the Barrier with the English Ministry and to give them his observations on the humours of the Dutch for peace. He announced his decisions to Heinsius, giving out that the journey was necessary for private reasons. Heinsius, however, did his best to dissuade the Duke, and when the journey became known the worst interpretations were put upon its object.[2] Marlborough left on the 29th of April, taking with him the Project.[3] The Barrier question had reached its second stage,

[1] Marlborough to Duke of Moles, 24 April 1709. Murray, IV, 488.

[2] H. Pesters, 30 April 1709, from The Hague. Record Office. The letter is a rather mutilated decipher, and it does not record to whom it was written.

[3] Lamberty's letters from The Hague, now in the Record Office, show how well—allowing for the Dutch constitution—the secret of this Barrier negotiation was kept both at this time and later when the Treaty was concluded. Of the Project, he observes: "Aucun des ministres qui le savent—car ce n'est pas généralement repandu parmi eux, n'a pu jusque ici avoir la copie de ce Mémoire qui est tenu fort secret. L'on a en général la notion par des membres de l'état que c'est une maîtresse pièce. Pour la juger telle il suffit de dire que c'est la production de la féconde et solide plume de M. Fagel, Greffier de MM. les États dont le sublime génie ne produit rien que dans la plus haute perfection. Aussi s'assure-t-on que la Cour de Grande Bretagne n'y trouvera rien à redire" (3 May 1709). This latter prediction proved just about as correct as the similar prophecies made on the subject of the Resolution of 17 Aug. 1706. (See above, p. 51.)

and passed from the region of promises to that of reality. A draft of the Treaty would in a few days be lying before the British Ministry, in very different circumstances from that brought back by Halifax in August 1706.

III

Marlborough arrived in London on the 2nd of May. These frequent journeys to and from The Hague awakened the liveliest interest in London. The probabilities of peace were eagerly discussed. Some declared he had come home to report peace offers; others, pretending to be more in the secret, argued that in a fortnight the campaign would have begun.[1] But the truth soon leaked out; it was not so much peace that had brought Marlborough to London as the Barrier. Marlborough desired a colleague to carry through that negotiation. Who should this be? From his previous experience in this particular negotiation, Halifax appeared the obvious person, and the Dutch quite expected that he would be chosen. On the other hand, there were two reasons against his receiving the post. In the first place, he had not been on good terms with the Dutch during his embassy at The Hague in 1706. In the second place, he had offended Marlborough and Godolphin by the animus which he had shown against them, when, thirsting for further diplomatic fame, he had applied in the spring of 1707 for the post of Plenipotentiary at The Hague in the event of a peace conference and had been refused.[2] Notwithstanding these objections, Halifax was now asked to go,[3] and the real reason for his not doing so was a very different one. Marlborough had written from The Hague to ask for a colleague, as it was necessary that someone should remain there during his absence at the army.[4] Such a request could not be refused, but this was felt not to be

[1] L'Hermitage, 3 May 1709. MSS., British Museum.

[2] Coxe, II, 92.

[3] There is a charming letter from Halifax to Marlborough, written on 24 April/5 May 1709, in the Blenheim Archives, hoping that his not going would produce no alteration in Marlborough's disposition towards him. In this silver-tongued masterpiece Halifax states that Somers and Godolphin had desired him to accept the commission.

[4] Marlborough to Godolphin, 24 April. Coxe Papers.

the true reason. Marlborough really wanted a second-in-command to take over the Barrier negotiation. Halifax was approached on the subject by Godolphin and Somers, but he refused the appointment and made no secret of his reasons. If Marlborough had foreseen, said he, that the Treaty entered into with the Republic would have gratified the English nation, he would not have been willing to divide with anybody the honour of completing it. The application for a coadjutor, therefore, raised the suspicion that he would like to shift on to the shoulders of this associate any odium that might arise.[1]

Accordingly, Lord Sunderland was proposed; but against him there was raised the objection of the vehemence of his procedure. The post was therefore offered to the youthful Townshend who had indeed, two years previously, been promised the post of

[1] L'Hermitage, 10 May 1709. British Museum. The passage as to Halifax's reasons for not going is taken from Hoffmann's report of 7 May, cited by Klopp, XIII, 227. These remarks of Halifax's, if they stood by themselves, might be put down as malicious libel. Unfortunately they are largely borne out by Marlborough's subsequent conduct towards Townshend, which points to a fixed determination on the Duke's part to make him a scapegoat. So long as the preliminaries seemed on the high road to success he was loud in his praises, "I cannot say enough of the pleasure I have in the company and assistance of Lord Townshend" (to Godolphin, 25 May). But when it came to the Barrier negotiation, all this changed. "Townshend is a very honest fellow but he does not understand the temper of the Dutch", he wrote at one time; at another, "Townshend's orders are full of obstructions". But he made no effort to instruct his colleague or to help him to clear away the obstructions. All through the summer he never corresponded with him about the Barrier and when he came to The Hague in the autumn, laid great stress to the Austrians upon the fact that he had known nothing of the negotiation for two months. More remarkable still is a passage in a letter in Portland MSS. written by Drummond to Harley from Amsterdam on 18/29 May 1711, in which he observes, "The Duke of Marlborough, I once I think wrote you, valued himself on having no hand in the Treaty of Barrier with the States. Some letters and expressions of his Grace to Prince Eugene and the Imperial Ministers being come lately by what I can hear to the ears of some of the principal ministers of this State, they in conversation put it on this foot that this Treaty of Lord Townshend's cutting off all his hopes of being Governor of the Spanish Netherlands and new conquests, makes him against it, and that he will never forgive Lord Townshend for concluding it without his knowledge" (*Hist. MSS. Comm.* XV, App. IV). It is no wonder that Townshend afterwards felt bitter towards the Duke. Onslow observes in a note to Burnet's *History* (VI, 112): "The Duke of Marlborough would have no hand in this treaty though joined in the same powers for it with Lord Townshend; of which I once heard that Lord talk with some indignation and reflect with some freedom on the Duke of Marlborough for it".

Plenipotentiary at The Hague, and whom Godolphin had wished to send over earlier in the spring. Hoffmann remarked of him that he was pliable and docile. He was, moreover, already known to the Dutch, among whom he had created a favourable impression on a former visit.

The next matter for consideration was the Project itself. It was accorded anything but a favourable reception. To Godolphin it appeared to afford very little consideration for King Charles, any more than for the Queen.[1] A Counter Project was therefore drawn up in accordance with the views of the English Ministry, on the basis of which the Treaty was to be negotiated. In this Counter Project every one of the important provisions of the Project, which have been noticed above, was radically altered.

1. From the long list of towns and fortresses claimed by the Dutch, Ostend, the key of the coast, and Dendermonde, the key of Brabant and East Flanders, were immediately removed, though otherwise the list remained practically unaltered (Art. VI).

2. The 7th Article of the Project, as it stood, seemed to belie the whole object of the Treaty. What the Dutch needed was protection against France in case of actual attack. The Project, however, gave the Dutch the power to fill the whole of the Low Countries with their troops on the mere rumour of war, and that from any quarter. France was therefore specified in the Counter Project as the attacking force, and the occasions for the use of these special powers further limited to cases of open war (Art. VII).

3. England refused to assist in finding an annual sum of 3,500,000 livres for the support of the Dutch Barrier fortresses. It was, in the opinion of Marlborough, utterly beyond the power of the Spanish Netherlands to provide such a sum.[2] Instead of this, a fund was to be formed from the revenues of such of the Barrier towns now given to the Dutch as had not belonged to King Charles II at the time of his death, and the garrisons and fortifications were to be maintained out of this fund, with this exception, the rights of the Spanish King to the revenues of

[1] Godolphin to Marlborough, 12/23 April 1709. Coxe, II, 398.

[2] Marlborough to Boyle, 23 April 1709. Murray.

the towns in the Low Countries were protected by a special clause (Art. IX).

4. The provision, by which King Charles III was forbidden to take possession of any part of the Low Countries until the final Convention between him and the States, was omitted (Art. XV).

5. The article relating to Guelders was so modified as to give offence neither to Prussia nor to Spain. The Queen was to assist in settling the question to the mutual satisfaction of King Charles and the States (separate article).

6. In return for their Barrier the Dutch were not only to "do their utmost to oblige the King of France to acknowledge Anne and the Protestant Succession", but to bind themselves not to make peace till this result had been achieved (Art. XXI).

In addition to these alterations two further articles were inserted; one to conciliate the Hapsburg brothers, the other to safeguard the commercial interests of England:

(*a*) The States General and England were to bind themselves not to make peace until the whole Spanish Monarchy had been recovered (Art. XX).

(*b*) Peace was likewise only to be made when the fortifications of Dunkirk had been demolished and the harbour rendered impracticable[1] (Art. XXII).

Such was the tenour of the Counter Project. We shall see at a later stage how the Dutch received the amendments.

On the 2nd/13th of May, Marlborough and Townshend were given their final instructions. These referred to (i) the preliminaries of peace; (ii) the Barrier Treaty. With regard to the former the instructions given to Marlborough on the 21st of March/1st of April were again insisted upon, and it was suggested that before a general peace a Grand Alliance should be

[1] This article was not of general importance to the Allies and was, moreover, particularly offensive to the States. "The proposal was not directed entirely against France but was also a warning indirectly to the Republic" (Hoffmann, 19 March, quoted by Klopp, XIII, 221). Later in the summer it seems to have occurred to some of the Dutch that by refusing to insist on this demand for the destruction of Dunkirk they would please France and perhaps obtain from her Cambrai for themselves. Noorden, III, 592.

renewed, and that "all the Allies should become mutual guarantees to one another of the several and respective conditions of the said peace". Moreover, as in the former instructions, the Allies were to be at liberty, in case the French had not agreed to the preliminaries by the opening of the campaign, to insist upon further conditions, so now it was to be understood that "in case the French do agree to the preliminaries demanded, there should be no cessation of arms till the Allies be fully satisfied that the preliminaries so agreed to will be made good to them".[1] With regard to the Barrier, the project of a treaty having been sent over, which the Queen "has considered and agreed to with such alterations as are reasonable", the Plenipotentiaries were to repair to The Hague and communicate to the Pensionary how far the project had met with approval. Moreover, a clause was added to bring these instructions into touch with the further concessions which, it was thought, France would probably, by this time, have made to the States at The Hague for their Barrier. It would not be unlikely that the revenues of these towns, which being on the frontier had suffered heavily from the war, would be insufficient for the cost of their maintenance. Marlborough and Townshend were therefore empowered, if this should prove to be the case, to add such further sums as should be reasonable, from the general revenues of the Spanish Netherlands. The chief interest of this clause lies in the way in which the idea was elaborated by the Dutch in the final treaty.[2]

On the day before the Plenipotentiaries received these instructions, Marlborough wrote again to explain his conduct to the Court at Barcelona. He sent to Stanhope, through Sunderland, a copy of the Project and Counter Project, and expressed the hope that the King would not think that the

[1] This provision for the security of the execution by Louis of the conditions appeared in its final form as the famous Article XXXVII of the preliminaries of May.

[2] Instructions to Marlborough and Townshend, 2/13 May 1709. Record Office. Printed in *Instructions to British Ambassadors*, vol. I, France, ed. Wickham Legge, p. 9. For the reference to the Barrier Treaty see Arts. XI and XIV, and particularly Townshend to Sunderland, 1 Nov. 1709. Record Office, and *Journal of House of Commons*, 14/25 Feb. 1712.

Queen "had been too easy in the matter".[1] He calculated that Charles would be grateful for the alterations of the Dutch scheme made by the English, particularly for the article relating to the restitution of the whole Spanish Monarchy. He was justified by the event—but to this we shall return later on.[2]

Marlborough and Townshend arrived at The Hague on the 18th of May. They arrived at the moment which has been referred to above, when the Dutch, having already received satisfaction as to their own claims, were insisting similarly on those of England.[3] There were still, however, difficulties to be settled with the Emperor and Savoy. No sooner was the portion of the Dutch Barrier demand included in the preliminaries settled, than other similar claims arose. The Empire and Savoy, too, required Barriers. "Everywhere", wrote Torcy, "you hear nothing but Barrier. The term is extended so far that they tell me that the Kingdoms of Naples and Sicily are a necessary Barrier to Tyrol."[4]

The English Plenipotentiaries informed the Pensionary that they had powers to settle the Barrier question, but to their surprise they found him backward in entering into negotiations. The reason of this, they discovered a few days later, was his desire to have first a general guarantee for so much of the Barrier as now appeared in the Preliminary Treaty. On the 29th they presented him with the Counter Project, of which he observed afterwards to Van den Bergh that it might form the basis of a useful arrangement if the revenues of the towns set apart for the maintenance of the Barrier expenses proved sufficient, a

[1] Marlborough to Stanhope, 1/12 May 1709. Murray. "I hope the King will not think the Queen has been too easy in the matter, since she can have no other view than to induce the States to insist on the entire Monarchy of Spain." Marlborough to Moles, same date: "Je me flatte que le Roi approuvera le projet de la Reine et les changements qu'elle propose pour adoucir cette affaire, puisque S. M. n'y entre que dans la seule vue d'avoir la monarchie entière pour le Roi, outre les villes que la France doit céder au-delà de ce que le feu Roi Charles possédait dans les Pays-Bas".

These letters show in what an awkward position the omission of the Spanish Monarchy article from the Treaty would leave Marlborough with regard to the Court of Barcelona. Moles and Charles each wrote to Marlborough in answer, 30 June 1709. Coxe Papers.

[2] Pp. 141 and 172 below. [3] P. 115 *note* 5, above.

[4] Torcy, *Mémoires*, II, 89.

point to which Van den Bergh was to give special attention.[1] "We foresee some difficulty in this matter", the English Envoys wrote home, "but shall in no way deviate from our instructions without further orders."

For the moment, however, the Barrier Treaty was put aside and the attentions of all were concentrated upon the peace preliminaries. To the various English demands Torcy gave his consent, though he complained that their claims as regards Dunkirk were "better suited to a garrison that was starving than to a treaty of Peace".[2] The article relating to the Barrier fortresses to be ceded by France came next. Objection to it came, not from France, but from another quarter. Sinzendorf, on the 23rd of May, arrived with fresh instructions from the Emperor. Eugene had sent to Vienna an account of the Dutch Project, the contents of which were such as to necessitate the despatch of an additional Envoy to stay all proceedings at The Hague contrary to the Imperial interests. The former points were recapitulated, and in particular Sinzendorf was not to admit of any definition of the frontier of the Southern Netherlands in the preliminaries—an event which would jeopardise any hopes of obtaining in that country the line of the Pyrenean peace—or of the question being decided without previous reference to the King of Prussia and the Electors Palatine and of Cologne.[3] The Dutch protested vigorously, so vigorously that Marlborough thought "all had been undone"; but they carried their point.[4] Article XXII of the preliminaries, in effect, defined the frontier of the Southern Netherlands, while it also gave Upper Guelders to the States. Sinzendorf and Eugene excused themselves to the Emperor for their compliance, by pointing out that they had thus obtained the more than counterbalancing advantage of

[1] Heinsius to Van den Bergh, 12 June 1709. Heinsius Archives.

[2] Marlborough and Townshend to Boyle, 4 June 1709. Record Office.

[3] Abstract of instructions to Sinzendorf. Wagner, *Hist. Josephi*, p. 270.

[4] "Finding this letter not gone when I came from the conference on Saturday night, Lord Townshend and I thought it very proper to stop the letters by the differences we found in the Conferences, by reason of the Dutch having inserted several articles concerning their Barrier which Prince Eugene and Ct. Sinzendorf declared they could not agree to, so that we separated that night in some anger. But I thank God we are now agreed as to that article." Marlborough to Godolphin, 27 May. Coxe Papers.

a universal pledge of all the Allies to the re-conquest of the whole Spanish Monarchy, that the Barrier article had only dealt with French towns and made no mention of the towns the Dutch wanted from the Spanish Netherlands, and that as for Guelders they had been forced by Dutch obstinacy to give in and felt less compunction in doing so as they did not see why more consideration should be paid to the feelings of the Prussian King than to those of the States, especially as the latter might in return assist in procuring an accession of territory to the Empire.[1]

This incident was the last serious difficulty on the side of the Allies in the negotiation and finally, on the 28th of May, the "Preliminaries of May" were presented to Torcy as the full and final statement of their claims. To this document Eugene, Sinzendorf, Marlborough, Townshend and the Dutch Deputies all appended their signatures. To all its provisions, with one exception, the French consent was eventually given.[2] The exception was Article XXXVII, which provided that if Louis had executed all the other articles and driven Philip out of Spain within the term of two months, then the cessation of arms should last until the conclusion of the treaty of peace. But in this one article lay the whole gist of the matter. The Allies had learnt that it was one thing for the French King to sign, and another to execute. The long series of negotiations which Louis had begun in January, in the hope of luring the Dutch from the Allies, had terminated in the united demand of England, Austria and the States that he should himself take the sword and expel his own grandson. Louis refused with all the superb dignity of which he was such a master, and his refusal was the signal for the renewal of war.

It is an extraordinary fact that hardly a single one of the Ministers who signed the "Preliminaries of May", or of the governments in whose names they were signed, really approved of them.

In England it was very generally agreed that France had been

[1] Wagner, *Hist. Josephi*, p. 282.

[2] See the forty articles with Torcy's observations on them in his *Mémoires*, II, 188.

leniently treated.[1] The majority were satisfied with the preliminaries because they were held to imply the recovery of the whole Spanish Monarchy.[2] Godolphin, however, thought otherwise. He was, on the whole, pleased at the rejection of the preliminaries just because he did not believe that they implied the recovery of the whole Spanish Monarchy. Two things struck him forcibly with regard to these preliminaries, and on these two impressions he based his policy for the year. The first impression was that France all along had intended a "chicane", as he called it, and never meant to fulfil the conditions. He stated his opinion decisively before the preliminaries had been drawn up[3]; he adhered to it steadily on hearing that Torcy had gone to Paris to submit the completed document to Louis[4]; and, when the news of its rejection arrived, his feeling was one of indignation but not of surprise. "It is plain", he wrote to Marlborough on receiving the news, "that the French have all along intended a deliberate insincerity about yielding up the entire Spanish Monarchy. I am very glad that by your great precaution and the firmness of Holland their artifice is pretty well discovered and so far eluded that I hope nobody will be the worse but themselves, for this shameful proceeding."[5] This deeply rooted distrust of the French intentions made Godolphin equally sceptical on the subject of the so-called "expedients" for Article XXXVII. He did not for a moment think that France would have complied with them. "It is plain", he

[1] L'Hermitage, 7 June 1709. On 4 June, speaking of Torcy's journey to Paris to obtain Louis' ratification, he writes, "Comme on ne doute pas qu'il ne la donne, on regarde ici la paix comme faite".

[2] Godolphin to Marlborough, 6/17 June. Coxe Papers.

[3] "What I most apprehend is the real difficulty of getting from France a solid effectual security for the performance of what they promise in the Preliminaries, and because cautionary towns have sometimes been mentioned as a proper security upon this occasion I beg leave to observe to you that cautionary towns unless they be Maritime towns can be of no security to us for the giving up of Spain. I am afraid France may design a chicane in that matter, tell us they can do no more than withdraw their troops, get a suspension of arms, and then leave us to get Spain as best we can." Godolphin to Marlborough, 16/27 May. Coxe Papers.

[4] "I shall always be in doubt about their yielding because of the nature of the thing itself." Godolphin to Marlborough, 27 May/7 June. Coxe Papers.

[5] Godolphin to Marlborough, 31 May/11 June. Coxe Papers.

pointed out, "that the French never intended to deliver up the entire Monarchy of Spain and therefore it is natural to believe they would have made use of the two months, to find some new chicane to gain more time for strengthening themselves."[1] The second impression which Godolphin derived from the preliminaries was that, on the whole, their rejection had been to the advantage of England, and this for the following reason. Even if some such effective guarantee were obtained from Louis that he would dispossess his grandson, and a truce were made with him on that basis, there would still remain the conquest of Spain to be undertaken. This task, Godolphin argued, would fall almost alone on England. Experience had lately shown how little could be hoped for from the Emperor, and, as for the Dutch, "I leave you to judge", he continued, "by all the rest of their proceedings what share they would take of the charge of that war after they were once easy and their frontier secure to them".[2] The continuation of a war against France and Spain in which all the Allies were engaged alike seemed to him preferable to a war against Spain undertaken by England alone.

In Vienna the preliminaries were condemned as altogether insufficient.[3] The Emperor was annoyed in particular with Article XXII relating to the Dutch Barrier and the cession of Guelders, and to the permission given them to have garrisons in Huy, Bonn and Liège; and also because much had been inserted that was properly matter for settlement between the Allies themselves without any French interference.[4] The far-off Court of Barcelona alone expressed pleasure. Charles remarked that they were "satisfactorily settled", though he noted that no stipulations had been made for the basis of the Peace of the Pyrenees—an omission which he hoped would be rectified in the final treaty.[5] Stanhope also expressed his pleasure at the preliminaries, which he thought "beyond what we could ever imagine or hope".[6]

[1] Godolphin to Marlborough, 13/24 June. Coxe Papers.
[2] Godolphin to Marlborough, 6/17 June 1709. Coxe Papers.
[3] Lamberty, v, 301. [4] Wagner, *Hist. Josephi*, pp. 282, 318.
[5] Charles to Wratislaw, 30 June 1709. "Korrespondenz", edited by Arneth, *Archiv für Oesterreichische Geschichtsquellen*, XVI.
[6] Stanhope to Marlborough, 22 June 1709. Coxe Papers.

On the other hand, the more thoughtful of the Envoys, who had vied with one another in showing themselves "well intentioned", awoke on the morrow to an inner conviction that these "good intentions" had carried them too far. In a conversation with Goslinga, who was indignant at the rupture of the negotiations and declared that he would have ratified the Treaty without Article XXXVII, Eugene answered, "I am very glad to find that those are your sentiments; they are mine too. In four campaigns we shall not obtain what we might have won by a stroke of the pen without spilling a drop of blood".[1] Marlborough observed to Schmettau, the Prussian Envoy, that he feared that Article XXXVII would spoil everything,[2] and his letters to Heinsius throughout the summer show that he was convinced that France could never be brought to consent to such a stipulation. "If I were in the place of the King of France," he wrote on one occasion, "I should venture the loss of my country much sooner than be obliged to join my troops for the forcing of my grandson."[3] Marlborough's protestations, which expressed the situation not inaccurately, would have been better made before the rupture of the negotiations than after. Previous to the 28th of May he had sheltered himself behind his unbending instructions, and assisted complacently in the process of piling up claims.[4] The truth was that the Allies had not stinted their demands, confidently believing that France would grant anything they chose to ask. The recall of Torcy was therefore surprising and disconcerting. It became obvious that, balked of their hopes, the various Plenipotentiaries were only too ready to find someone on whom to throw the blame.

Heinsius, as the spokesman of the Allies, was made the victim. Marlborough and Eugene, on returning to Brussels on

[1] Goslinga, *Mémoires*, p. 116.

[2] Lamberty, v, 288.

[3] Marlborough to Heinsius, 10 July 1709, "for yourself only". Heinsius Archives.

[4] Marlborough to Duchess, 31 May: "Since Torcy went away, I have a little time to myself. I have the satisfaction to tell my dear soul that I have now a prospect of living quietly with you. For I do verily believe the condition of France is such that they must submit to the conditions we have given them, and they are such as that I hope everybody will be pleased with them". Coxe Papers.

their way to the camp, expressed surprise that the Republic had suggested no expedient for Article XXXVII.[1]

> The Duke (wrote Albemarle to the Pensionary) let fall the observation that he had remarked in you much unbending firmness, and that as you had made no suggestion, he as well as Lord Townshend thought it was not their duty to do anything, and thus the affair was broken off. Prince Eugene also made similar statements. In fact I have noticed that they wished to shift the burden of the consequences of this business, and laid much on your shoulders.[2]

Heinsius was indignant at the injustice of these insinuations, but uncomfortable at the possibility of their existence.

> We arranged everything (he replied) in concert with the Duke of Marlborough, and we were always unanimous. It is surprising that, if my Lord Duke was really of the opinion you say, he should have given us no indication of it before Rouillé's departure. I must tell you that we acted in this business with all the circumspection in the world, in concert with the Deputies of the States General. Everything was approved by the States of Holland and I protest that if the whole thing had to be done over again, I don't see how we could do it otherwise.[3]

On the other hand, it was only to please the Allies that the Pensionary had shown his firmness. While the reproach was galling and unjust coming from Eugene and the Duke, it might have some semblance of reality in the mouth of the Dutch peace party, such as Buys. The breaking off of the negotiations had not been, in itself, a benefit to the States. The nation might ask their leader what advantages he had obtained in return. For the moment his honest endeavour appeared to the world in a curious light. The Dutch patriot had become the mouthpiece of the bigotry of the Empire and the infatuation of the Whigs.

IV

The rejection of the preliminaries affected the Barrier Treaty in two ways, both of which strengthened the Dutch and weakened the English position with regard to it. The States had attached enormous importance to their Barrier when it was only

[1] H. Pesters to Heinsius, from Brussels, 11 June 1709. Heinsius Archives.
[2] Albemarle to Heinsius, from Brussels, 11 June 1709. Heinsius Archives.
[3] Heinsius to Albemarle, 15 June 1709. Heinsius Archives.

one item in an advantageous peace. Now that it was set before them as the one compensation for the loss of that peace and for the continuation of a war which a strong and growing faction detested, the importance of the Treaty would be trebled in their eyes. If the first feeling of the burghers of Amsterdam in their disappointment was one of wrath against France,[1] the time would soon come when in the hopes of peace they would forget that wrong, or rather lay the blame of it on their own allies, from whom, with England's exception, they had not so much to gain.

In the second place, the English had often declared that if the French rejected the preliminaries they would no longer consider themselves bound by them, and after another campaign would exact additional concessions. Would it not be possible for the Dutch also to say that they would not be bound by the preliminaries but in another sense? Did it not seem as if that promise not to make peace without England, that chain by which their Barrier had for three long years been bound, was about to become a thing of the past? The peace party in the States might with some reason flatter themselves that a little duplicity would enable them both to have their cake and eat it. The attempt might have been, but was not, made—partly perhaps through the prudence, still more through the political honesty of Heinsius. Marlborough always believed (or pretended to believe) that the Dutch, when they had got their Barrier, would make peace with France. Townshend and the Whigs maintained that the settlement of the Treaty was the only way to keep them from doing so. After the conclusion of the Treaty the vigorous resolution of the States on the 14th of December to continue the war showed who was right.

But the task which devolved upon Heinsius from June to October was one of great difficulty, and in less competent hands would have been foredoomed to failure. He had to extract from the English such concessions as would satisfy the peace party in the States, and to kindle in the latter sufficient enthusiasm for the war to abide firmly by Article XXXVII of the preliminaries and so satisfy the Whigs. Even this, however, does not fully

[1] Walpole from The Hague, 11 June 1709. Record Office.

express the difficulty of the situation. All through the summer the French were occupied in endeavouring to find a way out of the "impasse" created by Article XXXVII, and the "ambitious windbag", Petkum, was kept constantly on the road between Paris and The Hague. We hear almost as much of "expedients" as of the "Barrier". But these expedients gave rise to a new source of disagreement between England and the States. As the object of the expedients was to obtain a security for the expulsion of Philip, the English demanded the handing over of at least three towns in Spain.[1] It was, moreover, considered essential that they should be maritime towns. If the reduction of Spain should after all prove impossible, thought the Whig chiefs, these towns might be very useful as commercial stations.[2] The cession of three towns in French Flanders was also insisted upon.[3] The latter requirement was the only one for which the Dutch were anxious. The Spanish towns had no interest for them. What added to the friction caused by this divergence of views was that the French King was only too ready to grant the demand of the States, but declared the English one to be utterly beyond his power as he had withdrawn his troops from Spain. Each successive visit of Petkum, therefore, impressed more vividly upon the Dutch the fact that it was English obstinacy that stood between them and peace. Well might Louis write to Villars:

If you stand out only this campaign without suffering serious loss, the conditions of peace will turn out differently, and the Dutchmen, who now stand under pressure of the allies whose strong active forces they see in the midst of their own land, will then recognise their true interest is that they should always unite with France, as they will thereby procure for themselves a rational barrier.[4]

[1] Such was also the feeling at Vienna, cp. Goslinga to Heinsius, "en Angleterre et à Vienne on ne croit pas qu'il y ait du salut à espérer à moins qu'on ait des places en Espagne", 2 Sept. 1709. Heinsius Archives, quoted by Noorden, III, 588.

[2] Boyle to Townshend, "No cautionary towns are of much significance in this case unless such as are maritime and essential to reducing Spain", 3/14 June 1709. Record Office.

[3] The towns in Flanders refer to the French Netherlands (Flanders, Artois, etc.) annexed in 1659, 1668 and 1678 and retained by France, but still referred to as "Pays Bas", e.g. *Recueil des instructions données aux Ambassadeurs et Ministres de France en Hollande*, II, 226.

[4] Louis to Villars, 3 June 1709. Pelet, IX, 25, quoted by Klopp, XIII, 347.

Such was the sea of conflicting interests through which Heinsius succeeded in steering his course. But this masterpiece of statesmanship kept the pilot throughout at a high state of tension. More than once the craft was all but on the rocks.

Marlborough's departure on the 9th of June to join the army, left Townshend sole English representative at The Hague. In that position he received very little assistance; most of his instructions from home were of a nature to add to, rather than solve, his difficulties; while Marlborough held persistently aloof. His answer, a copy of which he sent to Townshend, to a request made by Heinsius in August for his advice as to the question of peace, is typical of the Duke's attitude towards the former.

> The answer I gave him, (wrote Marlborough) which is the same I give your Excellency, was, that whatever my own notions were, I can have no other opinion than what is agreeable to the instructions we have from England; that your Excellency, being at hand, can better inform him what these are than I can do by letter; that you have so great a value for his integrity and foresight in this affair, that you will rely much on his opinion.

He therefore advised Heinsius to communicate his thoughts to Townshend and wait for the Queen's instructions, concluding his letter to Townshend with the following evasive remark: "this is the substance of what I wrote to the Pensionary, and indeed all of what I can say to your Lordship".[1] To this letter Marlborough's constant and confidential correspondence with Heinsius and Godolphin formed a striking contrast.[2] The question of the Barrier came up for discussion at the end of June and difficulties began at once. The Pensionary told Townshend that the consent of the States to the article that provided for the restitution of the whole Spanish Monarchy was impossible, and added his hope that, in view of the firm answer that he had just given to Petkum, the Queen would not insist upon it.[3] In reply to Townshend's request for further

[1] Marlborough to Heinsius, 10 Aug. 1709. Coxe Papers.

[2] Noorden in vol. III, chap. 6, quotes several of the former from the Heinsius Archives. In one case Marlborough concludes, "You see with what freedom I write to you, so that I must once more desire that you will never let anybody know of this letter" (10 July 1709).

[3] Townshend to Boyle, 5 July 1709. Record Office. The answer to Petkum was to the effect that France should give "encore d'autres places de sûreté" and that the expedient should be suggested by Torcy, not by Heinsius (Petkum to Torcy, 4 July. Legrelle, IV, 501).

instructions, Boyle wrote that it was "too nice a point" to give an answer upon at once. A fortnight later, Townshend, who had still received no further instructions, wrote again to the effect that the removal of difficulties connected with the Barrier would keep the Dutch firm. He received in reply the suggestion that the Treaty should be signed as now drawn up, and that a secret article should be added, providing that the Treaty should be in force but one year, except what concerned the Succession and the Barrier. This suggestion was to be made as if it were Townshend's own invention, and if accepted was to be referred for approval to London.[1] To Heinsius this idea seemed no improvement. He explained that a secret article was useless, as the Dutch constitution would necessitate the communication of the subject matter to all the provinces for their consent. Townshend reported this and waited, but still no satisfactory answer came from England. The Dutch, having now much less hope of penetrating into France during the present campaign, and regarding the demand for the cautionary towns in Spain as impracticable—they had just been informed by Torcy that Louis had withdrawn almost all his troops—became more and more impatient.[2] At last the wished for powers arrived and Townshend was able to inform the States that the Queen agreed that there should be nothing in the Treaty but what concerned the Succession and the Barrier. This meant, of course, the disappearance of both the articles referring to the Spanish Monarchy and the demolition of Dunkirk.[3] The concession had not come too soon. "The affairs of the Dutch", wrote Townshend, "are at this time in so happy a situation that it is not so much a question with them whether they can have a good Barrier, as from what hand they shall receive it."[4]

Why was the English Ministry so unwilling to yield, and why was it that, even when the concession was made, the precaution was taken of enquiring whether the Dutch after receiving satisfaction on this point would remain firm to the Alliance?

[1] Boyle to Townshend, 15/26 July 1709. Record Office.
[2] Townshend to Boyle, 2 and 9 Aug. 1709. Record Office.
[3] Boyle to Townshend, 2/13 Aug. 1709. Record Office.
[4] Townshend to Boyle, 20 Aug. 1709. Record Office.

The answer is to be found in Marlborough's attitude. The Duke, with that marvellous activity which enabled him to combine all the hardships of war with the most complicated diplomacy, had been following closely, by means of correspondence with Godolphin and Boyle, the negotiations at The Hague, as to which he had formed an entirely different opinion from that held in London.

The renewal of the war upon the rejection of the preliminaries had forced upon Marlborough the necessity of forming a new plan of campaign. This new plan was based upon the idea which was at the time predominant in Marlborough's mind—the demoralisation of France. In his correspondence with Godolphin, he constantly comes back to this point. "She is in so miserable a condition", he wrote at one time, "that when you shall insist only on what is in their power they must comply"[1]; at another time, "it will be a miracle if we have another campaign".[2] This firm belief in the desperate condition of France made Marlborough regard the continuation of the campaign in the Netherlands as needless and futile. It was *needless* because what Louis had offered would have placed him at the mercy of the Allies. "In my opinion," wrote the Duke to Godolphin, "if France had delivered the towns promised by the preliminaries, and demolished Dunkirk and the other towns mentioned, they must have been at our discretion, so that if they had played tricks so much the worse for themselves."[3] The campaign in the Netherlands was *futile* because it was an attempt to force France to do what she was incapable of doing.

> The positive orders (he declared in a confidential enclosure to Heinsius) that my Lord Townshend has, for the insisting on three towns in Spain, makes it impossible for me to express myself otherwise than I do in my letter; but I call God to witness that I think it is not in the power of the King of France, so that if you persist in having three towns in Spain it is in my opinion declaring the continuation of the war.[4]

[1] Marlborough to Godolphin, 3 Sept. 1709. Coxe Papers.
[2] Marlborough to Godolphin, 15 Aug. 1709. Coxe, II, 413.
[3] Marlborough to Godolphin, 16 June 1709. Coxe, II, 409.
[4] Marlborough to Heinsius, 4 July, enclosure "for yourself only". Heinsius Archives.

In conversation with Goslinga, the Duke expressed himself as so desirous of peace with France that the Dutchman sent word to Heinsius: "You have only to conclude peace and he will join with you".[1] Two letters received on the 22nd of August confirmed Marlborough in his previous conviction. These letters were from the Duke of Alba and Count Bergeyck, who, it was stated with sublime disregard for the progress of events, had been appointed by Philip as his representatives for the congress at The Hague. Philip went on to say—and this was the real import of the letter—that, if the two Maritime Powers would make peace with him, he would offer them the same commercial advantages as they had enjoyed under Charles II.[2] Such a statement, on the top of Philip's spirited declaration on the 4th of July that he would give his last drop of blood sooner than resign his kingdom, showed the absolute futility of attempted expedients for Article XXXVII.[3] On this basis Marlborough formed his new plan of campaign. The right course for England to pursue seemed to him to be that she should forestall the Dutch in patching up a peace with France, and at once make war resolutely on Spain for the complete re-conquest of that Monarchy. He believed the plan was feasible if properly conducted.

The reduction of Spain (he wrote to Godolphin) will never in my opinion be effected until the army in Catalonia and that in Portugal be in such a condition as that they may both march the nearest way to Madrid; for if we shall think of forming projects for the reducing of the provinces of Spain, the war is likely to last much longer than I shall live.[4]

If properly conducted he did not believe the war could last more than six months, a belief which he also communicated to Heinsius.[5]

[1] "Vous n'avez qu'à conclure; il y donne les mains." Goslinga to Heinsius, 1 Aug., quoted by Noorden, III, 588.

[2] The two letters are given in Murray, IV, 577–9.

[3] Philippe, *Lettre Circulaire sur la rupture des Préliminaires*. Lamberty, V, 306.

[4] Marlborough to Godolphin, 26 Aug. 1709. Coxe Papers.

[5] "(For yourself only) You say you find many who have great difficulty in continuing the war with Spain; they are of the same opinion and have the same difficulty in England. But for God's sake will not this difficulty be the

The importance, for our present purpose, of Marlborough's scheme was two-fold. (1) It must at the first blush appear a wanton continuation of the war.[1] For its successful execution, therefore, the English Ministry must be quite certain of the confidence of the country. (2) It necessitated the co-operation of the other Allies, principally of the Dutch. The latter would presumably be gratified at seeing a truce made with France sooner than they expected, and the consequent reduction of their expenses. They were to pay for this by being enrolled at once in a new alliance to be made between them, the English and the Emperor, for the re-conquest of Spain.[2] The old bond of allegiance upon which their Barrier had from 1706 been made conditional and from which they seemed almost to have escaped, was again to be placed upon them. Now the Barrier Treaty at the stage which it had reached in July 1709 seemed completely to undermine both these conditions, so essential to the success of Marlborough's scheme. But this was not all. The reasons for which it undermined these conditions appeared to him so far reaching that the accomplishment of the Treaty would bring about the downfall of the whole political system then existing. The Dutch demands were, he thought, such as would, if accepted, seriously imperil the English Ministry; and such as, when published, would completely paralyse the efforts of the Alliance.

The contents of the "Project" had been a great blow to Marlborough, and it would seem that, from the moment that he received that document, he determined to range himself in opposition to the Treaty. The Counter Project cut down the demands considerably, but it is doubtful whether he really approved even of the English reply. It still left to the Dutch

same two years hence, and Spain the more time they have given them, be the better able to defend themselves, for I think it is plain the French Ministers have it not in their power to recall the Duke of Anjou, and I think it is as plain that if England, Holland, and the Emperor will take vigorous resolutions, the war in Spain may be ended in 6 months" (Marlborough to Heinsius, 22 Aug. 1709. Heinsius Archives).

[1] "I am told in England this is thought a continuation of the war and a giving time to France to recover, so that whilst there are such devils as Harley in the world it is dangerous for honest men to give their opinion" (Marlborough to Godolphin, 26 Aug. 1709. Coxe Papers).

[2] Marlborough to Godolphin, 12 Aug. 1709. Coxe Papers.

Lier and Hal, the other places in the heart of the Netherlands, which, as Marlborough must have known, the Austrians would be even less ready to give up than those formerly asked of them. When he heard that the Dutch were raising objections to the two fundamental articles added by the cabinet for the benefit of England and the Alliance, the fire of disapproval that had long been smouldering burst out into open condemnation.

If the article with reference to the razure of Dunkirk were left out, this would probably mean that Dunkirk would never be razed. The demand was disliked rather than tolerated in the Republic and it was not likely that without compulsion the Dutch would join in forcing its acceptance upon France. But, further, Marlborough was not the man to be deluded into believing that the Dutch would rest content with what the Counter Project gave them.

When the States (he wrote) shall be acquainted with the orders Lord Townshend has received, he will find them every day more unreasonable in their demands. I wish I may be mistaken, for I have no wish but the Queen's and my country's service; but I am afraid I shall live to see this found fault with, since, in all probability, the Dutch will not be contented, unless they obtain some advantage on our trade.[1]

The Ministry would have to face Parliament and satisfy them as to why they had sold their country's interests in the Netherlands to a Republic, who refused to assist them in return to annihilate that nest of pirates which rendered their very coasts unsafe. Already the Ministry was none too secure. Marlborough realised that Godolphin, the Duchess, and he himself had no credit with the Queen,[2] and he had just learnt that the Tories, knowing him to be unassailable while the war lasted, were plotting to put an end to it, by stopping the supplies next session, so as thus to produce his downfall.[3]

The effects of the omission of the article for the re-conquest of the whole Spanish Monarchy would, it seemed to him, be hardly less disastrous. In the first place, the States, he thought,

[1] Marlborough to Godolphin, 26 Aug. 1709. Coxe Papers.

[2] Marlborough to Duchess, 5 Aug. Coxe, II, 415.

[3] Godolphin to Marlborough, 26 July/6 Aug. (Coxe Papers), reporting a conversation between Somers and Rivers.

would be sure to turn the omission to their own advantage. The assistance of the Dutch was essential to the accomplishment of that end, while without some such article to bind them, they would probably make peace without accomplishing it.

> Nobody (he explained to Sunderland) can be more persuaded than I am, that there is a necessity of endeavouring to give satisfaction to the States General as to the Barrier they desire; but at the same time, I am convinced it is the true interest of England to preserve the Monarchy of Spain entire, and if the clause for the entire Monarchy be left out of the Treaty for the Barrier, it is my opinion that in a little time you will be pressed for the giving of the Kingdoms of Naples or Sicily, or both, to the Duke of Anjou.[1]

He expressed the same conviction to the Duchess and concluded with the words: "I call God to witness that my concern proceeds from the love I have for my country, and my concern for such of my friends as are now in the Ministry".[2] In the second place, the Hapsburgs would be furious. When, on the 1st of May, a copy of the Counter Project was sent to Barcelona, Marlborough had particularly drawn the King's attention to the stipulation therein made for the re-conquest of the entire Monarchy. It was on this clause that the chief hope of the King's concurrence in the Counter Project had rested.[3] Should this clause now be omitted, Charles would have just reason to complain. Godolphin pointed out that a recent letter from Charles to the Queen had authorised them to proceed with the Barrier. He also urged that, even without such an authorisation, Charles' recent conduct with regard to Port Mahon[4] did not entitle him to consideration at the hands of England, and implored Marlborough to put an end to all jealousies in the Republic by himself undertaking that he would persuade the Queen to comply with the Dutch and make them easy about their Barrier.[5] Marlborough was immovable, and summed up his whole attitude towards the Treaty in the following "ultimatum",

[1] Marlborough to Sunderland, 12 Aug. 1709. Coxe Papers.

[2] Marlborough to Duchess, 19 Aug. Coxe, II, 415.

[3] Cp. above, p. 126.

[4] See following section.

[5] Godolphin to Marlborough, 31 July/11 Aug. and 2/13 Aug. 1709. Coxe Papers.

which is of such interest that we may be pardoned for inserting it in its entirety.

I am afraid you will find the advice given by Townshend prove very fatal to the interest of the Queen and England. I am sure you intend very kindly the advice you give me of my making myself so far master in this business as to be able to oblige the Pensionary and the States, by which I would have it in my power to conduct peace to the best advantage of England. I am of so different opinion that, as soon as the States shall know what is resolved, they will be so far from being grateful that they will be insolent and insist on such exorbitant conditions in the very Treaty of the Barrier that I will find difficulty even in the giving my consent. I wish with all my heart I may be mistaken; but I am sure there is a very growing party in Holland that will this winter by the encouragement they will receive by our leaving out the entire Monarchy, solicit openly for something to be done for the Duke of Anjou. Besides, the same party are of the opinion that the demolishing of Dunkirk is much more for the interest of England. I must observe to you that the letter writ by the King was in answer to that of the Queen with which the Counter Project was sent and the greatest argument was the care that was taken of the Monarchy, which by what is now ordered will be looked upon as abandoned, not only in Barcelona, but by many in England, so that if it can agree with the Queen's affairs, I should be glad that I might be excused from signing not being on the place. I am very sensible of what you say, that if I should openly oppose the treaty for the Barrier all the mis-intelligence that might happen between England and Holland would be laid to my charge, but on the other side to avoid one difficulty and run into another which is like to be so very prejudicial to the Queen and England is what I must beg your assistance in helping me to avoid.[1]

Again and again he repeated his remonstrances to the Treasurer, who was rendered by circumstances incapable of profiting by them. "Be assured", he warned, "that whenever England shall comply with the States as to the Barrier, as now desired, they will think it more their interest to be well with France than England."[2] That was the despairing cry of Marl-

[1] Marlborough to Godolphin, "for yourself, the Queen and the Duchess only". Without date, but evidently the enclosure to Godolphin referred to in his letter to the Duchess of 19 Aug. 1709. Coxe, II, 415. The letter quoted is in one of the few volumes of Godolphin's correspondence in the British Museum (Add. MSS. 28057).

[2] Marlborough to Godolphin, "for yourself only", without date. Coxe, II, 412.

borough's former policy. The spell, which had tamed the burghers of Amsterdam and for three years had chained their country to the war, was to be wantonly abandoned! But the cry rose from one who could not, or would not, see that things had entirely changed, that in 1709 the Dutch had broken the power of the spell, and that the time for this policy was past.

The negotiation for the Treaty thus proceeded in face of the Duke's opposition. For the first time since the commencement of the war, Marlborough had lost the direction of an important diplomatic transaction. It was for him the beginning of the end. In the following year his control over the peace negotiations was to slip from his grasp and that over the Ministry be wrenched from it. Twelve months later, he would be standing before the Houses, stript of his public honours, and charged, however falsely, with peculation. The first of Marlborough's three defeats was the least dishonouring of them. There was more of honest conviction and less of unpardonable weakness in the condemnation of the Barrier Treaty, than in his attempts to throw upon his Whig colleagues, in the last months of their ministerial existence, all responsibility for the continuance of the war, or in his consent to continue in the service under a chief who had in past years, as a dependant, thwarted and betrayed him. But even in his present attitude towards the Barrier Treaty, there was still the invariable mixture of motives which characterised so many of his actions. Behind his championship of the rights of the Coalition, whose chosen vessel he was, there still lay the fading phantom of the "Patent"; and, while he denounced with the enthusiasm of a patriot, he was aiming at a safeguard for himself. Beyond this, for the present crisis, he was in a large measure responsible. The spirit of exasperation and mistrust which had wound itself so firmly round the Barrier question was the outcome of his past procrastinating diplomacy. At this eleventh hour, his remonstrances were but counsels of perfection, to have adopted which, in August 1709, would have caused at one blow the secession of the Dutch.

Marlborough's opposition placed Godolphin in great embarrassment. Accustomed in time past to agree with his great colleague and, when differing from him, to yield, the Treasurer found himself compelled by the other members of the Junta, and no less by his better appreciation of the difficulties of the situation, to take an opposite course. The line of policy which he had adopted on the rejection of the preliminaries differed widely from that taken by Marlborough. He was opposed to patching up a peace with France at all: still more so, to patching it up on the security which Marlborough had thought sufficient. Whichever scheme, however, for the recovery of the whole Spanish Monarchy was adopted—the Treasurer's, of continuing the war actively on its present conditions, or Marlborough's, of making a truce with France and carrying the war into Spain—the co-operation of the Dutch was absolutely necessary. But as to the means of securing this co-operation the two statesmen differed even more completely. Marlborough believed that to grant the Dutch their Barrier on the footing they demanded, opened the door to secession on their part and in any case would render the recovery of the whole Spanish Monarchy impossible. Godolphin felt that to grant them their Barrier was the only way by which to keep them in the Alliance, and the only hope of obtaining their co-operation to the end in view. Herein the Treasurer showed that he had the greater grasp of the situation. All through the year he had watched the movements of the States with anxiety, as he recognised the strength of their position. He had stated, earlier in the summer, that he had never expected that the Dutch would tie themselves by a Treaty not to make peace until the entire Spanish Monarchy was restored, "though partly by persuasion and partly by resentment they had been induced to try the effect of the present campaign".[1] They must, therefore, he thought, be conciliated by all possible means. In the hope of bringing Marlborough to his point of view, Godolphin had, however, delayed committing himself, and he himself devised "expedients" for retaining the

[1] Godolphin to Marlborough, 10 July 1709. Coxe Papers. Heems also had thought that the preliminaries were, as far as the Dutch were concerned, the result of a moment of enthusiasm rather than of a settled conviction. "The difficulty", observed the Austrian resident at The Hague, "lies, not only in extracting something from France, but in keeping the Dutch state firm to what we demand, as most of the persons here had intended the Kingdom of Naples and Sicily for the Duke of Anjou" (Heems from The Hague, 10 June 1709. Austrian State Archives. Noorden, III, 583).

two articles of the Barrier Treaty, relative to Dunkirk and the whole Spanish Monarchy, until, as we have seen, Townshend was driven almost to despair. At last the urgency of the Whigs compelled the Treasurer to follow their advice and, in a moment of indignation against the Court of Barcelona, he gave his consent to the omission of the much debated articles.[1] When Marlborough's "ultimatum" of the 19th of August arrived, Godolphin had thus already taken the plunge to cement the bond of unity between him and the Whig leaders. Marlborough's letter was final and decisive. Henceforth the Treaty must proceed without the Duke's assistance and in spite of his opposition.[2] Nevertheless, Godolphin felt this wrench from his old bearings keenly. In his letter of the 14th of August he summed up the situation thus:

As to the matter depending about the treaty for the Succession and the Barrier, I find by all Townshend's letters that he continues not only firm but warm in his opinion, directly contrary to yours. And he is very positive that Heinsius and all those who are well intentioned will get the better of Buys and that party, if they can be able to give them this instance that the friendship of the Queen of England is more to be depended upon than any other, and that this will certainly take away the great handle by which Buys and his party gather strength in the States, instead of adding more strength to them as you and your letters seem to think it will. I must own I think that there is a good deal to be said for both these opinions and am therefore very far from taking upon myself to determine which is rightest.[3]

[1] Boyle to Townshend, 2/13 Aug. Record Office.

[2] Godolphin to Sunderland, 17/28 Aug. Coxe, II, 416.

[3] Godolphin to Marlborough, 14/25 Aug. 1709. Coxe Papers. There is a passage (pp. 397 ff.) in Mr Hugh Elliott's *Life of Godolphin* which calls for remark in this connection. He wrote the book, he says, partly with the intention of showing that Godolphin was not the pusillanimous devotee of Marlborough that Coxe makes out. In this attempt he is abundantly justified, but this being so, it is unfortunate that he makes an incident in which Godolphin appeared perhaps to greater advantage in comparison with his great colleague than in any other a subject for apology. Mr Elliott states, "As regarded the Grand Alliance the (Barrier) Treaty could have but one effect and that was to weaken it". Starting from this position, Mr Elliott argues that, as Godolphin knowingly consented—in the face of all the opposition Marlborough raised—to a Treaty which sapped the foundations of the Alliance, he must have been very certain and desirous of peace. He goes on to condemn the Treasurer accordingly on the principle of "si vis pacem para bellum". To argue like this is, we submit, to show a complete misconception of the difficulty of Godolphin's and the strength of the States'

He concluded by hoping that the renewal of the negotiations for peace might prevent a crisis, especially "when Townshend should begin to press the Dutch to enter into new measures for reducing Spain".

Godolphin had differed from Marlborough as to the manner of keeping the Dutch firm, but he took care that in their divergence of view the cause of it should not be lost. England had given in to the States about the two articles in the Barrier Treaty: it was very necessary that she should obtain the reward which should be the justification of the concession. Townshend was instructed to urge that the Dutch should enter into a new alliance with England and the Emperor for the recovery of the entire Spanish Monarchy.[1] The reception given to the latter demand at The Hague was unfavourable, but at the same time rendered it unnecessary. The Dutch realised its full meaning. Heinsius pointed out to Townshend that in his last answer to Torcy he had insisted on the three towns in Spain.

> England's latest demand would, therefore, occasion a jealousy here (he said) that she is disposed to conclude the war with France before a sufficient security is obtained for the speedy reduction of Spain. This would weaken the firmness the States have lately shown in case Torcy should return a fallacious answer.[2]

By this dexterous move the Pensionary warded off the blow. But the English concessions in the matter of the Barrier had done their work and the Dutch remained firm. The Ministry,

position at the time. Townshend's correspondence shows that Godolphin, as the head of the Whigs, yielded point after point to the Dutch, culminating with the ratification of the Treaty, not from a complacent optimism as to the speedy prospect of peace, but as a desperate resource to keep the Dutch firm to the allegiance. Godolphin was merely victim of the relentless laws of supply and demand, and throughout showed the most honourable unity of purpose and consistency.

[1] Townshend's instructions on this point were as follows: "Your Excellency cannot fail to observe that all the methods proposed in Holland and the best terms they expect from France for the conclusion of a General Peace will still leave d'Anjou master of the greater part of Spain and will oblige the Allies to considerable expense to drive him thence by force of arms. Measures therefore for that purpose, should be concerted and the several portions of the charge of that war between the Emperor, Great Britain and the States, should be adjusted as settled by treaty as soon as possible." Boyle to Townshend, 16/27 Aug. 1709. Record Office.

[2] Townshend to Boyle, 3 Sept. Record Office.

recognising that so long as they did so the new demand was unnecessary, let the matter drop.[1]

Heinsius had obtained the promise of their Barrier free from any written obligation to obtain the razure of Dunkirk, or the complete dispossession of Philip. Thus had he atoned to his countrymen for the rupture of the negotiations at The Hague in the first week of June. But now the discovery of a secret negotiation between the Courts of Barcelona and St James' came nearer than any previous difficulty to completely wrecking the Barrier Treaty.

V

The English dealings with regard to the cession of Minorca are interesting, not only for the profound effect their detection produced over the subsequent negotiation for the Barrier at The Hague, but also because they go a long way to account for the pertinacity with which England had been urging the claims of King Charles III. The whole transaction is, moreover, in itself a typical specimen of the diplomacy of that time. In 1706 the English had endeavoured, on the ground of money spent on the war in Spain, to extract from Charles a commercial treaty giving them special advantages. Charles had resisted, but the Ministry, availing themselves of the King's precarious position after Almanza, carried their point.[2] On the 10th of July 1707 a commercial treaty was arranged between the two courts, in which England was accorded various privileges with regard to dues on goods entering Spain. This treaty was ratified on the 9th of January 1708 and with it a secret article of infinitely greater importance. The latter provided that a commercial company should be formed of English and Spaniards, to trade in the Indies, and that in the meantime the English were to be allowed to trade in all ports of the Indies, to the extent of ten or eleven ships of five hundred tons each.[3]

[1] "So long as the Dutch continue to prosecute the same measures for recovering the whole Spanish Monarchy, the Queen will think it needless to enter into such a treaty. But whenever you perceive that they act in another manner it will be necessary to propose the treaty again" (Boyle to Townshend, 2/13 Sept. 1709).

[2] Landau, *Carl VI als König von Spanien*, p. 447.

[3] Garden, *Recueil des Traités*, t. II. It was further provided that if this

This concession was not only an infraction of the clause of the Grand Alliance, which forbade any of the parties to obtain a separate profit before a conclusion of a general peace, but was in itself a menace to the Dutch maritime trade.

But English ambition was still unsatisfied, when a successful siege brought the desired opportunity of indulging it. On the 30th of September 1708 Port Mahon was captured by the allied forces. It occurred to Stanhope that the retention of this place in English hands, a proposal which he soon afterwards enlarged into a claim for the whole island, would be very desirable, and the same view was taken by the English Ministers by whom the excuse of subsidies advanced by England was made to do duty again.[1]

Stanhope realised fully that such a measure would be very distasteful to the Dutch. They would find their trade with the Indies ruined by the secret article of the commercial treaty, while the possession of Minorca would enable the English to do them a corresponding injury in the Levant. He thought, however, that the fact that the Dutch were dependent upon the English for the Barrier would effectually prevent their raising any objection to his scheme.[2]

Marlborough feared its effect at The Hague.[3] Supported by the Ministers in London, Stanhope pushed the negotiation with an excess of zeal and a want of tact that deeply offended the Court of Barcelona. Charles resisted the demand as long as he could. In April, Craggs, during the temporary absence of Stanhope, obtained from Count Stella the concession that the whole island should be given to the English for a mortgage for the expense of the fortifications and that they should specify so great a sum as they should think fit "to put it out of possi-

company could not be set up, Charles was to give the English the "mêmes droits d'un commerce libre aux Indes dont jouissaient les Espagnols".

[1] Stanhope to Sunderland, 9 Nov. 1708. Mahon, *War of the Spanish Succession in Spain*. Instructions to Stanhope, 9/20 Dec. 1708, "It is highly just, as reasonable that we should keep the said town of Port Mahon in our possession as some sort of security". Record Office.

[2] Stanhope to Sunderland, "A main objection which I am sensible may be made, is the jealousy it may give to the Dutch: whether this may not be obviated and the Dutch satisfied by our giving way to their pretensions in Flanders, I humbly submit to your Lordship". 15 June 1709.

[3] Marlborough to Stanhope, 26 Jan. 1709. Murray.

bility of being redeemed".[1] A remark lower down in the letter containing the above statement, shows the spirit in which the negotiation was carried on by the English. Oblivious of the fact that the "subsidies" argument had already been used twice, Craggs continued:

Your Lordship may observe that thus far it has not been mentioned of diminishing any of the Queen's charges of the war which may stand good for any other view that Her Majesty may have, On the contrary, Major General Stanhope, before he went away, and I have since, always represented this thing as the greatest advantage in the world to the King of Spain.[2]

But on the English General's return to Barcelona, the King tried again to amuse him by evasive answers. He explained to Wratislaw that he was doing his utmost to put off the evil day, but that he began to realise that the English would keep the island whether he liked it or not.[3] Losing patience, Stanhope presented a Memorial on the 18th of May, demanding the surrender of Minorca in order that his Queen might establish there her full sovereignty until the subsidies sent out by her had been fully repaid, and also that the King should issue a decree expressing his "sincere gratitude to the Queen" for all she had done for him.[4] Charles tried polite procrastination once more. Stanhope, to show the King's dependence upon England, ordered a British regiment, which had been landed to strengthen Staremberg's army, to reimbark and proceed to Minorca. There was nothing left now for Charles but to give in. He promised the renunciation on condition of the right of redemption and of the consent of the Emperor and the States. It was an advantage to transfer the negotiation from Barcelona to London, as he would thus escape from the pressure of the discourteous Stanhope. He sent therefore to Gallas and Hoffmann the draft of a treaty which, in the last extremity, and subject to the

[1] Craggs to Sunderland, 29 April 1709, in the volume of original letters in the Coxe Papers.

[2] This was the light in which Marlborough, after the transaction had become public, endeavoured to present it to Wratislaw. Marlborough to Wratislaw, 26 Sept. 1709. Murray.

[3] Charles to Wratislaw, 15 May 1709. Arneth.

[4] Stanhope's Memorial quoted in Landau, p. 538.

Imperial consent, they might conclude. At the same time Gallas was informed that he need not suppose that the treaty was seriously meant; the draft had only been transmitted to propitiate the Queen.[1] Stanhope also sent a copy of the letter home with a covering letter of complaints.

The behaviour of these people (he declared) in relation to Minorca has made me lose my temper with them, which I shall be very sorry for, if it should in the least prove prejudicial to the great interests which Your Grace is to manage for all the world with the Dutch; but this Court does not deserve from England nor from Your Grace the least part of the management you have for them, and if it does not interfere with any other views your Grace may have for the public good, they would be very rightly served if we complied with the demands of the Dutch, how exorbitant so ever.[2]

Craggs took this letter and the project of the treaty with him and started for London, there to receive further instructions. He arrived at The Hague in the second week of July and set out the next day for the Army.[3] He reported the situation of affairs to Marlborough and started for London, taking with him a letter from Marlborough to Godolphin, in which the former observed that

the circumstances of Charles are such, that his interest will always oblige him to endeavour to be well with the Queen, so that this proposal, which is now sent by Stanhope, if it be thought good for England, he must comply with it, though I believe you will find Count Gallas makes difficulties.[4]

Craggs arrived in London on the 19th/30th of July, with the project of his treaty. Godolphin was disappointed with the project. "One may plainly see", he wrote Marlborough, "that it was chiefly framed to get rid of Stanhope's pressing importunity and without any intent of bringing it to a conclusion; and therefore I did expect as you seem to do, that Count Gallas would be instructed to make difficulty about it." Count Gallas, however, exceeded all anticipation in that

[1] Sketch of the Treaty of 15 June enclosed in Gallas to Emperor, 16 July 1709. Moles to Emperor 15 and 16 June 1709. Landau, p. 539.

[2] Stanhope to Marlborough, 15 June 1709. Murray.

[3] H. Walpole from The Hague, 12 July. Record Office.

[4] Marlborough to Godolphin, 18 July. Coxe Papers.

respect. On the 21st July/1st August an interview took place between him, Godolphin and Sunderland. The English Ministers told him that they were aware that Charles had sent him full powers. Gallas answered very shortly that it was true that he had such powers, but that he had likewise a direction not to make any step in that matter till he had received instructions from Vienna. "This answer appeared to us so very trifling", wrote Godolphin, "that we are sending back Mr Craggs soon to Mr Stanhope, with such variations as shall be thought proper here, and with instructions to press the conclusion of it there."

"By this and everything else", he continued, "that he has hitherto done, you will easily see that we have no great reason to manage Charles' interests even with you, in Flanders, any further than they are agreeable to our own."[1] It was this interview that seems to have removed the remaining scruples of the Treasurer to omit the clause relating to the Spanish Monarchy from the Barrier Treaty. A few days later the instructions to Stanhope were drawn up and he was given full powers to conclude the cession of Minorca—whether of the whole island, or of a part—as a purchase or as a pledge.[2]

From the beginning this transaction had been carried on by the Court of Barcelona under the strictest secrecy, a course in which Eugene, to whom Charles communicated the negotiation, entirely concurred. The danger was that if the States came to know of it, they would place their pretensions in the Netherlands still higher.[3] But in spite of all precautions the news leaked out, and Charles, after all, found among the Dutch more protection against English greed for annexation than among the English against the Dutch. The course pursued by Stanhope had been widely different. He communicated the affair to the representatives of the Allies at Barcelona, asking for their support;

[1] Godolphin to Marlborough, 22 July/2 Aug. 1709. Coxe Papers.

[2] The instructions dated 31 July (O.S.) ran: "Te (Stanhope) constituimus plenipotentiarium de praedictae insulae Minorcae jure vel in totam vel pro parte in nos sub idoneis conditionibus transferendo, sive per modum venditionis sive oppignerationis communicandi, tractandi, et concludendi". Record Office. Rather sweeping terms for the quasi-denial which the Whigs were about to make of the affair.

[3] Eugene to the Emperor, 17 July 1709. *Feldzüge des Prinzen Eugen.*

so that when Gallas received the first intimation of it from Charles, he found the Savoy Minister in London already informed on the subject and the same information soon reached the Portuguese Ambassador through his colleagues in Barcelona.[1] Through some such channel the news must have reached Vryberg. He sent home an account, obtained presumably from Gallas, of the latter's interview with the English Ministers on the 1st of August. A few days later he approached the Austrian on the subject again. He reported that the Pensionary approved of the breaking off of the negotiation, and asked how things stood. Gallas answered that he had explicit orders in case of further urgency to explain that as the engagements of Charles III bound him towards both the Sea Powers, his ambassador could not without the previous knowledge of the States General, meddle in a matter of such importance. Vryberg rejoined: "This answer removes all my fears. For in fact Minorca in English hands would be as hazardous for the republic as Ostend". Gallas could inform the Emperor that, if he and his brother wished to use the States General as the cat to pull the chestnuts out of the fire, these were at all times quite ready to do so.[2]

Such was the condition of affairs when to their consternation, the English Ministry learnt from The Hague that news of the Minorca negotiation had reached the Pensionary.

VI

On the 23rd of August Townshend wrote that Heinsius had been informed by letters from Spain that her Majesty was in treaty with King Charles for Port Mahon, but that, refusing to believe that her Majesty would enter into separate bargains for any part of Spain, he would not mention it to any one else. "I told him," added Townshend, "'that I did not believe the

[1] Gallas to Emperor, 16 July and 30 July in the Austrian State Archives, cited by Landau, p. 540. Charles to Wratislaw, 23 Nov. 1709. In this letter Charles observed that his belief was, that Stanhope had published the affair to do himself credit in the eyes of his countrymen.

[2] Gallas to the Emperor, 27 Aug. 1709. Austrian State Archives, cited by Landau, p. 542 and Klopp, XIII, 281.

Queen had entered into any such treaty'. But being acquainted on what account Mr Craggs lately went to England I must desire you will let me know what I am to say to the Pensionary in case he presses me on the subject again." The English Ministers felt uncomfortable; Godolphin told Boyle to write "that the Queen will do nothing of that kind that shall be uneasy or disagreeable to the States".[1] Townshend's next letter was infinitely more disquieting. From a conversation with Sinzendorf, Heinsius and another influential member of the States, he had gathered that the Pensionary not only knew all about the Minorca affair but had also discovered the existence of the secret treaty, although he did not know its exact terms. The Spanish Envoy Sinzendorf had denied its existence clumsily and a few days later made a clean breast of it. "If these things be true," said Heinsius, "and get air among the Provinces, it will be the absolute ruin of all those who are most zealous for a strict friendship between Her Majesty and the States, and nothing can prevent this State from concluding a peace with France on any terms." Townshend, thoroughly alarmed, had told him that he was persuaded her Majesty had entered into no engagements in relation to Port Mahon and that he knew nothing of a treaty relating to commerce in the West Indies.[2] The English Ministers were still more awkwardly placed. There was nothing for it but to make a virtue of necessity, as Godolphin wrote to Marlborough, and, in palliation of their duplicity, to lay stress upon the incomplete state of the negotiation regarding Minorca, though that was just the feature of the affair at which they themselves were so vexed.[3] It is, however, only fair to Godolphin to add that, believing the English object to be unattainable, he urged that the attempt to obtain it should be put an end to honestly. "What reason is there", he asked, "to give a jealousy to our friends for a thing which at last we shall never be able to obtain?"[4] The excuse of incompletion was impossible for the treaty of commerce,

[1] Godolphin to Marlborough, 1/12 Sept. 1709. Coxe Papers, and Boyle to Townshend, 23 Aug./3 Sept. 1709. Record Office.

[2] Townshend to Boyle, 6 Sept. 1709. Record Office.

[3] Godolphin to Marlborough, 1/12 Sept. 1709. Coxe Papers.

[4] Godolphin to Marlborough, 29 Aug./9 Sept. 1709. Coxe Papers.

which had been formally ratified.[1] On this subject Boyle wrote to The Hague that the concession was only a reasonable reward for the vast charges to which England had been put over the war in Spain, and that doubtless the States would expect the same advantages.

> To show how sincere and friendly Her Majesty is to the Dutch, (he continued) she will join with them in procuring the same advantages of trade with Spain in the West Indies for both Nations; provided the States will insist at the next treaty of peace, that the English shall be put upon the same foot and have equal benefit of trade as the Dutch in all the dominion of France.[2]

Though Heinsius expressed himself to the British Minister as well satisfied, he disliked the suggestion that the States should admit Britain to a share in concessions received from France.

> They say they are willing (he wrote) that we should enjoy the same advantages, but they add a clause which surprises me, namely that this is to be on condition that they enjoy the same advantages, as we, in French dominions. The latter is altogether different, for we are not the masters there. But all this signifies that the English keep their eyes open everywhere and will not scruple to take advantage of us.[3]

In the end he had no cause for vexation, as the Barrier Treaty bound the English to share the concessions in the Spanish dominions and said nothing with regard to France. Townshend

[1] From Portland's account it would appear that the English tried to deny the commercial treaty also. His letter is interesting as it brings out very well how this incident weakened the position of England in their relations with the Dutch. He writes, "Touchant le traité pour Port Mahon on le nie absoluement, assurant que comme on vous l'a déjà dit cela n'a été que le pensée ou le projet d'un seul homme mais qu'il n'en est sûr n'en sera jamais rien. Pour celui qui regarde des Indes Occidentales on le nie aussi, mais moins positivement à ce qu'il me semble et quand (j)ay insisté un peu fortement sur la verité de la chose, ceux à qui j'ay parlé m'ont assuré que s'il en était quelque chose il faudrait que cela fut fait devant qu'ils étaient dans le Ministère. Mais ce qui me semble etre le meilleur c'est qu'on semble que s'il en est quelque chose cela ne (? est) l'intérêt indispensable d'Angleterre de estre et demeuré runy (réunis) avec les Etats-Généraux et que l'on fera voir par les effets que l'on veut et est porté à faire tels transport et engagement qui ne laisseront pas bien aucune jalousie de ce que l'on voulut ici" (Portland to Heinsius, 6/17 Sept. 1709. Heinsius Archives).

[2] Boyle to Townshend, 2/13 Sept. 1709. Record Office.

[3] Heinsius to Portland, 27 Sept. 1709. Heinsius Archives.

was forced to content himself with a verbal promise on the subject.

The Ministry were, however, to pay heavily for their duplicity though for the moment prospects brightened. In a haughty letter from Torcy to Heinsius (very different from his previous communications) he remarked, "I no longer know myself what judgement to have, seeing that so many advances and offers are rejected in Holland". This letter arrived at The Hague and would have, the Pensionary thought, an effect of which the Frenchman would soon repent.[1] The moment chosen, moreover, was peculiarly unfortunate. The letter arrived together with the news of the victory of Malplaquet. This battle was treated almost as a victory in France—but the Allies imagined it to be France's dying effort.[2] While, therefore, the prospects of a speedy and advantageous peace increased, the question of the Barrier seems to have hung fire. The attention of the diplomatists at The Hague was for the moment concentrated on the affairs of the north where the overwhelming defeat of Charles XII at Pultowa had produced an upheaval in the political system that seriously threatened the west of Europe. On the 25th of October, however, the consideration of the Guarantee Treaty was resumed, but Rotterdam and Leyden insisting still upon Ostend, no progress was made.

It was in these circumstances that Townshend concluded the Barrier Treaty. It is clear that he was in no way responsible for the commercial concessions which were made to the Dutch. Although not contained in the original instructions, Boyle's letter of 2/13 September authorised them. It has been generally represented that the difficulties in connection with the Treaty arose because Townshend had exceeded his instructions; in this, the provision which subsequently gave the most trouble, Townshend was acting within his powers.

[1] Townshend to Boyle, 13 Sept. Torcy to Petkum, 5 Sept. 1709. Legrelle, IV, 503.

[2] "La dernière bataille a plutôt relevé le courage de la nation qu'elle ne l'a affaibli" (Torcy to Molo, 27 Sept. 1709, quoted in Legrelle, IV, 504). "Tout le monde croit communement que ce sera la dernière épreuve que les Français voudront faire de leurs forces avec celles des alliés" (L'Hermitage from London, 17 Sept. 1709. MSS., British Museum).

By the 29th of October the Treaty was completed, signed and sent to London. Townshend enclosed a brief note pointing out that he had in some places gone beyond his instructions, but he expressed the hope that when he had time to lay before the Queen his reasons for these changes, she would be pleased to ratify the Treaty.[1] After the conventional clauses as to the renewal of alliances, the Treaty[2] contained provisions for the Succession to the throne of England: the States General pledged themselves "to assist and maintain" the Protestant Succession as ordained by parliament, and to make no peace with France until Louis XIV had acknowledged the Succession and had expelled the Pretender from his dominions (Arts. XIII and XX). In return, the Queen of Great Britain pledged herself to obtain certain concessions from France and from the future sovereign of the Southern Netherlands, on behalf of the States General.

As many towns and fortresses as possible were to be conquered in the Southern Netherlands. At the general congress for peace, the Queen should "use her endeavours...that all the Spanish Low Countries and what else shall be found necessary, whether conquered or unconquered, shall serve as a Barrier to the States" (Arts. III–V). To this purpose, the States should garrison Nieuwport, Knocke, Ypres, Menin, the town and citadel of Lille, Tournay and its citadel, Condé, Valenciennes, "and the places which shall henceforth be conquered from France", Maubeuge, Charleroi, Namur and its citadel, Lier, Hal (to be fortified), Forts Perle, Philippe and Damme, the Castle of Ghent, Dendermonde and Fort St Donas in entire possession. The fort of Rodenhuysen was to be demolished (Art. VI). These garrisons, a formidable array, would secure to the Republic the military and economic control of the Southern Netherlands which they desired.

Strategically, the fortresses fall into three groups:

(1) Maubeuge, Charleroi and Namur, together with the temporary garrisons in Liège and Huy (first separate article), would serve for the defence of the Sambre and Meuse.

[1] Townshend to Boyle, 29 Oct. 1709. Record Office.
[2] The Treaty is printed below in Appendix E.

(2) Dendermonde, Ghent, Lier and Hal, the Forts of Perle, Philippe and Damme, constituted an inner line of defence, serving as communication between the United Provinces and the outer line of fortresses, and at the same time making a strong defence of the Scheldt.

(3) (i) Nieuwport, Furnes, Knocke, Ypres and Menin; (ii) Lille, Tournai, Condé, Valenciennes "and what more may be conquered from France" [1] made a strong line of fortresses from the coast along the frontier.

From the economic standpoint, Antwerp and the southern exits of the Scheldt were dominated by Fort Perle, Bruges, Ghent and Fort Damme; the Bruges Canal was controlled by Fort St Donas, Fort Sluis (already in possession of the Dutch) and Knocke; Nieuwport and Fort St Philippe connected Ostend and the interior; Dendermonde, Lier and Hal commanded the towns further inland. [2]

In addition to the right to garrison these fortresses, the Dutch were to be given certain powers: in the event of threat of war from any power, to garrison any other fortresses deemed necessary (Art. VIII); to make what repairs and fortifications they pleased in those towns which they were by treaty to garrison; to send into them, without hindrance and without being subject to any duty, "arms, materials for fortifications and all that shall be found necessary for the said garrisons and fortifications" (Art. VIII). They might appoint governors, commanders, etc., responsible only to themselves, "still preserving the rights and privileges as well ecclesiastical and political of King Charles III" (Art. IX), and they might freely exercise the Protestant religion.

As to revenues, the Dutch were to have the possession of the revenues of towns conquered from France and not in the possession of Charles II at the time of his death, together with an income of one million livres per annum, to be paid from the revenues of the Spanish Low Countries as they were at the death of Charles II (Art. IX).

Article XV contained securities for Dutch trade; the rights

[1] See Appendix C, the New Conquests.

[2] Cf. Noorden, p. 598.

of the Treaty of Münster were re-affirmed and tightened up. It was laid down that seaports on the coast of the Southern Netherlands should be controlled in the same way as those "rivers, canals and mouths of the sea on the side of the United Provinces". Further, all commercial privileges granted in any of the Spanish dominions to the inhabitants of Great Britain should apply equally to the subjects of the States General.

Finally, the States were to have immediate enjoyment of those privileges, while the Archduke might not enter into possession of the Southern Netherlands until he had agreed to these conditions (Art. XIV).

Two separate articles were appended; by one the States were to be given an extension of territory in Flanders; by the other they were to enjoy full possession of the Upper Quarter of Guelderland, in accordance with the 52nd Article of the Treaty of Münster: they were also to be permitted to garrison Liège, Huy and Bonn until otherwise agreed upon with the Emperor.

On 1 November Townshend despatched the promised explanation of the alterations he had made in the English Counter Project.[1] These alterations fall into three groups, strategic, financial and commercial.

(1) In the first place, Townshend had agreed to the inclusion of a greater number of fortresses in the Barrier than warranted by his instructions. In particular, he had gone against the wishes of the Ministry by the inclusion of Dendermonde, a town situated in a commanding position on the Scheldt, necessary, the Dutch declared, to prevent the enemy from cutting off their communications with the more outlying provinces. The Dutch had claimed it in lieu of Ostend, from which they had desisted in the face of English opposition. It was unfortunate for these arguments that Dendermonde should be equally objectionable to the English for the same reason as Ostend, that it was commercially important. It is significant that Article XV, by which the provisions of the Treaty of Münster were re-affirmed, was considered as further compensation for the omission of Ostend. There can be little doubt

[1] Townshend to Boyle, 1 Nov. 1709. State Papers Foreign, Holland, 233, Record Office.

that the Dutch aimed at commercial strength, under cover of strategic necessities.

As to Dendermonde, Townshend could see no possibility of injury to English trade so long as Ostend, "the key of our direct commerce with these countries", was not included in the Barrier. Goods imported at Ostend were sent from Ghent to Brussels without passing through Dendermonde. Finally, "when goods have paid Royal duties or Customs they are free for other towns in Flanders, thus including Dendermonde". A further security lay in the reservation of the civil power in the Southern Netherlands to the Emperor.

All danger to commerce being thus forestalled, Townshend trusted that the Queen would not disapprove of Article VI, which provided not merely for the addition of Dendermonde, but of "some other towns and fortresses not mentioned in our Project, most of them being pursuant to my instructions, and none of them being of any use other than to make ye Barrier strong and sufficient". These towns were Charleroi, Fort St Donas and Fort Philippe: since the States were to garrison all the exposed places from Nieuwport to Namur, he saw no harm in the inclusion of the first[1]; as to the forts, he did not think their cession would have any "ill consequence", since the States already held Damme and Perle by the English Project, Lilo and the mortgage on St Mary, and had previously been in possession of the "Ecluse" to which St Donas was annexed.

(2) It followed naturally upon the inclusion of additional fortresses, and having due regard for the devastation of the country by the war, that the sources of revenue suggested in the English Project were insufficient. In his instructions of 2 May 1709[2] Townshend was authorised to make up any

[1] Townshend to Boyle, 26 Nov. 1709. S.P.F.H. 233.

[2] "Whereas it is expected that several towns now belonging to and in the hands of France, should be given up and yielded by the Treaty of Peace, to be garrisoned by the Forces of the States General for the security of their Barrier, if, therefore, the revenues of such towns etc, so delivered up and garrisoned, be not found sufficient to answer the necessary expenses for that service: in such case you have liberty to consent to the adding of such further sum or sums as shall be thought requisite and reasonable for that purpose, out of the incomes and revenues arising in general from the Spanish Low Countries" (2 May 1709. Instructions to Marlborough and Townshend). See Wickham Legge, *Instructions to English Ambassadors in France*, vol. I.

deficit. This he had now done, by the addition of the 1,000,000 livres per annum to be paid from the revenues of the Southern Netherlands in the possession of Charles II at the time of his death, to those revenues from conquered towns, not in possession of Charles II at that time, and now added to the Barrier.

(3) As has been indicated, the commercial provisions of Article XV were considered by the States General as compensation for the omission of Ostend from the Barrier. They further claimed "that there was nothing in this Article but what they had a right to by the Treaty of Münster". The Article contained two provisions; first, that in accordance with the Treaty of Münster,

> commodities in and out of the Harbours of Flanders, shall be and remain charged with all such duties and other imports as are raised upon commodities going and coming along the Scheldt...the Queen of Great Britain promises and engages, that Their High Mightinesses shall never be disturbed in their right and possession, in that respect, neither directly nor indirectly, as also that the commerce shall not, in prejudice of the said treaty, be made more easy by the Sea Ports, than by the Rivers, Canals and Mouths of the Sea on the side of the United Provinces, either directly or indirectly.

To this there could be little objection: it was what it purported to be, a more stringent and more detailed enunciation of the rights of the Treaty of Münster[1].

The next words concealed a very real innovation, a provision which was not embodied in the English Counter Project, but for which Townshend had received authorisation in Boyle's later correspondence,[2]

> and whereas by the 16th and 17th Articles of the same treaty of Münster, His Majesty, the King of Spain is obliged to treat their High Mightinesses as favourably as the subjects of Great Britain and the Hans Towns, who were then the people most favourably treated: Her Britannic Majesty and their High Mightinesses promise likewise, to take care that the subjects of Great Britain and their High

[1] It was later objected that as England had not been a party to the Treaty of Münster, this confirmation was mistaken, if not illegal.

[2] Boyle to Townshend, 2/13 Sept. 1709. Cf. p. 154.

Mightinesses shall be treated in the Spanish Low Countries, *as well as in all Spain*, *the Kingdom and States* belonging to it, equally and as well the one as the other, as favourably as the people most favoured.

Thus, whatever the terms of the suspected monopoly in the West Indies, ratification of the Barrier Treaty would admit the Dutch into a share of these gains. Protest was useless; Townshend had learned his lesson from the Pensionary and repeated it faithfully: to insist on omitting this part of the Treaty would at once react, with consequences fatal to the Whigs, on the Franco-Dutch negotiations. Indeed, not only must this passage be included but no time was to be lost in doing so.[1] Finally, since Sinzendorf had declared in the name of King Charles that the Dutch should have the same benefits as England, Townshend could see no use in further delay.[2]

Townshend completed his defence[3] by the promise of further benefits to England: in return for the Barrier Treaty, the Dutch would support the English claim to Hudson Bay, at future peace conferences. Finally he re-affirmed the greatest value of the treaty. "I am every day more fully convinced", he wrote on the 19th of November,[4] "that nothing can so perfectly establish Her Majesty's credit and interest here, and keep this people from running into separate measures in relation to the peace, as perfecting the Barrier Treaty."

That he judged accurately was later demonstrated in the rupture of negotiations at Geertruidenberg (1710). There the Dutch, entrusted with the sole conduct of affairs, remained loyal to the English demands, leaving the French determined never to negotiate with them again,[5] and, at the same time profoundly disappointing the peace party in the Republic.

Without foreknowledge of this future benefit, the Lords of

[1] Townshend's report to Boyle, of his conversation with the Pensionary, 1 Nov. 1709. S.P.F.H. 233.

[2] Cf. 26 Nov. 1709, where Townshend reiterates his belief that in any case Charles would have made similar concessions to the Dutch. S.P.F.H. 233.

[3] The chief letter of defence was written on 1 Nov. 1709, but additional arguments were given in letters throughout November. S.P.F.H. 233.

[4] Townshend to Boyle. S.P.F.H. 233.

[5] "Elle (Sa Majesté) avait vu de la part des Hollandais, tant d'éloignement pour la paix, tant de hauteur, tant de mauvaise foi, qu'Elle ne pouvait plus s'adresser à eux pour entamer une nouvelle négociation" (De Torcy, *Journal Inédit*, p. 308).

the Council sat in London, dismayed at the terms of the Treaty. To the chagrin of Townshend, they did not immediately grasp the force of his reasoning.[1] They pointed out, very pertinently, that it was the States who had always insisted that nothing should be included in the Treaty but what was relevant to the Barrier and Succession, and that the clause relating to Spanish concessions was not merely irrelevant, but was of "so nice and so extensive a nature as to require a distinct and more deliberate consideration", than a prompt ratification would warrant.[2]

The Ministry had other objections: the increased number of fortresses, the proviso that Charles was not to be installed until the Dutch had been satisfied in the financial question,[3] the separate engagement as to Guelderland and the temporary garrisons in Liège, Huy and Bonn.

Townshend replied in several letters, for the most part a recapitulation of his former arguments,[4] reinforced by some unpalatable truths as to the real responsibility for the innovation of Article XV.[5] He offered, in consolation, his opinion that it was doubtful whether Charles had ever meant to keep to his agreement with the Queen,[6] and pointed out the possible value of the good offices of the Republic, when the English came to a commercial agreement with France.

On the 8th/19th of November, Boyle reported that the Treaty had been ratified, after a discussion so prolonged that he had time only to announce Her Majesty's decision.[7] A week

[1] Townshend to Boyle, 10 Dec. 1709, "I am under the greatest affliction imaginable that the Treaty is thought liable to so many objections". Record Office.

[2] Boyle to Townshend, 8/19 Nov. Record Office.

[3] Art. 14.

[4] S.P.F.H. 233, 1, 3, 10 Dec. 1709.

[5] "I am fully perswaded that nothing of this nature was ever intended to be inserted in the Treaty, till one of the King of Spain's Ministers had informed them of Her Majesty's having some time since concluded a treaty of commerce with his master" (to Boyle, 26 Nov. S.P.F.H. 233).

[6] "Besides if one may judge of the dispositions of the Court of Barcelona by the behaviour of their Ministers, there is reason to think they were never heartily disposed to the performance of that treaty. Otherwise, they could not have been guilty of such imprudence, as, by discovering it at this time, to have endangered the creating of jealousies between Her Majesty and the States upon whose friendship their hopes of obtaining the whole lies" (to Boyle, 26 Nov. S.P.F.H. 233).

[7] To Townshend, Foreign 'Entry' Book 75, Record Office.

later Townshend received the reasons for the ratification: there was little hope of alterations when Townshend had committed himself so far, and when the Treaty had gone to the Provincial Estates of the United Provinces. In the opinion of the Council, to insist on any alteration would

necessitate the breaking off entirely of this Treaty of Succession and Barrier, which are points of too great consequence to be hazarded at this juncture, when coldness, jealousies and misunderstandings between Her Majesty and the States might be of the last ill consequence, especially when some steps have been lately taken, which seem to lead towards he renewing of the negociations of peace and finishing our great work.[1]

Townshend was therefore to ratify the Treaty: at the same time he should point out that this was "a signal proof of Her Majesty's affection for the States". But an effort was to be made to rid the English of at least one of its obligations. On the ground that the Queen disliked separate articles and the first separate article in particular, as irrelevant and "very much enlarged" with "unnecessary precautions" which might offend some of the Allies, Townshend was to withhold ratification.

The King of Prussia was the ally most in question. His friendship was essential, not merely as a member of the Coalition, but as a Power with interests in the Baltic, whose co-operation might be useful in the impending struggle between the various northern Powers. These considerations, wrote Boyle, "seem to require that the prince should rather be managed with a due tenderness and indulgence, than shocked with an unreasonable repetition of what has already disgusted him so much".

The reference is to the allocation of the Upper Quarter of Guelderland to the States General.

I thought (replied Townshend) all difficulties on that head were entirely removed. Upon the whole, I could not judge it for Her Majesty's service, at a time when we were labouring to keep this people steady to carry on the war against France and recovering the

[1] The reference is to Petkum's departure from The Hague to the Court of Louis XIV; the negotiations of Petkum were the cause of much anxiety to the Ministry. Boyle to Townshend, 15 Nov. Record Office.
Cf. Noorden, III, 600.

whole Monarchy of Spain, to give them the least Jealousie Her Majesty was not disposed to afford them Her assistance in securing to them the advantage which had so nearly concerned their safety and had been already stipulated to them by the Preliminary Treaty.

Heinsius was even warmer on the subject.

It was true (he said to Townshend) the King of Prussia, though he had no right to it, had made several instances to keep it (Guelders) as a security for the sums of money owing to him by the Crown of Spain, but the States thought they had already done enough to satisfy him, having obliged themselves by Treaty to give him that assistance towards obtaining satisfaction in all his just demands upon the Crown of Spain, and having given him fresh assurance of their continuing firm to their engagement in their answer to the Memorial of his Minister....The King of Prussia may with as good reason require them to pay those debts, as fix upon a method of payment so against their right and to their prejudice.[1]

In such a situation, Townshend was of the opinion that it was "vain to suppose the States would ratify the Treaty without the Article which was of so much consequence to their Barrier".[2]

At last the Ministry gave way, although "a little surprised that the Pensionary expressed himself so warmly". Boyle sent Her Majesty's ratification of the separate article, together with a protest against "the menacing insinuations" of the States General. Townshend was to withhold the ratification while he made one last effort to evade it, by suggesting that since the question was settled in the preliminaries of 1709, it was unnecessary to make any further engagements on the subject.

It was easy for the Pensionary to point out that this very fact took away all possible objections the Queen could have to its inclusion in the Treaty. As to the importance attached to it by his masters, the States General, "he believed the very knowing any difficulty had been made on this article might be attended with dangerous consequences at this critical juncture".[3]

The Republic had won on every count: on the 17th of December the Treaty was completed by the ratification of the second separate article.

[1] Townshend to Boyle, 3 Dec. 1709. S.P.F.H. 233.
[2] Townshend to Boyle, 3 Dec. 1709. S.P.F.H. 233.
[3] Townshend to Boyle, 17 Dec. 1709. S.P.F.H. 233.

CHAPTER V

Reception of the Barrier Treaty

I

IN tracing the course of the negotiations which led up to the Barrier Treaty, very little reference has been made to the part played by the Powers other than the two immediately concerned with the exception of the Minorca incident. By this means a clearer consecutive narrative could be obtained. At the same time, such a method involved no great departure from the actual conditions, for the negotiation pursued its course with very little interference from without. Prussia and Spain were the two outside parties most concerned, but the obstinate refusal of the States to give in in any way to the former, and the curiously inactive part played by Sinzendorf while representing the latter, enabled the English and the Dutch to arrange matters almost as they pleased. Notwithstanding this fact, there is a considerable interest in tracing the effect, first of all of the rumours, and then of the actual discovery, of the Treaty, upon the policy of Frederick and the Hapsburg brothers. As late as the 7th of January 1710 Townshend imagined that the affair was still kept secret. "Though most of the ministers have some suspicion of it," he wrote, "I cannot find that they are apprised of the substance of any one article." In this he was mistaken.

II

Frederick's interest in the Barrier Treaty lay almost exclusively in the article relating to Guelderland. His three diplomatic aims were: (1) the recovery of Orange and certain Burgundian lands in Franche Comté from France; (2) an agreement as to Orange with the Prince of Nassau;[1] (3) the settlement of his monetary claims on Spain, either by the cession to him of Guelders (a province which from its juxtaposition to

[1] Frederick and the Prince of Nassau were co-heirs of William III.

his isolated possession of Cleves would be of particular value to him) or by some other method. Of these aims the last alone brought him into immediate opposition to the Barrier Treaty.

The town of Guelders had been taken by the Confederate troops on the 12th of December 1703 and had remained under a Prussian garrison ever since. It was the King's constant wish to convert this occupation into a permanent right. He lost no opportunity of urging his claims. He importuned the Court of Barcelona to cede the province to him in liquidation of his monetary claims; and the Ministers of the unfortunate Charles, who could not dispense with the Prussian troops, were forced to cultivate to an unexampled perfection the art of diplomatic evasion.[1] Schmettau, at The Hague, was not less on the alert. His suspicions were aroused during the Barrier negotiations of November and December 1706, but Stepney assured him that nothing was being done prejudicial to his master's interests.[2] Marlborough also had been of opinion that, considering the humour of the Prussian Court, it would be advisable to keep it out of the negotiation until the conclusion was in sight.[3] More than two years of silence followed but it was at last broken by the Duke himself with his letter to the King on the 26th of April 1709, to which reference has already been made, warning him of "the pretensions of the States".[4] This letter found the King in a frame of mind in which "he would have liked to put on his cuirass and show these ungrateful and insolent people their proper places".[5] Having, however, to be content with diplomatic methods and realising that the situation had become critical, he went the round of the Courts of Europe for co-operation in the accomplishment of his design, applying in succession to the Dutch Republic, England, Spain and France.

Amidst the chorus of approval with which the preliminaries of May were handed to Torcy, the Prussian Minister's voice alone struck a discordant note. He complained that his master's

[1] Moles to Emperor, 29 Nov. 1707, cited by Landau, p. 446.
[2] Stepney to Marlborough, 21 Dec. 1706. Stepney Papers.
[3] Marlborough to Stepney, Dec. 1706. Murray.
[4] P. 119 *note* 2.
[5] Instructions to Grumbkow, 27 and 29 April 1709, cited by Noorden, III, 604.

interests had been neglected, and presented a Memorial to the States in which he made a double suggestion. The first proposal was that Prussia and the States should divide the province of Spanish Guelders between them; the second was that if the States decided not to make any claims for that province except for garrisons in Venloo, Roermond, and Stevensweert—which would afford communication with their outpost of Maestricht—the King of Prussia should keep Guelders till satisfied by Spain as to his pretensions[1]—a provision which would have given him a long lease. The States refused both invitations. They replied that in the preliminaries they had stipulated for nothing beyond what they had a right to by the Treaty of Münster. They fully recognised that the King had claim on Spain and they would help him to obtain payment, but "they could not believe that he would seek satisfaction to their prejudice in a territory to which they had a right".[2]

There was more to be hoped for from England. Marlborough had followed up his first letter with a second, assuring the King he would do his best to induce the Queen to obtain such satisfaction for him as he might most desire.[3] In London, however, Spannheim tried vainly to advance matters beyond the region of empty promises. The most he could obtain was a reply to the effect that, "as to the claims which the King of Prussia has upon the Crown of Spain for very considerable sums of money, in consideration of which he is at present in possession of the Upper Quarter of Guelders, the Queen has promised already to assist him to obtain satisfaction and will not forget to join in all means suitable to the attainment of that end".[4] The English Envoys at The Hague feared that even these expressions would be thought in the Republic to have gone too far in recognising the Prussian occupation, especially as Heinsius

[1] Lamberty, v, 273, etc.

[2] Resolution of States General of 10 July 1709, contained in Townshend's correspondence, British Museum MSS., also at Record Office.

[3] Marlborough to King of Prussia, 21 May 1709. Murray.

[4] Draft of Memorandum to Spannheim enclosed in Boyle to Marlborough, 1/12 July. Blenheim Archives. Marlborough approved, 18 July (Murray), and the Memorandum was handed to Spannheim "without any material alteration". Boyle to Marlborough, 15/26 July. Blenheim Archives.

showed no inclination to meet Prussia half way.[1] But the English Ministry being very unwilling to add to their difficulties by precipitating this matter, disregarded the objection.

Frederick made a third attempt during the summer, trying again at Barcelona. Koenigshausen was sent to extract the consent of Charles if possible.[2] Spannheim received the impression that the request had been favourably entertained. On the 10th of September, Boyle wrote to Townshend that Spannheim had informed him by word of mouth that Charles was ready to leave the town of Guelders to Frederick. "Her Majesty", he added, "would be willing to use her good offices to the satisfaction of the King of Prussia but she would do it in such a manner as to give no disgust or jealousy to the Dutch."[3] Townshend questioned Sinzendorf as to the truth of Spannheim's statement, but could not ascertain that Charles had given much more than an open answer. Charles' real sentiments, like those of a true Hapsburg, were that he would not under any consideration give up the place either to the States or Prussia.[4]

Lastly, dissatisfied with the Allies, the Prussian Monarch started negotiations with France. These lasted, with interruptions, from September to February, but it is doubtful whether Grumbkow, who transacted the negotiation, did not do his utmost to frustrate its success.[5] At all events nothing came of it.

[1] H. Walpole from The Hague, 19 July 1709. Record Office. By the same post Townshend wrote, "In my opinion you should be very cautious how you express yourself as to the part of Guelders, which is now in that King's possession, lest you give offence here".

[2] Raby to Marlborough, from Berlin, 4 June. Coxe Papers.

[3] Boyle to Townshend, 30 Aug./10 Sept. Record Office.

[4] Charles to Marlborough, 23 Oct. 1709. Coxe Papers.

[5] This is a point of some interest. Grumbkow was so much a confidential agent of Marlborough that one is predisposed to believe anything he wrote to him. But his words derive striking confirmation from the perfectly independent passages quoted by Legrelle from Torcy's *Journal*. Grumbkow wrote, 21 Dec. 1709, to Marlborough thus: "Je dirais de plus et je sais que votre Altesse ne me trahira pas, qu'on est actuellement en négociation avec le parti contraire, et que l'homme qui vous écrit y a été employé, ce qu'il n'aurait jamais fait, s'il ne l'avait fait dans le dessein de traverser la négociation, et de la faire échouer, et qu'un autre qui y devait être employé, et dont les vues étaient bien différentes des siennes, n'y eût réussi".

From Legrelle, IV, 530: "L'agent Prussien omit de parler des points essentiels, d'Orange, de Neufchatel, de la reconnaissance du titre royal....Au

Frederick had tried everywhere, and had nowhere met with success. From England alone did there seem any real chance of help. Circumstances had, however, been too strong for the English, and they had been obliged to consent to the ratification of the separate article. Having consented, they could only count the hours until the storm burst. By the middle of December, it was known at Berlin on what day the Treaty had been signed. The King was piqued with the Queen of England because not a word had been said to him about it. The great attention shown to the Dutch was in strong contrast to the secrecy preserved towards him.[1] Moreover, it was already rumoured that in the Treaty Guelders had been assigned to the States. Three weeks later the whole truth leaked out.

They have now got here (wrote Raby on the 18th of January 1710) the heads of the treaty lately made between the Queen and the States General, and seem very angry at that Article relating to Upper Guelder, which they say is not according to the hopes that the Queen and your Grace have often given the King in that matter.[2]

Each successive letter from the British Minister testified to the growing resentment of Frederick, which culminated, after the manner of Prussian kings, in a refusal to eat or appear in public.[3] The result of this indignation appeared in the instructions immediately sent to Schmettau to the effect that if the King's demands were not complied with in four or five weeks, his troops were to be recalled.[4]

surplus Grumbkow n'exhiba aucun pouvoir écrit, aussi ne conclut-il rien. 'Peut-être', remarqua Torcy, 'que ce prince voulait seulement exciter la jalousie de ses alliés en ménageant des conférences dans les Pays-Bas avec un homme envoyé par le roi'". Torcy, *Journal*, pp. 60–2.

[1] Grumbkow to Marlborough, 21 Dec. 1709. Coxe Papers. It looks very much as if Marlborough was the cause of the news of the treaty reaching Berlin as he was, cf. section III, with Austria. This much is certain: (1) that Marlborough and Grumbkow were to arrive together from the campaign at The Hague. Grumbkow to Torcy, 22 Oct. 1709, quoted at length in Legrelle, IV, 522; (2) that Grumbkow knew quite well about "the treaty" as he calls it; Grumbkow to Marlborough, 21 Dec. 1709; (3) that he arrived in Berlin on the 18 Dec. 1709, i.e., just in time to communicate his news before writing this letter. Raby to Duke of Marlborough, 28 Dec. Coxe Papers.

[2] Raby to the Duke, 18 Jan. 1710. Coxe Papers.

[3] Raby to the Duke, 4 Feb. 1710. Coxe Papers.

[4] Raby to the Duke, 25 Jan. 1710. Coxe Papers. Townshend to Boyle, 28 Jan. 1710. Record Office.

England must find some remedy. This was attempted in two directions. Townshend had on the 26th of November/7th of December been instructed to consider with the Pensionary the possibility of an expedient for satisfying the debt claimed by Prussia from Spain without interfering with the States' right to Guelders. To pacify Schmettau, who confronted him with a draft of the Treaty, Townshend therefore suggested that the States should engage to obtain satisfaction for the King of Prussia, who till then should remain in possession of Guelders. As king Charles's debts were so very numerous, argued Townshend —much as Stanhope and Craggs had done over the Minorca Treaty—it was not likely the Crown of Spain would ever be in a position to pay them. Prussia would thus be left in perpetual possession, and the dispute was really only one about words. Schmettau expressed himself satisfied.[1] The drawback to this suggestion was that there was not the slightest prospect that the States would be brought to consent to it. Meanwhile, another scheme had to be devised in England, for as Boyle informed Townshend, the firm belief there that the Dutch would insist on Guelderland, forbade their making such a suggestion to Spannheim as that made by the English Envoy to Schmettau.[2] In this matter, however, the Whigs seemed to have obtained the benefit of Marlborough's help. The latter was quite alive to the necessity of retaining the Prussian troops in the service. He therefore requested Grumbkow to send him full information as to the extent of the pretensions of Prussia on the Spanish Monarchy, as this should be the basis of proposals.[3] This line of negotiation was the one eventually attended with success. A set of proposals was drawn up in accordance with Grumbkow's information, submitted from England to the King, and accepted, though with renewed expressions of the injustice of his treatment and the magnanimity of his forgiveness.[4] Prussia was to recover at the conclusion of peace the Principality of Orange and the lands in Franche Comté, and an

[1] Townshend to Boyle, 14 and 24 Jan. 1710. Record Office.

[2] Boyle to Townshend, 10/21 Jan. 1710. Record Office.

[3] Marlborough to Grumbkow, 6/17 Jan. 1710. Murray.

[4] King of Prussia to Marlborough, 22 April 1710, 6 May 1710. Blenheim Archives.

indemnity should be given her for the loss of Guelders.[1] It is typical of the general upheaval of diplomatic conditions that the next three years were to produce in Europe, that in the final settlement Prussia received exactly the reverse of what was here offered. Orange and the Burgundian lands passed to France, while the young King Frederick William I, with the help of France and England, and a bribe of 50,000 thalers to Raby (then Lord Strafford), succeeded in rounding off his frontier with the much coveted district of Upper Guelders.[2]

III

Townshend, on the day on which he signed the Barrier Treaty, wrote home: "the Imperial and Spanish Ministers know nothing as yet of the conclusion of this treaty; for after their behaviour in relation to what has been negotiated at the Court of Barcelona for the service of Her Majesty and her subjects, I thought they deserved very little regard on this occasion".[3] But though their Envoys might be kept in the dark as to details, both Charles and Joseph were well acquainted with the main drift of the negotiation at The Hague, for they knew the contents both of the Dutch Project and the English Counter Project.

Copies of the Dutch document and the English reply were sent to Stanhope on the 1st/12th of May, together with letters from the Queen, Sunderland and Marlborough. Towards the end of June, Stanhope presented the documents to the King, but he must have found some difficulty in his endeavour to explain to His Majesty how the Counter Project "showed the great regard and tenderness with which the Queen did espouse and assist his interests". Charles, indeed, declared himself extremely satisfied and grateful—but to these utterances Stanhope attributed the same value as to the King's similar professions recently on the subject of Minorca.[4] It appears,

[1] Marlborough to Grumbkow, 12/23 April 1710. Murray.

[2] Erdmannsdörffer, *Deutsche Geschichte*, II, 291. But see p. 300, Note 4 [Editor].

[3] Townshend to Boyle, 29 Oct. 1709. Record Office.

[4] Stanhope to Sunderland, 28 June 1709, in the Sunderland Papers at Blenheim Palace.

however, that, as Marlborough had hoped would be the case, the differences between the Project and Counter Project did make a good impression at the Court of Barcelona. They saw there how much the Queen had pared the pretensions of the Dutch, and this gave the King a hope that he would be able to beat them down still lower. "I promise myself", he wrote to Marlborough, "that these Dutchmen shall climb down in the matter of the places and forts they claim in the centre of the Netherlands, and that they shall be satisfied with what shall be considered just and equitable, that is to say, with places on the frontier of France." The Duke of Moles also laid stress on this point; the Dutch claims could only have been made "to defy the King". The Court was quite willing that the States should have a strong barrier as a reward for all their labours, and to be able to "compel France to live in peace", but the list of places proposed in the Project extended practically to a domination of all the principal towns in the Netherlands.[1] The end in view at Barcelona was still "the restitution of the whole Spanish Monarchy without any dismemberment on the foot of the peace of the Pyrenees".[2]

About the same time as the Counter Project reached Barcelona, the news arrived of the presentation of the preliminaries of May. With the latter Charles would appear to have been, on the whole, provisionally satisfied. But beyond the omission of any reference to the Pyrenean Treaty, he observed to Wratislaw that too great concessions had been made as to the Barrier, especially as regards Guelders. He was willing that, besides their Barrier *against France*, the Dutch should have one line of communication across the Meuse. But this must not be Guelders, partly, so as not to offend Prussia, and partly on the ground of religion. To establish their communication with the outpost of Maestricht, which they already possessed, he would, if necessary, allow them garrisons in Venloo, Roermond, and Stevensweert.[3]

[1] Charles to Marlborough, 30 June 1709; Moles to Marlborough, 30 June 1709. Spanish volumes of Coxe Papers.

[2] Charles to Marlborough, 16 June 1709. Coxe Papers.

[3] Charles to Wratislaw, 30 June, 23 July 1709. "Korrespondenz", ed. Arneth. Charles was too weak in the exceptionally difficult position in which he found himself at Barcelona to be anything but a failure. He lacked the

Charles forwarded instructions to Sinzendorf on these points, but seems to have relied chiefly on the credit and authority of Marlborough for seeing his wishes put into execution. "We shall be able to restrict our concessions greatly," he wrote to Wratislaw, "if only we could have England on our side." But Charles had another string to his bow. Marlborough had three times been offered the Patent and on each occasion had returned a guarded refusal. Charles now considered that "his hands were no longer tied", and fell back on what had probably long been a favourite scheme of his. He proposed to confer the Government of the Netherlands on Eugene. Although he had just written to the Duke to express the hope that the Netherlands might soon be under "his good government", he now urged at Vienna the appointment of Eugene as the only person who held both the Imperial confidence and the affections of the Dutch. The Prince should decide the Barrier question and bring back to the Netherlands a golden age of patriotism. The Emperor concurred but thought it unwise to confer the appointment yet for fear of arousing the hostility of Marlborough, and Eugene himself was fully agreed as to the advisability of delay.[1]

On the whole, Charles' reception of the double blow to his position in the Low Countries, dealt by the Counter Project and the preliminaries, was characterised by a colourless complacency. He failed to realise the importance of the fact that the former was stamped with England's approval and that Austrian Ministers

magnetic qualities which alone could have turned the scale in Spain in his favour. But one has far more sympathy for him than for Joseph, who treated his younger brother more or less like a colony to be tolerated and bullied at pleasure. Charles had a conscience, and he throughout stood up consistently for the Catholic religion, whether in Guelders, or in Minorca, or by a refusal to assist the French Protestants in the Cevennes. He bore the iniquitous arrangement with regard to Milan, forced on him by his brother, till his indignation at the deeds done in his name there drove him to threaten Joseph with the exposure of the secret abdication before the eyes of all Europe.

[1] Charles to Marlborough, 16 June 1709; Charles to Wratislaw 30 June, 23 July, 14 Sept., 23 Nov. 1709 to Feb. 1710; Eugene to Charles, 18 Jan. 1710. *Feldzüge des Prinzen Eugen.* The three occasions referred to by Charles were 23 Sept. 1706, 5 Aug. 1708, and 2 Feb. 1709. The attitude of Marlborough in the first two cases has already been referred to (above, p. 85 and p. 92). For the change which came over Marlborough's feelings in this matter in 1709, and for the attitude of the Viennese Court, see the General Note on Marlborough and the Patent below, Appendix A.

were among the signatories of the latter. With an optimistic confidence in the result he entrusted his "poor Netherlands"[1] to Marlborough, Eugene, and Sinzendorf, of whom the first was about to withdraw his influence from the negotiation, the second thought it too soon to bring his to bear, and the third was at all times incapable of exerting any. The next thing Charles was to hear was that the Treaty had been concluded.

In the meantime, the attitude of the Emperor towards the Barrier question had been such as to produce among the English Ministers the belief that if difficulties were made in the matter by Sinzendorf, they would proceed more from the court of Vienna than from Barcelona.[2] On the receipt of Eugene's letter of the 19th of April, describing the terms of the Project, the Emperor had sent Sinzendorf with additional instructions to The Hague. The failure of the Count and Eugene to comply with these instructions had annoyed him, when to add to his resentment, a copy of the Counter Project reached him from Barcelona. The reception given to this document at Vienna was very different from the "satisfaction and gratitude" with which Charles had accepted it. It mattered little that the terms of the Counter Project were less harsh than those of the Project. Without England's consent the Dutch proposal was mere waste paper; the Court saw at once what Charles had not seen, that England had abandoned them. This, to them, spelt disaster.

By the letters from Barcelona (wrote Wratislaw to Marlborough) we have a Counter Project that England has drawn up for the pretended Barrier of the Dutch. I confess it struck me with consternation and I fear that Parliament will have to go back on it one day when they learn that under this name of Barrier the Dutch will render themselves masters of the Netherlands, or hold them under a dependence so tyrannic that it will be better to abandon them altogether than possess them under those conditions. You will excuse my writing with this frankness, but, believe me, I foresee a terrible disaster on this subject.[3]

[1] Charles, writing to Eugene on 14 Sept. 1709, hoped "that he would exert himself for the poor Netherlands as if he were already stadtholder". A. R. von Arneth, *Prinz Eugen*.

[2] Godolphin to Marlborough, 31 July/11 Aug. 1709. Coxe Papers.

[3] Wratislaw to Marlborough, 7 Aug. 1709. Blenheim Archives.

Marlborough's answer added to, rather than diminished, Wratislaw's anxiety; for it informed him that great difficulty would be found in getting even this Counter Project accepted in the Republic.[1]

I am of your opinion (the Austrian wrote back) that the business of the Barrier is in as bad a way as it could possibly be. It will be difficult to find a remedy, for England abandons us, and Stanhope's proposition as regards Port Mahon will make these Dutch restive and perhaps throw them into the arms of the French, if England insists on that point. If that is her intention, believe me, we are lost.[2]

Wratislaw might fulminate and Charles issue instructions in complacent expectation, but the only chance that the Hapsburg brothers possessed of effectually checking the progress of the negotiation lay through their common Ambassador at The Hague. Sinzendorf received a rescript, bidding him watch the Dutch who, "under the pretext of a barrier against France, wished to get the entire Catholic Netherlands into their power",[3] and this was followed by repeated instructions to put to a veto on the negotiation in a more forcible manner.[4] Fully empowered by both Courts, he was in a particularly strong position to exert an influence on the course of the Treaty. Marlborough had a conversation with him at Brussels shortly after the arrival of the instructions from Spain, and was of opinion that these alone would be sufficient to cause considerable opposition.[5] Yet the fact remains that the only two respects—to judge from Townshend's letters—in which Sinzendorf influenced the course of the Treaty were, firstly, in his partial responsibility for the Minorca affair being known at The Hague, and secondly, in his declaration that Charles intended to give the Dutch equal trading rights with the English in his dominions—the declaration which finally induced Townshend to accept Article XV.[6] What was the reason of this inaction? Was it that Townshend omitted from his letters to give an account of objections actually raised

[1] Marlborough to Wratislaw, 25 Aug. 1709. Murray.
[2] Wratislaw to Marlborough, 7 Sept. 1709. Blenheim Archives.
[3] Imperial Rescript, 28 May 1709, cited by Noorden, III, 602.
[4] Noorden, III, 602.
[5] Marlborough to Godolphin, 1 Aug. 1709. Coxe Papers.
[6] Townshend to Boyle, 6 Sept., 26 Nov. 1709; to Sunderland 1 Nov. 1709 Record Office.

by the Austrian Minister? Or was Sinzendorf unable to make his presence felt? The latter view seems to be the more correct. The statement made by Townshend on the 29th of October, that "the Imperial and Spanish Ministers as yet knew nothing of the conclusion of the Treaty", if true, shows that it was possible to keep Sinzendorf in the dark to an extent which would have been impracticable with a really first-rate diplomatist. Moreover, in the correspondence between the Austrian Minister and Marlborough which followed the discovery of the conclusion of the Treaty, the former appears as one completely at a loss and seeking for advice. But there is above all a passage in Arneth's *Life of Eugene* which seems to place beyond doubt the fact that Sinzendorf was a weak man.[1] Be that as it may, the months passed, and the negotiation proceeded, till at last the Hapsburg brothers found themselves face to face with an accomplished fact.

It seems uncertain how Sinzendorf and Eugene (then at The Hague on his return from the campaign) were first acquainted with the conclusion of the Treaty. Suspicion attaches, however, to Marlborough. He arrived at The Hague on the 3rd of November, but can have remained there only a few days, for he was in London on the 8th/19th of November. During his stay, however, Marlborough had a confidential conference with the two Austrians, in which, with very little regard for the probable wishes of the Ministry at home,[2] he discussed the question of the Treaty and

[1] The passage is in vol. II, pp. 54, 55. It was considered very necessary to send a competent Minister to The Hague to represent Austria in the peace negotiations of May 1709. Wratislaw was thought of, but he preferred to stay at Vienna to counteract the influence of Salm and direct affairs himself. The Emperor therefore agreed to send Sinzendorf, though he doubted whether the latter had the strength of character to stand against plots and obstructions. He was sent because there was no one better.

[2] The orders of the Whig government were that "to prevent a premature discussion with the Imperial Court, the Barrier Treaty was to be kept secret between the Sea Powers", Vryberg to Heinsius, 10 Dec. 1709, cited by Noorden, III, 502. "Dieu soit loué que le traité de Barrière soit fini; je comprends bien la nécessité du secret, s'il se pouvait garder". Portland to Heinsius, 1/13 Nov. 1709. Heinsius Archives. "Lord Townshend has at last finished the Treaty for the Barrière and the Succession, upon which I congratulate you. I believe this ought to be made a secret if that were possible." Somers to Newcastle, 29 Oct./9 Nov. 1709. Portland Papers, Hist. MSS. Comm. XIII, App. 1 and 2.

declared that not only had he had no part in its conclusion, but had heard nothing of it. "It was done by my second, and without my knowledge", he explained to Heinsius.[1] From the subsequent correspondence it is clear that he left the Austrians under the impression that on his return to London he would oppose the ratification of the Treaty and do so with every prospect of success. As a result, probably, of this interview Eugene and Sinzendorf waited upon Townshend to remonstrate against the Treaty. They observed that it could only be compared to forcing a master to give up the keys of his own house, that nothing worth having in the Netherlands was left by the Treaty to Charles, and nothing was said about the recovery of the Spanish Monarchy. Townshend first attempted dissimulation; then he admitted that the Queen had seen no other way in which to soften the resentment of the States over the Minorca affair, adding that it was the imprudence of the Archducal Envoys in this matter that had brought things to a crisis. The only consolation he could afford them was the information that the Treaty had not yet been ratified.[2] At once Sinzendorf sent over Heems to dissuade the Queen from ratifying it, by dilating upon the injuries such a treaty would do to English trade in the Netherlands. The Count congratulated himself upon having acted in time to prevent such a consummation;[3] but Gallas in London knew better than to imagine that any success could come out of this errand. Eugene and Sinzendorf also tried expostulations with Heinsius. The Pensionary had found out Marlborough's feelings with regard to the Barrier Treaty;[4] but,

[1] Report of Count Gallas from London, 13 Dec. 1709, cited by Klopp, XIII, 351.

[2] Wagner, *Hist. Josephi*, p. 320.

[3] Referring to his interview with Townshend, Sinzendorf wrote to Marlborough: "Il m'a répondu après plusieurs préambules qu'il était bien vrai qu'on traitait comme on l'avait fait depuis quelques années mais que la chose n'était pas encore conclue; j'ai cru qu'il était nécessaire de vous avertir de ceci, et de vous faire connaître qu'il aurait été assuré si je n'en avais parlé à ce lord de la manière que je l'ai fait" (6 Dec. 1709. Blenheim Archives).

[4] "Milord Duc partit avanthier et sera peutêtre arrivé dès à présent. Je ne le crois pas content du traîté de la Barrière. J'espère pourtant qu'il s'y conformera et que nous serons bientôt en état de changer les ratifications" (Heinsius to Portland, 19 Nov. 1709. Heinsius Archives). It is a significant fact that the Barrier Treaty is never once mentioned in the correspondence

confident of the support of the Whig leaders, he could now adopt a haughty tone. The Austrians were informed that if the Emperor should wish to withdraw from the stipulations of the May preliminaries, the States would seek an arrangement with France in order to safeguard their right in some other way.[1] In the meantime Marlborough, having returned to London, in a correspondence which presumably was kept secret from his colleagues, continued to initiate Sinzendorf into the mysteries of the Barrier Treaty. On the 22nd he wrote to the latter saying that the Treaty had been ratified with the exception of a separate article touching Guelders, Bonn, Liège and Huy, which had not been confirmed;[2] Sinzendorf in reply thanked Marlborough for his confidential communication and hoped that the action taken in England would be for the good of the Emperor and the common cause—rather a distant hope under the circumstances. But this was the first he had heard of the separate article, and he was therefore very desirous to know if he might rest upon the assurance that England would never agree to the cession of Guelders to the Dutch or allow them to have garrisons in Bonn, Liège or Huy. "I pray you to indicate to me", he continued, "what my line of conduct ought to be in case the States propose to enter into negotiation with us as regards the Barrier. It would be well for this purpose if you could inform me of the expedients which you think might be proposed to redress that which has slipped too far."[3] Sinzendorf should have known that things had slipped beyond the possibility of redress. More disillusionment was to follow. Marlborough's next letter stated that the separate article had been ratified, though only on full consideration of "the fatal consequences" that might follow the slightest misunderstanding between

between Marlborough and Heinsius after April 1709 until the almost sarcastic observation of the Duke's of 29 Nov./10 Dec.: "The kind proceedings of the Queen as to your Barrier I hope will put it out of doubt, even with the most malicious, that the Queen will always be ready of giving sincere marks of her unalterable friendship to the States" (Heinsius Archives).

[1] Eugene and Sinzendorf from The Hague, 16 and 18 Nov. 1709. Austrian State Archives, cited by Noorden, III, 603.

[2] Autograph letter in the late Mr Alfred Morrison's collection. *Hist. MSS. Comm. Report*, IX, Appendix.

[3] Sinzendorf to Marlborough, 10 Dec. 1709. Blenheim Archives.

"Great Britain and the States". The next clause in the letter proves almost indisputably that Marlborough was acting the part of secret adviser to the Austrian Ministers, for he continued: "If by any chance the proposal should be made to enter into negotiation with you about the Barrier, I think the best way would be for you to manage to put matters off until the Prince of Savoy's return and mine, so that we may together take careful measures as to our future course of action".[1] This letter disappointed Sinzendorf.

I flattered myself (he wrote in answer) that the engagement of England had not gone so far. We must not believe, that the Associated Circles of the Empire in general will concur in the establishment of the Guarantee and in the signature of peace, unless the Articles which regard it are digested on the foot of the constitution of the Empire.

He begged Marlborough therefore to reflect well on this Treaty and on those begun between England and King Charles, urging that the true interest of the Queen, the Emperor, and the States, lay in neither of the three gaining any advantage over the others. He still looked to Marlborough to devise some scheme "that they might get out of this affair". "Remember, my Lord," he concluded, "to what despair the Spaniards were driven by the Treaty of Partition."[2] Marlborough understood this letter as accusing him of participation in the Treaty—a charge which, as at the conference they had had at The Hague, he vigorously denied.

"I did not hear a word about the affair", he wrote, "for more than two months; the first thing I learned on arriving at The Hague was that this treaty had just been signed on both sides. I thought I had explained myself sufficiently then for no such suspicion to have been cast upon me."[3] These remarks deserve rather more than passing attention, when it is remembered that they came from the pen of one of the two Plenipotentiaries specially instructed to negotiate the Treaty, and were written

[1] Marlborough to Eugene, 29 Nov./10 Dec. 1709; to Sinzendorf, 13/24 Dec. Murray. Eugene had left The Hague in November to return to Vienna.

[2] Sinzendorf to Marlborough, 27 Dec. 1709/7 Jan. 1710. Coxe Papers.

[3] Marlborough to Sinzendorf, 3/14 Jan. 1710. Murray.

on the very day that orders were sent by the writer's colleagues to the other Plenipotentiary to "keep the Guelders business secret as long as possible".[1] Before Marlborough's letter reached its destination an event occurred to heighten the difficulty of the situation at The Hague.

The "Minorca incident" was not yet closed. England had not yet paid the full price for this "ill-starred thing", as Godolphin termed it. It was certainly to the advantage of the Whigs that the Barrier Treaty had been concluded before two letters from Moles to Marlborough and the Emperor, intercepted and sent into Holland by Louis, were published at Amsterdam. The burden of both these letters was Stanhope's recent action with regard to Minorca. In the first, Moles appealed to the Duke against the action of the general who had confronted the Court with the powers sent to him from England, and wished to complete the transaction without taking any notice of the difficulties caused by the Grand Alliance and the Aragonian Coronation Oath. Moles protested again that Charles could not give way without exposing himself to the reproaches that he would naturally have to expect from the Dutch, at such a manifest violation of the Treaty of 1701. Moreover, he complained bitterly that Stanhope's conduct had destroyed any chance of keeping the thing secret.[2] To the Emperor, Moles poured out the tale of his indignation at the "extreme efforts and excessive warmth" which still characterised the conduct of Stanhope, who had informed him frankly that the fate of Spain depended upon the answer "yes" or "no" to his scheme. The decision of the Queen to support Stanhope seemed to the Spanish Minister to show the complete dishonesty of England in the matter.

The assurances (he complained) that the Counts of Sinzendorf and Gallas have continually given us, and the promise given by the Queen's Ministers to the Dutch envoy in London that the affair

[1] Boyle to Townshend, 3/14 Jan. 1710. Record Office. To Vryberg Marlborough behaved very differently. The Dutchman found him very reserved in the matter of the mutual guarantee. Vryberg to Heinsius, 5 Dec. 1709. Heinsius Archives.

[2] Moles to Marlborough, 26 Nov. 1709. Copy in the Blenheim Archives.

should be spoken of no more, have shown us that at London they succeeded in cajoling the Dutch by such declarations, while they pressed the negotiation more effectually than ever by withdrawing the means necessary for the conduct of the war.[1]

Louis was not mistaken as to the effect that the publishing of these letters would produce in the States. Though Heinsius remained firm,[2] the peace party began to raise its head. Sinzendorf became despondent.

Our affairs (he wrote to Marlborough) are horribly embroiled; attempts are made to impose on the King of Spain, and with the consent of England, a condition under which the Low Countries cannot be accepted. Garrisons are to be stationed in the places of the Empire to which we cannot accede; Minorca is occupied, and a treaty of commerce concluded, which throws this State into despair and reduces the monarchy of Spain, with the other dismemberments of Portugal as to Savoy, to a situation which I know not how it can be desired or maintained. How can one hope to guarantee a peace like this, even could one succeed in making it? But I hope for everything (he concluded) from your wisdom.[3]

Not three months had passed since the signing of the Barrier Treaty and the clouds were gathering between England and the Dutch; moreover, the Treaty itself had brought the long struggle between the Republic and the Empire to a head. In both cases the tension must be relieved by concession or the Alliance could hardly stand the strain. In neither case was it

[1] For a short account of the letters, see Lamberty, VI, 5–8. The letter quoted in the text is given at length as an enclosure in Townshend's letter of 24 Jan. 1710 to Boyle (Record Office). It is clear from the letter to the Emperor that the Court at Barcelona now despairing of secrecy in the matter had determined to make what advantage they could out of its publicity and endeavour to enlist Dutch sympathies on their side. The last paragraph of the letter contains the following remarkable statement: "En attendant on a cru convenable...d'en écrire au Comte Sinzendorf qu'il communique à M. le Pens. ces nouvelles instances...et à la seule fin de prouver au même la bonne foy de Sa Majesté, puisque les expressions, avec lesqu'elles le dit Pens. expectora au Baron Sinzerling lui parlant de cette affaire, n'étaient pas moindres que les États Gen[x] *souhaittent que Sa Majesté se contentât du seul appuy de l'Angleterre parce que eux, las de la guerre, feront une Paix particulière*".

[2] "The letters might have had ill consequences but for the Pensionary's good sense" (Townshend to Boyle, 24 Jan. 1710. Record Offices).

[3] Sinzendorf to Marlborough, 24 Jan. 1710. Coxe Papers.

the Dutch who gave way. Their double diplomatic victory marks the highest point to which their fortunes rose throughout the war.

Ever since the indications of resentment with which the news of the Minorca incident was received in the Republic, the wisest of the English statesmen had doubted the wisdom of pursuing the undertaking. It was Stanhope who remained insatiable, to gain credit in his country's estimation. The Ministry now felt that the Project must be definitely dropped.[1] Townshend acting under instructions, informed the Pensionary that the orders sent to Stanhope in relation to the Treaty about Minorca were despatched a considerable time before the assurances given by him (Townshend) that the Queen would do nothing in that matter that might be uneasy or disagreeable to the States—assurances which he now repeated.[2] These were no empty professions. Eugene spoke the truth when, two months later, he wrote that "at the English Court they think no more of it, but have requested Gallas so to settle the affair that it shall no more be brought into question as they have entirely abandoned it".[3]

There remained for the Emperor a far more bitter humiliation. The news of the Barrier Treaty filtered into Vienna partly through Eugene in person, and partly through Sinzendorf's despatches. The news was received with indignation and amazement. Hearing from Marlborough that the separate article had been ratified, Eugene replied that it was as impossible

[1] There is an interesting letter by Palmes, engaged at this time on a special embassy at Vienna. He was against the undertaking, but on utilitarian grounds. Describing an interview with Wratislaw, he writes: "He in a passion told me what passed between the King of Spain and Mr Stanhope on the subject of Port Mahon and what little regard we had in England in that affair to a solemn Treaty. I had but little to say on that subject for I think it scarce worth while to alarm our allies and those that are no allies and to be at vast expense to fortify a place which when all is done upon the breaking out of another war the French with good reason will take from us before we can have in England the news of its being besieged" (Palmes to Marlborough, 5 Feb. 1710). In passing it may be noted that at Utrecht the States did not get the Barrier Treaty of 1709, but England did get Minorca. Cf. Part II.

[2] Boyle to Townshend, 20/31 Jan. 1710. Townshend to Boyle, 7 Feb. 1710. Record Office.

[3] Eugene to Charles, 26 March 1710. *Feldzüge des Prinzen Eugen*.

as the rest of the Treaty.[1] But the Court were powerless to resist. In their impotence they turned upon the long-suffering Charles.

That my Lord Townshend's Queen (wrote Wratislaw) has ratified his treaty with the Dutch is an amazing and lamentable thing, which shows how little England is to be relied on and how good it would have been if your Majesty had come to a close and timely understanding with the States General concerning the Barrier Treaty. The Commercial Treaty concluded by England with your Majesty will have given them a great advantage; this evil you might easily have prevented if you had chosen to break off communication with the Queen before the conclusion, instead of continuing it so long as fortune happened to keep it secret. But now that these powers have an understanding with each other, the remedy will be difficult.[2]

Charles could merely reply with more airy schemes for rectification at the final peace. For the present he had to confess that both the Barrier and Guelderland went exactly as the Dutch desired. "But in this", he lamented, "there is little to do when the Allies part my garments among them."[3] The consciousness of defeat was bitter to the Emperor; the confession of it to a Republic he had invariably belittled, was worse.

Happily matters have not yet arrived at such a point (ran the rescript to Sinzendorf) that we and the Empire must subject ourselves to the tutelage and supremacy of the States General. Before this should come to pass, other means might be found whereby the safety of the United Provinces could be provided for, without humiliating Ourselves and the Empire. Upon this declaration you must firmly and seriously insist until the Act comes on for signature.

It was, however, foreseen in this same rescript that the Sea Powers would prosecute their plans and would incorporate the Barrier Treaty in its unaltered form in the treaty for the peace.

[1] Eugene to Marlborough, 1 Jan. 1710. *Feldzüge des Prinzen Eugen*. Wratislaw, to whose correspondence with Marlborough one generally looks for the most authoritative expressions of Anglo-Austrian diplomacy, on this occasion maintained a gloomy silence. He merely referred to the "close" correspondence which Eugene and Sinzendorf had had with the Duke, and contented himself with observing, "J'avoue que le cœur me manque parce que je vois on prend certaines maximes en Angleterre qu'on n'avait pas de mon temps et qui nous coûteront cher pour l'avenir, à moins que votre prudence et fermeté n'y rémédie point" (22 Jan. 1710. Blenheim Archives).

[2] Wratislaw to Charles, 8 Jan. 1710. *Korrespondenz*, edited by Arneth.

[3] Charles to Wratislaw, 11 Feb. 1710 and 10 March 1710. *Ibid*.

"Then and then only", continued the Imperial command, "you will agree as for yourself, to sign the treaty, but even then not otherwise than under the enclosed reservation, and under an express protest which is to be filed in the records and to be submitted to the authorised ministers."[1]

It was just nine years since the Republic had launched its bark on its adventurous journey for the recovery of the Barrier. For five years, while expectations were remote, it had glided uneventfully down the widening estuary of the war. But with the battle of Ramillies and the reconquest of the Southern Netherlands it had passed out into the open sea of international jealousy and quivered at the shock. For four long years it had been buffeted by the winds of British self-interest and the waves of Austrian hostility, till at last, piloted by the skill and devotion of the Pensionary, it had reached its haven of rest. Misfortune was again at hand, when the Republic was to become the plaything of French spite and English party spirit; and there was a day to come, as yet far distant, when another Joseph would declare that Austria and France were one, and bid the States recall their garrisons, for the Barrier was no more. But for the moment the Dutch were victorious.

[1] Imperial Rescript, 31 Jan. 1710. The whole passage is taken from Noorden, III, 604.

PART TWO

THE DUTCH BARRIER

FROM 1709–19

BY

ISABEL A. MONTGOMERY

CHAPTER I

Introduction

I

WITH the signature of the Townshend Treaty in 1709 the first period in the history of the Barrier comes to a close. At this point certain facts emerge which are of influence in the history of the two later periods, from 1710–14 and from 1714–19.

In the first place, the Treaty of 1709 marks the highest point of success in the policy of those who, under the leadership of Heinsius, favoured a close alliance with England, and its necessary corollary while the Whig Ministry was in power, the continuation of the war.

As has been shown, the prospect of peace had been constantly before the Republic from 1706 onwards. Peace was urgently required; the succession of wars against France had crippled the finances of the country and the prolongation of the war necessitated the burden of fresh loans. With war came a still more serious loss, the decrease in trade, upon which the very life of the country depended. Such was the state of finances, that the colleges of the Admiralty were not only without money for the building of new ships; but were unable to repair and maintain the old.[1] Trade suffered from war restrictions as well as from lack of money: it was the constant aim of English merchants to prevent traffic between the Dutch Republic and France, for trade had continued between the two countries during the first years of the war.[2] As a result the great trading towns, led by Amsterdam, gave their support to the party which considered that by peace with France the interests of the Republic would best be served.

In 1709, the year in which the Barrier Treaty was signed, the menace of a Baltic war made the Dutch still more anxious to

[1] Bussemaker, *Gids*, 1899, p. 44.
[2] State Papers Foreign, Holland, 1701–9. Record Office.

extricate their country from the toils of the coalition in order to protect trade in the north, if possible by mediation.[1]

Despite the overwhelming attractions of peace, Heinsius favoured a close alliance with England. He was able temporarily to unite the two parties in the Republic by holding out the prospect of the English guarantee of all that the Dutch could desire in the Spanish Netherlands, short of annexation. To this was added a pledge of importance to the trading towns, the promise of a share in concessions in the West Indies.[2]

For these benefits the States General decided to continue the war. To all appearances the Republic stood as high as it had ever done. The Dutch had been in the enviable position of choosing between the offers of France and England and they had been able to dictate their own terms.

Nevertheless, Heinsius was to find that he had been mistaken; he had built upon the shifting sands of an alliance with a party in Britain whose continuation in power was artificially maintained by the prolongation of the war. The fall of the Whigs and the revolution in foreign politics made by their successors Heinsius could not, perhaps, foresee, but what after all was the value of the Barrier Treaty for which he had risked so much?

Upon examination it cannot but be admitted that the advantages of the Treaty were largely illusory, in consequence of certain inherent defects. In the first place, the possession of extensive military and economic advantages in the Southern Netherlands did not necessarily constitute a strong defence against France, since it would alienate the inhabitants of the provinces and their future sovereigns. Secondly, it was improbable that the Archduke would accept the terms of the Treaty when he had repeatedly made proposals which fell far short of its provisions. Thirdly, in addition to the hostility of the Archduke and the King of Prussia, the Treaty might lead to friction between the Maritime Powers themselves on account of their commercial interests in the Southern Netherlands.

With these considerations the conclusion is inevitable that Heinsius bought the Barrier Treaty at too high a price. The

[1] Townshend to Sunderland, 18 Oct. 1709. S.P.F.H. 233.
[2] Cf. p. 154.

opportunity to make peace with France was lost, and the war, which was already beyond the resources of the Republic, was prolonged for three years. More than ever, therefore, did the compensation of the Treaty appear necessary. On this account the Dutch, and in particular those like Buys, who had forsaken their convictions to obtain the Treaty,[1] were the more deeply committed to the precise execution of its terms. This determination alienated what little sympathy the Tory Ministry ever cherished towards the Republic. It explains the feeble policy of Heinsius from 1711–13, when, abandoned by his chief ally, he turned now to this side, now to that, consistent only to the vain hope of preserving the advantages of the Townshend Treaty.

The negotiations of 1709 had one unforeseen result: on account of the critical circumstances in which they took place, the controversy between Townshend and the Ministers in London over the inclusion of commercial privileges in the Treaty and of towns of importance to trade as Barrier fortresses had been concealed.

As a result, the Dutch felt a misplaced confidence in the extent to which the Whigs really supported the Treaty of 1709. During the period when the Tories were in office this misconception was strengthened by the intrigues to overthrow the Ministry, in which the promise of Spain for the Emperor and a good Barrier for the Dutch was the basis upon which the opposition sought to lure the Allies from negotiations at Utrecht and renew the war.

It was the cause of bitter disappointment to the Dutch when, on their return to power in 1714, the Whigs refused to push the claims in which they had formerly acquiesced. This disillusionment, as well as the betrayal of Dutch interests in the peace negotiations, contributed to the coolness and ultimate estrangement between the Maritime Powers.

[1] Cf. Townshend to Boyle, 25 Feb. 1710. S.P.F.H. 243. At Geertruidenburg Buys would have made conciliatory offers to France, "if he had thought he had strength enough to support (them) with the States on his return".

II

Mention has been made of the possibilities of friction between the Maritime Powers in the Southern Netherlands as a result of the Treaty of 1709. Disputes broke out from the moment the Treaty was signed. Once they felt secure the Dutch proceeded to avail themselves of their economic advantages to the full.

English dissatisfaction arose from two causes—the preponderance of the Dutch in the Condominium and their greater facilities for the commercial exploitation of the conquered provinces. In reality, the English demand for equality of government was solely to enable them to participate in commercial privileges, or at least, to restrict the Dutch to an equality with themselves.

To appreciate the situation, it is necessary to glance back to the seventeenth century, in which the basis for the economic control of the Southern Netherlands had been laid down.[1] These provinces, so prosperous in the Middle Ages, lost their commercial supremacy after the break up of the Netherlands in the sixteenth century. The jealousy of the Northern Provinces proved fatal to their trade and in addition they were weakened by internal rivalries and by the indifference with which the Spanish kings regarded the interests of their distant subjects. Two facts further contributed to the decline of commerce in the Southern Netherlands. In the first place, the Dutch were successful in blocking the Scheldt, the natural outlet of trade.[2] Secondly, the measures taken by the Spanish kings during the eighty years' war reacted unfavourably on Brabant and Flanders. Their mode of retaliation against the Dutch was to prohibit trade between their subjects in the Southern Netherlands and the United Provinces, a prohibition impossible to enforce without completely destroying the trade of the Southern Netherlands. Accordingly it was relieved by the grant of licences to trade in various goods, upon payment of what came

[1] This brief account is based on Gachard, *Histoire de la Belgique*, and Huisman, *La Belgique Commerciale*.

[2] As a war measure the Scheldt had been closed since 1585: this was made permanent by the Treaty of Münster, 1648.

to be a regulated tariff of dues. At the conclusion of the war these tariffs were continued, not as a political weapon, but because the King of Spain had found in them a useful source of revenue.

The economic control of the Southern Netherlands thus depended on the manipulation of these tariffs. Unhappily for the inhabitants, the Spanish kings preferred to sacrifice their trade rather than cede an inch of territory at the close of hostilities.[1] The result was a succession of tariffs favourable to whichever country had the upper hand, France, Britain or the United Provinces.

The highest point of Anglo-Dutch achievements was attained in the tariff of the 21st of December 1680.[2] The significance of the manipulation of the tariffs may be perceived in the contrast between the duties on goods imported into the Southern Netherlands and on those exported from these provinces to the Dutch Republic. While the Dutch might import their manufactures (such as brandy and spirits) at a low rate, they encouraged the export of raw materials (such as wood, iron and stone) for which they were dependent on the Southern Netherlands.

For the benefit of England, duties on "Indian goods, woollens and leathers" were lowered, while in England high protective duties were retained on silks, woollens, laces, linens and velvets, the chief products of the Southern Netherlands. It was the age of "Colbertism" and the Maritime Powers were not slow in the exploitation of its principles to the full.

The tariff of the 21st of December 1680 was not for long enjoyed by the Maritime Powers. In the last decades of the century, the Spanish Netherlands fell under French influence. Their governor, Maximilian Emmanuel of Bavaria, and his chief Minister, Count Bergeyck (Superintendent-General of Finances and Minister of War), attempted to imitate France by the adoption of protection. Beginning with small modifications of the tariff in 1690 and 1697, Count Bergeyck codified in 1699 the protective and retaliatory measures he had introduced.

It is unnecessary to dwell further on this phase of the history

[1] Huisman, pp. 8–20. [2] *Idem.* p. 22.

of the Southern Netherlands, but it is interesting to notice that the protective measures were abandoned as much because of the rivalry between the towns of Brabant and Flanders, as on account of Anglo-Dutch protests.[1] Count Bergeyck became unpopular and was forced to modify his measures. In May 1701 the prohibitions were removed and the Maritime Powers were again permitted to carry goods within the Southern Netherlands upon payment of a duty of 2½ per cent. *ad valorem*.

On the outbreak of the war, in the same year, Count Bergeyck took fresh measures against the Maritime Powers. In 1703 all trade with members of the Grand Alliance was prohibited, while trade with France was encouraged by a favourable tariff. These efforts did not increase the prosperity of the provinces: they were, in effect, merely a change from one subjection to another.[2] The conquest of the Southern Netherlands by the Maritime Powers and the establishment of the provisional government gave to the English and the Dutch a sense of security, in which their mutual jealousy developed. While they were united in the desire to obtain a favourable tariff, each power wished in secret to exclude the other from special privileges.

It has been shown in the preceding chapters[3] how reluctantly the Dutch had admitted the Queen into a share in the Condominium and how they had taken advantage of the English apathy to gain predominance at Brussels.

The first step taken by the Maritime Powers was the reintroduction of the tariff of November 1680 in the Southern Netherlands. After the establishment of the Provisional Government, this became a "loi stable" in these provinces. Double duties were imposed on all transactions with France and with those parts of the Southern Netherlands occupied by Maximilian Emmanuel, Namur and Luxemburg.

That these measures favoured the Maritime Powers at the

[1] Huisman, p. 45.

[2] Huisman, p. 45, writing on the assumption of powers in the Provisional Government in 1706: "Pour nos pays, qui venaient de subir six années consécutives la sujétion française, s'ouvre un intérim de dix années d'anarchie gouvernementale, qui offre le plus désolant tableau au point de vue économique".

[3] Cf. pp. 18–32.

expense of the Southern Netherlands may be illustrated by the effect on the finances of those provinces. The fall in revenue was so alarming, that, in view of the need to maintain the allied armies in Flanders, certain of the restrictions had to be modified. On the "Four Species"[1] the inhabitants of the Southern Netherlands were permitted to return to the tariff of 1699, on condition that if the revenue so gained exceeded that of the tariff of 1680, the excess should be devoted to the payment of the troops.

After the conclusion of the Barrier Treaty the Dutch felt sufficiently secure to make use of their mastery of Brussels. The unequal advantages of which they availed themselves arose in two ways. In the first place, by Article VIII of the Barrier Treaty, all things "necessary and convenient" for the garrisons of towns included in the Barrier could enter these towns free of duty. This facilitated the introduction of manufactures underhand. When it is remembered that such towns as Dendermonde, or Ghent, were keys to Brabant and Flanders, the disabilities of English merchants in the competition with Dutch traders may be understood. It is surprising that among the criticisms of the Barrier Treaty by the Whigs, the loose wording of this article should have passed unperceived. It is not until the time of St John that complaints are noticeable.

In Article XV the Queen agreed that the ports of Flanders, Ostend and Nieuwport, should be subjected to the same restrictions as those upon the Scheldt; this meant that all goods were required to pay heavy duties before they could enter the Southern Netherlands.

Although the tariff lightened certain duties, the effect of these restrictions was to favour the Dutch trader; while he could send goods free of duty to the Barrier towns, his English rival had to pay the "Royal Duty" or customs at Ostend. Secondly, the Dutch claimed the sole right of administering the "pays conquis", or country captured from France. In virtue of this right they had set up "comptoirs" on the frontier dividing the "pays conquis" from the Southern Netherlands, at which officers appointed by themselves collected the duties on goods

[1] Wine, salt, vinegar and brandy. Cf. Huisman, p. 46.

exported to towns within the "pays conquis". These duties were collected to pay for the administration of the country, but in reality they were a commercial weapon used against the English traders. To export goods into the "pays conquis", the English must pay double duties, while the Dutch went free. Since the Dutch edict of the 23rd of September 1706, British goods had paid on average 8 per cent. more than Dutch. In the case of fish, a trade in which the two countries had long been rivals, and a trade on which eighteenth-century economists set much store, the English paid as much as 15 per cent. more on Yarmouth red herring, pickled herring and salt salmon.[1] A further increase on all goods except those coming from the United Provinces was made by a Placard of the 31st of October 1710.[2] These duties applied equally to goods sent to the "pays conquis" for consumption there, or going beyond them to other markets.

These grievances, wrote William Drummond, when he was appointed to redress them, "Townshend could not or would not rectify".[3] When the opportunity presented itself, the complaints of English traders, no less than those of the Emperor and the King of Prussia, combined to influence the recasting of the Barrier Treaty.

[1] Laws to Bromley, 8 May 1713. S.P.F. Flanders, 62.
[2] Laws to Bromley, 13 July 1713. S.P.F. Flanders, 62.
[3] Drummond to Laws, 23 April 1713. S.P.F. Flanders, 62.

CHAPTER II

First Relations between the New Ministry and the Dutch

I

It has often been pointed out that the true distinction between Whig and Tory lay in their attitude to the Church of England. A secondary, but by no means unimportant distinction might be traced in the general attitude of the Tory party to their continental allies,[1] in their jealousy and suspicion of those allies, and in particular, of their closest ally, the United Provinces. This attitude of mistrust now displayed itself with the sudden blaze of a fire which had for months been smouldering underground. It is essential to remember, amid the denunciations of the English policy which culminated in the Treaty of Utrecht, that the revolution in foreign politics occasioned by the fall of the Whig Ministry was not wholly unexpected. In their period out of office, the Tories had clearly indicated their desire for peace. It was in their relations with the Allies, and especially with the Dutch, that the last Ministry in the reign of Queen Anne alarmed and mortified the Coalition. A new régime set in, in which the Allies were alternately bribed or threatened and were never entrusted with the secrets of English policy. The effects of this sudden change were nowhere more severely felt than in the Dutch Republic. However grudgingly the confidence of the Whigs might sometimes have been given, the States had hitherto directed the previous peace negotiations in conjunction with the Queen.

Now the Dutch were to be ignored, even deceived, by their former ally; they were to be excluded from negotiations where they had formerly taken a leading part. In such circumstances,

[1] Cf. St John to Plenipotentiaries, 9 June: "All nations, except my own, are to me indifferent, and as the several circumstances of affairs may bring one or other of them nearer to the interest of Britain, so will I..be more or less a friend to any of them". S.P.F.H. 248.

it is not surprising that the readjustment of their policy required some years; until December 1712, when they finally capitulated to the demands of the Tory Ministry, they continued toilsomely in the old tracks, in the belief that with the resumption of their share in the negotiations, they could regain their lost prestige. These efforts we shall follow in the history of events to 1712.

II

With the internal situation in England we are not here concerned: the machinations of Harley, the attitude of the Queen, her religious principles and her dislike of the Junto, the reactions of the Sacheverell Trial—these are relevant only in their combined result, the fall of the Whig Ministry in 1710.

In the months immediately preceding its disruption, the Ministry had enjoyed an abnormal existence, abnormal since it depended on the prolongation of a war in which the fruits of victory had long been within their grasp. From the day on which the Marquis of Kent, the first to fall, received his dismissal the collapse proceeded slowly but relentlessly. The dismissal of Sunderland, son-in-law of Marlborough, in June 1710, was a more alarming portent. At The Hague the Grand Pensionary noted its reaction on the conduct of the French at Geertruidenberg; it was evident that they hoped to prolong the negotiations until a change had taken place in the English Ministry. In alarm, Heinsius repaired to Townshend: "I find that all I could say to him on this occasion", wrote the latter,[1] "was not enough to remove the bad impression they had received".

This alarm was expressed not, as Townshend feared,[2] in a hasty agreement with the French, but in a resolution of the States General deploring the changes in the Ministry. This brought upon the Dutch a rebuke for meddling with domestic politics, in addition to the protestations of the Junto, that their position was secure; both messages were delivered by the uneasy Townshend in his "civilest and softest manner".[3]

[1] Townshend to Boyle, 27 June 1710. S.P.F.H. 235.
[2] 18 July 1710. S.P.F.H. 235.
[3] 28 July. S.P.F.H. 235.

The fate of the Ministry was sealed in early autumn by the appointment of Harley and St John to the offices occupied by Godolphin[1] and Boyle. Marlborough, it is true, continued to hold office, but his sphere of influence was restricted to the battlefield. Townshend's days at The Hague were plainly numbered and he was uninformed as to the policy of his superiors. Heinsius had to seek his information from another source.

A fresh chapter now opened in Anglo-Dutch relations, one in which the fate of the Barrier Treaty was to play a part of great importance. Outwardly, all was the same, but below the surface new currents were stirring in the waters of diplomacy.

The new Ministry gave instructions for the continuation of the war, as if their accession to power had left the policy of England undisturbed; preparations were made for the new campaign and Norris and Wishart went, as usual, to The Hague, to discuss the respective quotas of ships, of men and of money for the coming year (1711). Only in the Queen's speech at the opening of parliament,[2] was there a new note—she intimated her earnest longing to obtain for her subjects remittance from the burdens of the war.

The campaigns of 1710 had not been as encouraging as the Allies could desire. In the Southern Netherlands the war had come to a stalemate; notwithstanding all their strength, the allied armies made no progress. In Spain they had suffered actual defeat, at Brihuega and at Villa Viciosa; after these victories Philip became virtual master of Spain, the Archduke being once more confined to Catalonia. The Emperor had long left that scene of operations to the Maritime Powers, "as a thing he is no way concerned in",[3] wrote the virtuously indignant St John, and the King of Portugal, though nominally an ally, was reluctant to co-operate with the Archduke.

Peace was long overdue; the Allies were now in a less advantageous position than when they had rejected the overtures

[1] In Harley's case, the Treasury was put in commission for a year when Harley, who during that time had been Chancellor, became Lord Treasurer, with the title of Lord Oxford.

[2] 25 Nov. (O.S.) 1710.

[3] St John to Drummond, 17 Nov. 1710. *Bol. Cor.* I, 23.

of France in 1709, or even earlier in that year. It was the aim of St John to free his country from the war, without sacrificing the advantageous terms offered by De Torcy and embodied in the May preliminaries. This was the more difficult, since in the winter 1710–11 the position of the Ministry was by no means safe. A precipitate overture of peace might produce a revulsion of feeling in the country, bringing with it the return of Marlborough and his colleagues into power. It was to avoid such a catastrophe that the Tories simulated a desire to carry on the war. In secret they were laying the foundations of a separate peace with France. The readjustment of relations with the Dutch was the concomitant of such a policy, both to ensure stability at home, by the parade of co-operation with the most important ally, and to extract the best terms from France, by the employment of that same weapon.

For these reasons, the first policy of the Ministry was not unfavourable to the Republic, if the Dutch would accept English guidance. It was necessary, in order to preserve the secret, that these sentiments should be expressed by a channel other than the present ambassador, Lord Townshend,[1] or the equally "Whiggish" Vryberg, the Dutch representative in London. The new note of insistence that the Dutch, as indeed all the Allies, should exactly fulfil their obligations to the Coalition, if they wished for the continued co-operation of England, was, in itself, a hint of withdrawal. It remained for the Ministry to make a direct bid for the participation of Heinsius in their policy.

The person chosen for this delicate task was William Drummond, a Scots merchant, residing at Amsterdam. Drummond had lived many years in Holland[2]: his acquaintance with the leading persons of that province, his fluent Dutch and his knowledge of the intricacy of the Dutch constitution and politics made him an invaluable assistant in the plans of St John and Harley, with both of whom he was on confidential terms. The selection of a comparatively unknown person had the

[1] In his *History of the last Ministry of Queen Anne*, p. 102, Salomon suggests that Townshend was not at once recalled because his presence in London might have been an embarrassment to the as yet insecure Ministry.

[2] Twenty-one years, on his own account. Drummond to Buys, 25 Jan. (O.S.) 1712. British Museum Add. MSS. 20985.

further advantage of avoiding the attentions of the curious. Unsuccessful in his career—he was bankrupt in 1713—Drummond pursued the instructions of St John with a fidelity which earned him an unenviable reputation. The Whigs regarded him as a rogue and "a snake in the grass",[1] the Dutch, as a betrayer of the country which he had almost, if not quite, adopted.[2]

Drummond's task was to persuade the leaders of the Republic that through him the Ministry would indicate their true policy.[3]

In reality, St John intended that they should be informed of what for the moment it pleased the English Ministry to tell them.[4] The first illustration of this plan occurs in the months of November and December 1710.

As early as the 14th of November 1710 St John explained the situation to Drummond: the good understanding between the Dutch and the Whigs had rested upon a false basis; the previous Ministry had made concessions in order to prolong the war which it was no longer in the "true interests" of Britain to continue.

Three days later,[5] he contrasted the respective advantages of the bargain between the two countries:

Holland, however, gains a great Barrier, and keeps her Trade uncramped by prohibitions. I doubt Britain, were this war to conclude

[1] Richardson to Tilson, 6 Sept. 1714. S.P.F.H. 251.

[2] Add. MSS. 20985. 21 Jan. 1713, Drummond to Buys on the false charge that he (Drummond) has become a bad Englishman instead of a good Dutchman whereas (Portland MSS. 25 April 1713, Drummond to Oxford) Buys "is a little mistaken for I never was a burgher, only an inhabitant".

[3] E.g. St John to Drummond, 14 Nov. (O.S.) 1710. *Bol. Cor.* I, 19: "I enclose a letter to M. Buys: my correspondence with him shall be very frank and open. There is nothing of more real concern than to keep up a good understanding between the two countries, and that can never be maintained long if one side is as much deceived as Holland has been about the true intent and state of the other". Cf. St John to Drummond, 2 March (O.S.) 1711. *Bol. Cor.* I, 86: "I am very heartily glad to hear that the Pensionary places that confidence in you, and shows those marks of friendship in you which your behaviour and common good offices have deserved. They will find every day, more and more, the accounts which you have given them of this country to be true; and will come, it is to be hoped, at long last to judge better of our affairs than they have done".

[4] Cf. Klopp, *Der Fall des Hauses Stuart*, XIV, 40, and Salomon, p. 105.

[5] St John to Drummond, 17 Nov. (O.S.) 1710. *Bol. Cor.* I, 23.

tomorrow with the evacuation of Spain and the Indies, would have no particular advantage above the common one, except such as would be very precarious, since it would depend upon Austrian gratitude.

The hint of jealousy of the Barrier is clear, but although St John desired that Drummond would indicate the change of feeling as to the continuance of the war,[1] he made no mention of the Barrier.

It is unfortunate that the replies from Drummond to St John have not been preserved,[2] but we may infer the questions put to him by Heinsius in their interview, from the unequivocal reply of St John on the 3rd of December (O.S.)[3]: "The Barrier which the States have obtained, we are perfectly satisfied with; we look upon Holland as the frontier of Britain and upon these two nations together as the bulwark of the Protestant interest.[4] *Suffer no jealousy of another kind to prevail*".

With such assurances, it is not surprising that the Dutch believed themselves to have the full confidence of the Ministry. It remained for St John to dispel their doubts as to the security of his party in office. In the beginning of January he made this clear to Drummond[5]:

I take it for granted that your people are made to believe there are divisions among the Queen's servants, and that this New Ministry

[1] St John to Drummond, 28 Nov. (O.S.) 1710. "We are as sensible as he (Marlborough) or anyone can desire us to be of the effort which the Dutch make: but we hope they will be so too, of the weight which we have taken on ourselves. Our trade sinks, and several channels to it, for want of the usual flux, become choked and will in time be lost; whilst in the meantime the Commerce of Holland extends itself and flourishes to a great degree. I can see no immediate benefit likely to accrue to this nation by the war, let it end how and when it will, besides the general advantage common to all Europe of reducing the French power: whilst it is most apparent, that the rest of the confederates have in their hands already, very great additions of power and dominion....You know me well enough to be assured that I speak thus not as being cool in this war, or in any affection to the States. No man living is warmer for both than myself: but I would not willingly have these good words abused any longer and under pretence of carrying on the war, and pleasing Holland, unnecessary expenses be thrown upon us, rapine and extortions be established for ever." *Bol. Cor.* I, 26.

[2] While the correspondence of Drummond to St John is not preserved we are fortunate in having the letters of Drummond to Harley (Portland MSS., *Royal Hist. MSS. Commission, 15th Report, parts* 3–5) as a substitute.

[3] *Bol. Cor.* I, 35.

[4] This reads like one of the most zealous Whig pamphlets!

[5] 5 Jan. (O.S.) 1711. *Bol. Cor.* I, 60.

is come to no consistency, and by consequence cannot for any time support itself; but these reasoners are deceived; we are built on a better bottom than they imagine.

While Drummond was thus engaged with the Dutch, spurred on by perpetual reminders of the necessity of preserving amicable relations with them,[1] St John was accomplishing the more difficult task of the first approach to France. The earliest intimation that Britain would make concessions in Spain and the Indies appears in a note from Gaultier to De Torcy, dated the 28th of December 1710.[2] As the prospect of a general congress came nearer, it became necessary to decide on a meeting place. The English Ministers did not wish to negotiate in England for fear of an agitation against peace.[3] Harley's suggestion was to allow the negotiations to take the form of a resumption of the Geertruidenberg Conferences,[4] but the refusal of De Torcy to trust himself once more to the Dutch made it necessary to decide upon another place and method.

After some weeks, the English demands were sent to France to be recast as an "overture" from De Torcy, which might be disclosed at the convenience of both parties. St John could now approach the Dutch with confidence.

III

The question of the appointment of a successor to Lord Townshend had been discussed in England during the winter months. The cautious Harley, who was not unfavourable to the inclusion of a Whig or two in the new Ministry,[5] attempted to secure the appointment of Lord Halifax, who was already experienced in Anglo-Dutch affairs,[6] but the suggestion was abandoned in favour of a proposal to send Colonel Hill, brother of Mrs Masham, to The Hague. The colonel's illness necessitated

[1] St John to Drummond, 19 Jan. (O.S.) 1711. *Bol. Cor.* I, 77. "Go on in God's name to cultivate harmony between our friends the Dutch and us. It is the best service which any man can do to both nations."

[2] Salomon, p. 55, on the difference made since the Archduke had lost Spain. Cf. Salomon, p. 53 and Weber, pp. 13–14. Gaultier had been in association with Jersey and Harley since July 1710.

[3] Weber, *Friede van Utrecht*, p. 1.

[4] Salomon, p. 56.

[5] Salomon, p. 96.

[6] Cf. Negotiations of Barrier Treaty, pp. 40–50.

another choice and, after some dispute, the appointment was conferred on Lord Raby, then Ambassador at the Court of the King of Prussia. The choice of Raby was to have great influence on the subsequent relations with the Dutch. Raby was a descendant of the friend and statesman of Charles I, Thomas Wentworth, and he was always insistent upon the respect due to his position and to his descent.[1] He had served bravely in the wars and had subsequently been successful in his diplomatic career at Berlin. His pride, his Prussian connections, and the fact that he was superseding the popular Townshend were enough to account for the atmosphere of "prejudice and prepossession"[2] in which he found himself on his arrival at The Hague. Notwithstanding his previous service, neither Raby nor his colleague in the negotiations at Utrecht (the Bishop of Bristol) was "of much parts", if we are to believe Swift.[3] "Strafford", continues Swift, "has some life and spirit but is infinitely proud and wholly illiterate."[4] Nevertheless, St John was optimistic as to his choice and wrote to Drummond,[5] "the warmth which you apprehend in him (Raby) we will take care to cool; and, upon the whole matter, you will find him to be the best we could at present send you". He added in a later letter,[6] that, although "some cases may happen where it will be reasonable and even necessary for him to take a little more upon him than has usually been practised by our Ministers at the Hague...the cases will be few, and he will have strict and clear orders in them"—a definition of powers very necessary in the case of the dictatorial Raby.

In matters of policy, Raby sought to guide rather than to be guided, and his early despatches from The Hague contain longer instructions to St John than that gentleman then saw fit to give

[1] Cf. his well-known refusal to be Plenipotentiary at Utrecht if co-ordinate with a man of such humble rank as Prior.

[2] Drummond to Harley, 10 March 1711. *Royal Hist. MSS. Commission*, 15*th Report*, App. 3, Portland MSS.

[3] *Journal to Stella*, ed. Bohn, p. 338.

[4] N.B. In reproducing extracts from Strafford's letters I have kept to his own spelling and punctuation, as to make corrections might lead to unjustifiable alterations. (In certain passages of his letters it is impossible to make sense of his writing.)

[5] 9 Feb. (O.S.) 1711. *Bol. Cor.* I, 85.

[6] 2 March (O.S.) 1711. *Ibid.* p. 89.

to the Ambassador. Added to this, Raby was of a suspicious nature which easily found cause for offence,[1] and the little knowledge which he had of the relations between Drummond and the Ministry was the subject of many remonstrances to St John.[2] To soothe him, Drummond professed great admiration for the Ambassador and pressed him to visit him at Amsterdam, but Raby haughtily repulsed these overtures.

Throughout the course of his appointment at The Hague Raby had the disquieting knowledge that the secrets of policy were shared with, if not better known by, another, and that the successful conduct of negotiations did not depend upon Her Majesty's Ambassador alone.[3]

On his side, Drummond wrote to Harley of his hopes that the new Ambassador would quickly learn "that it was solidarity and good sense that prevail here, and not outward show, punctilio or compliments, which please often a German Prince better than a learned speech of advice".[4] Nevertheless, he reiterated his desire not to offend Raby by disclosing the confidential terms which existed between himself, Heinsius and Buys.[5]

[1] Cf. St John to Drummond, 15 May (O.S.). *Bol. Cor.* I, 206. "My Lord ambassador Raby is a very good man, but he has the misfortune of being a little too apt to take umbrage and to be punctilious."

[2] St John's letters to Raby (afterwards Earl of Strafford) repeatedly deny the understanding between Drummond and the Ministry. The fiction was kept up as may be seen in the following interesting illustration. Drummond to Oxford, 1 Nov. 1712. The Hague (Portland MSS.) "My Lord Strafford told me as a compliment at my arrival here last week that he had recommended me to the Pensionary and had given such an account of me that he had declared his desire to see me. I could hardly think that the Old Gentleman had kept so long secret that he knew me, and I had been even the evening before with him to show the injustice to us in the Spanish Netherlands."

[3] Cf. the following letter from his brother Peter, which can hardly have been reassuring to the recipient. *Wentworth Papers*, ed. Cartwright, p. 212. Peter Wentworth to Strafford, 25 Nov. 1711. "The last week Mr Drummond and his wife was here and very much caressed by Mrs Masham, and her friends cry him up for one that has been a great support of our credit abroad, and very instrumental in laying the ground of this good peace we are likely to have; but I must do them the justice that to me they own that you have the honour of doing your Queen and country eminent service in this affair."

[4] Portland MSS., *Royal Hist. MSS. Commission*, *15th Report*, App. 4. Drummond to Harley.

[5] *Ibid.* App. v, p. 7, and postscripts on letters to Buys and Oxford, e.g. 26 June 1711 to Harley: "I must not omit to beg of your Lordship to take as little notice of my discourses with the Pensionary to Lord Raby as possible.

It was characteristic of Raby that he, almost immediately, took sides in the disputes between the leading statesmen and the Republic. Prominent among the great officials who served the States General were Anthony Heinsius, the Grand Pensionary, Willem Buys, Pensionary of Amsterdam, the Greffier Fagel, and Bruno van der Dussen, Pensionary of Gouda.

In 1711 Heinsius was seventy years of age; despite his age and the severe attacks of illness which sometimes incapacitated him, he continued to take a leading part in the affairs of the Republic. In policy he had inherited the traditions of his friend and master, William III, with whom he had for many years struggled against the powers of France. He believed implicitly in the value of the English Alliance and, as has been shown, in the necessity of a strong Barrier against France. Although of a reserved nature,[1] Heinsius was popular with the English statesmen with whom he came in contact; even the quarrelsome Raby was on good terms with him, though the latter complacently attributed this to his "delicate flattery", to which he believed the Pensionary "very sensible".[2]

Very different was the Grand Pensionary's colleague, Willem Buys, of whom Drummond once regretfully observed[3] "he has not that tranquility (sic) of mind which the Old Gentleman has". Buys was a man of unprepossessing manners, at once talkative and secretive.[4] "Speaks English well enough, but is plaguily political" was Swift's verdict when he dined with him at the Masham's, "telling a thousand lies; none of which passed upon any of us."[5] Buys' reputation as a talker was widespread: Raby, who took a dislike to him on account of his correspondence with Drummond,[6] dubbed him "wiseacre", "babbler" and "whip'd cream Buys, who has many words and little to the

I would not gladly give his Excy. any umbrage, and I fear he is easily touched"; and Add. MSS. 20985, Drummond to Buys, 21 Jan. 1713: "I beg you not to mention this letter to the English Ministers".

[1] Drummond to Harley, 4 Aug. 1711. Portland MSS.

[2] Strafford to St John. S.P.F.H. 239.

[3] Drummond to Harley, 8 Sept. 1711. Portland MSS.

[4] 9 June. Cf. S.P.F.H., 245, Bolingbroke on Buys: "I am well enough acquainted...to know that he would try any temper". To Plenipotentiaries at Utrecht.

[5] *Journal to Stella*, p. 301.

[6] Cf. pp. 203 and 211.

purpose".[1] As Pensionary of Amsterdam, Buys shared the interests of the oligarchic and pacific party, of which he was the leader, throughout the war. He had earned the dislike of Heinsius by his readiness to make peace in defiance of the Grand Pensionary's understanding with the Junto. Heinsius summed up his view of Buys, professing that it was the general opinion, that his colleague gained himself some enemies, "by taking too much upon him, and being very tenacious, and his constant pushing everything for the private benefit of his town, whether for the universal benefit or not, created a jealousy against him".[2]

To the party of Buys belonged the powerful Regents of Amsterdam. Heinsius was supported by Fagel, Duivenvoorde and Bruno van der Dussen, his "kinsman and favourite". The latter was the more useful, on account of his indirect relationship to Corver, one of the Regents of Amsterdam,[3] and was in a sense a link between Buys and Heinsius during the negotiations at Utrecht.

In his dealings with this internecine rivalry, Raby displayed great lack of statesmanship. On account of the association he soon suspected between Buys and Drummond, the ambassador listened the more readily to the tales of Heinsius, until he was convinced that it was Buys who was the strongest opposer of the English negotiations for peace, a misunderstanding which had serious effects.

IV

When Raby arrived at The Hague, in the spring of 1711, the ground had been well prepared for him by Drummond. The Dutch had no fears for the security of the Barrier Treaty, although they were on the alert for negotiations between England and France. They were soon to be undeceived: had they but known it, Raby's instructions hinted at an unforeseen development:

[1] *Wentworth Papers*, p. 30.

[2] Drummond to Oxford, 25 Oct. 1712. Portland MSS.

[3] *Ibid.* Van der Dussen a man of "a great deal of cunning and a strong constitution and by birth and marriage related to the chief men of Amsterdam, Dort, Gouda and Schiedam".

You will be pleased to use the Ministers you treat with in the gentlest and softest manner possible, (wrote St John[1]) and rather to overact the part than otherwise; after which, whenever the honour or interest of Britain comes to clash with the Dutch, your Excellency will show a firmness which your predecessors never did show, and be by so much the more justified, by how much more tenderly you have indulged them before.

It was at this time, when the English had almost reached a settlement of general principles with De Torcy, that the Dutch, through Buys and Drummond, made a bid for a real understanding between the Maritime Powers, as a foundation for a joint negotiation with France.

For some months previously, Buys had been in correspondence with St John on terms which he might be justified in thinking confidential.[2] On the 6th of April St John instructed Drummond to inform Buys of his desire to open negotiations with France.[3] He concluded with the following passage: "I must once more repeat my apprehension that we cannot treat advantageously, perhaps not safely, with France, till Britain and Holland know the minds of each other more exactly than it can be pretended they do".

The offer was seized upon; Buys proposed that he should come to England to discuss peace. Drummond recommended the acceptance of this scheme and added that to facilitate negotiations he was willing to accompany the Dutchman. Buys suggested that the preliminaries of 1709 would serve as a basis for the new negotiations.[4] Even Raby testified to the sincere desire for peace of the Pensionary of Amsterdam, in one of the first letters he wrote on his arrival at The Hague.[5]

[1] 23 March (O.S.) 1711. *Bol. Cor.* I, 127. [2] Cf. p. 199 *note* 3.

[3] *Bol. Cor.* I, 142. "You should let M. Buys know that you have wrote to those to whom it was proper in Britain, as he desired you to do, and the answer given to your enquiry is, that the Ministers of the Queen are desirous of making peace, as in making war, to have a perfect good understanding with the States; that the method proposed for carrying on a treaty in case we are obliged to sink below the terms formerly insisted upon, may be very agreeable, provided the Queen be from the first let into the whole secret."

[4] Weber, pp. 110–11.

[5] Raby to St John ("Privet"), 21 April 1711. Add. MSS. 22205. "Pensionary Buys told me plainly that they were unfortunate they had lost their occasion (i.e. at Geertruidenberg), and now they must make a peace, not being able to support the war any longer. I asked him if they had offers

When matters had arrived at this stage, a change was made in the Dutch policy by Heinsius. On the pretext that the death of the Emperor necessitated further deliberation, he decided to suspend the negotiation.[1] It was true that the succession of the Archduke to the whole Hapsburg inheritance was an event as menacing to the peace of Europe as the accession of a Bourbon to the throne of Spain, and one which upset the calculations of the English. Heinsius had, however, other motives for his action.

In the first place, jealousy of Buys led him, with the help of Duivenvoorde, to attempt to divert negotiations to his own hands. The first step was taken on the 5th of May, when Duivenvoorde disclosed to Raby the transactions between Buys and Drummond, which had hitherto been kept secret from the Ambassador.[2] "He asked", wrote Raby, "why we would not sooner trust the Pensionary Heinsius and his friends, who, he could assure me, was heartily for a peace." Duivenvoorde suggested that he himself should obtain proposals from France which would at once be forwarded to the Queen. He concluded by saying that he knew that he and Heinsius were suspected by the Ministry on account of their friendship with the Duke of Marlborough but "they saw all his failures". They therefore implored Raby to inform St John, Harley and Lord Shrewsbury, privately and particularly, of their peaceful intentions, and not to treat through Buys.[3]

Raby finished his report to St John with reproaches that the secret had been kept from him; he condemned the use of the unworthy Drummond and pointed out that he, the Ambassador, was the proper channel for such communications.

When the news reached England, St John perceived that Heinsius was jealous of Buys.

What happened relating to Monsieur Buys' project gives me much speculation (he wrote[4]). I look upon the Grand Pensionary to have been the prompter of the Gentleman who spoke to the Ambassador,

of peace by any other canall. He answered me not, but that he was assured the French had one open in England, but I assured him he was mistaken, there was none I knew of."

[1] Cf. Salomon, p. 110.
[2] Cf. Weber, p. 111.
[3] Raby to St John, 5 May. Add. MSS. 22205.
[4] St John to Drummond, 8 May (O.S.). *Bol. Cor.* I, 199.

and his view, without dispute, was to break any private correspondence which might have been carried on betwixt us and Holland, of which he was not the leader.

It is probable, however, that Heinsius had another motive for breaking off negotiations and for wishing to be the first in the field with France. He had just heard that the Ministry wished to change the Barrier Treaty. The first intimation of this policy was sent on the 19th/30th of April.[1] This letter and those which followed it breathe a spirit very different from the assurances of the winter months.[2]

> I have but just time to add two words about the Barrier Treaty (wrote St John). Your Excellency must be of opinion, as we all are here, that this was the measure of a faction who made their court to Holland at the expense of Britain. I will undertake to show, in almost every article of it, something more or less scandalous. Your Excellency will therefore, please, with that address you are master of, to incline the Dutch to a composition upon it. The Queen is engaged by her ratification and therefore cannot directly refuse to make it good: but there are others who are under no tie of submitting to it.[3]

These "others" were the Imperialists, who, as St John was probably well aware, had already pressed the Dutch to recast the Treaty on terms more favourable to the Archduke.[4] If this threat were not enough, St John warned the Dutch that the English commercial classes would never permit the Treaty to remain as it was.[5]

[1] St John to Raby. *Bol. Cor.* I, 153.

[2] Cf. pp. 199–200.

[3] St John to Raby, 19/30 April. *Bol. Cor.* I, 153.

[4] Raby to St John, 24 April (N.S.) 1711. S.P.F.H. 239. Raby reports that Sinzendorf, "finding these people here not so high as formerly", was urging them to settle the Barrier "otherwise than 'tis by the preliminaries and their treaty with us, telling them that neither the Emperor nor King Charles can ever consent to it as it is". Raby adds that Sinzendorf has hopes that the Dutch will agree to this and concludes, "indeed they seem at present here extreemly dejected, complain extreemly for want of money to carry on the war, and the eager wishers for a peace cry out extreemly for one".

[5] To Raby. *Bol. Cor.* I, 153. "It may not improperly be let fall that we have great ground to complain of the subjects of Holland on the coast of Africa and the Indies, and there is no small difficulty in keeping our merchants from making very loud remonstrances on these heads: but if the Barrier Treaty comes to be publicly known it will be absolutely impossible to keep the ferment down. All ranks, all parties of them will unite in their protestation against it."

A second letter followed, even more fiery than the first:[1]

the last and great sale of the British interest was made in the Barrier Treaty: under the pretence of rendering Holland safe...we have given to the Dutch, by that infamous compact, extent of country, the only thing they wanted to enable them to be superior to us in trade. This, my Lord, has been the price at which the good harmony has been created and maintained. I believe, and I have reason to believe that they begin to think in Holland we shall no longer prove so blind as to suffer the national interest to be bartered by a faction.[2]

This condemnation of the Treaty does not take into account the advantage gained by the Whigs in the prolongation of the war, since it was not one calculated to appeal to the party excluded from power by this manœuvre. Nevertheless, it is only fair to admit that peace was postponed until the new Ministry was able to conduct negotiations still more favourable to their interests, though not to those of their Allies.

The Tories objected to the Barrier Treaty not only on account of the commercial advantages it bestowed upon the Dutch, but also because precise execution of its terms would hinder the prospects of a speedy peace with France. Louis's position was stronger than in 1709 and towns such as Tournai and Lille could be obtained only by prolonged negotiation, or possibly by additional concessions.[3]

Once the preliminary understanding had been reached with De Torcy, St John felt himself in a position to intimate his plan of changing the Barrier Treaty. The moment was at hand; when St John wrote the letters just quoted he was awaiting the "Propositions" from France which arrived before the 27th of April (O.S.).

Meanwhile Duivenvoorde was at Breda where he hoped to meet De Torcy. A week later he returned having accomplished nothing. He told Raby, however, that he was confident that when the French made terms it would be with himself.[4]

[1] St John to Strafford, 20 April (O.S.). *Bol. Cor.* I, 156.

[2] Weber, p. 113, does not make it clear that the Barrier Treaty was attacked before Heinsius broke off negotiations. He refers to this letter as "an energetic and sharp protest", but the concluding lines demonstrate that the Dutch had changed from their previous attitude of confidence in the Ministry.

[3] Cf. Weber, p. 114.

[4] Raby to St John, 12 May. Add. MSS. 22205.

The insinuations of Heinsius were not without effect: on the 19th of May, Raby advised St John that "'tis certainly ye best way, if we would have peace to leave it by their channel, than by ye other project, for Buys is not a man to be relied solidly on".[1]

Whatever hopes Heinsius and Buys cherished with regard to negotiations, they were both frustrated by the unexpected announcement that the Ministry had received "Proposals" from De Torcy which were considered satisfactory. These included a Barrier for the Dutch which should be "agreable to England and the English nation".[2] St John betrayed how little trust he had in Heinsius and his friends in the concluding paragraph of the letter accompanying the propositions:

> the fear that the Dutch will conceive of our obtaining advantageous terms for Britain will naturally put them on trying underhand for themselves, and endeavouring to make us dupes of the peace as we have been of the war. Your Excellency will therefore please to be watchful to discover any proceedings of that kind.[3]

The duties of Raby in this respect were less important than this letter indicates, since St John had forestalled any possibility of Franco-Dutch negotiations by an agreement with De Torcy on the subject.[4] To the advances made once more by Duivenvoorde and later by a Regent of Rotterdam,[5] De Torcy replied that he preferred, after his treatment at Geertruidenberg, to negotiate alone with England.

V

On the 25th of May Heinsius made his reply to St John's communication; the States General were willing to negotiate, but upon a clearer basis, that of preliminary propositions, such

[1] Raby to St John, 19 May. Add. MSS. 22205.

[2] St John to Raby, 27 April (O.S.). *Bol. Cor.* I, 172.

[3] *Ibid.*

[4] De Torcy, *Mémoires*, III, 30, cited by Klopp, XIV, 103–4.

[5] These advances were made not as De Torcy wrote by Petkum, but by Hennequin. Cf. Klopp, XIV, 103, who cites Robethon's *Bericht vom* 23. *Mai.* This is corroborated in Raby to St John, 2 June 1711. Add. MSS. 22205, when he writes "every little Burghermaster as Henneken (*sic*) at Roterdam... at liberty to go to frame what Propositions they please".

as those of 1709.[1] Next day Raby wrote to St John to explain the attitude of the Dutch.

I may assure you... that tho' they do all they can to hide it from the enemy...yet they are as weary of the war as we are, and very heartily desirous of a good and lasting peace, and ready to join in any method Her Majesty shall think proper to obtain it...they look on this proposition (in the same manner as you do) to be as yet very dark and general, and they see how the enemy would create jealousies between the Queen, this Republick and the other Allies, but they are satisfied it will have no effect and relye entirely on the justice and prudence of Her Majesty in this affair according to our Alliance, and don't question but she will be pleased to make the French explain themselves more particularly.[2]

St John replied coldly: the States General must trust to their ally in this negotiation and must not prevent the English from seeing how far the French would enter into it.[3] His opinion of Dutch policy he expressed to Drummond.[4] "I cannot look for the Pensionary Heinsius to be for any peace unless it be such an one as he has the sole direction of—which will not be the case whenever we are happy enough to treat."

To Raby, the suspicious character was Buys: "I must own", he wrote,[5] "I apprehend more Mons. Buys than the Pensionary Heinsius since he has a much narrower soul and understanding than the other who is certainly right that the more we seem eager for a peace, the further we are off a good one".

The unfortunate Buys was aware of the Ambassador's suspicions and of the readiness with which Raby listened to the Grand Pensionary and his faction. He made an effort to overcome these prejudices.[6] He begged Raby to give him a private interview. The two withdrew to a pleasant garden some miles from The Hague, where they could converse unobserved. There Buys, with his habitual flow of language, sought to persuade the Englishman that he was heart and soul for peace. He pointed out in vain that it was he who had been overruled

[1] Cf. Weber, p. 113.
[2] Raby to St John, 26 May 1711. S.P.F.H. 239.
[3] St John to Raby, 22 May (O.S.). *Bol. Cor.* I, 225.
[4] St John to Drummond. *Bol. Cor.* I, 314.
[5] 2 June to St John. Add. MSS. 22205.
[6] Following abridged from Raby to St John, 12 May. Add. MSS. 22205.

by Heinsius at Geertruidenberg and again in April. His words were to no purpose; Raby's mind had long been made up. He would never forgive Buys and Drummond for keeping their correspondence with St John a "mistery" from him.[1]

In the episode of the broken negotiations of April, the English Ministry found an excellent pretext for withholding their confidence from the Dutch. "From that hour to this", wrote St John,[2] "I have thought no more of the matter, knowing Buys to be very light under a very solemn appearance: and besides we wanted no help of theirs to begin this negotiation or to justify our conduct in it."

The refusal of Heinsius to admit De Torcy's "Propositions" as a basis for peace was the signal for the English to adopt a new tone to the Dutch. Henceforth they made no pretence of communicating the progress of their negotiations with De Torcy. "Britain has gone much too far in weaving her interest with that of the Continent", wrote St John significantly; "...it will prove no easy task to disentangle our affairs without tearing or rending."[3]

The first effort in this direction was the attempt to revise the Barrier Treaty. Raby held out hopes of "a reasonable explication...if the Dutch were rightly managed",[4] since they were alarmed at the protests of the Emperor's Ministers against it.

St John instructed the Ambassador to take leave of The Hague for some weeks, on the ground that he had been given permission to return to London for his marriage and to receive an earldom. The real motive for his recall was to report on Dutch policy with regard to the Duke of Savoy[5] and to communicate the Pensionary's attitude to the proposed revision of the Barrier Treaty, since England "would be glad to compound the matter with as little ill will as possible".[6]

[1] Raby to St John, 12 May 1711. Add. MSS. 22205.
[2] St John to Raby, 6 May (O.S.). *Bol. Cor.* I, 185.
[3] 29 May (O.S.), to Raby. S.P.F.H. 241.
[4] Raby to St John, 26 May. S.P.F.H. 239.
[5] The Dutch were disinclined to agree with the Ministry's project of strengthening the Duke in order to preserve the balance of power between the Bourbons and the Hapsburgs.
[6] St John to Raby, 1 June (O.S.). S.P.F.H. 241.

Some days before he left The Hague, Raby expressed his views on the subject.[1] He condemned the Barrier Treaty on two grounds. In the first place, the Dutch might make a separate peace and yet hold the Queen to her guarantee of the Barrier.[2] Secondly, by Article XV—"that extraordinary unparalleled clause"—they might claim a share in any advantages granted to England by the King of Spain.

Raby suggested that the English should threaten to revise the whole Treaty; this would frighten the Dutch into compliance with the Ministry's methods of negotiation with France and at the same time into altering the objectionable article. It is noteworthy that Raby, while denouncing the Treaty on these grounds and on the general charge that it contained not one article in favour of England, did not attack the Treaty on the pretext that it strengthened the Dutch unduly in the military sense in the Southern Netherlands. Raby's final recommendation is interesting in the light of English policy in the spring of 1712. If the Dutch refused to comply with the Queen's demands she should insist that her troops should remain in some of the Barrier fortresses.

In Raby's opinion it was impossible to exclude the Dutch from negotiations with France, since he feared that they would make their own terms unless they were taken into the secret.[3] In this he was mistaken. On the 3rd of August Prior returned from his mission to Paris accompanied by Mesnager, the Envoy of the French Court. By the end of September the negotiation was concluded by the signature of three conventions to be communicated to the Allies when both parties saw fit to do so.[4] The first concerned the interests of England, which were fully and precisely stipulated; the second, designed for immediate communication to the coalition, concerned the Emperor and

[1] "Privet" to St John, 2 June 1711. S.P.F.H. 239.

[2] *Ibid.* "Their portion, thanks to the Barrier Treaty, is already cut out for them. One word at any time ends their war with France nor do I remember one article on our side in that treaty that makes voyd our engagement to them, in case they make a separate peace with France."

[3] Raby to St John, 2 June 1711. S.P.F.H. 239. "We must for our own sakes go on, hand in hand with these people."

[4] Cf. Weber, p. 58.

the Dutch;[1] the third was an agreement as to the provision for the Duke of Savoy.

As a result, when Raby, or as he must now be named, the Earl of Strafford, returned to The Hague in October, St John had arrived at an understanding with France which gave him the upper hand with the Dutch. Before this power could effectually be put into practice, new difficulties arose in connection with the struggle to assemble the peace congress. For this we must turn to a new chapter in the course of events, the mission of Willem Buys to England.

[1] *Actes et Mémoires concernant la Paix d'Utrecht*, I, 163. "Articles Préliminaries de la part de la France pour parvenir à une Paix générale. Septembre 27, 1711.

1. Qu'elle reconnaîtra la Reine de la Grande Bretagne en cette qualité comme aussi la succession de cette Couronne, selon l'establissement présent.

2. Qu'elle consentira volontiers et de bonne foi qu'on prenne toutes les mésures justes et raisonables pour empêcher que les couronnes de la France et de l'Espagne ne soient jamais réunies en la Personne d'un même Prince.

3. L'intention du Roi est, que tous les Princes et Etats engagez dans cette guerre sans aucune exception, trouvent une satisfaction raisonnable dans le Traité de Paix que ce sera: et que le Commerce soit rétabli et maintenu à l'avenir à l'avantage de la Grande Bretagne de la Hollande, et des autres Nations qui ont été accoûtumé de trafiquer.

4. Comme le Roi veut aussi maintenir exactement l'observation de la Paix, lorsqu'elle aura été conclue, et l'objet que le Roi se propose étant d'assurer les frontières de son Royaume sans inquiéter en quelque manière que ce soit, les Etats ses voisins, S. M. promet de consentir par le Traité qui sera conclu que les Hollandois soient mis en possession des Places fortes, qui seront spécificés dans les Pais Bas, qui serviront à l'avenir de Barrière pour assûrer le repos de la Hollande contre toutes sortes d'entreprises du côté de la France.

5. Le Roi consent aussi, qu'on forme une Barrière sûre et convenable pour l'Empire et pour la maison d'Autriche."

6. (Dunkirk to be razed in exchange for an equivalent to be arranged at future peace Conference.)

7. (All interests of all Princes and States to be discussed at future Conference.)

CHAPTER III

The Struggle to Assemble the Peace Congress

I

DURING the absence of Strafford, Lord Orrery[1] took charge of affairs at The Hague. Although personally agreeable to Heinsius,[2] his silence on all important questions was felt to be an ominous sign when Anglo-French negotiations were on foot.

From Amsterdam, Drummond wrote in vain counselling frankness: Heinsius was inclined to friendship with England,

> but I cannot say very open; but I discover this, that he will not speak plain about the peace, *and if you will have him into it*, you must be pleased to write the Queen's Instructions first to him; or get Lord Strafford to tell them, plainly and resolutely. His absence at present is very surprising to them and, in my poor opinion, does harm.[3]

Drummond, like the Dutch, did not realise that the absence of communication was intentional, as the Ministry did not wish to show their hand until Mesnager had come to an agreement with them.

From the Dutch point of view, the absence of Strafford was doubly to be deplored, since they had no minister in England. The former Ambassador, Vryberg, had died in office in July 1711 and had not been replaced. Buys was suggested for the post, but Heinsius was unwilling to send him to England until he knew the intentions of the Ministry with regard to peace.[4]

Drummond feared that the Ministry's silence would encourage Dutch intrigues with Marlborough and he finished his

[1] Orrery and the Dutchman Van den Bergh were Joint Governors of the Southern Netherlands.

[2] Drummond to Oxford, 24 July. Portland MSS. "The Grand Pensionary has an extreme good opinion of his (Orrery's) integrity and loves his serious grave way of doing business."

[3] Drummond to Oxford, 11 Aug. Portland MSS.

[4] Drummond to Oxford, 11 Aug. Portland MSS.

warnings with a final appeal for frankness—"be pleased to write plain to Buys".[1]

This counsel produced no change in London. St John pursued his old course of giving assurances of Her Majesty's friendship, without in the least divulging the secrets of her policy.

We are as earnestly and zealously for a new alliance to subsist between the two nations in time of peace as the Pensionary can be (he replied[2]). We will think on our side, and you must do so on yours, how to make it as clear and strong as possible, and when my Lord Strafford goes over, he will meet the Dutch Ministers more than halfway in this affair.

Britain will act honourably to the last: no peace without the States is to be had; or even was thought of here, but a peace must be in concert with them.[3]

As the settlement with France drew near, the letters took a sharper note[4]:

You will do well to insinuate (that Her Majesty) is Queen of Britain, and that the interests of this island are not any longer to be deemed the property of other people. Certain it is, that she will use Holland as her best and nearest ally; let the Dutch take care to observe the same conduct and the union of the Queen is indissoluble.

This warning was provoked by St John's irritation at the Dutch efforts separately to approach De Torcy. Nevertheless, "after the British Ministry had morally broken the Alliance, it was inevitable that the Dutch should take further steps in this direction".[5] Even Strafford had pointed out that this must be the outcome of English policy.[6]

Finding that they could learn nothing from either France or England, the States General decided to send Buys to England as Envoy Extraordinary. This was the final effort of Heinsius to remove his country from the position of isolation into which

[1] Drummond to Oxford, 11 Aug. Portland MSS.

[2] To Drummond, 28 Aug. (O.S.). *Bol. Cor.* I, 340.

[3] Cf. Weber, Appendix A, p. 401. Heinsius was further encouraged by his correspondence with Lord Oxford. The purport of Oxford's letters was to conceal from him the progress of the Mesnager negotiations, while pretending to take him into the confidence of the Ministry.

[4] St John to Drummond, 21 Sept. *Bol. Cor.* I, 363.

[5] Klopp, XIV, 103.

[6] Raby to St John, 2 June 1711. S.P.F.H. 239.

it had been manœuvred by the Ministry. Some weeks earlier he had despatched Drummond with the same intent but to no purpose.[1]

Buys was charged "to inquire what the English were doing in relation to the pourparlers with France, and to assure Her Majesty of the States' Attachment to the Queen and to her interests": to concert the plan of a negotiation with France and to elicit those parts of the Barrier Treaty considered prejudicial to English interests. Finally he was to concert a new alliance between the Maritime Powers to subsist in time of peace.[2]

These instructions and the subsequent meeting of Buys and Strafford show that the States were totally unprepared for the extent to which negotiations had progressed.

Buys set off for Helvoet Sluys towards the middle of October. He was detained there by contrary winds which hastened the arrival of the ship in which Strafford had set sail, bearing the long delayed communication of the Queen's intentions. Strafford and Buys met at the port on the 20th of October. Buys at once displayed his instructions and listened with painful anxiety to the Ambassador's communication.

Strafford's instructions[3] were "a remarkable piece of work, in which the secret negotiations with France were made to appear as if they had taken place with the knowledge of the Republic".[4] He was empowered to reveal the Mesnager overture and the convention which concerned Allied interests.[5] As to England, he was to say no more than "we have made no particular stipulation for ourselves that may clash with the interests of Holland". Next, he was to assure the Dutch that "No concession whatsoever can tempt us to embrace the blessings of peace, unless our good friends and Allies, the States General, have all reasonable satisfaction as to their Barrier, their Trade and in all other respects".

After this, Strafford was to "insinuate strongly to the

[1] Cf. Weber, p. 119. Drummond arrived in England at the end of September.

[2] Helvoet Sluys. Strafford to St John, 20 Oct. 1711. S.P.F.H. 239.

[3] Printed in Wickham Legge and *Bolingbroke's Correspondence*, I, 398.

[4] Cf. Klopp, XIV, 196.

[5] Cf. p. 214 *note* 1.

Ministers of Holland how just reason we should have to be offended, if they should pretend to any further uneasiness upon this head".

The fears of Buys would not be allayed by the next passage relating to his country.

> You will represent very earnestly to them, how much it is for the interest of Holland itself rather to compound the Barrier Treaty than to insist upon the whole, since it is notorious that the House of Austria and several of the Allies are, and must necessarily continue, utterly averse to it...nothing can be more odious to the People of these kingdoms than many parts of the Treaty

and "only the greatest care and industry" could "calm the minds of those who are acquainted with this guarantee and make them keep it secret".

Strafford was to conclude "by desiring that they (the Dutch) will give all possible dispatch to the choice of a place of Treaty, and that the passports of the French Plenipotentiaries may be hastened". In this demand lay the only weak point in the strong position of the Ministry after the conclusion of the Mesnager Convention. They wished the Congress to take place in the United Provinces rather than in England and for this they were dependent on the co-operation of the States General. This would demonstrate the continued concert between the Maritime Powers and give the lead to the other Allies, while it would be of use if De Torcy sought to take too much advantage of the isolation of the Allies. Secondly, the Ministry was not yet strong enough to risk holding the Congress in England, where the Whigs might seize the opportunity to stir up popular feeling against the negotiations.

The instructions concluded in a threatening tone; if the Dutch or the Imperialists should object to the Convention as an insufficient basis for a congress, or should they propose a return to the preliminaries of 1709, Strafford was "to insinuate that the French might very probably have been brought to explain themselves further, had they not perceived the extraordinary uneasiness, impatience and jealousy, which during their transactions discovered itself among the Allies"—a passage in which it is tempting to conjecture that Swift gave his assistance, particularly when accompanied by St John's recommendation to deliver it in "a fair as well as a peremptory manner"![1] If the Dutch insisted on continuing the war, the Queen would take her part, but on a different footing: "We can no longer bear that disproportionate burden that has every year increased upon us, nor that deficiency which our Allies, in every part of the War, are guilty of".

St John calculated that after the communication of these instructions, "the best resolution the States can take is soundly and frankly to follow us".[2]

The effect of Strafford's communication at Helvoet Sluys, was for once, to stem the eloquence of Buys. The Dutchman confessed himself "extremely ambarrased to find matters had advanced so far" and suggested that he should accompany Strafford to The Hague to receive new instructions from the States General.[3]

II

On the 21st of October Strafford and the Grand Pensionary held their first meeting.[4] Strafford read his instructions and inquired if Buys was empowered to draw up a new Barrier Treaty, in order to concert "a reasonable Barrier". Heinsius replied that no such powers had been given and pointed out that the Queen had not only concerted, but also ratified the Townshend Treaty.

Strafford argued that the Treaty could not stand since the Emperor would never agree to it, and since it was unfair to the English, for whom no advantages—not even the demolition of Dunkirk—were stipulated. Finally the French would never permit the Treaty to remain as it was, since they desired as equivalent for Dunkirk "a town or two" out of the Barrier.

Heinsius was not unprepared for this demand, as he had previously received a letter in which Drummond informed him that to please the Dutch, the Ministry would assemble the peace

[1] St John to Strafford, 9 Oct. (O.S.). S.P.F.H. 241.

[2] *Ibid.*

[3] Strafford to St John, 20 Oct. S.P.F.H. 240.

[4] Report of Heinsius to the States of Holland, 22 Oct. 1711. Archives of Gouda, B. 12, 17. Notulen gehouden ter Vergaderinge van de Heeren Staeten van Holland ende W. Vriesland, 1709–13.

congress on Dutch territory and that if the States would not insist on the Townshend Treaty entire, all would go well with them.[1] He was, however, unprepared for the vagueness with which Dutch interests were laid down in the Mesnager convention and he suspected that English claims had been safeguarded by some secret agreement. In this, as we have seen, he was correct, although the secret was preserved for many months.

When the two statesmen parted, Heinsius promised that Buys should receive fresh instructions when the States General had come to a resolution on this new turn of affairs. Strafford was confident that this Resolution would be favourable to English plans. His hopes seemed to be confirmed by a conversation he held three days later with the Pensionary of Amsterdam,[2] which left him positive that the Dutch had "come to themselves" and would speedily

> take the Ply of acquiescing to what the Queen has proposed and Buys will be instructed to desire in an honourable manner the Queen's assistance and friendship in promoting their pretentions, so that the French may not cut them too short of their hopes, at least of their Barrière which is what they most apprehend and what they have most at heart. For Buys could not help saying that had the Queen but taken care to secure them "spécialement" their Barrière, they would have been well satisfyed, and he still hopes by his eloquence to persuade my Lord Treasurer and you of the necessity there is that they should have that settled according to their famous treaty, before any other part of the negotiation is settled upon.

Buys pointed out that those, like himself, who suggested that they should come into the Queen's measures were "silenced by saying that they must be enemies of their country who could be for a peace, where not only was their Barrière not specifyed, but at the same time every reason imaginable was given them to believe it was designed to be taken from them". Nevertheless, Buys was of the opinion that many people "weary of the war would rather give up a town or two in the Barrière than risk

[1] Drummond to Heinsius from London, 8/19 Sept. 1711. Heinsius Archives, 51 A. N.R.A.

[2] Strafford to St John, 24 Oct. S.P.F.H. 240.

their entire ruin by keeping up a war against the Queen's inclinations" and believed "that even the Warrior Party" might be brought to accept this view.

This interview with Buys, who was genuinely pacific, led to a misunderstanding of the temper of the Republic. This may be seen from St John's letter to the Queen of the 17th of October (O.S.).[1] On receipt of Strafford's communication,

> a great consternation appeared at first in the Ministers of the States, but they have taken the Ply of acquiescing in Your Majesty's good pleasure, *and Mr Buys is instructed accordingly*. I find the fear of losing the exorbitant Barrier they have obtained is the greatest, if not the only check upon them, and that will soon be removed when they are appraised of Your Majesty's generous conduct and kind inclinations towards them.

This last passage refers to the proposals sent through Drummond to Heinsius in a letter of the 9th/20th of October.[2] The changes were to be made in order to protect English interests and to provide the compensation to France for the demolition of Dunkirk. "I fear", wrote Drummond, "that you will find the Equivalent that the French require for Dunkirk somewhat extravagant." England would never permit the States to garrison Nieuwport on account of the dangers to English trade. They must be content with Furnes, Ypres, Menin, Lille, Tournai, Ath, Mons, Namur, Charleroi and Upper Guelderland. A glance at the Townshend Treaty will show the significance of these changes: the disappearance of Condé, Valenciennes and Maubeuge might be looked on as an equivalent for Dunkirk, but Knocke, Nieuwport, Ghent, Dendermonde, Lier, Hal and Forts Perle, Philippe and Damme, towns of the Inner Barrier, were omitted because the Dutch might use their privileges there to frustrate English commercial competition. The addition of Ath and Mons, towns in the Outer Barrier, was poor compensation for so extensive a departure from the terms of the Townshend Treaty.

It was after this communication that on the 24th of October

[1] *Bol. Cor.* I, 412.

[2] Heinsius Archives, 51 A. This letter is partly quoted by Weber, p. 114.

the States General deliberated on their course of action. Although Strafford heard[1] that Heinsius made his report

with all the seeming impartiality imaginable...the cry was artificially spread that England would allow them no Bariere (*sic*)...that he would be an enemy to his country who would be for losing all the hopes for recompense they had for this war, in their Bariere.

Even Buys was carried away by the magnitude of the changes proposed in the Barrier and declared to Strafford that

there was not a man in the Republic would consent to send packets (passports for the congress) for the French Plenipotentiaries till they were assured of their Bariere and commerce.[2]

The States General resolved that the Mesnager convention was made in terms so general and so obscure ("si peu clair"), that they seemed a subject for lengthy consideration.

And Their High Mightinesses have strong apprehensions, that in entering into a formal negotiation with it as basis, the peace negotiations will be subject to delays, uncertainties and other great inconveniencies...for this reason Their High Mightinesses have ordered his Excellency M. Buys...to communicate their apprehensions to Her Majesty, and to make the representations necessary in an affair of such importance.[3]

Contrary to English expectations of acquiescence (which persisted despite this warning), Buys was sent to London to obstruct the negotiation instead of to facilitate it. His first object was to change the method of the negotiation to the old safeguard of 1709, of preliminary propositions.[4]

It was not so much the probable partition of the Spanish inheritance[5] as the curtailing of the Barrier Treaty which made the Dutch return to the preliminaries of 1709. The Treaty had been the price of their continuance in a war for which, since the re-conquest of the Southern Netherlands, they had lost all

[1] Strafford to St John enclosing the Resolution of the States General of 24 Oct., 24 Oct. S.P.F.H. 240.

[2] Strafford to St John, 24 Oct. S.P.F.H. 240.

[3] *Ibid.* enclosed by Strafford.

[4] Cf. De Torcy, *Mémoires*, p. 84. "Les Préliminaires de 1709...étoient regardés comme une règle dont les Etats Généraux ne pouvoient s'écarter sans risquer la ruine de leur pays, et l'assujettissement de toute l'Europe à la puissance de la maison de la France."

[5] They had, it will be recollected, been not unfavourable to a partition since Geertruidenberg.

interest, and by which they stood to lose, the more it interrupted trade.

"The first question I was asked", reported Strafford after a conference on the 26th of October,[1] "and what indeed is all in all (was) what! is there not a Treaty which might have been mentioned as the Bariere for us, and former Preliminaries of Peace in which our Bariere was specified?" Later he added, "I will be answerable that if you will sattisfy them in the Bariere they desire, and in their Tariff, they care not how general France is to all the rest of the Allies". He then warned St John that Buys would attempt to make the Queen desist from a congress until Dutch interests were secured precisely. He perceived that the Dutch position was weak, since De Torcy refused to negotiate with them and the Emperor was irritated by the demands made upon him in the Barrier Treaty. "If you seem resolute upon your measures", continued Strafford, "and (show) that you won't be amused, you may bring them to anything in spight of the intreagues of those at home, who would buoy up a party here, and make them believe that if they stand out, they will gain their point."

Despite his advice to Heinsius "to entrust Mons. Buys so fully of what they may give up and what they think absolutely necessary to insist on, that no delay might be pretended for further instructions",[2] Strafford realised that the Grand Pensionary was in a dangerous position: "It were well", he advised St John,[3] "that the Dutch knew immediately what Bariere and Tarif for the security of their commerce could be obtained, and then the cry of their being no Bariere designed for them would be stopped in advance". Heinsius had been responsible for the continuation of the war in order to gain the Townshend Treaty and it was difficult for him to abandon it. Strafford noticed at the Conference of the 26th of October that "the Pensionary's discourse was as well to justify himself to his Brethren as to me, that he was sincerely for a peace".[4]

The next letter which Heinsius received from Drummond

[1] To St John. S.P.F.H. 240.

[2] Strafford to St John, 26 Oct. S.P.F.H. 240.

[3] *Ibid.* 30 Oct.

[4] *Ibid.* 26 Oct.

was, however, still less reassuring. Drummond was requested to warn the Dutch that if the Townshend Treaty became known, there would be a popular outcry in England. Neither the Queen nor her Ministers would be able to prevent the ruin of Townshend, since they did not approve of the Treaty, nor did the party of the Duke of Marlborough. Finally, wrote Drummond,[1] England was determined on a speedy peace, and if the Dutch refused to send the passports for French Plenipotentiaries, the Queen would make her own peace in England.

It was true that Louis XIV had offered to negotiate on English soil,[2] but, as has been pointed out,[3] the Ministry were unable to accept the offer, on account of the danger of a revulsion of feeling in favour of the Whigs.

Heinsius was aware that the Ministry was not yet strong, particularly in the House of Lords. He decided, therefore, to play a waiting game. Buys was given no authority to grant passports, nor was he instructed to determine a meeting place for the Congress, or to change the Barrier Treaty. His powers with regard to the Barrier were merely to inquire into English grievances. In only one sense were his instructions positive; he was to propose the method of negotiation by preliminary propositions. At the same time he was charged to find out if the Ministry had made any agreement in the interests of England with De Torcy.[4]

Buys needed little persuasion to undertake this task, although he had formerly worked for peace. He and Heinsius were united to preserve the Barrier.[5] The States General were determined not to yield the passports until the Treaty had been saved.

III

From the despatches of Strafford during the month of October 1711 it was clear to the Ministry that they could have enlisted the Dutch on their side if they would agree to retain the Barrier Treaty. "'Tis there the Shoo pinches", wrote Strafford.[6]

[1] 16/27 Oct. Heinsius Archives, 51 A.
[2] De Torcy, *Mémoires*, p. 84.
[3] Cf. p. 218.
[4] Weber, p. 125.
[5] Weber, p. 126.
[6] To St John, 4 Nov. S.P.F.H. 240.

If the Tories had agreed to this, they would have cut the ground from the feet of the Whigs and greatly strengthened their own position. To force the Dutch to change the Treaty was to run the risk of cabals against themselves, but this they decided to hazard, rather than share the Assiento with the Republic or allow the Dutch so strong a position in the Southern Netherlands.

For these reasons the struggle to assemble the Congress turned upon the Barrier Treaty. Without it the Dutch determined not to grant the passports, while the Ministry was equally determined that the Dutch should first consent to the Congress and then modify the Barrier in order that England might avoid the odium of openly repudiating the Treaty.

When Mesnager left London for France on the 13th of November, St John requested that he would elicit French proposals for the Barrier. Mesnager objected that the Dutch would abuse any show of compliance. "We have often informed them", replied St John,[1] "that after the enormous expenditure which England has made, she considers herself to have the right to form the Barrier they claim. It is not to our advantage that the Barrier should be so extensive or so strong." It remained to be seen whether England or the States would win in the struggle.

Buys arrived at the end of October to plead the claims of his country. The interviews between the Dutch Ambassador and the Ministers and the audience with the Queen have been so fully described in *Der Friede von Utrecht*[2] that their contents may be briefly summarised here. First Buys demanded negotiation by preliminary propositions: next he demanded to know the precise terms of the equivalent for Dunkirk. This, wrote St John,[3] would be hotly disputed, "since Holland will think it hard to have a town or two less in the Barrier on account of the demolition of Dunkirk: and since Britain will be apt to complain if this thorn should not be taken out of their side for the sake of giving one more town to the Dutch".

[1] De Torcy, *Mémoires*, p. 77.
[2] Weber, p. 126 *et seq.* 22, 24, 30, Oct. (O.S.).
[3] St John to Strafford. *Bol. Cor.* I, 427.

Buys asked what preparations the English were making for a renewal of the war in the spring and spoke of his masters' desire to make a new alliance to subsist in time of peace between the Maritime Powers. St John listened with a seeming deference, which deceived Buys into thinking that it was still within his power to change the policy of the Ministry.

In the meantime Heinsius was informed, through the medium of Drummond, that the English could not understand why Buys displayed no powers to change the Barrier Treaty, as they were persuaded that the Dutch could never wish to maintain a treaty which would prejudice relations between the Maritime Powers. Drummond concluded by earnestly desiring the Pensionary to direct his countrymen to acquiesce in the Queen's plans.[1]

The conflicting reports of Buys and Drummond made it hard for Heinsius to decide between compliance and resistance. If he chose the latter, he might improve relations with the Emperor who was enraged not only by Anglo-French negotiations, but by the dismissal of his minister in England for prematurely publishing the Mesnager Convention, which he had been shown in confidence.[2] Nevertheless, the Emperor had not encouraged Heinsius to think that he would be favourable to the Townshend Treaty. As a result, on the 7th of November Strafford noticed the first signs of weakening on the part of the Dutch. He received a visit from Slingelandt, one of the party which was in close touch with the Whigs.[3] Slingelandt "went so far (as) to own there were severall things the Austrians objected to against the Treaty of Barrier which ought to be changed and...perhaps the States might desist from Bon; nor a town or two more or less in the Barrier be of great consequence, nor enough to break off the rest". Strafford took the occasion to remark once more, on the unfair character of the Treaty in which the Dutch obtained everything and the Queen little or nothing. "'Twas not ours, but the fault of your own Ministers they asked no more for you", was the reply of Slingelandt.[4]

[1] Drummond to Heinsius, 26 Oct./6 Nov. Heinsius Archives, 51 A.

[2] Cf. Coxe, *Life of Marlborough*, III, 253.

[3] Slingelandt and Townshend were on confidential terms. Their correspondence is at the N.R.A., The Hague.

[4] Strafford to St John, 7 Nov. S.P.F.H. 240.

On the same day, Van der Dussen, too, showed a disposition to better relations with England. He apologised for the letter of remonstrance for changes in the Ministry written by the States General to the Queen.[1]

Three days later, on the 10th of November, Strafford observed that Heinsius was "down o' the mouth", in consequence of a letter from Buys, who had not "such hopes for the success of his Rhetorick as when he left this place".[2] The interviews with Oxford on the 30th of October (O.S.) and on the 2nd of November (O.S.) had convinced Buys that it was impossible to impede the concert between France and England. If they were to gain anything, the States must give way on the method of negotiation and join forces with England, since their present isolation was becoming dangerous.[3]

The Ministry combined persuasion with force and offered on the 2nd/13th of November[4] the tariff of 1664, if the Dutch would agree to a Barrier "which would not make their best friends jealous".

Meanwhile feeling in the Republic was still high. In a resolution of the Council of Amsterdam on the seven preliminary articles signed by Mesnager, they "unanimously resolved to oppose as much as possible...peace...upon the foot...of the said preliminaries".[5] The Dutch felt that by yielding to England they might lose their independence.[6]

This attitude was fostered by the Emperor and the Whigs. Marlborough and Cadogan were at The Hague. Eugene was shortly expected.[7] "The King of Spain does all he can", wrote Strafford.[8]

From Milan Charles despatched a sharp letter to the States in which he denounced the Mesnager Convention as inadequate, and demanded Dutch support in holding out for a treaty on

[1] Strafford to St John, 7 Nov. S.P.F.H. 240.
[2] Strafford to St John, 10 Nov. *Ibid.*
[3] Weber, p. 129.
[4] Drummond to Heinsius. Heinsius Archives, 51 A.
[5] Dayrolles (Secretary at The Hague) to Tilson, 3 Nov. S.P.F.H. 238.
[6] See Appendix D, p. 376, in which a specimen of the type of pamphlet then in circulation is given.
[7] Strafford to St John, 15 Nov. S.P.F.H. 240.
[8] *Ibid.*

terms no other than the preliminaries of 1709.[1] This letter was at once presented along with a memorial by the Imperial Envoy, Count Goes.[2]

Still the Pensionary made no move: he spoke to Strafford "in the old tone of its being hard to make them agree to come in blindfold into a negotiation of a general peace upon such vague terms".[3] Strafford wrongly suspected that it was Buys who counselled resistance.[4] He was right in his judgment that Buys was determined to preserve the Barrier Treaty as far as possible, but he did not realise that Buys now believed that this could only be obtained by acquiescence in the demands of England.[5]

The English Ministry accused Buys of acting contrary to the instructions of his government, by withholding the passports for the French Plenipotentiaries and by counselling resistance to the demand for them. On both charges he must be acquitted, as may be seen by his report to the States of Holland on his return to The Hague,[6] and in the correspondence of Drummond. On the 4th/15th of December Drummond wrote to Heinsius that he was "of the opinion that a wrong has been done to His Excellency (Buys) and that he has explained himself as much as the States gave him instructions to do".[7]

On the 9th of November Buys suggested to St John that in the absence of instructions from his masters, he would draw up a plan of the alliance between the two countries. He offered to sign this "sub spe rati". St John made an evasive reply to this and to a further suggestion on the part of the Dutchman

[1] Printed in *Actes et Mémoires concernant la Paix d'Utrecht*, p. 1.

[2] *Ibid.* p. 216.

[3] Strafford to St John, 15 Nov. S.P.F.H. 240.

[4] *Ibid.* "I must advertise you that Buys, however he might be made easy in other things, is one of the most violent supporters of the Extensive Bariere of anyone in the whole Republic, so you must manage him accordingly." Cf. Strafford to St John, 24 Nov. S.P.F.H. 243. "I need not repeat to you the character of the man you so well know, you hear his words and I have told you I had it from a friend of his he is one of the most violent men in the country for the Extensive Bariere."

[5] Cf. p. 227.

[6] Gouda Archives, 14 Jan. 1712. Buys, in his report, referred to these charges and quoted from his correspondence with Fagel when in England, to show that he was blameless. His report was approved and he was thanked by the States for the conduct of his embassy.

[7] Drummond to Heinsius, 4/15 Dec. Heinsius Archives, 51 A.

that he should detail the changes desired in the Barrier Treaty.[1] It was St John's policy to obtain the passports first.

At The Hague, in obedience to instructions, Strafford made a final effort to extract the passports. On the 19th of November he handed in a Memorial to the States, demanding that they should without delay come in with the Queen's measures.[2]

Next Strafford turned his attention to particular Deputies; those of Guelderland were obstinate and the Deputies of Overyssell, Groningen and Zeeland—whom Strafford suspected of being in the pay of the Emperor—were instructed not to consent until the States General was unanimous.[3] On the morning of the 21st of November he had an interview with a Deputy from Guelders, in which they came "to pritty high words", and Strafford "thought it necessary to use all his fierté against him". Later in the day Strafford despatched a peremptory note to Heinsius, saying that England could wait no longer and that the States must at once come to a decision.

Strafford's firm tone made an impression on the irresolute Pensionary. The latter was encouraged by Drummond and by the misguided Buys to believe that if the passports were sent, the Ministry would be more agreeable to the preservation of the Barrier Treaty, in essentials if not in detail.[4] On the afternoon of the 21st Heinsius and the recalcitrant Deputies withdrew behind locked doors. He emerged triumphant and a Resolution in compliance with the Queen's demands was taken. Utrecht was named as the meeting place of the Congress and the passports were despatched to Buys for presentation to the English Ministry.[5]

The news of this Resolution was received with joy by the Tory party. Tears came into the eyes of Mrs Masham: "God be thanked", she said, "that the States have made such a friendly Resolution. This will prolong the Queen's life". Oxford expressed his gratification, acknowledged that Strafford

[1] St John to Strafford, 9 Nov. (O.S.). *Bol. Cor.* I, 467.
[2] Klopp, XIV, 200.
[3] Strafford to St John, 21 Nov. S.P.F.H. 240.
[4] Cf. p. 227.
[5] Strafford to St John, 21 Nov. S.P.F.H. 240.

had used too harsh words to the Dutch and vowed that he should be instructed to be more agreeable in future.[1]

IV

As the States General had bowed to the wishes of the Queen, they expected that the Ministry would become more explicit as regards their policy, in particular with regard to the Barrier. Strafford shared this view.

You say (he wrote to St John[2])...that Buys was not very well able to defend your objections to the Barrier Treaty. I should be mighty glad to hear from you what are these objections, and I do believe I could make use of them to H.M. service. I am often in discourse on the matter, and when they cry to me, what do you think fit for our Bariere, we don't care it should be so extensive, and perhaps we shall be easier than you imagin upon it, *but let us know some Bariere you design us*.

The Deputy Goslinga, with tears in his eyes, declared that he had not slept all night on account of the charge that he had betrayed his country. Strafford assured him that the Queen would secure the demands of all the Allies except the recalcitrant Emperor. "I really take this to be the true plan your Lordship has set down," he wrote to Oxford,[3] "and that you will do all you can (that) this Republic should be sattisfyed."

Strafford was of the belief that his countrymen ought not to trust too much to the "bonne foi of France",[4] and pointed out that as the Ministry had promised "the free concert and communication of the Queen", if the States would send the passports, the States now awaited the communication of her intentions with regard to the Barrier. If the terms were reasonable, he was convinced that the Dutch "would act heartily with the Queen...but if it was otherwise, tho' they must and will submit to the Queen's negotiations yet they will do all they can to thwart it".[5]

This letter reached St John at a time when he was not in a

[1] Drummond to Heinsius, 17/28 Nov. Heinsius Archives, 51 A.

[2] 24 Nov. S.P.F.H. 243.

[3] Strafford to Oxford, 8 Dec. *Royal Hist. MSS. Comm. 15th Report*. Portland MSS. 9.

[4] *Ibid.*

[5] Strafford to St John, 24 Nov. S.P.F.H. 243.

position to make any reply. De Torcy's answer to his request for details on the Barrier fell short of even his expectations: "all he could say in his efforts to find them satisfactory, was that they were very obscure, but that he hoped to reach an end of all disputes".[1] Buys was aware of the arrival of De Torcy's offer: as it was not communicated to him, he readily deduced that it was unfavourable to the Republic.[2] Still worse, his next meeting with Oxford and St John convinced him that by yielding in the matter of the Congress, the Republic had not saved the Townshend Treaty.

Buys suggested the project of De Torcy, made in 1710.[3] This entitled the Dutch to Furnes, Poperingen, Lille, Condé and Maubeuge. He demanded in addition places which had since that time been conquered: Douai, Bethune, St Venant, Aire and Bouchain.

St John attacked the Treaty in three ways. While agreeing to the addition of the New Conquests, he was of the opinion that

> if we obtain for the barrier of the States from France, besides those towns belonging to Spain which they are to have (i.e. the Inner Barrier), Furnes, Ypres, Menin, Tournai, or even the first of these two last, together with the Chatellanies and counties belonging to them, we make a very good bargain, and such an one as the Dutch ought to be contented with.[4]

Privately St John hoped to gain more for the Dutch, but he was for the moment hindered by the French project, which he told Strafford in confidence, was "no manner of use".

In his conversation with Buys, St John did not communicate this opinion, but turned to another part of the Treaty to which he objected. The Queen would assist the States to obtain the garrisons in the Inner Barrier "provided such of them was excepted, as would render the trade of Britain to the Spanish Low Countries precarious, and even put it into the power of the States whenever they thought fit, to shut that door upon us".[5]

[1] Weber, p. 134. Cites *Bol. Cor.* I, 479.
[2] Weber, p. 135.
[3] St John to Strafford, 4 Dec. *Bol. Cor.* II, 39.
[4] St John to Strafford, 4 Dec. *Ibid.* 32.
[5] St John to Strafford, 4 Dec. *Ibid.*

Buys replied that on this pretext all the towns might be objectionable and desired to know what towns were to be excepted. The answer was Nieuwport, Ghent and Dendermonde. Buys pointed out that Nieuwport had been substituted for Ostend in the Treaty of 1709, and maintained that one or other was necessary to prevent attack by sea. Ghent and Dendermonde were required to preserve communication between the Outer Barrier and the Dutch Republic. He argued that an Outer and an Inner Barrier were necessary and that the fortresses had been chosen by their best generals, who were the best judges of military security—an innuendo against the wisdom of politicians. Finally, since the Maritime Powers were allies, a strong Barrier was as much for the security of England as for the Dutch Republic.[1] It was a repetition of the argument between Townshend and Heinsius, this time with the advantage to England. Neither side gave way and the problem was left unsolved until Utrecht.

St John's third objection to the Treaty concerned the injuries to English trade: these have been explained in a previous chapter.[2] After prolonged discussion, Buys agreed that it was only just that these grievances should be removed[3]—if they existed, a matter on which he professed himself ignorant. He argued that they were no objection to Article XV of the Treaty as such, but were merely a question of the administration of the New Conquests.

The dominating factor in this acquiescence was the suggestion that when the Dutch came to treat on the Barrier with the Emperor or the French they would require English support, which would not be forthcoming without "a previous and formal engagement that the subjects of Great Britain shall trade on as free and as advantageous a foot" as those of the Republic.[4] The question of Nieuwport, Ghent and Dendermonde was again brought forward: Buys hoped "that the Queen would not from imaginary fears expose the States to a real danger". St John replied that the retention of those towns would be "An eternal

[1] Buys to Fagel, 15 Dec. Legatie Archief, 74. N.R.A.

[2] Chap. I (Part II).

[3] *Bol. Cor.* II, 38.

[4] St John to Strafford, 4 Dec. *Bol. Cor.* II, 40.

ball of dissension between the two Nations", and argued that the plea for security was founded on "panick terror", on which grounds the Dutch might as well claim Antwerp while they were about it. Since the country was to belong to an ally, "the States ought to have whatever is really essential to the security of their Barrier against France, but no more".[1]

V

By their capitulation to the Ministry's desires, the Dutch had gained nothing. The Barrier Treaty was attacked in England and the only possible alternative, approach to the Emperor, seemed excluded by their participation in the arrangements for the Congress.

On receipt of this news, the Emperor had written an angry letter to the States, in which he expressed his displeasure at their desertion[2]. In the conferences of the Allies, Strafford remarked that the pro-Austrian party in the Republic disliked his frequent reference to the concert of the Maritime Powers.[3]

In this situation the Dutch had little chance of obtaining their Barrier. Their only hope lay now in the overthrow of the Tory Ministry. All eyes at The Hague were turned to the coming session of Parliament.

In the beginning of December, Strafford learned that reports of the Ministry's instability were sent by Buys. "He draws false inferences from several...things, as that of the Parliament being prorogued to be a sign that the Ministers know they won't approve what they have done."[4] In the opinion of Buys, if the States had only delayed the resolution to send the passports, "the very mob would have...obliged the Ministers to have assured the States of the entire Bariere as settled by my Lord Townshend, besides the Parliament would have forced them to it".[5]

It was natural that these reports should prejudice the Ministry

[1] *Bol. Cor.* II, 40.
[2] Strafford to St John, 2 Dec. S.P.F.H. 243.
[3] Strafford to St John, 8 Dec. *Ibid.*
[4] Strafford to St John, 8 Dec., on the authority of "the most dear and intimate friend of Buys". *Ibid.*
[5] *Ibid.*

against Buys, although as has been shown, the latter had advised the States General to acquiesce in English policy. This did not prevent him from hoping that the Tory party would be defeated when the peace negotiations were brought before Parliament. "We are not deceived," wrote St John on the 30th of November (O.S.), "they want to know our secret and engage the Queen... (and) appear to negotiate, to see what Parliament will do, and the effect of Whig Cabals."[1] Buys was as hopeful as any, but he was not as Strafford insinuated,[2] an active participant in Whig intrigues.

The "plot", as the Tories called it, centred round the reply of the Elector of Hanover to the Ministry's communication of negotiations with France. The Elector's opposition was not due, as the Whigs represented, to fear for the Protestant Succession, but to the dangers anticipated from the cession of the Spanish crown to a Bourbon.[3] The Memorial in which the Elector stated his views recommended a closer union with the Emperor and gave unqualified approval of a strong Barrier for the Dutch.[4]

With this document Bothmar was despatched from Hanover to England. On his arrival he communicated the terms of the Memorial to the Whigs and to Hoffman, the Austrian Minister. Buys was also taken into the secret, but he did not approve of the terms of the document. This was consistent with his longing for peace, to obtain which he had always been willing to

[1] To Strafford. *Bol. Cor.* II, 26.

[2] Strafford to St John, 7/18 Dec. S.P.F.H. 243. "The party (i.e. the Whigs) in England is strongly knotted with them here, and no stone will be left unturned to baffle what you have undertaken: I have alarmed some to-day against the behaviour of Buys who, though he wishes for peace, is made, unknown to himself, their tool for carrying on the war." The charge against Buys was unjust, as will be seen in the part he played in the presentation of the Bothmar Memorial.

[3] Cf. Salomon, pp. 116–22.

[4] Klopp, XIV, 688, App. 8. Bothmar Memorial, Art. V. "Il sera bon de désabuser ceux qui s'imaginent que la Barrière aux Pays Bas ne regarde que la sûreté de la Hollande, et de leur faire comprendre qu'elle regard tout autant celle de la Grande Bretagne, laquelle ne se trouverait pas moins en danger que la Hollande, si la France devenoit maîtresse des Pays Bas. C'est une verité qui a esté reconnue de tout les temps par les bons Anglois, et mesme sous le règne de Charles II lequel, malgré ses liaisons avec cette Couronne, ne voulut pas permettre qu'elle en fist la Conqueste, de sorte que la Barrière qui ferme à ce dangereux ennemi l'entrée aux Pays Bas est un intérêt commun aux deux Puissances Maritimes."

partition the Spanish inheritance. Nor was he instructed by the States General to participate in the publication of the Memorial,[1] therefore the Ministry's accusation of complicity was wholly unfounded. It is significant that some days before Parliament met, it was the gossip of London that "the Whigs begin to rail at Mr Buys, and make him a sort of Monster, calling him a Tory Dutchman".[2]

The Ministry instructed Drummond to inform the Dutch that they were confident of success when parliament met; they had heard, wrote Drummond,[3] that Buys was working against peace. It were better that the States General should be informed that the Lord Treasurer expected a majority of 40 in the House of Lords, and 200 in the House of Commons, in favour of peace. If the Dutch did not oppose peace, they would be given Douai, Valenciennes,[4] Furnes, Ypres, Menin, Lille and Tournai from France: Luxemburg, Charleroi, Namur and "good communications" in the Spanish Netherlands. The Ministry were gravely displeased at the lack of confidence on the part of Buys. All foreign Ministers were warned to trust the party in power and not to pay attention to the cabals of the Whigs.

Strafford feared the effects of St John's attitude to the Barrier. He hoped to pacify the Dutch until parliament had taken its resolution on the peace, but in his opinion it would be better if he were to negotiate with Heinsius on the Barrier, rather than that the Ministry should lose time in argument with Buys, "the greatest stickler" for the Townshend Treaty.[5]

St John replied that Strafford might elicit what Heinsius and Goslinga were willing to yield, while Her Majesty would do the like with France. "Her part in this affair is that of a mediator",[6] he concluded. This was a retraction from Her Majesty's promise to guarantee the terms of the Barrier Treaty.

The attention of the Allies was now directed to the English

[1] Salomon, p. 138.

[2] Peter Wentworth to Strafford, 25 Nov. (O.S.). *Wentworth Papers*, ed. Cartwright.

[3] Drummond to Heinsius, 4/15 Dec. Heinsius Archives, 51 A.

[4] St John to Strafford. *Bol. Cor.* II. Valenciennes had been reincluded in the Barrier by St John as a concession to Buys on 4 Dec.

[5] Strafford to St John, 11 Dec. S.P.F.H. 243.

[6] St John to Strafford, 4 Dec. *Bol. Cor.* II, 31.

parliament. On the 6th of December (O.S.) the Bothmar Memorial was published in the Whig *Daily Courant*. The time was well chosen: parliament was to meet on the day following. It is possible that the Ministry would have carried the day had it not been for the surprising coalition of one section of the Tories with the Whigs. The disgruntled Tories were led by Lord Nottingham, whose expectations had been in various ways disappointed by the Ministers. Out of revenge, he agreed to support the Whig amendment against peace, if, in return, the Whigs would vote for his Occasional Conformity Bill. After some hesitation, Marlborough, who had returned to England from The Hague, agreed to join the Whigs[1] and the Nottingham Tories.

The result of this intrigue was the carrying of the Whigs' amendment that no peace should be made which gave Spain to a member of the House of Anjou, by 62–54 votes in the Lords. This blow was by no means compensated by the defeat of the amendment in the Commons, by a majority of 126. The Ministry was now in a grave position. Its continuation in power depended upon peace. The peace negotiations rested on the understanding of a partition of the Spanish dominions and this understanding was imperilled by the vote in the House of Lords.

The coolness of the Lord Treasurer saved the situation: it was he who bolstered up the feeble Queen and persuaded her to stand firmly against a Whig or a mixed Ministry. Both De Torcy[2] and Heinsius[3] were informed that the Tories would maintain their ascendancy, but the more excitable St John betrayed his nervousness in a letter to Strafford,[4] written a few days previous to that of the Lord Treasurer to Heinsius.

For God's sake, my Lord, speak to those on whom you judge it will have a good effect: tell them plainly that they are upon a wrong track: that their Minister here mistakes; that we have promised and will perform all they can ask relating to their Barrier and their Trade, and that Monsieur Buys is very unfair in his proceedings if he has not told them so much: but that we proceed in some respects

[1] Salomon, p. 125.
[2] St John to De Torcy, 15/26 Dec. *Bol. Cor.* vol. II.
[3] Oxford to Heinsius, 15/26 Dec. Cf. Weber, p. 137.
[4] 12 Dec. (O.S.). *Bol. Cor.* vol. II.

on a new scheme of politics: that this country comes more and more to its senses: and that the single dispute now is whether they (the Dutch) will join the faction against the Queen, or with the Nation for her.

The Whigs, Buys and Bothmar were indiscriminately blamed.

Your Excellency will please...to speak of this event as produced by a trick (wrote St John in a firmer letter[1]) and one which will turn upon the contrivers of it and upon the actors in it. You will please to show great dryness and reserve to the Pensionary and the Dutch Ministers, letting them know the Queen thinks herself ill-treated.

He concluded by affirming the Queen's resolution to stand fast, even if it meant a separate peace.

Buys now incriminated himself by taking advantage of the confusion to propose that England and the States General should sign a separate article in which they should enumerate the conditions which were a *sine qua non* of peace.[2] In this way he incurred the stigma of participation in the plot, from which he undoubtedly sought to extract an advantage to his country.

St John was not to be frightened into such a proposal and coldly replied that the Queen had neither time nor inclination for such an engagement and that she expected "some satisfaction to those objections upon that infamous Treaty of Barrier" before she could tie herself to the Dutch.[3]

The Lord Treasurer was no less severe: he told Buys that since the Allies "had encouraged an impotent attack on the Queen and the Nation, they must reap the fruits of it and make the peace for themselves, but they should not (as was their aim), make one for Britain". Finally, he said it was impossible for him to do anything more on behalf of the Dutch: "for myself," he said, "I had endeavoured to keep everything fair and easy during the war...but their intrigues had made my moderation unpracticable".[4]

Oxford had previously pursued a more moderate policy

[1] St John to Strafford, 8/19 Dec. *Bol. Cor.* vol. II.
[2] Cf. Weber, p. 141.
[3] St John to Strafford, 12/23 Dec. S.P.F.H. 240.
[4] Oxford to Strafford, 8/19 Dec. *Bol. Cor.* vol. II, 50.

towards the Dutch[1]: now he went over completely to the side of St John. His firm tone alarmed Buys, who delivered up the passports for the safe conduct of the French Plenipotentiaries on the 12th of December, despite the opportunity for delay.

The final triumph of the Ministry over the Whig party was achieved by the creation of twelve Peers, which restored the balance of the House of Lords in their favour. On the same day Marlborough was deprived of all his offices. From these blows the strength of the Whigs never recovered throughout the peace negotiations, and the Ministry was able to pursue its policy successfully, despite further cabals on the part of the Opposition and the Allies.

VI

On the 28th of December (O.S.) Buys took leave of the Queen, who presented him with £1000, double the sum usually presented to an Envoy Extraordinary. St John hoped this would please him[2]; since Buys was to play an important part in the negotiations at Utrecht, it was advisable to soften his memories of his stay in England. In his final interview with the Lords of the Council Buys was unable to penetrate the secrets of the Ministry's intentions with regard to his country. The conversation was diverted to the more congenial task of complaining of the Emperor's deficiencies and the Minister parted with "the greatest civility on both sides".[3] Despite these civilities, Buys returned from his embassy with the bitter consciousness of defeat. He had not prevented the assembly of the peace congress: he had not saved the Barrier Treaty: "all he brought with him was a worthless document reaffirming the Alliance between the Maritime Powers".[4]

The prestige of the United Provinces was lowered by this defeat. The step which led them to grant the passports to England alienated the sympathies of the Emperor. Their grudging submission, and the sympathy between Heinsius and

[1] Cf. his efforts to send Halifax as Ambassador instead of Strafford and suggestion that the peace negotiations of April 1711 should take the form of a resumption of negotiations at Geertruidenberg.

[2] St John to Strafford, 28 Dec. S.P.F.H. 241.

[3] St John to Strafford, 28 Dec. *Bol. Cor.* II, 109.

[4] Weber, p. 143.

the Whig leaders left the Tory Ministry with a feeling of resentment. The States were thus more firmly tied to an ally whom, as the history of the next few months proved, they did not intend to trust.

Buys now determined to save what he could of the Barrier Treaty. He realised that in the Southern Netherlands, Dutch ascendancy would not be permitted to the extent promised in the Treaty of 1709. There was one part of the Treaty, however, which would be of great advantage to his own town if he could secure its execution. This was the promise, in Article XV, that the two parties would share all private advantages granted in the Spanish dominions. This entitled the Dutch to a share in the Assiento, which had been secured for England by the secret agreement with France in 1711.

Before he left England, Buys had made one attempt to make sure of this benefit. During the insecurity which followed the vote of the House of Lords on the 7th of December, he suggested to the Tories that upon condition that they would yield to the Dutch "half the advantage of trade" which they were to have, he would procure a resolution of the States counter to that of the House of Lords. "This is a meanness", wrote St John indignantly to Strafford,[1] "which those who have the honour to serve the Queen are incapable of submitting to. Let the peace be a good one for Holland, but let it be most advantageous for Britain, who suffered most by the war." In reply to this letter, Strafford forwarded an *Amsterdam Gazette*, from which it was plain "that these people, thinking themselves secure that England designs them a Bariere and Tarif, are now looking out for some advantage in the West Indies".[2]

A few days later Strafford reported that "everyone has it in their mouths that England must let them in for half their advantage in the West Indian Trade, or else they must loose (lose) the negotiation out of their hands and then this state will have it in theirs, and those Patriot Lords may see the service they have done their country by their hearty advice".[3]

[1] 15/26 Dec. *Bol. Cor.* II, 76.
[2] Strafford to St John, 1 Jan. 1712. S.P.F.H. 243.
[3] Strafford to St John, 5 Jan. 1712. *Ibid.*

Buys had received the impression that the Tory Ministry would not survive the next session.[1] A year later he confessed to Drummond that he had been misled by the tone of the debate in the House of Lords, from which he "believed that the Queen and her Ministry would give them any terms to take the declaration of King Philip's continuing on the throne on them".[2] Believing that they could not carry out their intentions without Dutch co-operation, his hopes for preserving some parts of the Townshend Treaty rose again.

Strafford summed up the situation in a letter to the Lord Treasurer[3]:

> The Dutch are easily freightened, and mightily dejected and humble when they are so; and they do as easily conceive hopes and grow sanguine, and then are as much delighted as they were depressed before: they then fall to the play which they like best, which is making use of the conjuncture, to screw all things to their own particular advantage, and to hinder what they can, the encrease of power or commerce to their rival, as they undoubtedly take Great Britain to be.

[1] Strafford to St John, 15 Jan. 1712. S.P.F.H. 243. "He told me plainly that the party of the Whigs would be much stronger than that of the Tories before the end of the next session."

[2] Drummond to Oxford, 25 Oct. 1712. Portland MSS.

[3] Strafford to Oxford, 5 Jan. 1712. Portland MSS.

CHAPTER IV

The Repudiation of the Townshend Treaty

I

On the 29th of January 1712, after some disputes as to procedure, the Congress of Utrecht was opened. Hitherto the English Ministry had avoided all the difficulties of such extensive negotiations, but now their troubles were to begin. It was the task of the English Plenipotentiaries to reconcile the demands of the Allies to a comprehensive scheme and to force the Dutch to revise the Barrier Treaty. France, whose sole important ally was the Elector of Bavaria, saw that she might profit by this conflict of interests and all the skill of Louis and De Torcy was called into play to isolate the Allies by exciting jealousies amongst them. Their task was simplified by the natural resentment of all the Allies against England, who had assembled the Congress after privately arranging terms for herself.

If the negotiations at Utrecht were prolonged until the opening of the new campaign, the Tories would have difficulties in London as well as at Utrecht. The disposal of the Spanish crown and the Barrier were two of the chief aims of the war and they had been left unsettled by the Mesnager Conventions.[1] If the Opposition could prove that the new Ministry had in any way neglected these interests they might bring the people to their side again, defeat the Tories and resume the war.

Until the question of the Spanish Succession was settled the Tories were not strong enough at Utrecht to impose a new Barrier on the Dutch. It is therefore necessary to indicate

[1] Cf. p. 214 *note* 1. On the disposal of the Spanish crown the two parties bound themselves "to take just and reasonable measures to prevent the union of the Crowns of France and Spain in the person of one Prince"; i.e. no conclusion as to the successor to the Spanish crown was made—it might be Philip or it might not. Similarly the Dutch Barrier was not defined, nor were the towns which Louis would cede to augment the fortresses in the Spanish Netherlands.

briefly the stages of Anglo-French negotiations on account of their influence on the Barrier settlement.

When the Congress opened, Strafford and his colleague, the Lord Privy Seal, were unaware of the real intentions of the Ministry. Their instructions were supplemented week by week, according to the progress of negotiations between St John and De Torcy.[1] As to the Barrier, St John had already received indication that De Torcy might make unsatisfactory proposals[2]; when the French terms came on the 11th of February the Ministry was dismayed by their disregard of the interests of the Allies. It was in part the result of the desertion of the Allies by the leader of the Coalition; further, since the Ministers had met with the reverse in December, Louis was ready to take advantage of their temporary weakness to raise his demands.[3]

Louis proposed that the Archduke should renounce his claim to Spain in favour of Philip: in return, Philip was to give up Naples, Milan and Sardinia. Not only did Louis now withhold Strasbourg from the Barrier of the Empire, but he also demanded Tournai and Lille, two strongholds of the Netherlands frontier as well as Aire, St Venant, Douai and Bouchain to complete the Barrier of France. These proposals aroused consternation at Utrecht.

The English had to make the best of the situation. At the suggestion of Lord Oxford, Gaultier was told to notify his master that the Queen was pacifically inclined; if Louis would make an offer more palatable than that of the 11th of February the Ministry would secure from Parliament the presentation of a petition to the Queen for a peace on such a basis. After this the Allies would have to come in, or fight alone in the new campaign.[4]

The deaths in the French royal family, which now occurred, necessitated a change in policy. The Duke of Burgundy died on the 18th of February and the death of his eldest son on the 8th of March, left one life, that of Louis' sickly great-grandson, between Philip and the throne of France. After some deliberation, Oxford and St John decided that the claims of Orleans

[1] Cf. Salomon, pp. 140–1.
[2] Cf. p. 231.
[3] Cf. Salomon, p. 141.
[4] Cf. Salomon, p. 141.

and Berry were insufficient as a safeguard against Philip if he should desire to gain the throne of France. Accordingly, Philip should decide between the two crowns: if he chose to wait for the succession to the throne of France, the Spanish crown, with the Indies, might be given to the Duke of Savoy. The possessions of the Duke, with the inclusion of Sicily, would then be transferred to Philip. Should Philip succeed to France, Sicily would be ceded to the Emperor, but he might add the remainder of his new possessions to France. This project was conceived by Lord Oxford: in his opinion there was little chance that Philip would reject France on such terms and, in sending the scheme to the Ambassador from the Court of Turin, Oxford did not even mention the possibility of an alternative.[1]

The scheme was then broached to the Emperor through Eugene. The Prince, while vetoing the alternative that Philip should be King of Spain, was not unfavourable to the elevation of Savoy. In his account of this negotiation, Salomon, refutes the theory of Weber that these negotiations "were only to amuse the Emperor" and were never seriously intended.[2] Salomon bases his assertion on the fact that Oxford did not calculate that Philip would chose the crown of Spain. It will be seen in the course of the Barrier negotiations that Oxford had an additional reason for approaching the Emperor: he wished to prevent a rapprochement between Vienna and The Hague by which the Barrier Treaty would be settled without English intervention. With this in view, it was scarcely likely that he would take the risk of offending the Emperor at this time by proposing a settlement which he did not intend to execute.

Finally, the scheme would be pleasing to the House of Lords; in December a resolution had been carried in which it was declared that no peace should be made which gave Spain to a member of the House of Anjou.

These negotiations continued until April 1712 when De Torcy gave a favourable reply. In the meantime we must turn to the Barrier negotiations during these months.

[1] Salomon, p. 145.
[2] Salomon, p. 146 and Weber, p. 270.

II

"There is a spirit of habitude among our Allies", observed Strafford to St John,[1] "to impose what they can upon us, and when they see they can't, to submit." It was in this frame of mind that the English approached the Dutch.

The Queen's instructions[2] regarding the States fall into two sections: the first concerned the commerce of the Republic. The Dutch were to be granted a favourable tariff, that of 1664, with France; further, they were to be given commercial privileges of the Treaty of Ryswick and the exemption of the toll of 50 pence per ton on Dutch vessels trading to French ports.

As to the Barrier, the Plenipotentiaries were to insist "that the Most Christian King do yield...Furnes, Ft Knocke, Menin, Ypres, Lille, Tournai, Condé, Valenciennes, Maubeuge, as likewise Douai, Bethune, Aire and St Venant...to be garrisoned in such manner as is or shall be agreed on between us and the States General or others concerned."

These gains were not to be secured unconditionally to the Republic: under the guise of "explanations", parts of the Townshend Treaty were to be greatly altered.

You are, however, (continued the instructions) to take especial care not to suffer these Articles in favour of the States General to be concluded, until the Treaty of Succession and Barrier be so explained as to remove those apprehensions which we have as to the consequence of it in some points...Whereas by the Treaty of Barrier the Commerce of these our kingdoms to the Spanish Netherlands, and to such places as shall by the virtue of the said Treaty accrue to the said States General, is exposed to be lost, or at least to become precarious: and whereas the Sieur Buys, their Envoy Extraordinary, has himself acknowledged the reasonableness of our apprehensions, and the justice there is that we should be secured against any prejudice which we have reason to fear may arise to us from those great accessions which they have, at the expense of the Blood and Treasure of Our subjects, acquired, You are therefore...to insist that Nieuwport, Dendermonde, the Castle of Ghent and such other places as appear to be rather a barrier against us than against France, be either not put in the hands of the Dutch, or such expedients be found for the doing thereof, as may secure the Ingress and Egress of Our

[1] 8 Jan. 1712. S.P.F.H. 243. [2] 23 Dec. 1711. *Bol. Cor.* II, 96.

subjects in all the Low Countries as fully and effectually as if the said Barrier had not been granted to the States General.

The intent of the Ministry was clear: they would guarantee the Barrier to be won from Louis and the Emperor, only if they received such securities. A later passage in the instructions ordered

that special provision be made that our subjects may not suffer in their commerce by any omission in the 15th Article of the said Barrier Treaty: that it be expressly stipulated that the subjects of these Our Kingdoms shall trade as free, with the same advantages and privileges, and under the same impositions and no other, as they used to do when those places were in the hands of France or Spain, or as the subjects of the States General themselves have done, or shall at any time hereafter do.

In furtherance of the removal of these grievances, which will be dealt with in a later chapter,[1] St John had for some weeks been in close touch with the Commissioners for Trade and Plantations, who, at his instructions, had summoned merchants to report upon their treatment in the Barrier towns.[2] For a second reason, which was not mentioned in the instructions, the English wished to change Article XV. They did not intend to share the Assiento with the Dutch and they accordingly wished to drop the clause by which Townshend had consented that each party should share new commercial privileges with the other.

As a final precaution, the instructions contained the provision that the Dutch might garrison any additional fortresses in the Spanish Netherlands, not as in the Townshend Treaty, "in case

[1] Cf. pp. 311 *et seq.* The Provisional Regulation.

[2] See *Journal for the Commissioners of Trade and Plantations*, C.O. 391/22, p. 30, 10 Dec. 1711. "Mr Levinus Dorpere attending as he had been desired, and being asked what New Custom Houses had been erected, and what new duties the Dutch had laid or exacted upon the trade and manufactures of Great Britain going out of the Spanish Low Countries into the New Conquests, which they are possessed of by the Barrier Treaty, he communicated to their Lordships an order of the Council of State of Flanders relating to the said duties, which he thought by computation might amount to about 8 per cent." Cf. 18 Dec. and 21 Jan. 1712. When "Levinus Dorpere presented a Memorial...of what he judges will be advantageous to the Trade of Flanders". 4 Feb. Report on the State of British Trade in foreign parts from Consuls, for Ostend and Bruges.

of apparent attack", but in the special event of "apparent attack on the part of France".

These instructions have been given in detail as it is necessary to emphasize their resemblance to the Project of the Second Barrier Treaty, which was sent to the Republic in December 1712. After a year of negotiations, the Dutch obtained precisely what St John had decided upon for them in December 1711, with the exception of certain towns in the Outer Barrier which Louis would not yield to them.

III

Since an agreement on the Barrier between the Maritime Powers would expedite and simplify negotiations with France, Strafford attempted to settle the matter before he left The Hague for Utrecht. On the 8th of January he approached Heinsius with the suggestion that before the opening of the Congress they might agree as to the Barrier and tariff. To his disappointment, he met with an evasive reply: the Pensionary preferred to wait till Utrecht, when both Buys and Bristol would have arrived from England.[1]

Arrived at Utrecht, the first business of the English Plenipotentiaries was to confer with the Dutch[2] on "Essentials of our Negotiation".[3] The differences of opinion on the Barrier Treaty were at once revealed and the Conference lasted seven or eight hours without result. "Buys, my lord," wrote Strafford to Oxford after it was over,[4] "shows his and his country's meaning but too clear, which is having surprised us in the Barrier Treaty they will try to keep us to it."

The first dispute at the Conference[5] was concerned with the Dutch powers to treat. These, they said, were only "to hear

[1] Strafford to St John, 8 Jan. S.P.F.H. 243.

[2] The Dutch Plenipotentiaries were Buys, Van der Dussen, Rechteren, Goslinga, Renswoude, Knjphausen, Gockinga and Geldermalsen; of these the first four were most influential.

[3] Plenipotentiaries to St John, 26 Jan. S.P.F.H. 244.

[4] Strafford to Oxford, 26 Jan. Portland MSS.

[5] The account of this Conference is abridged from the lengthy letter of Plenipotentiaries to St John, 26 Jan., S.P.F.H. 243, enclosing a Memorandum with English proposals and Dutch remarks.

and reply as they found agreeable" on the elucidations of the Barrier Treaty. Strafford failed in his attempt to make them alter this to powers "to hear and reply as the case demanded".

This point being adjusted in favour of the Dutch they reserved their reply on the proposal altering Article VIII to "the case of apparent attack on the part of France". As to trade, they assured the Englishmen that they were willing to put Britain on an equal footing in the Southern Netherlands on condition that the Queen would accord them equal privileges in Spain and the West Indies. This brought them to Article XV, round which the dispute grew hottest. Buys said bluntly that his greatest objection to any change was that the Article engaged the Queen to procure the same advantages in the Spanish dominions. These comprised two benefits: in the first place, there was the Assiento. On this Buys proposed an expedient "letting them into the half or some other proportion of it". Strafford replied that the Assiento had never been shared by any previous holder of the privilege and that the Queen would not depart from this custom. The second privilege was as yet unattained. By their instructions,[1] the English Plenipotentiaries were enjoined "in settling the trade of Our subjects to the Spanish dominions...to endeavour to obtain such exemptions upon all goods and merchandizes of these kingdoms as shall amount to an advantage of at least 15 per cent." The Dutch were determined that the Queen should not obtain this privilege and claimed that by the Treaty of Münster they were entitled to treatment as favourable as that of the most favoured nation in Spain. "We should scarcely have struggled so much", wrote the Plenipotentiaries, "...if only the Assiento had been here concerned. The 15 per cent. was what we endeavoured to provide for."

The difficulty of the 15 per cent. was settled later in an unexpected fashion. In April Mesnager, the French Plenipotentiary, refused to include it among the commercial concessions to England, an act which the Ministry ascribed to Dutch influence.[2]

The last conflict in the Conference between Strafford and

[1] *Bol. Cor.* II, 104.

[2] Cf. p. 266.

Bristol and the Dutch was concerned with the confirmation of the Treaty of Münster in Article XV of the Barrier Treaty. Strafford demanded that the Dutch should refrain from passing goods free to the Barrier fortresses under pretext of the Treaty of Münster.[1] To this the Dutch replied that they would have pleasure in finding an expedient "to prevent Frauds on the one side and retarding Transport on the other", a reply which suggests retaliation on the part of English merchants. The Conference broke up with bitter feeling on both sides.

St John wrote that "Her Majesty was very much afflicted" at the conduct of the Dutch. "I am afraid", he continued,[2] "that our friends in Holland will find the National Sentiment expressed in harder terms upon this subject than ever the Senses of the Queen or of her Ministers was." It would be easy to revive a feeling against the Republic, "which used at all times more or less to appear in Britain against the Dutch". The Queen's grievances against the Townshend Treaty were well founded and she would not depart from her instructions for their removal.

Had they but known it, the persuasions of the English were not without effect. Before the first Conference, on the return of Buys from England, Heinsius had consulted with the "gentlemen of the respective Admiralties" on the taxes at Lille and Tournai. They "were of the opinion that it was unreasonable that there should be so great an inequality" and suggested that the goods of England and the Republic should be put upon an equal footing. But as the taxes had been introduced to pay for garrisons in the New Conquests, they suggested that the equalisation should consist in making Dutch goods pay the duty imposed on English goods at the "Comptoirs" or customs houses which they had introduced on the frontier between the Southern Netherlands and the New Conquests.[3]

At the "Besoigne" of the States of Holland on the 11th of February it was suggested that the duties should be paid on

[1] Cf. explanation on pp. 193–4.

[2] St John to Plenipotentiaries, 27 Jan. (O.S.). S.P.F.H. 245.

[3] 22 Jan. 1712. The Pensionary's account to the States of Holland, Gouda Archives.

the footing of the tariff of 1671 with France,[1] but two days later it was agreed that the affair should not at once be terminated, in case the English might raise new difficulties. In the meantime the Dutch Plenipotentiaries should be instructed merely to inform the English that the grievances would in course of time be reduced.[2] In this change of front, it is possible to trace the influence of the hitch in Anglo-French negotiations consequent upon the meagre offers of Louis on the 11th of February.

Yet although the Dutch Plenipotentiaries were more moderate on the subject of the duties in the New Conquests, their inactivity did not relieve the tension. The three Conferences,[3] on the 5th, 9th and 11th of February, produced only one concession on the part of the Republic. At first the Dutch had "warmly contested" the demand that Nieuwport, Ghent and Dendermonde should be withdrawn from the Barrier. After hours of discussion they said they might desist from Nieuwport, upon an assurance that they would be permitted to garrison the town in time of war.

If they expected in return some concession on Article XV, they were disappointed. After two Conferences on the subject both sides parted "in some uneasiness...seeing very evidently that for want of an agreement on this point, their general concert, which daily becomes more necessary, was at a standstill".

Strafford and Bristol wrote to St John, however, to ask if they might make some concession as to Ghent and Dendermonde in order to gain Dutch compliance on Article XV. The Dutch, too, felt the need of fresh instructions, and Buys and Goslinga left Utrecht to report matters at The Hague. On their return they declared to the English Plenipotentiaries "they were ready to examine and settle all to our content *provided we would in the first place agree to their proposition of absolute equality*", that is, in return for fair treatment of Britain in the Southern

[1] 11 Feb. 1712. The Pensionary's account to the States of Holland, Gouda Archives.

[2] *Ibid.* 13 Feb., and Amsterdam Archives. 13 Feb., Deputies to Amsterdam.

[3] Plenipotentiaries to St John, 5, 9 and 11 Feb. from which the account of pp. 249 and 250 is taken. S.P.F.H. 244.

Netherlands the Dutch demanded a share of trade in the Spanish dominions. Strafford and Bristol argued that the equality intended by the Treaty of Münster meant "equal liberty and security for both sides" without reference to a private contract given to England. This the Dutch refused to admit: they declared that the Assiento meant "the certain ruin of the traffic they have formerly had by way of Cadiz, the loss of which, they say, their people will never endure". Finally the States General had come to a resolution by which their Plenipotentiaries were instructed to insist on Article XV, Ghent and Dendermonde, although they might give way on Nieuwport.[1]

A deadlock was reached in the Conference of the 11th of February on the Assiento. "Buys was in this debate much stiffer than any of them", wrote the English Plenipotentiaries,[2] who concluded that this was due to pressure from Amsterdam. But Buys had received a stimulus to his hopes of an equivalent for the Assiento from Lord Oxford through the medium of Drummond.

On the 25th of January (O.S.) Drummond sent Buys a letter which can only be described as full of duplicity.[3] It began by warning the Dutch that, despite the efforts of Eugene, who was then in England, the Queen stood firm to her desire for peace. Next, it described the mortification of Marlborough on his fall from power. As to the Barrier Treaty, Eugene had declared that the Emperor would never accept the Southern Netherlands on such conditions, "on which yesterday it was decided to lay the same Treaty before Parliament, together with everything concerning the war". Finally, St John wished Drummond to assure Buys that he had acted openly and to warn him that the Queen had no need of foreign assistance to make peace.

There was nothing novel in these warnings but they gave a convincing air to the letter. It was in the next paragraphs that the snare lay. In a conversation with St John and Oxford Drummond reported himself as having said that he had known the Dutch for one and twenty years

[1] Secret Resolutions of the States General, 10 Feb. Legatie Archief, 76.
[2] Plenipotentiaries to St John, 12 Feb. S.P.F.H. 244.
[3] 25 Jan. (O.S.). Add. MSS. 20985.

and that they were to be won by fair words and conduct, but not by threats. On this my Lord Treasurer, who was also present, said, "we threatened no-one, but were pushed to extremities: that all the jealousies in Holland proceeded from the Slave Trade to the West Indies, which England had demanded for herself", whereon I said (continued Drummond) "that if the Dutch were not permitted to have an equal share in this trade, an equivalent might be found for the commerce of the Dutch". On which Lord Oxford answered "*Must we propose such an equivalent, let that come from Holland and we shall obtain it.* Have we not done enough for Holland during the war, to show them that we are willing to help them to a good peace, but if they will oppose the reasonable proposals of the Queen in order to get the peace out of her hands, we must tell the nation why they grudge us it, and let every good Englishman see what the interest of his own land is, and if such a peace is not better than the war...". "Sir", continued Drummond to Buys, "arguments of such a nature begin to prevail so strongly here, that I hope means may be found to prevent further estrangement between the two Nations, whose concord is so highly necessary."

The schemes of Oxford are difficult to penetrate, but in this letter it seems clear that he was willing to "amuse" Buys with his project of an equivalent for the Assiento, either to soften the coming shock of Parliament's decision on the Barrier, or to keep the Republic on the side of the Ministry until negotiations with France were on a more detailed basis. When it is recollected that Buys still entertained the notion that the Ministry depended upon Dutch co-operation,[1] it is not surprising that he should fall into the trap. It was well baited, for an equivalent for the Assiento was of the utmost importance to Amsterdam, the town of which he was Pensionary. For the next four months, as will be shown in the ensuing chapter, Buys occupied himself with his schemes for this equivalent, to which the English had no intention of agreeing.

Meanwhile, the English Plenipotentiaries drew up an amendment to Article XV in the shape of an additional clause

by which the liberties and other commercial advantages which subjects of either party have enjoyed, or shall enjoy, shall in no way be prejudiced by the context of this Article. It is further agreed that the subjects of the Queen shall in future enjoy in all places in the

[1] Cf. p. 240.

Spanish Netherlands and the Barrier...all the Privileges, Exemptions, Liberties and Facilities of trade, either in importation or exportation, that they enjoyed formerly or when the French held them.

Neither side pledged themselves to accept this proposal. Negotiations were suspended until the English reply should come.[1]

The Dutch had the more reason to come to an agreement with England when they heard that Louis not only proposed to keep Aire, St Venant, Bethune, Douai, Tournai and Lille, but also to exclude six kinds of goods from the tariff of 1664, and to make them pay according to the tariff of 1667. The disadvantage of this proposal is explained by the different purposes of the two tariffs: that of 1664 had been drawn up by Colbert to provide a good revenue and was therefore favourable to the introduction of Dutch goods while the tariff of 1667 was prohibitive.[2] The question of the tariff was bound up with the Barrier because Louis refused to make concessions in the Netherlands unless the tariff was arranged to his satisfaction.

Alarming as was this news, the fate of the Townshend Treaty in the House of Commons concerned the Republic still more. When the Dutch Plenipotentiaries heard that the Treaty was to be laid on the table of the House of Commons, they hastened to Bristol and Strafford to discuss once more the alterations required by the Ministry.[3] They reiterated their intention to rectify the commercial inequalities in the Southern Netherlands: they made a new concession in their suggestion that they would give way on Article VIII: still they had no instructions to desist from Ghent and Dendermonde or from Article XV. Another Conference on the 16th of February produced no concessions on either side[4] and on the 19th of February the States General came to a resolution[5] by which they declared that while they were willing to make reasonable explanations of the Treaty, they

[1] Plenipotentiaries to St John, 12 Feb. S.P.F.H. 244.
[2] Elzinga, *Het Voorspel van het Oorlog van* 1672, p. 228.
[3] Plenipotentiaries of the States General to Fagel, 13 Feb. Legatie Archief, 76.
[4] Plenipotentiaries to St John, 16 Feb. S.P.F.H. 244.
[5] Resolutions of the States General, 19 Feb. Legatie Archief, 76.

affirmed their right to "enjoy to the full" the Townshend Treaty, which was "a great foundation of security...for this State...and the means of keeping up a good confidence with Her Majesty".

The obstinacy of the Dutch sealed the fate of the Barrier Treaty in Parliament. On the 16th/27th of February it was repudiated as scandalous and prejudicial to the interests of Britain. Townshend and all who were concerned in drawing up the Treaty were voted enemies of the country.[1]

The correspondence between Boyle and Townshend was accepted as a justification of this act, since it showed that the ambassador had exceeded his instructions. This was supplemented by "*Some Remarks on the Barrier Treaty by the Author of the Conduct of the Allies*", a pamphlet in which Swift once more came to the rescue of the Ministry. This pamphlet,[2] by omitting the real reason for which the Treaty had been conceded to the Dutch, presented a damaging case against the Republic. Swift pointed out the change in the States General's conception of the Barrier. Next he set forth in his incisive style the advantages to the Dutch, expatiating the while on the injuries to English trade: Article XV he summarised as "Perfect Boy's Play: Cross I win, Pile you lose". Against this he set the one so-called benefit to England, the articles by which the Dutch were given the right to meddle with the English Succession. It looked, as Swift pointed out, as if the Dutch were in the position of the Roman Empire, making a treaty with some minor Prince!

The numerous Whig pamphlets[3] which appeared were unable to parry this blow: they could not deny that the advantages were to the Dutch, or that at present British trade suffered. Swift had made it impossible for them to advocate such an increase of the strength of the Republic, by which in his words, "we shall see our Neighbours who in their utmost Distress called for our

[1] Gachard, *Histoire de la Belgique*, pp. 226–7.

[2] In the British Museum (first ed. 27 Nov./8 Dec. 1711) and in collected editions, e.g. Bohn.

[3] Those at the British Museum are: *The Treaty between Her Majesty and the States General for securing the Succession...and the Barrier...considered*, 1712. *The Dutch Barrier Ours*, 1712. *The Barrier Treaty Vindicated*, 1712.

Assistance, become...even in time of Peace, Masters of a more considerable Country than their Own: in a condition to strike Terror into us with 50,000 Veterans ready to invade us, from that country which we have conquered for them!"

It is true that in order to pursue their mistaken policy of continuing the war the Whigs had agreed to include in the Barrier Treaty terms which were prejudicial to the trade of England. But the argument that the Treaty made the Dutch too strong is scarcely tenable, when the impoverished condition of the country is considered. The Assiento was at the bottom of the repudiation of the Treaty and this price the Whigs had been prepared to pay in order to prolong the war, however grudgingly they may have granted the concession.

The practical grounds—apart from the moral—for condemning the repudiation of the Treaty, and the desertion of the Dutch by the Tory Ministry, are to be found in the lowered prestige of the Dutch Republic. Not only was the final Barrier ineffective—as was proved in the War of the Austrian Succession—but the Dutch were never again so useful an ally. Doubtless the Republic had overtaxed its strength and was entering on the first stages of decline; but it is equally true that English policy contributed to and accelerated this process. The Dutch Republic was the natural guardian of the Southern Netherlands, the weak spot in the north-western division of the continent. A Franco-British alliance, such as continued for some years after Utrecht, might postpone, but could not avert an eventual attack on the Emperor in these Provinces.

CHAPTER V

The Dutch Attempt to Save the Barrier

I

"SHARP handling does better with these people than the best words", observed Strafford,[1] but there were limits to what the Dutch would suffer, even after the submission to England in December 1711. It has been shown that Heinsius gave way to the Ministry in the hope that the Townshend Treaty would not suffer material alteration. After the repudiation it was inevitable that the Dutch should seek to preserve the essentials of the Treaty by some expedient.

Their efforts may be divided into two groups: those of the "Warrior party" were directed towards a settlement with some country other than England. With these negotiations Buys and those of his persuasion had no part: throughout the Congress at Utrecht Buys never attempted to break away from England. However recalcitrant he might be in conferences with Strafford and Bristol, he did not believe that the States had anything to gain by turning elsewhere.

At this period Heinsius was in a perplexing situation. The desertion of England had deprived him of his one chance of a Barrier Treaty on a basis satisfactory to his country. If he turned to the Emperor, it was with misgivings, since previous negotiations had shown him how unlikely it was that a satisfactory arrangement could be made. For seven months he pursued a vacillating course, negotiating now with one side, now with the other.

When the news reached Utrecht that the Barrier Treaty might be repudiated, Strafford suggested to St John that this might lead the Dutch to bargain privately with France, in order to obtain a tariff and a barrier more advantageous than that offered

[1] To St John, 9 July 1712. S.P.F.H. 243.

by the Ministry.[1] On the 1st of March the English Plenipotentiaries heard a rumour "that a person shall come privately (from France) to settle with the Dutch the principal points of negotiation".[2] There is no trace in French instructions or in the correspondence of Heinsius of such a person. It is probable that the story had no foundation. In the first place, the French offers of the 11th of February were, as has been shown, even less favourable than those of England, in which Tournai was still included. Secondly, the French had no reason to depart from their previous declaration that they would not negotiate with the Dutch, the more so when they were still in close touch with the English.

More worthy of attention was Strafford's fear of a rapprochement between the Emperor and the States General. "The Dutch have had great opportunities to ingratiate themselves with the Imperial Ministers," wrote Strafford on the 12th of February,[3] "and can scarce fail of obtaining that way some advantage in Spain; in case they bring any advantage to bear." The bond of union was dissatisfaction with the English. Strafford's suspicions were further excited by the suggestion, made by Fagel during the Ambassador's visit to The Hague, that the Maritime Powers should co-operate with Heems, the Austrian Minister, in the provision of forage for the troops in the Spanish Netherlands.[4] As the Dutch had previously been jealous of arrogating any share of the arrangements for these Provinces to the imperialists, and as it was technically an infringement of the Barrier Treaty to admit the Emperor into a matter concerning the Southern Netherlands before he had come to an agreement with the Maritime Powers, Strafford surmised that the two countries had arrived at a secret understanding.[5]

Strafford broached the subject to Heinsius who denied that any agreement had been made, but he was unable to convince

[1] Plenipotentiaries to St John, 12 Feb. S.P.F.H. 244.
[2] Plenipotentiaries to St John, 1 March. S.P.F.H. 244.
[3] Strafford to St John, 12 Feb. S.P.F.H. 243.
[4] Fagel to Heems enclosed in Strafford to St John, 26 Feb. S.P.F.H. 243.
[5] Strafford to St John, 26 Feb. S.P.F.H. 243.

the Ambassador that there had been no settlement with Sinzendorf.[1]

Heinsius spoke the truth when he said that no agreement had been arrived at. But he had been in negotiation with Sinzendorf on the subject since the end of January. On the 21st of January,[2] the two Ministers held a conference to discuss the fate of the Spanish Netherlands. Sinzendorf began by saying that he did not know if it were to the advantage of the Emperor to take over these Provinces, since he feared the numerous burdens to be laid upon them. Heinsius replied that the Barrier Treaty of 1709 would afford a basis for negotiations. Sinzendorf suggested that they should negotiate secretly "in order to prevent all jealousies". Heinsius was willing, and authority to treat was given by the States General on the 22nd of January.[3]

The negotiation became more general when, in March, the English opposition attempted to unite the Emperor and the Maritime Powers for the continuation of the war. The basis of this alliance was to be a pledge to restore Spain, by conquest or by negotiation, to the Emperor. In return, the Maritime Powers were to be rewarded by trade privileges in Spain and the Spanish dominions.[4] Unless the Barrier could be satisfactorily arranged, the Dutch would not willingly co-operate and a conference on the 9th or 10th of February[5] had shown the Pensionary that Sinzendorf might be as difficult on this point as Strafford himself. In the first place, Sinzendorf said that the Emperor would not cede one place in the New Conquests to the Republic: further he would not permit the States to garrison Ghent and Dendermonde[6]: finally he would not apply the

[1] Heinsius to Buys, 24 Feb. Add. MSS. 20985.

[2] Report of the Pensionary to the States of Holland, 22 Jan. Gouda Archives. Weber, p. 214, quotes the report of Heems in March, as the beginning of negotiations on the Spanish Netherlands; in reality this was the second attempt to settle the Barrier as Sinzendorf made this effort in January.

[3] Gouda Archives.

[4] Cf. Salomon, pp. 150–1.

[5] Gouda Archives, 10 Feb.

[6] Cf. Remarks of the Imperialists which Swift appended to his pamphlet on the Barrier Treaty. These remarks were sent by Strafford to St John by whom they were received 29 Sept. 1711. S.P.F.H. Treaty Papers, 50. Among these papers are documents which must have supplied Swift with his material—The Treaty, the English Counter Project, the "Remarks of the Imperialists" and "Observations on the effect of the Treaty on British Commerce".

revenues of the New Conquests to the upkeep of Dutch troops in the Barrier, though he was prepared to pay them from the revenues of the Southern Netherlands as they were in the time of Charles II, with some additional payments.

The Dutch had to decide which was the lesser evil: on the one hand, if they chose the English terms, they had a chance of support in their claims to a better revenue;[1] on the other, if they joined the Emperor in the continuation of the war, they might yet obtain concessions in the Spanish West Indies. From neither side did they have much prospect of Ghent and Dendermonde.

Heinsius tried both sides. On the 8th of March Strafford was surprised to find the Dutch "as forward as they have hitherto been otherwise". They at last consented to transmit the English amendment of Article XV to the States General and asked if, in return, there was any probability that they might be given Ghent. The Plenipotentiaries reported this to St John and said that though they were "very earnest for Dendermonde", Ghent was of more importance to the Barrier.[2]

At the same time Heinsius was watching the outcome of conferences between Sinzendorf and Count Rechteren, one of the Deputies at Utrecht and a well-known supporter of good relations with the Emperor.[3] The opportunity arose after a conference of the Allies on the 5th of March.[4] To avoid notice, Sinzendorf and Rechteren left together for a country walk. The Austrian opened the conversation by reproaching the Maritime Powers for concluding the Barrier Treaty. Rechteren replied that up till then, the Emperor had failed to offer a "good and secure Barrier". Sinzendorf answered that the Emperor was disposed to give the States reasonable satisfaction without further delay. Rechteren then asked if the Emperor would include the New Conquests in the Barrier: this, he argued, was only reasonable, since the Republic was as much interested as

[1] The English Ministry had raised no objection to the article concerning revenue, as this was at the expense of the Emperor.

[2] Plenipotentiaries to St John, 8 March. S.P.F.H. 244.

[3] *Nieuw Nederlandsch Biographisch Woordenboek*, Count Rechteren.

[4] The account of this interview is summarised from Rechteren to Heinsius, 5 March. Heinsius Archives, 77 A.

the Emperor in the security of the Spanish Netherlands. Sinzendorf said that, without conceding anything, he would like to hear Rechteren's proposals. With equal caution, the Dutchman replied that without knowledge of the States General's opinion, his private conception was that the Republic could invest two lines of fortresses. The first, the Outer Barrier, consisted of places conquered from or to be ceded by the enemy. For the second, or Inner Barrier, he proposed a line from Ostend (or if the English objected from Fort Damme) including Ghent, Dendermonde, Fort St Marguerite, along the River Rupel as far as Mechlin, along the Rivers Dyle and Demer and concluding at the Meuse. The land and places north of these rivers—Antwerp and Lier for example—should be put in possession of the Dutch with power to fortify them. The Inner Barrier would, in his opinion, be more efficacious than their present arrangement with England.

In reporting this conversation to Heinsius, Rechteren had to admit that Sinzendorf had at once raised objections to a project which would put the Dutch in possession of Antwerp. Nevertheless, Rechteren had hopes of overcoming this and other difficulties: he trusted to the Emperor's need of help from the States General. He concluded by urging Heinsius to strike at once.[1]

Meanwhile the English Ministers were not idle. Three days after the repudiation of the Barrier Treaty, a fresh set of instructions was drawn up. These were to be delivered by a kinsman of the Lord Treasurer, Mr Harley. The instructions are dated the 19th of February,[2] but the hitch in Anglo-French negotiations caused the Ministry to delay Mr Harley's departure until the end of March.

From the tone of the instructions, it is clear that the Ministry wished to avert a separation on the part of the States: "if even now the States General will enter into a closer union with the Queen, explain the Treaty of Barrier in such a way as to secure Britain from the ill consequences apprehended from it, and go hand in hand with us at the Conferences at Utrecht, we may obtain for the whole Alliance a safe and advantageous peace".

[1] Rechteren to Heinsius, 5 March. Heinsius Archives, 77 A.
[2] Printed in *Bol. Cor.* II, 181–91.

Nevertheless, Harley's Mission was to be the Queen's ultimatum, for the passage quoted continues "but if this measure is not taken by them, the Queen must save her own country and such of the Allies as will join her".

As Harley's embassy was delayed till April,[1] the Ministry turned to Drummond. Drummond approached Van der Dussen on the 15th of March.[2] The latter told him frankly that he had no hopes of arriving at a settlement with Strafford. Drummond proposed that negotiations should continue secretly with the more amiable Bristol, but this suggestion was thwarted by the Bishop himself, who very properly refused to keep his colleague in the dark. (No doubt his fear of Strafford had much to do with this decision.) Drummond then tried another plan by which he might win Van der Dussen to the side of England. On a plea of interest in Van der Dussen's tile-making factory, he drew the Dutchman apart from Buys during a visit to the Dutch Deputies. Van der Dussen responded readily to this approach and, after some persuasion, agreed to permit a report of his conversation with Drummond to be made to Strafford. He suggested that he should leave Utrecht for his country house, ostensibly to give directions about his business; in reality he would go in secret to The Hague, to persuade Heinsius "to concert matters with the Queen's Ministers and to remove all jealousies". Van der Dussen said that he must have a week to undertake this task and begged that Ormond should be instructed to prepare for another campaign. Further he urged that an expedient must be found for assuaging the jealousy conceived by the trading towns against the Assiento—"anything, though not worth a hundred pounds a year...hundreds of Antient and good families ruined by the fall of the West India Company were to be pitied...and some small consideration was to be had for them".

Drummond replied that the Lord Treasurer was "not against this", thus bearing out the tone of his letter to Buys in February.[3] Further, he said he would himself undertake to

[1] Cf. p. 265.

[2] The following is abridged from Drummond to Oxford, 15 March. Portland MSS.

[3] Cf. p. 250.

procure an order from the Queen's Ministers that if the English South Sea Company were unable to perform the whole contract with Philip, they would employ the Dutch rather than any other country to fulfil it and "if any small benefit not prejudicial to English Trade and Plantations could be thought upon for the benefit of the Dutch West India Company, he would find the Queen and her Ministers would come very heartily into it". Van der Dussen seized upon this idea and suggested Porto Rico, "a small and almost uninhabited island near Curaçoa".

The conversation turned to the Barrier: Van der Dussen asked if the Queen would support their demand for Valenciennes. Drummond replied that the States must not count upon this but that

> in the Barrier Treaty, the Queen would show the greatest complaisance *and even put hardships on the Emperor* if the States should take care to deserve better of the Queen than the Emperor did; but that they must lay aside the 15th Article entirely and settle the commerce on a just and equal foot with England in the Spanish Netherlands, and a new Barrier.

As to Dendermonde and other places, the Dutch "would be made easy". Nieuwport, Van der Dussen agreed to give up.

The Ministry's next step was a sharp warning to Buys from the Lord Treasurer himself.[1] The Whigs, he wrote, had made no headway since December. As to the policy of the States, he continued

> I hope you are perswaded...of my study to cultivate a good and perfect understanding between the two Nations. For God's sake let not groundless fears, the Ambitions and Revenge of private persons be too hard for the well intentioned of both Nations. Let not those arts sow those seeds of distrust which may prove mischeveous to both. I told you, Sir, plainly all that England asked. Envy not the Assiento, which is all we are like to purchase with a hundred millions laid out in two wars. We are a people a great while before we take harm, but then it is very durable. I would be very sorry that Unreasonable backwardness to let Britain enjoy this small benefit should soure the Nation.

[1] Oxford to Buys, 8/19 March. Add. MSS. 20985.

The news from Parliament emphasised this warning. Sir Thomas Hanmar had just drawn up his famous indictment of the part played by the Allies,[1] a proceeding which left poor Heinsius "very melancholy"[2] and, as usual, undecided on a course of action.

The weight of English policy had, however, some influence on negotiations between Sinzendorf and the Dutch. When Strafford paid a visit to The Hague to "have an eye on Sinzendorf", he surmised that though the Austrian was active he did not seem to have made much progress.[3] In this he was correct. Negotiations were suspended: Sinzendorf awaited Eugene's arrival at The Hague[4] and Heinsius had ordered Rechteren to make no further advances for some days.[5]

On the 1st of April Sinzendorf and Rechteren held a further conference at Utrecht, in which Sinzendorf still refused to agree to the fortresses which Rechteren claimed, despite the assurance of the latter that the States General would leave civil, ecclesiastical and financial rights to Charles. Sinzendorf raised the religious question which, he said, would be of as great difficulty in the Upper Quarter of Guelderland as in the Barrier fortresses. Rechteren replied that this and other difficulties might be solved and urged that Sinzendorf should cede the Inner Barrier to the Dutch.[6]

The English Ministry had handled the situation successfully. Drummond's conversation with Van der Dussen had given the Dutch just sufficient hope to make them over firm with Sinzendorf and to irritate the Emperor. The arrival of Eugene had made the situation no better: the Imperialists were dissatisfied with the Dutch on another point, their evasive reply to the suggestion that if England refused to transport Imperial troops to Catalonia, Dutch vessels should perform this service.[7]

[1] The Commons Representation. See *Actes et Mémoires de la Paix d'Utrecht*, I, 470. The States replied by a Resolution and Memorial to show that the proceedings of the Commons were unjust. *Ibid.* pp. 497 and 506, 1 April 1712.

[2] Drummond to Oxford, 29 March. Portland MSS.

[3] Strafford to St John, 25 March. S.P.F.H. 243.

[4] Weber, p. 214.

[5] Rechteren to Heinsius, April. Heinsius Archives, 77 A.

[6] *Ibid.*

[7] Weber, p. 264.

The final blow at the rapprochement between the Imperialists and the Dutch was Oxford's project for the elevation of the House of Savoy. As has been indicated, Eugene was not unfavourable to this plan[1] and was disinclined to listen to the Whigs, when they attempted to unite the Emperor and the Dutch in renewing the war. The uncompromising attitude of the Dutch regarding the Barrier confirmed Eugene in his belief that his master would be better served by good relations with England.

On the Dutch side, there was reluctance to pursue the war. In May, when the Imperialists renewed the subject, Heinsius asked what safeguards would be taken to prevent the union of the Imperial and the Spanish crowns. All Sinzendorf could reply was that when the Emperor had two sons, he would divide the Hapsburg inheritance once again.[2] As the Emperor had been married for five years and was still childless, this was an unsatisfactory reply. Heinsius answered that it was not the time for new alliances, though the States would never leave the Emperor, an answer which Sinzendorf interpreted as an indication that the Dutch would never separate from England.[3]

II

Meanwhile Buys pursued his policy of saving part of the Barrier Treaty by an arrangement with England. As has been indicated, he still believed that the Ministry was dependent upon Dutch co-operation. He had been encouraged in his expectations by Oxford's letter in which it seemed probable that the Ministry would buy Dutch support by some concessions in the West Indies.[4]

The letter promised to the Dutch "an equivalent". Buys took this to mean that though the English would never admit the Dutch to the Assiento to supply slaves to the south coast of South America, some port on the north coast, or some island near the coast, might be allotted to the Dutch as a port to which they could send a certain number of slaves, whom they might

[1] Cf. p. 243. [2] Cf. Salomon, pp. 150–2.
[3] Sinzendorf's Report, 18 May, 1712. Weber, p. 265.
[4] Cf. p. 250.

use to make up any deficit on the part of English traders. The letter from Oxford was dated the 25th of January. Its results were seen immediately. On the 19th of February Strafford reported that in speaking of the Assiento, Buys "had a greater air of assurance than formerly: he has some opposers in the States, but he is backed entirely by Amsterdam in this matter of trade and commerce, which they would have equal with the English, and they are supported by the Pensionary and his faction at The Hague".[1]

After the repudiation of the Barrier Treaty, Buys concentrated on obtaining this equivalent for the Assiento. Just as Heinsius watched the negotiations between Rechteren and Sinzendorf, so he awaited the outcome of negotiations between Buys and the English Plenipotentiaries.

The first task of Buys was to settle with his masters as to what he should suggest as the equivalent. He wrote to the Burghermasters of Amsterdam for their advice. The Burghermasters "interrogated a well informed person who had often been in the West Indies".[2] This gentleman informed them that the right to import negroes sometimes brought with it the opportunity to enter the harbours of South America and to trade without the knowledge of the King of Spain, "as had happened more than once to himself", he naïvely admitted.

It was on account of this underhand trade that the Dutch feared to concede the Assiento to England to the exclusion of themselves. If they, as well as the English, could gain some footing in South America, they might avail themselves of similar opportunities. Accordingly Buys flattered the English Ambassador by offering him a "famous entertainment", after which he returned to Strafford's house, where the two men talked till midnight.[3] Buys protested that "he was still for peace and so was Amsterdam", and that if the Ministry would but allow them some concessions in the West Indies, they "would declare for peace tomorrow, and such a peace as France would accept, and

[1] Strafford to Oxford, 19 Feb. Portland MSS.

[2] Burghermasters of Amsterdam to Buys, 2 March. Add. MSS. 20985.

[3] Strafford to St John, 16 March. S.P.F.H. 243, in which this conversation is reported.

what for the vote of the House of Lords we (the English) could not come at". Strafford, who had received no instructions with regard to the equivalent[1] replied "plainly as a friend, not as a Minister", that there was no hope. This made Buys "very uneasy": he explained his desire to obtain an equivalent for the Assiento, though he admitted that it was impossible to continue the war, "however they had worked their people to be mad for it". He agreed that it was impossible for the Emperor to retain Aragon, Catalonia, Valentia and Muria. As to the Barrier, he "did as good as own" that the States must give up Aire, Bethune, Bouchain, St Venant and Douai, but he would hear of no equivalent for the demolition of Dunkirk and would rather leave it fortified than yield up Lille.

On receipt of this information, the Lord Treasurer wrote the letter of the 8th/19th of March, in which he, too, bade Buys forget the Assiento.[2] The idea of an equivalent had, however, taken root and on the 22nd of March, when Strafford visited Heinsius at The Hague, the Pensionary said that his countrymen could "never think of any peace in which they must loose (lose) the joint right they have with the English in the trade of Spain and the West Indies". As Strafford was more than a match for Heinsius, the two "argued long and warmly on the subject".[3] When Strafford left The Hague he recorded his impression that "all these people seem bent not to leave the 15th Article out of the Treaty of Barrier, let what will happen".[4]

St John's reply was to despatch Harley with instructions dated the 21st and 23rd of February,[5] which contained the "two cardinal points on which negotiations turn", the Queen's ultimatum to the States and the offers to France.[6] Harley arrived on the 3rd of April; the first days of his visit were occupied in negotiations with the Dutch.[7] One point of

[1] Strafford's instructions were exactly to the contrary: cf. St John to Strafford, 16 Feb. (O.S.). S.P.F.H. 241. "Cut off their hopes of our consenting to share with them the Assiento."

[2] Cf. p. 261.

[3] Strafford to St John, 22 March. The Hague, S.P.F.H. 243.

[4] Strafford to St John, 25 March. *Ibid.*

[5] Cf. p. 259.

[6] St John to Plenipotentiaries, 16 April. *Bol. Cor.* II, 264.

[7] Plenipotentiaries to St John, 6 April. S.P.F.H. 244.

importance to Anglo-Dutch relations was his instruction to drop the English demand for the reduction of the 15 per cent. on goods going to Spain.[1]

On the 8th of April a conference was held between the English Plenipotentiaries, Buys, Rechteren and two other Deputies.[2] The Dutch were pleased to hear that the 15 per cent. had been dropped and expressed their readiness to concede the towns demanded by France, except Lille, Valenciennes and Tournai. "At present", wrote Strafford,[3] "they show a great desire to concert sincerely measures with us, which we are ready to do on our side. We shall see what temper they will be in when they return from the Hague. They are extremely subject to be governed by appearances and events."

The Resolution taken by the States General produced only one change: their Plenipotentiaries were authorised to suggest an equivalent by which the Dutch might take part in the slave trade.[4]

When the Plenipotentiaries returned to Utrecht, a conference was held on the 14th of April.[5] Strafford argued that they could not discuss the slave trade, the Assiento "being of a private Nature only a temporary contract such as other Nations had entered into without any objections".

The Dutch then asked the terms of the Assiento and were told that it was similar to that granted to the Portuguese and to the French, "with an establishment on the river Plate...only to give...such convenience as the Portuguese then had". This reply concealed the innovation in the Assiento, the right to send one ship yearly to trade in South America.

For the present, the Dutch said they could take no further

[1] Cf. Plenipotentiaries to St John in cipher, 15 March. Add. MSS. 22205. "The explication given by Mr Mesnager is that our goods designed for America shall not pay any duty which the others do, to the amount of 15 per cent. We thought that was to extend to goods consumed in Spain but he averred it was never so intended." The Plenipotentiaries gave way in April. They were instructed by St John "to render this concession of the Queen a means of bringing the Dutch to reason and to compliance with H.M. measures". St John to Plenipotentiaries, 12 April. S.P.F.H. 245.

[2] Secret Besoigne of the States of Holland. Add. MSS. 20985.

[3] Strafford to St John, 8 April. S.P.F.H. 243.

[4] Secret Resolution of the States General, 9 April. Legatie Archief, 76.

[5] Plenipotentiaries to St John, 14 and 15 April. S.P.F.H. 244.

steps, until they received orders as to the details of the equivalent they should demand for the Assiento.

The conversation then turned to the Southern Netherlands. The Dutch promised, as usual, to redress the commercial grievances of Britain and asked once more if they might keep Ghent and Dendermonde. In accordance with Harley's instructions,[1] the Plenipotentiaries assented, on condition that the Queen might retain Ostend and Nieuwport. The Dutch were amazed: it was, as they wrote to The Hague,[2] an attempt to introduce a new system of Barrier. They tried in vain to make Strafford and Bristol desist from this demand, and the Conference broke up leaving them in confusion.

The 15th of April saw all parties busy on the Barrier. It was the day on which the French made their new offers.[3] For the Dutch, they proposed that the Southern Netherlands should be ceded to the Emperor, with the exception of the Upper Quarter of Guelderland and of Luxemburg, which was designed for the Princesse des Ursins. As equivalent for the demolition of Dunkirk Louis demanded Charleroi, Nieuwport, Ypres and Tournai and for the French Barrier, Douai, Bethune, Aire St Venant and Bouchain. Finally he was prepared to grant the tariff of 1664, with the exception of four species, to be arranged.

On the same day, Harley made a report of his embassy at The Hague.[4] Feeling in the country, especially at Amsterdam, was very bitter against England, on account of the Assiento. The commercial advantages alone were, he thought, sufficient "to make these craving envious people averse to any peace on such terms for the good of their Neighbours". He found Heinsius more tractable than he had expected. The old man was "not a little pleased" at Harley's visit and with his manner of negotiation which contrasted with "the harsh usage which he and others have had from some employed by the Queen". He admitted to Harley that he was averse from "meddling with

[1] 23 Feb. *Bol. Cor.* II, 181.

[2] Deputies to Fagel, 14 April. Legatie Archief, 76. But see Introduction, d'Avaux's Negotiation, 1701.

[3] Plenipotentiaries to St John transmitting the French offer, 15 April. S.P.F.H. 244.

[4] Thomas Harley to Oxford, 15 April. Portland MSS.

the parties in England", a confession which was not, in view of later events, very sincere.

Baron van Wassenaer, with whom Harley also spoke, promised that if the equivalent for the Asiento were granted, "he would take all the pains he can to gain those that are averse". He thought that even the Emperor might be persuaded to agree to the demands of the Ministry.

The peaceful disposition of Heinsius, together with the project for giving Spain to the Duke of Savoy, raised English hopes. The Ministry could not, or would not, realise how much the conduct of the Dutch depended on the Assiento.

During the month of April, Buys was in correspondence with Bassecour, one of the Pensionaries of Amsterdam, upon the details of the equivalent. Bassecour interviewed Willem van Coppenol on the West India trade.[1] Coppenol, himself a merchant, was of the opinion that despite the Assiento

> neither the French nor the Portuguese had done very well out of it...they had to pay the King of Spain a large douceur for their privileges...and he did not know if private trade by smuggling were possible. Ships arriving at the Coast of Spanish (S.) America, did not trade with Governors, but with particular persons who had need of slaves, a system which offered many delays and sometimes led to long and costly journeys.

He thought the fears of English competition much exaggerated, since the English company was not sufficiently flourishing to export the number of slaves required. The deficit would have to be supplied by other countries. If the Dutch were permitted an establishment at Curaçoa they might export slaves thence to the mainland.

The cautious Bassecour reminded Coppenol that "his simple conjecture was no sure way to success". As he feared that the English company might be able to maintain the monopoly, and believed that Coppenol's report was made "with more zeal than precision",[2] he consulted with certain other merchants.[3] These men were apprehensive lest the English might obtain the

[1] No date, but among the papers of the week from 12–19 April 1712, Bassecour to Buys. Add. MSS. 20985.

[2] Second letter from Bassecour to Buys. Add. MSS. 20985.

[3] *Ibid.* Simon Burg, Couturier, Pieter Hinke.

right to import slaves to Buenos Ayres, a settlement more important than Porto Bello or Cartagena, which the Spaniards had therefore never previously included in the Assiento. They inquired if the English would be given the right to erect forts or colonies, since they might build these on the coast at the mouth of the River Plate, which was navigable as far as Buenos Ayres. The right to erect forts they feared, since it almost inevitably led to private trading on the sly. So long as private trade was interdicted, they did not fear the Assiento, if they might have the right to send slaves to Curaçoa.

As a result of these councils, Burghermaster de Haas approached Drummond on the subject. Drummond wrote to Oxford advising him "to procure or show endeavour to procure, for the Dutch or their West India Company, the Assiento to the North parts of the Spanish West Indies, seeing they realise you will supply the whole South Sea Coast". If the English would do this, the Dutch would

> hasten matters to their satisfaction, but without some douceur of this nature, they protest to me, and I can too visibly see it, it will be impossible to moderate the minds of the people...who are animated to an incredible degree at present by encouragement from your side and connivance here....They are to come to no resolution of peace (he continued) unless England will assist them to obtain...Porto Bello, Cartagena or Porto Rico, a small island for the Curaçoa trade, and all the sincere wishers of peace here hope your Lordship will obtain the Queen's orders to procure it from the French.[1]

Drummond sent similar advice to the Earl of Strafford, but the latter thought that the Dutch could be made to enter into a peace without the equivalent. He founded his opinion on the inability of Heinsius to come to terms with the Emperor, and on the fears of the States General that if they did not give way, the English would persist in their demand for Ostend.[2]

Heinsius seemed disposed to placate the Ministry, for he procured a resolution of the States General promising to redress English grievances in the Southern Netherlands.[3]

[1] Drummond to Oxford, 15 April. Portland MSS.
[2] Strafford to St John, 19 April. S.P.F.H. 243.
[3] Resolution of the States General, 16 April. Legatie Archief, 76.

About the same date,[1] Strafford had a private conversation with Somelsdyk, a member of a noble family with interests in Surinam, in which he told the latter plainly that England would never permit the Dutch to have concessions in the West Indies similar to the Assiento.

Nevertheless, the Dutch clung to the idea of an equivalent. On the 22nd of April Buys received a letter on behalf of the West India Company to say that, without a foothold on the continent, at least on the north side of South America, the company would be ruined.[2]

At Utrecht, the Dutch in pursuance of their instructions, asked for the precise terms of the Assiento. Bristol gave them a copy of the contract granted to the French.[3] This was a deliberate deception, if not on the part of Bristol, at least of the Ministry, since the copy omitted the clause permitting the English to send the annual ship for trade. On reading the French contract, the Dutch were "extremely content and enlightened at that communication as enabling them to give quite a different account of the matter from what it had been represented, and seemed not uneasy at the firmness we (the English Plenipotentiaries) expressed that it was impossible to admit them into any share of it".[4]

This copy of the French contract was forwarded to Amsterdam, the town which, under the leadership of Buys, had been most resolute on the equivalent. The opinion of Amsterdam would be of immense influence in the decision as to whether the Dutch should persist in the demand for concessions in the West Indies. After some days of deliberation[5] the town came to a Resolution which is quoted in full[6]:

1. The English Merchants want to have the right to import slaves to Vera Cruz, Cartagena and the Northern side of South America. No objection.

[1] Somelsdyk to Buys, undated, but about 14–30 April. Add. MSS. 20985.
[2] Bors van Waveren to Buys, 22 April. Add. MSS. 20985.
[3] Bristol to St John, 26 April. S.P.F.H. 244.
[4] *Ibid.*
[5] Drummond to Oxford, 10 May. Portland MSS.
[6] 11 May, Resolutions. Amsterdam Archives.

2. To import 500–600 slaves to South America (i.e. Buenos Ayres). No objections, *so long as no merchandise is imported*, and neither fortifications nor settlements are erected.

3. Concerning the wish of the English to import slaves to the Pacific, two ships per year, objections are made because it is feared that those ships will be used not only for the importation of slaves but for merchandise as well.

In spite of these objections, the Dutch do not fear this Assiento very much, as hitherto Assientists have never been very successful, and considering the antipathy between England and the Spanish Nation which will cause many difficulties, it will be better for the Dutch that the Assiento should be between Spain and England, rather than between Spain and France.

With this Resolution, the plan of an equivalent was dropped, although suspicions lingered at The Hague that the English might have obtained concessions for trade.[1] Events leading to the "war of Jenkins' Ear" showed that the Regents of Amsterdam were justified in their prediction of friction between Spain and England. Yet had they known of the clause permitting trade they would never have allowed their Deputies to advise the States of Holland that "the whole Assiento as given to France can be abandoned to England".[2]

A year later, in June 1714, Buys found that he had been tricked. In the negotiations of the Treaty between the Republic and Spain, both the French and the Spanish Ministers owned to the article permitting one ship to trade annually in the South Seas.[3] On this news, Buys, with justice, "complained extremely" because the Plenipotentiaries had assured him that the pact contained nothing beyond the French Assiento. It was this assurance, he told Strafford, which had led the Dutch to drop Article XV of the Barrier Treaty and their project of an equivalent.[4]

[1] Deputies to Amsterdam, 13 May. Amsterdam Archives. The suspicion was voiced by the deputies of Rotterdam in an assembly of the States of Holland. The deputies at Utrecht continued till the end of May to discuss the Assiento.

[2] Deputies to Amsterdam, 12 May. *Ibid.*

[3] Plenipotentiaries to Bolingbroke, 9 June 1713. S.P.F.H. 246.

[4] 17 June 1713. *Ibid.*

III

Although the point of the Assiento was dropped, it became apparent that Harley's mission to The Hague would be without result, as the Dutch would not withdraw their claim to Ghent and Dendermonde. Impatient at this obstinacy, the Ministry decided to obtain an excuse for abandoning their ally.

Accordingly, St John was not displeased when Heinsius, pressed by Strafford to communicate peace proposals, gave an evasive reply.[1] If the States delayed, he wrote to Strafford, France and Britain might make peace alone "and this may be done with a much better grace, if after repeated incitations to open their minds, the Ministers of Holland should continue still silent, than it could be if they freely declared their sentiments and entered into formal concert with your Lordships".[2]

The Ministry had by this time received a favourable answer from De Torcy to their proposal that Spain should be given to the Duke of Savoy. On the 10th/21st of May St John was emboldened to send instructions to Ormond, Marlborough's successor in the field, to avoid both siege and battle until further notice, as news was expected from Spain which would render useless the opening of a new campaign.[3]

The secret of these instructions was not well preserved and all the enemies of the Ministry combined to raise difficulties for Oxford and St John. At home Godolphin came forth from his retirement to lead the Opposition in a last attack upon the Ministry.[4] News of this impending attack made Heinsius more obstinate at The Hague.[5]

St John expressed regret that the Dutch continued "to listen to the bubblings of a faction here",[6] but his real feelings were indicated when he told Strafford that without the Dutch, the English might "render the terms of the Treaty more solidly advantageous to Britain".[7]

[1] Strafford to St John, 30 April. S.P.F.H. 243.
[2] St John to Plenipotentiaries, 29 April (O.S.). *Bol. Cor.* II, 300.
[3] Cf. Weber, p. 250.
[4] Cf. Salomon, pp. 150–1.
[5] Van der Dussen to Buys on his suspicions that "Heinsius will do nothing as he awaits news from England", 29 May. Add. MSS. 20985.
[6] St John to Drummond, 2 May. *Bol. Cor.* II, 307.
[7] St John to Strafford, 10 May. *Ibid.* p. 310.

The States' Plenipotentiaries were not unaware of this design: they showed themselves "extremely nettled" when Strafford observed with a sneer that it was surprising that they had the title of Plenipotentiaries when they had no powers to conclude.[1] They proposed to visit The Hague to ask for fresh instructions. On their return, Strafford found that matters had advanced no further.[2] They refused to discuss any matters except the Barrier. Strafford excused himself from further negotiation on the ground that he could do nothing while his colleague Bristol was ill. This delay convinced Count Rechteren that the Ministry intended "to make the Dutch odious to the English Nation" by demonstrating their unwillingness to come to terms.[3]

Rechteren would have been confirmed in his suspicions if he had seen a letter from St John to Thomas Harley of the 10th of May (O.S.).

> I confess I begin to wish that the Dutch may continue still to be dully obstinate (wrote St John[4]) rather than submit to the Queen's measures, since we do not want them either to make or superintend the peace and since it will be better settled for England without their concurrence than with it. Does it not make the blood curdle in your veins to hear it solemnly contested in Holland whether Britain shall enjoy the Assiento, an advantage which the enemy yielded to us?

The next step was the temporary recall of Strafford, who left for England on the 24th of May,[5] and an order to Bristol and Harley[6]

> to let all negotiations sleep in Holland, since they have neither sense, nor gratitude nor spirit enough to make a suitable return to all the offers sent lately by the Queen....Her Majesty will look on herself as under no obligation to them, but will proceed to make the peace, either with or without them...the rule prescribed to my Lord Privy Seal for his conduct is, that he absolutely decline treating with the Ministers of the States either on the subject of the amendments to the Barrier Treaty, or of the general policy of peace, or of any other subject whatever.

[1] Strafford to St John, 6 May. S.P.F.H. 244.
[2] Strafford to St John, 17 May. S.P.F.H. 244.
[3] Rechteren to Heinsius, 19 May. Heinsius Archives, 77 A.
[4] St John to Harley, 10 May (O.S.). *Bol. Cor.* II, 323.
[5] Bristol to St John, 24 May. S.P.F.H. 244.
[6] St John to Harley, 17 May (O.S.). *Bol. Cor.* II, 327.

This order was communicated by Bristol on the 2nd of June: Rechteren and Kniphausen flew into a rage and it was with difficulty that Buys succeeded in calming them.[1] Rechteren noticed that the Bishop was as much astonished at his orders as any of the Dutch.[2]

This news was followed by the death blow to all hopes of the overturning of the Ministry. It had been the object of the Whigs, in conjunction with Eugene and the Dutch, to force the Ministry to begin a new campaign. Eugene held a council of war and challenged Ormond to produce his instructions. The States General followed his lead by a letter of remonstrance to the Queen at Ormond's inactivity.[3] The Opposition concentrated on an attack in Parliament from which great results were anticipated. Even Marlborough joined forces with Godolphin, though he had been reluctant to attack the Ministry in December 1711.

The Opposition demanded that Ormond's instructions should be laid before Parliament in order that better co-operation with the Allies might be secured. By this they hoped to force the Tories to reveal their quasi-armistice with France and to defeat them in a vote on the negotiations for peace, since hostilities had been stopped before Philip's renunciation of the crown of Spain had been received. The debates ended in a triumph for Oxford and St John. In the Upper House, Oxford replied that Ormond had sent home a plan of a siege and had been asked to express his views on peace before he carried out his intention. As for peace negotiations, these were progressing so successfully that in a few days the Queen would lay her plans before Parliament, and he who would place obstacles to such an arrangement would do so only because the terms were so advantageous to Great Britain: in former treaties English interests had been shamefully neglected and it was now reasonable that they should be well considered.

In the House of Commons, St John made a similarly evasive speech; adding that "the poison of a faction" could not disturb

[1] Bristol to St John, 3 June. S.P.F.H. 244.
[2] Rechteren to Heinsius, 2 June. Heinsius Archives, 77 A.
[3] Cf. Salomon, pp. 150–1.

the Ministry and that if a battle had been avoided, it was for the reason which had often before occurred, that it had been opposed by the Dutch.

As a result, in both houses the Tories carried the vote and the Commons added an address of confidence in the Queen. The Opposition was completely routed and Marlborough declared it would have been better policy not to have raised the issue.[1]

On receipt of this news,[2] Heinsius realised that it was impossible to avert English negotiations with France. A momentous decision was before the States General: should they yield to the Queen, or should they join the Emperor, who gave every indication that he would continue the war alone? If they joined with England, they would have to accept a peace on terms which were as yet hidden from themselves. After months of negotiation, nothing was settled as to their Barrier, and tariff, and they had been forced to abandon their hopes of an equivalent for the Assiento. The initiative in any decision lay in the hands of Heinsius, in whose past experience the Republic had never accepted terms dictated by another ally. There were not wanting those to counsel him to rebel against this fate. Rechteren urged fortitude: "they must, like a good captain, try to bring the ship to the harbour as much through storms as in fair weather and before the wind".[3] Since the English were so unreasonable as to force the States to such extremities, it was better to fight on with the Emperor and the Elector of Hanover. In this and later letters Rechteren urged the renewal of preparations for war, the reorganisation of finances and the increase of Dutch troops.[4]

This feeling of resentment against England was shared by the common people. Pastors preached with the approbation of their listeners against Tories as Papists, quoting Charles II and James II as examples: from the pulpit the wish was openly expressed that Oxford should lose his head.[5] The Dutch were

[1] See Salomon, pp. 151 *et seq.*

[2] Bristol to St John writes that the Dutch were "disappointed at the wise and resolute behaviour of Parliament", 17 June. S.P.F.H. 244.

[3] Rechteren to Heinsius, 6 June. Heinsius Archives, 77 A.

[4] 6, 24, 28 June. Heinsius Archives, 77 A.

[5] Bristol's Memorandum. "What is consulted and now Adoing in the United Provinces", 24 June. S.P.F.H. 244.

exhorted to prepare for further warfare. "There are so many... indications of ill temper", wrote Bristol,[1] "that it is difficult, perhaps dangerous, not to suspect them."

Many pamphlets were addressed to Heinsius full of warnings against England, as a country which had thrown in its lot with France and Spain to undermine the strength of the Republic.[2] The old jealousy between the Maritime Powers revived and the pamphleteers hinted that the Tory Ministry, if not actually Papist, was against Presbyterianism.

Bristol had hopes that Amsterdam would give the lead to the peace party, as the Regents were desirous of ending the war.[3] Drummond was more pessimistic and was the more trustworthy on account of his knowledge of that city. He informed Oxford that the town would insist on Lille, Tournai, Namur, Charleroi and Ypres in the Barrier, and on the tariff of 1664 entire, particularly for whalebone and whale oils.[4] "Lord Strafford is now much longed for," he continued, "and though His Excellency has not the good luck to be universally beloved, yet they rather will that he should return than a new one." This was a reference to the rumour that Sir Thomas Hanmar would be sent, a man disliked and feared by the Dutch on account of his report to Parliament on the conduct of the Allies.[5]

Heinsius inclined more and more towards resistance, but he temporised in the hope that he would find out the terms arranged by England. This policy seemed the more advisable since the Ministry had met with an unexpected check, which might overthrow their plans and force them to renew the war. The courier from Spain reported that, despite the offer of Savoy, Philip had elected to remain king at Madrid. Oxford's policy was reduced to nothing: the hope of an understanding with the Emperor fell to the ground as Spain would go to a member of the House of Anjou, and, until new terms were arranged with France, Ormond was in a dangerous position in the field. Worst of all, De Torcy sought to take advantage of the situation

[1] Bristol to St John, 24 June. S.P.F.H. 244.
[2] Cf. Archives of Holland, 2950, No. 72.
[3] Bristol to St John, 17 June. S.P.F.H. 244.
[4] Drummond to Oxford, 16 June. Portland MSS.
[5] Cf. p. 262 *note* 1.

to procure remission from one of the most important conditions of the armistice—the evacuation of Dunkirk. He proposed to delay this until the conclusion of peace.

It is impossible not to admire the collected behaviour of the Tories: once more they extricated themselves from their difficulties without loss to England, a task which they facilitated by further sacrificing the interests of the Allies. Oxford decided that the best plan would be to put his cards on the table, to announce to the world that England would make peace if Philip would renounce the throne of France.[1] The Queen appeared in Parliament and declared that the chief aim of the war had been secured[2]: the crowns of Spain and France would never be united. She was in a position to disclose advantageous terms for England. As to the Empire, the Rhine would be its frontier. Louis would evacuate Breisach, Kehl and Landau and restore the Rhine fortresses he had captured. The Emperor would be given the Netherlands, Naples, Sardinia, Milan and the Tuscan ports. Time pressed and it was not yet possible for her to detail the interests of the other Allies, with the exception of the Duke of Savoy, who would be rewarded with special concessions for his sacrifice of Spain. Despite the efforts of the Whigs, a vote was carried in favour of these terms.

Oxford gauged accurately the impression which would be made by this speech in Paris. De Torcy forwarded a satisfactory project for the armistice, in which he promised to obtain Philip's renunciation of the throne of France within a specified time after the conclusion of hostilities. Dunkirk, he promised to evacuate at once. Thus, by the 11th/22nd of June, all difficulties were overcome.

In the United Provinces, the vagueness of the Queen's reference to Dutch interests heightened the universal consternation then prevailing. "They appeared extremely allarmed that all the fruits of the last three years were cut off," wrote Bristol,[3] "as also two or three towns of which they said that there was a report Lille and Tournay were to be too (*sic*)." Bristol pointed out to the Dutch Plenipotentiaries that the

[1] Salomon, p. 153. [2] Weber, pp. 270–1.
[3] Bristol to St John, 24 June. S.P.F.H. 244.

Queen's speech was not an ultimatum and that each ally might negotiate further for himself. "They took it otherwise and concluded that no more was to be got, and that such a Barrier would be their ruin."

Bristol replied that the Republic "had subsisted and flourished without any Barrier at all and consequently must the more do so with such a one as they might (now) have, which for ought I know may be better in the negotiation than is yet expressed". He told them that they must wait till Strafford returned to know the details of the negotiation.

Goslinga went privately to Bristol, to see if he would be more communicative unofficially. Bristol informed him that the Queen was making a suspension of arms, but refused to reveal the terms on which it would be concluded. Goslinga replied that his country would be thrown upon the charity of France, from which only God's mercy could save them.[1]

The suspense was short-lived: on the 28th of June Bristol informed the Deputies of the terms on which they could come into the Suspension of Arms.[2] These terms were neither more detailed nor more advantageous than those offered by Harley in April 1712: the tariff of 1664 "except certain species", the Barrier of 1709 "except two or three towns", and an explanation of the Treaty of 1709 with the Queen. It was clear that the English were determined to force the Republic to agree to their terms.

The Dutch "represented this proceeding"—the general terms for the Allies—"as the unavoidable ruin of Europe, and some of them seemed uncertain whether it was more advisable to expire with the common liberty, or to submitt to France and scramble for a share in the common plunder of the world". As to their disappointment with their own terms, Bristol warned the Ministry that he did not know "what to expect from the unreasonable Rage of these People nor where it will end".[3]

When he heard that Philip was to keep the throne of Spain, the Emperor turned once more to the Republic. Sinzendorf

[1] Goslinga to Buys, 28 June. Add. MSS. 20985.
[2] Deputies to Fagel, 28 June. Legatie Archief, 76.
[3] Bristol to St John, 28 June. S.P.F.H. 244.

roused himself from his usual lethargy and acted with unwonted skill. On the day after the news of the projected armistice, he informed the Dutch that it was in his power to offer a new alliance for the conquest of Spain; for which his master promised an army of 108,000 men.[1] This speech was effective: Rechteren eagerly considered whether others among the Allies would be prepared to join the Emperor, and was hopeful that the Duke of Savoy would be discontented with his compensation for the loss of Spain.[2]

The States General had now to decide upon its policy. The Deputies of Amsterdam remarked with truth that the Republic "had little to do with an affair which England could execute by herself", and that therefore it was of no avail to add conditions to the Suspension of Arms.[3]

The arrival of Strafford with the details of the Barrier and tariff roused the town of Amsterdam, eager though the Regents were for peace. Strafford's instructions were dated the 20th of June/1st of July[4] and were communicated by the Plenipotentiaries to the Dutch in the Chamber of Trèves, at The Hague on the 8th of July.[5] The armistice with France was justified on the grounds that the Dutch had refused to concert measures with England. "This proposition you are to repeat and insist upon as undeniably true and sufficient to justify Our Conduct throughout the whole course of negotiations" ran the instructions.

Then followed the tariff for the excepted species. The significance of the losses incurred by the exception of four species from the tariff of 1664, which the Dutch had hoped to gain entirely, may be grasped by a comparison of the three following tables. The tariff of 1664 was most favourable, and that of 1667 most unfavourable to the Dutch. That of 1699 by which the four species were now to pay approximated more nearly to the tariff of 1667.

[1] Weber, p. 296.
[2] Rechteren to Fagel, 1 July. Legatie Archief, 76.
[3] Deputies to the Regents, 2 July. Amsterdam Archives.
[4] Instructions to Bristol and Strafford, 20 June. S.P.F.H. 245.
[5] Plenipotentiaries to St John, 9 July. S.P.F.H. 244.

	1664[1]	1667[2]	1699[3]
Woollens	40 livres per piece	80 livres per piece	55 livres per piece
Whalebone	3 " "	—	20 " "
Whale oils	3 " per vat	12 livres per vat	7 livres 10 sous per vat
Fish	16 " per lath	—	40 livres per lath
Refined sugar	15 " "	22 livres 10 sous per lath	22 livres 10 sous per lath

The increase on whale products and on refined sugar would hit the town of Amsterdam particularly, as sugar refining and soap boiling were two of its most important industries. It is worthy of note that the duty on woollens approximated most closely to that of 1664: it is not unlikely that when making this provision, the English remembered that it would be of greatest importance to their country if they could also obtain the tariff from France.

As to the Barrier, the Dutch were not to give up all hope of Tournai and Condé, but the Queen thought the demolition of Dunkirk "reasonably purchased" by the cession of Lille. This was a cause of satisfaction to the Queen on other grounds,

since our Trade is so essentially concerned in the manufacture and commerce of this place and since they have already shown the Disadvantages they intend to put our Trade under by continuing so great a duty on our subjects whilst theirs are exempted from it notwithstanding the frequent representation of our Plenipotentiaries.[4]

On the following day, another conference was held regarding the general interests of the Allies.[5] Heinsius, Fagel and Slingelandt were present as well as the Dutch Plenipotentiaries. The Dutch pressed for the inclusion of Strasbourg in the Empire, a request to which the English gave a non-committal answer. Strafford then declared that he would not hold another conference until the Dutch instructed their Field Deputies to suspend hostilities. To St John he sent one of his illiterate notes in his own writing[6]:

Count Sinzendorf is the great Ingien (Engine?) that setts all at work and gives the money amongst them. They are certainly ambarrassed

[1] From tariff sent by Deputies to Fagel, 25 July 1712. Legatie Archief, 76.
[2] Elzinga, *Het Voorspel van het Oorlog van* 1672, p. 228.
[3] From tariff sent by Deputies to Fagel, 25 July 1712. Legatie Archief, 76.
[4] St John to Plenipotentiaries, 24 June. S.P.F.H. 245.
[5] *Ibid.*
[6] Strafford to St John, 9 July. S.P.F.H. 243.

and know not which course to take. Bothmar is a great man amongst them and talks so extravagently I can't but wonder at it they are freightened out of their Witts; one time they are fore one thing and the next minute for another. At noon we had worked them up to be with the Queen for the cessation, but this evening they were staggering and would not come to a resolution for an immediate cessation. However with much ado I got the letters to their deputies not to enter into any action for six days.

Strafford left The Hague that night for the allied camp, where he was to assist Ormond in the preparations for the suspension of hostilities. Bristol returned to Utrecht and the Dutch were left to come to a decision.

Outward quiet reigned but the war party in the Republic slowly gained the upper hand. Drummond, always the first to gain news of the feeling of the Dutch, reported that they would insist upon additional terms before they agreed to the armistice: the Townshend Treaty, the tariff without exception, and Strasbourg for the Emperor.[1]

Two important conferences[2] were held between the Dutch Plenipotentiaries and the high permanent officials at The Hague. The minutes of these meetings were reported in the precise hand of Buys. Opposite his own name he wrote the words "for the suspension of arms without any additional conditions". He had one supporter—Goslinga. The others, Van der Dussen, Van Randwyck, Van Geldermalsen, Van Wassenaer and Kniphausen followed Slingelandt who proposed that Strasbourg and Sicily should be given to the Emperor and that the fortress of Hunningen should be razed.

At the second conference, on the 12th of July, Buys "adhered to his advice of yesterday", but he admitted that the English ought to explain clearly their intentions as to Ghent and Dendermonde. He was joined on this occasion by Renswoude as well as by Goslinga, but the majority was against them.

Buys realised that, having so far capitulated to England, nothing was to be gained by forfeiting the assistance of the Ministers who held the reins of the negotiations in their hands.

[1] Drummond to Oxford, 12 July. Portland MSS.

[2] 11 and 12 July. Add. MSS. 20985.

Heinsius favoured the policy of Slingelandt: the failure of the Whigs to overturn the Ministry convinced him that the only way in which the Republic might gain her ends was by responding to the overtures of the Emperor.[1] Heinsius and Sinzendorf had achieved a closer understanding than had been the case for months since the disclosure of the Barrier Treaty. Former jealousies were lost in the common hatred of Great Britain. As a result, the "warrior party" daily gained ascendancy over Buys.

Still Heinsius wavered: the States of Holland drew up a resolution in which a middle course was adopted. At the suggestion of Rotterdam, the Queen was asked to suggest new proposals for the armistice and to suspend the withdrawal of her troops until the Dutch had communicated with the other Allies.[2]

Eugene wrote a sharp letter to the States General remonstrating against this delay. He advised the Dutch to refuse the armistice and at once to join in preparations for the new campaign.[3]

On the 13th of July, the States General submitted a resolution to the Provinces entitled "Points of Importance to be agreed before the Armistice is made".[4] These points were five in number:

1. Strasbourg for the Empire.
2. Sicily for the Emperor.
3. The immediate withdrawal of Maximilian Emmanuel from the Southern Netherlands on conclusion of peace.
4. Lille, Tournai and Condé for the States.
5. The tariff of 1664 entire for the States.

The Provinces were unanimous in their accession to this resolution. So high did feeling run in the States of Holland, that the whole proceedings were held up until the little town of Alkmaar could be persuaded to withdraw instructions that its

[1] Weber, pp. 296–7. [2] *Ibid.*

[3] *Ibid.* p. 297. Cf. Bristol to St John, now Viscount Bolingbroke. The Imperialists "do all they can to soothe the opiniatreté of the Dutch and encourage them to reject the suspension of arms", 23 July. S.P.F.H. 244.

[4] Deputies to Amsterdam, 27 and 29 July. Amsterdam Archives.

Deputies should insist on the preliminaries of 1709 as a basis for the armistice.[1]

The Queen's reply was that she would support them in obtaining modifications of the tariff with regard to woollens, fish and whale products. De Huxelles would not relent as to sugar. As to the other points she made no answer.[2]

The result was seen in the battlefields: Ormond found that he could not prevent the Dutch from joining the Imperial troops. Under the leadership of Eugene, the united armies left the English camp on the 16th of July.[3]

On the 19th of July,[4] Strafford reported to Bolingbroke that the armistice had been successfully arranged.

> I can now wish you joy (he wrote) of the most glorious situation it is possible for the Queen of Great Britain to be in, after such violent attempts to break her measures. She has now a bridle on France by Dunkirk, and on the States and Imperialists by Ghent[5]... and yet her Allies (cannot) accuse her of leaving them in the least, and 'tis both in reality and in the letter, their leaving her.

In the ensuing chapter it will be seen that the States General did not long pursue their fortunes apart from England.

[1] Deputies to Amsterdam, 27 and 29 July. Amsterdam Archives.
[2] Plenipotentiaries to Fagel, 23 July. Legatie Archief, 76.
[3] Weber, p. 267.
[4] Strafford to Bolingbroke, 19 July. S.P.F.H. 243.
[5] Bolingbroke arranged with De Torcy that English troops should enter Ghent.

CHAPTER VI

The Submission to England and the Settlement in the Southern Netherlands

I

THE movement of the allied troops culminated in a few days in a pitched battle at Denain on the 24th of July. The decisive victory of France convinced the Dutch that it was impossible to fight longer without England. At the same time, by raising the hopes of Louis XIV it made it harder for Heinsius to obtain even those terms they had first rejected.[1]

Louis's new demands concerned the interests of the Republic. De Torcy had almost come to an agreement with the English Ministry that the Duke of Savoy should be compensated for the loss of Spain at the expense of the Emperor, from whom Sicily would be withheld. After the battle of Denain, Louis replied that he was willing that Sicily should be given to the Duke on condition that the Spanish Netherlands were ceded to his faithful ally, the Elector of Bavaria.[2] This, he pointed out, would be easy of achievement, since the Queen already held Bruges, Ghent and Dunkirk.

The English Ministers were not prepared to grant this request, for fear of an outcry in Parliament if they should so much disregard the interests of their Allies, the Emperor and the Dutch. As they remained firm, Louis proposed to compensate the Elector by permitting him to remain in Namur, Luxemburg, Charleroi and Nieuwport until he was reinstated in the Empire or by giving him the island of Sardinia with the title of King.[3] These difficulties necessitated Bolingbroke's

[1] Weber, pp. 307–8.

[2] Dollot, pp. 371–5. Philip had made over his rights to the Spanish Netherlands to Louis XIV in January 1712, on condition that the Princesse des Ursins should be given a principality. Louis XIV had compelled Philip to make this cession in order that the Elector of Bavaria might be put in possession of those places still held by French and Bavarian troops.

[3] Weber, pp. 308–10.

journey to France in August 1712. While he was there, he obtained Sicily for the Duke. It was further decided that France and Britain should arrange the terms of peace, leaving the Allies to decide whether to come in with them or not.[1] Until these terms were settled, Bolingbroke determined not to give the Dutch the opportunity to make peace with France.

It was not so easy to keep the Dutch from negotiations after Denain. "This turn of affairs has given credit to Burghermaster de Haas' management at Amsterdam," wrote Drummond,[2] "and he has new life to push on the good work of a peace, which he is as hearty for as one would wish." De Haas deplored the loss of Lille and the exceptions of the tariff of 1664, though he was aware that "if they had come in sooner as we had often advised and pressed them, the Queen could have obtained that (the tariff) for them".

The first step towards England was taken on the 8th of August, when the Dutch refused to make a new alliance with the Emperor; Heinsius admitted that after Denain the States could go no further.[3] Eugene was well aware that there was little more to be gained from them.[4]

Bolingbroke summed up the situation when he wrote to Strafford in September[5]:

> it was very easy to foresee that the general intimacy between this Republic and the Court of Vienna would not be of any long duration. Their several views with respect to the Spanish Low Countries must of necessity set them at variance. Surely this consideration would have prevailed on wiser men to have modelled the Barrier Treaty to the Queen's satisfaction and in all other instances to have courted her friendship instead of provoking her resentment.

In short, Bolingbroke knew that the Dutch would come back to Britain, and he was prepared to wait until he could impose terms to his own satisfaction.

The sole difficulty was to prevent the return of the Dutch to negotiations until Anglo-French affairs were adequately settled.

[1] Weber, p. 310, 19 Aug.
[2] Drummond to Oxford, 6 Aug. Portland MSS.
[3] Weber, p. 326.
[4] A. R. von Arneth, *Prinz Eugen*, II, 499, 18 Aug. Eugene to La Serraz
[5] Bolingbroke to Plenipotentiaries, 26 Sept. S.P.F.H. 245.

As early as the 9th of August, Strafford informed Oxford that the Dutch would willingly capitulate at the price of Tournai and Condé, "to save the party who really wish well to your Lordship and your Ministry, from being reproached by the others as being betrayers of their country".[1]

By the 19th of August the Dutch intimated their desire to renew conferences with France.[2] This further irritated the Imperialists who insisted that the French must make the first offer, leaving the Allies to answer it.[3]

Fortunately for the plans of Bolingbroke a dispute arose on the 21st of August between France and the States General over a point of diplomatic prestige.[4] The original cause was a fight between the servants of Count Rechteren and those of Mesnager. The quarrel was kept alive until December as much by the management of the English Plenipotentiaries as by the obstinacy of the Dutch. Until Louis received the satisfaction of an apology and Count Rechteren's dismissal, there could be no direct approach to France. In this position of isolation the spirits of the Dutch Ministers fell to their lowest ebb.

During this period, the English Plenipotentiaries advised Bolingbroke that the Dutch should be given Tournai.[5] Strafford considered the fortress essential, as without it the Dutch would have no stronghold commanding Brussels, Louvain and Antwerp, except the unimportant fortress of Ath.[6] In the same letter (an

[1] Strafford to Oxford, 9 Aug. Portland MSS. "I desire to know clearly which you would have, that we should force the Dutch into the Queen's measures and clip their Barière so short that it might be of no great use to them if ever they should fall out with our Nation and so show them what is the Queen's resentment for their obstinate behaviour during all this Negotiation...or would your Lordship all at once end the war and have the States General submit entirely to the terms of the Queen's speech and renew a strict union and friendship with Her Majesty...now is the time to do what you will."

[2] Plenipotentiaries to Bolingbroke, 12 and 19 Aug. S.P.F.H. 244.

[3] Deputies to Amsterdam, 17 Aug. Amsterdam Archives.

[4] Plenipotentiaries to Bolingbroke, 21 Aug. S.P.F.H. 244. The management of the negotiations between the French and the Dutch on this point is to be found in detail in this volume of the State Papers. See also Weber, p. 327.

[5] Cf. 2 Sept. "Those amongst the Dutch who appear to be the most cordially disposed to such a peace as may establish a good harmony between us and the States...we find...firmly resolved to have Tournai and Condé yielded to them" (Plenipotentiaries to Bolingbroke, S.P.F.H. 244).

[6] Strafford to Oxford, 13 Sept. Portland MSS.

unofficial note to Oxford), Strafford suggested a new Barrier, one which might have given satisfaction to the Dutch. He proposed that the Emperor should garrison the Flanders fortresses, Knocke, Furnes, Ypres, Ostend and Nieuwport, while the Dutch should occupy Mons, Oudenarde, Menin, Charleroi, Namur and Tournai. According to Strafford the revenues of Ypres were more than those of the other fortresses, which would please the Emperor, while the Dutch would have Tournai, and strong defences on the Lys and Scheldt, without restricting English commerce.

> I am really not partial to the Dutch (concluded the complacent author of this scheme) but to Her Majesty's honour and your Ministry's: for if we obtain them Tournay and fix the Barrier as I mention it, I defy envy itself to say the Queen has not left the Dutch secure against France, even with the loss of Maubeuge, Valenciennes, Douay, Lille, Bethune, Aire and St Venant.

It is interesting to notice that although the Ministers of the Republic were convinced that they could no longer fight on, popular feeling was still dangerously high against England. Crowds threw stones at the windows of Strafford's house and those of the Ministers of Savoy and Prussia. In the streets an effigy of Bolingbroke was broken on the wheel.[1]

The first indication that the Ministry would relent was received at the end of September. Bolingbroke informed the Plenipotentiaries that, if the Dutch would submit to the English terms, "the Queen's compassion and the National pity would be moved...a wise and plain answer...would be the best Resolution which perhaps this Republic ever took".[2]

The Dutch were not long in taking the hint. On the 5th of October[3] Buys, Van der Dussen, Renswoude, Goslinga and Kniphausen visited the Plenipotentiaries. First they repeated their demand for Tournai and Condé and for an assurance that the Spanish Netherlands would be ceded to the Emperor and not to Maximilian Emmanuel, which would be to put them virtually in the hands of France. For this they would agree to

[1] Strafford to Bolingbroke, 16 Sept. The Hague. S.P.F.H. 243.
[2] Bolingbroke to Plenipotentiaries, 17/28 Sept. *Bol. Cor.* III, 71.
[3] Plenipotentiaries to Bolingbroke, 5 Oct. S.P.F.H. 244.

allow Louis Bethune, Aire, St Venant, Bouchain, Quesnoy, Douai, Maubeuge, Valenciennes and Lille, and come to an agreement on the four species. As to Strasbourg and Sicily, they were content to be guided by the Queen, who must be as anxious as they were to serve the Emperor. It was "a complete submission made at the Emperor's expense: with it, the French king's dreams of a separate peace were dissipated".[1] The Ministry realised that they could not deny peace to the Dutch without danger in England. "We shall not dare leave them behind us," wrote Bolingbroke, "...some of our best friends among the Tories would, in such case, join to condemn us."[2]

On the 30th of September (O.S.) Bolingbroke wrote to De Torcy to demand Tournai for the Republic, saying that it was in the hands of Louis to give peace to Europe. Just as in the case of Philip's renunciation of France, De Torcy gave way, because his country needed peace.[3] On the same day Bolingbroke expressed his opinion on Dutch policy in a letter to Strafford.[4]

> The Dutch do seem to take the right pli at last, but, give me leave to say, it is the only tolerable one which is left for them to take: for I fear neither their throwing themselves into the hands of France, nor their adhering to the Emperor's chimerical project: one is mad, the other is silly. They can never expect that France will give them better terms without the Queen than with her, and the proposals which come from Vienna have not as much as the force of probability to invite.

Matters were settled in Council with the Queen: Van Borselle was given a reassuring interview by Bolingbroke, in which the only cloud was the English Minister's remark that English troops would not evacuate Ghent and Bruges until the Queen was satisfied as to the commercial privileges of her subjects in the Southern Netherlands.[5]

Strafford was summoned to England to receive fresh instructions regarding the terms for the Republic.[6] He left with the

[1] Weber, p. 334.
[2] Bolingbroke to Prior, 29 Sept. (O.S.). *Bol. Cor.* vol. III, p. 124.
[3] Weber, pp. 335–7.
[4] Bolingbroke to Strafford, 30 Sept. *Bol. Cor.* vol. III, p. 133.
[5] Bassecour to Buys, 4/15 Oct. Add. MSS. 20985.
[6] Bolingbroke to Strafford, 30 Sept. (O.S.). S.P.F.H. 245.

assurance that Heinsius had changed his attitude to England.[1] At Amsterdam, Corver and De Haas were whole-heartedly for England.[2] Van der Dussen was overheard to mutter, "let us but gain time and matters will fall out more and more to our advantage", but if he was not drunk when he said this, as Buys explained to Drummond,[3] he was alone in his opinion.

II

The first days of November passed quietly, except for the Rechteren-Mesnager dispute. Despite his conviction that the Dutch could do nothing with France, Bolingbroke was careful to prolong the quarrel,[4] as the fishing rights off the coast of Newfoundland still delayed the English settlement with De Torcy.

Meanwhile the peace party in the Republic anxiously awaited the return of Strafford.[5] When he arrived on the 7th of December, his instructions[6] were to force the States "to agree entirely to lay aside the whole Barrier Treaty". If they would give their "immediate and absolute concurrence" in the conclusion of peace, Tournai was to be included in the Barrier. They were further requested to support the Queen's project for the Duke of Savoy and to permit the Elector of Bavaria to remain in Namur, Charleroi and Luxemburg until reinstated. Then followed the Project of the Barrier Treaty[7]: the Plenipotentiaries were "to show...that all alterations, additions and omissions, which are made, are only such things as are necessary to rectify mistakes and explain things doubtful in the former Treaty".

As this project was adopted almost word for word as the new Treaty, it is given here in full. The project was sent in Latin

1 Drummond to Oxford, 25 Oct. Portland MSS.
2 *Ibid.*
3 *Ibid.*
4 Bristol to Bolingbroke, 15 Nov. S.P.F.H. 244.
5 Bristol to Bolingbroke, in cipher, 2 Dec. S.P.F.H. 244. "Some of the States' Ministers seem to be in the utmost pain that My Lord Strafford's return is so long retarded, and the States thereby left in very dangerous uncertainties and those that are for peace very much exposed."
6 Instructions to Bristol and Strafford, 11 Nov. S.P.F.H. 245.
7 *Ibid.*

and in English. It begins with a note on the Latin copy, in English:

The first Separate Article (i.e. of the Treaty of 1709[1]) is entirely omitted because by the declaration which the States General made to the King of Prussia when he was last in Holland, they seemed to have themselves given up the Point of the Upper Quarter of Guelder and it would be rediculous of them to insist to engage the Queen to obtaine on their behalfe a point which they have yielded. An agreement must be made with the Emperor as to Bon, Huy and Liège: my Lords are of the opinion that the first should be garrisoned by the Emperor and the last by the Dutch.

The second Separate Article concerning the extension of Dutch territories into Flanders is to stand as it is in the former.

The Preamble and Article I declared the Barrier Treaty of 1709 to be null and void, as it contained provisions prejudicial[2] to the interest of Britain.

Article II pledged the Dutch to maintain the succession "as established" in Great Britain.

Article III pledged the Queen "to employ her utmost efforts in the Treaty of Peace not only that the Spanish Low Countries, but such other Towns or places as shall be found necessary, whether conquered or not conquered may be made use of to obtain a Barrier for the said States General".

Article IV. "...the States General may put garrisons in the following places, Furnes, Ft Knocke, Ypres, Menin, the town and citadel of Namur, the castle of Ghent, the Forts of Perle, Philippe and Damme, the Fort of Sluys being yielded to the said States General and Fort Rodenhuysen to be razed."

Article V. "In case of an actual warr with France, or an apparent attack on the part of France", the States General may put troops in any of the places in the Spanish Low Countries.

[1] Cf. Appendix E.

[2] In Latin "injuriosi". "Whereas in the Treaty which was concluded the 29 of October 1709...about the Succession to the Crown of Great Britain and the Barrier of the United Provinces several articles and clauses are contain'd, which require more ample Explanation, and which without some equitable Amendments, are already *prejudicial* and may hereafter prove dangerous to the welfare and Interest of her said Royal Majesty's subjects...."

Article VI. The States General may send into the places, fortresses, etc., where they shall have garrisons, without hindrance and without paying any duties, munitions and materials necessary for garrisons and fortifications.

Article VII. The States General may put, in the places mentioned in Article V, officers, governors, etc. "who shall not be subject to any other orders relating to the security and military government of the said places...but only to their High Mightinesses...yet without prejudice to the rights and privileges, as well Ecclesiastical as Political, of the Emperor Charles VI".

Article VIII. The States General may repair the said fortifications and towns.

Article IX.

Whereas it is agreed that the propriety and sovereignty of all the Spanish Low Countries shall belong to His Imperial Majesty...all the Revenues, except such part thereof as shall be necessary for the support of the Civill Government of the Towns, Fortifications etc. which are by this Treaty to be made part of the Barrier and which did not belong to the late King Charles II at the time of his death, shall be received by the said States General for the maintenance of Garrisons...upon this express condition, that the States General shall not by virtue of this Article, or on any other pretence whatsoever, assume a Power of laying on the said places any new impositions. (Further) to the States General, out of the clearest and best funds of such parts of the Spanish Low Countries as were in the possession of Charles II, at the time of his death, shall be paid the sum of one million florins, at the rate of 100,000 crowns each three months.

This article assigned to the States the same revenues as the first Barrier Treaty, but in the interest of England it limited their powers to increase them by additional duties. The revenue was further limited by the omission of Lille, Condé and Valenciennes, which were to be returned to France, and which were big towns with large revenues. Article VI of the first Barrier Treaty had promised "what more be conquered from France" and these towns, Aire, Douai, Bethune, Bouchain and St Venant were also to go to France.

Article X. No town, fortress, etc., to be yielded to France or to any Prince of the French line.

Article XI. The Queen of Great Britain "to prevail upon His Imperial Majesty to enter into a Treaty" on the Barrier with the States General and "to use her good offices until the said Treaty be concluded".

Article XII.

And whereas the supreme power in the Spanish Low Countries has ever since the reduction of them, been vested in Her Majesty and in the Lords the States General and their troops...it is hereby agreed that the Government of these Provinces shall not be altered, nor any of the said Towns and Fortresses evacuated until the trade and interests of the subjects of Great Britain shall be settled to Her Majesty's satisfaction and the Barrier of the States General be secured in the manner above stated.

This elaborate statement of what the Maritime Powers required before they would admit the Emperor into the Southern Netherlands, was new. They demanded satisfaction because they were conscious that their administration of the Southern Netherlands and their desertion of the Emperor in the peace negotiations gave the Emperor grounds for discontent, even for revenge.

Article XIII.

And whereas experience has already shown how necessary it is in the most effectual manner to prevent not only the obstruction and interruption or other Grievance, which may be occasioned to British Commerce by giving to the States the Jus Praesidii in so many places on the Rivers, Canals or other parts of the Spanish Netherlands, but also to prevent All Frauds and Collusions which may be practised by the abuse of the Privilege granted by the 6th Article of this Treaty, it is agreed that the subjects of the Queen of Great Britain shall in future, as well in time of war, as in time of peace, enjoy in all the places of the Barrier which shall be yielded to the States General, all the Privileges, Exemptions, Libertys and facilities which have already been granted or which shall hereafter be granted to the subjects of the States General in the said Spanish Netherlands and in the places of the Barrier, in such manner that no officer either civil or military shall ever be allowed to interrupt or retard the passage of Goods belonging to the subjects of Great Britain... (States General to punish offenders) and...the said States General do further oblige themselves to give sufficient and effectual orders and to cause the same to be strictly observed, that on account of the

Carriage of Provisions, Ammunitions etc. whereof mention is made in the said 6th Article no Frauds be committed in respect to the Dutys payable on Goods and Merchandises which shall never be laden nor carryed on the same vessells or other Carriages with the aforesaid provisions, ammunitions etc. and to the intent that all the particular Rules be established for the full and effectual observation of this generall Treaty it is hereby agreed that commissarys shall be appointed on each part who are to meet fifteen days after the signing this Treaty...to regulate together, and with those of His Imperial Majesty, if he shall think fit to appoint any, all matters relating to the commerce of the Spanish Low Countries or the Places of the Barrier.

As this article will be fully discussed in a later section on "The Provisional Regulation of Trade in the Spanish Netherlands", we shall pass to the final articles, XIV and XV, by which the troops for the mutual guarantee were arranged at 10,000 on the part of the Queen and 6000 of the States General, "to be increased if either party desire it", and by which provisions were made to invite Princes to join the Treaty, and for the ratification of the Treaty.

On his arrival at The Hague, Strafford immediately sent a page to ask if he might have a conference with Heinsius. He came at 6.30 in the evening of the 6th of December to the Pensionary's house, where he read his instructions in detail. From the minutes which the Pensionary took down in his own hand,[1] it is apparent that he was fully aware that the States General would have to act with unwonted speed, if they were to take advantage of this offer. Two or three weeks was the longest time which the Queen would permit for the States General to arrive at a Resolution.[2]

Within four days, the Queen's terms were despatched for the decision of the Provinces,[3] while Strafford left for the Congress, to detail his orders to the Dutch Deputies at Utrecht.[4]

It is interesting to notice how the old spirit lingered in the Republic: thus the deputies from the town of Rotterdam, whilst

[1] 7 Dec. Heinsius Archives, 76 A.

[2] Strafford to Bolingbroke, 9 Dec. S.P.F.H. 243. Cf. Strafford to Bolingbroke, 14 Dec. "It would be a matter of 16 days at the least." *Ibid.*

[3] Resolution of the States General, 10 Dec. *Ibid.*

[4] 15 Dec. Gouda Archives.

agreeing that they ought to come in with the Queen, could not refrain from adding "that although they wished to seek Her Majesty's friendship, the State must be careful of its own well-being. If they followed England so blindly, perhaps the world would think they had been intimidated by hard expressions and threats".[1]

The loss of the Upper Quarter of Guelderland was the greatest stumbling block to agreement with the English Ministry. As Heinsius pointed out to Strafford, if it were not mentioned in the Treaty, it would be impossible to procure it from the Emperor.[2] The Deputies of Amsterdam were near the mark when they suggested that the English were prepared to yield it to the King of Prussia, although Orrery, who was at that time at The Hague, assured them that it was merely reserved for the Emperor.[3] Even Sinzendorf, though he denied that the Emperor had ceded Guelders to them in the previous March, admitted that his master "had been near giving it up, except that the Dutch could not give an equivalent".[4]

The next difficulty was that the Dutch asked Strafford to change parts of the project "which seem so hard a reflection on the States to sign as if they had contrived and drawn up the last Treaty to cheat us", wrote Strafford. The Ambassador replied that the Queen might soften any hard expressions in the project, but she refused to change the sense of the Treaty in one article.[5]

From Almelo came the last protest of the warrior party: in the bitterness of his enforced retirement Rechteren wrote to Heinsius,

I find Strafford's communication so full of difficulties (*Haaken en Oogen*), that without altering the whole, I cannot see how this State and the other Allies can find in it any security at all, the more that a compulsory agreement will lead to slavery...and so I beg you to confide in me and to ask the Province of Holland and the Regents

[1] Account of the Assembly of the States of Holland, 15 Dec. Gouda Archives.

[2] The town of Guelders was still held by the King of Prussia, 14 Dec. *Ibid.*

[3] Deputies to Amsterdam, 16 Dec. Amsterdam Archives.

[4] Strafford to Bolingbroke, 14 Dec. S.P.F.H. 243. Cf. p. 258.

[5] *Ibid.*

if I may not co-operate to manage things for the best interest of our dear Fatherland.[1]

No notice was taken of this communication. On the 19th of December Heinsius held a conference with the Deputies of Foreign Affairs, and with Buys, Goslinga, Van der Dussen and Randwyck. These gentlemen counselled agreement with the Queen's project, though remarking that it contained some things that were painful to the Republic. It was suggested that they should ask for Fort St Marie, in compensation for Dendermonde.[2] Next day Heinsius reported this conference to the Province of Holland. He informed the Deputies that the Provinces of Utrecht and Friesland had consented to come in with the Queen's measures. It was the opinion of the Ridderschap that the demands for Bonn and Upper Guelder were not sufficient to hold up the Treaty. The Deputies of Leyden agreed, though they added that "Dendermonde ought to be ours".[3]

Strafford heard that the Deputies of Amsterdam were empowered to acquiesce in the project, in the hopes that the four species and the Upper Quarter of Guelderland would be given as a reward.[4] Bolingbroke had no intention, however, of settling the Dutch tariff until he had first concluded an agreement with De Torcy over the fishing rights off Newfoundland, for fear that the Dutch might be ready to sign a peace without England.[5]

Though the French Plenipotentiaries were "surprized and uneasie" that Strafford and Bristol had received no instructions on the four species, De Torcy calculated rightly that the Ministry would force the Dutch to accept the tariff of 1699 for them[6]: in December the Dutch were not aware of this bargain.

On the 3rd of January 1713 the Dutch Plenipotentiaries informed Strafford that they were empowered to agree to the new Barrier Treaty.[7] Before they would sign, they awaited the

[1] Rechteren to Heinsius, 20 Dec. Heinsius Archives, 76 A.
[2] Memorandum by Heinsius, 19 Dec. *Ibid.*
[3] 20 Dec. Gouda Archives.
[4] Plenipotentiaries to Bolingbroke, 20 Dec. S.P.F.H. 244.
[5] Bolingbroke to Plenipotentiaries, 9 Dec. (O.S.). S.P.F.H. 245.
[6] Plenipotentiaries to Bolingbroke, 23 Dec. S.P.F.H. 244.
[7] Plenipotentiaries to Bolingbroke, 3 Jan. 1713. S.P.F.H. 246.

Queen's answer to a letter from the States General, asking if fresh instructions might be sent to the English Plenipotentiaries on certain points. This letter was delivered by Van Borselle on the 30th of December (O.S.). "It was a joyful moment for the Ministry to have the capitulation of the States at last within their hands."[1] Their exultation was turned to exasperation when they heard that simultaneously the Whigs had received a copy of this letter to the Queen. It was considered, wrote Bolingbroke to Strafford,[2]

> an affront and Indignity...I mention this the rather, and dwell the longer upon it, because we have good reason to believe that the States are running once more into that dangerous Error, which has cost them already so dear, of depending upon efforts to be made upon our side of the water, to disturb the Queen's affairs, and that in this view they will keep us in suspense, in expectation of what may be done in Parliament to strengthen them in perplexing the Treaty... cure them of any such expectations.

As to the Dutch suggestions, continued Bolingbroke's reply, the first, that the Preamble should be dropped, "cannot be granted as it gives one of the reasons for making the New Treaty". The second suggestion, that to the Dutch guarantee of the Protestant Succession the words "as now determined" should be added, Bolingbroke refused as "very extraordinary". "Your Lordships may observe", he continued, "the invidious affectation of the States in their remark on this article and you would do well to let them know how much the Queen is obliged to them for assisting her in the laws of Great Britain." In view of Bolingbroke's connection with the Old Pretender, this retort is interesting as an early indication of the way in which he was to turn.

The third demand in the States General's letter concerned additional towns for the Barrier. These were Condé, Dendermonde and Fort St Marie. The first was refused on the ground that after the resistance and defeat of the Allies, the Queen was not now in a position to ask it for them. As to Dendermonde, it was in too important a position on the Scheldt to be given

[1] Weber, p. 350.
[2] Bolingbroke to Plenipotentiaries, 7 Jan. (O.S.). S.P.F.H. 248.

to the Dutch. Fort Marie was similarly refused as "a bridle to Antwerp".

Fifthly, the States demanded a clause in the Treaty stipulating for equality of trade in the Spanish Netherlands. "Such precautions are necessary for us as they have no occasion for", was all the reply they were given, "as it is the Dutch who are to have the occupation of the Spanish Netherlands".

In reality, at Orrery's instigation, the Ministry contemplated the conclusion of a private agreement with the Emperor, by which they might gain commercial privileges superior to those given to the Republic.[1]

The sixth request, that the Treaty of Münster should be confirmed by the Barrier Treaty, the Ministry refused to allow. Nor would they agree to guarantee Upper Guelderland to the Dutch (Article VII), or do more than make an agreement with France as to the tariff for the four species (Article VIII).

(Finally), the Queen thinks that if the States are seriously inclined as they pretend, to root up and take away all seeds of diversion, there can be no pretence, no room whatsoever, to object to the signing of the Treaty forthwith as it now stands.... Your Lordships will observe to them that this is a surer and a more decent way of prevailing with the Queen to back and assist them in their disputes with the Emperor and with other Powers, than by endeavouring to tye Her Majesty down by formal Articles, to every Usurpation, little or great, that they have a mind to make upon the Revenues and Privileges of the Spanish Netherlands.

This refers to the attempt on the part of the Republic to arrange securities for the payment of the million assigned to them out of the Spanish Netherlands as they were at the time of Charles II's death.

The Queen's answer was communicated to the Dutch on the 28th of January. On the evening of the 30th, they made a handsome apology for the communication of their letter to the Whigs at the same time as to the Queen. They declared themselves ready to accept the Treaty unaltered, if the Plenipotentiaries would change certain expressions in the Preamble. They proposed that the new Treaty should be made on account

[1] Cf. pp. 305 *et seq.*

of certain parts in the Townshend Treaty which were "prejudicial" and not "willfully harmful", as the English project stated. Strafford was willing to accept this alteration, and on the same night the Treaty was signed and sent to England for ratification.[1]

The history of the negotiations leading up to this Treaty has shown the essential difference between the first and the second Barrier Treaty. Throughout the months which followed their return to office, the Ministry aimed at reducing the power of the Dutch in the Southern Netherlands and in this they had succeeded.

In the first place the number of fortresses to be garrisoned by the Dutch was severely limited. The line of Inner communications—Dendermonde, Lier and Hal—was gone. On the French frontier, Lille, Condé, Valenciennes, Nieuwport and Maubeuge, which were specifically promised by the first Treaty, were omitted, as also Douai, Aire, St Venant, Bethune and Bouchain, which might be claimed as coming under the promise of "what more be conquered from France".

The inclusion of Mons was an inadequate substitute for these losses and for the omission of Liège and Huy and for the limited acquisitions in the Upper Quarter of Guelderland on the east.

Despite these omissions, the Treaty was a considerable advance upon the Treaty of Ryswick, as the Dutch were given Furnes, Fort Knocke, Ypres, Menin, Tournai, Mons, Charleroi and Namur on the Outer line; Ghent for communication with the United Provinces, and the Forts of Perle, Philippe and Damme, with a promise of extension of Dutch frontiers for control of the Scheldt. Further they were provided with an adequate revenue for the upkeep of these fortresses.

Finally, the restrictions on Dutch powers in the Southern Netherlands were made solely with the intention of safeguarding English commerce: hand in hand with England the Dutch might still exploit these provinces to the utmost.

[1] Plenipotentiaries to Bolingbroke, 30 Jan. S.P.F.H. 246. The change was the substitution of "damnosi" (prejudicial) for "injuriosi" (meaning harmful with the suggestion that there should be compensation). The Treaty is printed in Appendix E.

III

The Barrier Treaty of 1713 finished, there remained for consideration certain points arising out of it: the settlement with France, the disposal of Guelderland and the Provisional Regulation of trade in the Spanish Netherlands.

Close on the signature of the Barrier Treaty followed the settlement of the Rechteren dispute. On the 31st of January the French Plenipotentiaries announced themselves satisfied and the Dutch were once more free to negotiate with France.[1]

The cardinal point of these negotiations was Tournai. This had been promised to the Dutch on condition that the Elector of Bavaria should remain in the Southern Netherlands until reinstated, and that the four species should be excepted from the tariff of 1664.[2] When it came to negotiations with France, the Dutch received an unpleasant surprise: Mesnager claimed that while the Ministry had stipulated for Tournai and the Tournesis for the Dutch, they had agreed to certain exceptions in the Tournesis, namely the Bailliages of Mortagne and St Amand.[3] Further, from the Châtellanies of Ypres, the French claimed the Bourg of Commines and the Bailliage of Bailleul.[4] These fortifications were of importance, in the case of Tournai, as ensuring freedom of communications between Arras and Douai with Condé and Valenciennes. The Châtellanies of Ypres were necessary to secure communications with Lille.

In the project of the Barrier Treaty, no mention of such exceptions had been made. The English Plenipotentiaries had in good faith assured the Dutch of Tournai and Ypres entire. On the 2nd/13th of December Bolingbroke despatched a letter to Strafford in which he apologised for his "carelessness" in omitting to state these exceptions: "how far they may be reasonable or unreasonable," he concluded, "I am afraid we are too little acquainted with the geography of that place to determine".[5]

[1] Plenipotentiaries to Bolingbroke, 31 Jan. S.P.F.H. 246.
[2] Plenipotentiaries to Bolingbroke, 6 Jan. *Ibid.*
[3] De Torcy to Bolingbroke, 12 Oct. 1712. Enclosed in Bolingbroke to Plenipotentiaries, 2 Dec. 1712. S.P.F.H. 245.
[4] De Torcy to Bolingbroke, 26 Oct. *Ibid.*
[5] Bolingbroke to Strafford, 2/13 Dec. *Ibid.*

At the first conference between the French and the Dutch, on the 3rd of February, the French claimed their rights in accordance with Bolingbroke's promise. At first the Dutch were inclined to insist on a "quid pro quo" in the four species,[1] but on the 17th of February they capitulated,[2] possibly in the hopes of obtaining the support of the English Plenipotentiaries in the matter of Guelders.

With regard to Upper Guelderland, the Ministry were, on the whole, indifferent: Prussian support counted for little now that the war was over and, on the question of merits, Bolingbroke wrote that "the behaviour of all the Allies has been so equally bad to the Queen that it is not to be expected that she should side very warmly with Holland against Prussia, or Prussia against Holland, or take much part in the disputes between the Dutch and the Imperialists".[3]

At Utrecht, however, the King of Prussia had a warm supporter in the Earl of Strafford, who retained his affection for the Court at which he had formerly been Ambassador.[4] Accordingly Strafford despatched a long letter to Oxford in favour of the King, recapitulating the old arguments: the Dutch had produced no equivalent in accordance with the Treaty of Münster: the Queen had entered into no engagements on that head in the Grand Alliance: the Dutch had maintained Maestricht for years without additional communications: finally, "give it to the King of Prussia and you fix an eternal obligation on that Prince and his descendants... you have a Prince of the Empire on your side, and a check on the Dutch".[5] Similarly he advised Bolingbroke that it would be "worth the Queen's while to gain the young king's affection and confidence".[6]

Bolingbroke was lukewarm: he decided "neither to perplex

[1] Shrewsbury to Bolingbroke, 20 March. Cf. *Bol. Cor.* III, 505.

[2] Plenipotentiaries to Bolingbroke, 17 Feb. S.P.F.H. 246.

[3] Bolingbroke to Plenipotentiaries, 28 Jan. S.P.F.H. 248.

[4] See p. 171. Rive, *Nederland en Pruissen*, also insinuates that Strafford had been bribed by the King of Prussia. I have found no trace of this transaction, although money was of great importance to Strafford and his letters are full of his difficulties. On the other hand, a violent partisanship on honourable grounds is not out of keeping with his character. Further he loved to increase his importance by guiding the policy of the Ministry.

[5] Strafford to Oxford, 24 Jan. 1713. Portland MSS.

[6] Strafford to Bolingbroke, 18 March 1713. The Hague. S.P.F.H. 246.

nor retard" peace on this question. He thought that after the Barrier Treaty of 1713 the Dutch had claims to the Queen's support: as to the new King of Prussia

> the Queen is of opinion that there is little to be built on so uncertain a character as that of this Prince, and if one may judge by the manner in which he sets out, it must be rather the Interest of Britain to hinder him from having a footing in the Netherlands than to give him one there. His army, it seems, is to be his Mistress and war his Trade; he will therefore employ the one and promote the other wherever he has to do. Whereas it ought to be our aim always to keep war out of a country that is in our Neighbourhood.[1]

Behind this leaning towards the Dutch, Bolingbroke concealed his real policy. If the Dutch were given Upper Guelderland, he hoped that they would be more willing to further the interests of the Princess des Ursins, whose ascendancy over Philip V had been of service in the past,[2] and might be of use in the future. This was the more necessary as there were signs of a rift between the Courts of Madrid and Versailles.[3] The reward suggested was a Principality worth 30,000 crowns a year in the Spanish Netherlands.[4] Luxemburg was proposed, but the Princess had a preference for Limburg, which was agreeable to Bolingbroke as it was not part of the Barrier against France.

The next step was to inform the Emperor that this was a "sine qua non" of peace.[5]

Strafford raised the claims of the Princess at a conference on the 22nd of February.[6] It was inevitable that the Dutch should resent the intrusion into the Spanish Netherlands of a Princess connected with Philip, when the Barrier Treaty had stipulated that no place should be ceded to a member of the House of Anjou. Nevertheless, the English acquiescence in their claim to Guelderland was tempting. The sincerity of the Ministry is

[1] Bolingbroke to Plenipotentiaries, 3 March. S.P.F.H. 248.

[2] Bolingbroke to Plenipotentiaries, 16 March. The Princess had helped to assign the Asiento to Britain. Cf. Bolingbroke to Plenipotentiaries, 3 July. "This lady's power is seemingly absolute." *Ibid.*

[3] Bolingbroke to Plenipotentiaries, 10 Feb. *Ibid.*

[4] Bolingbroke to Plenipotentiaries, 3 Feb. *Ibid.* and Drummond to Oxford, 9 Jan. Portland MSS.

[5] Bolingbroke to Plenipotentiaries, 3 March. S.P.F.H. 248.

[6] Plenipotentiaries to Bolingbroke, 22 Feb. S.P.F.H. 246.

vouched for by a cipher letter written some days later by Bolingbroke to the Plenipotentiaries: "Her Majesty is of opinion that in the present circumstance of affairs, it is much more her Interest with respect to what is to come, as well as much more reasonable for her on account of what is past, to give satisfaction to the lady rather than to the king".[1]

The hope of Upper Guelderland was the more tempting, since the Dutch were at that moment in negotiation with the Emperor on the subject. The Emperor, feeling his growing isolation,[2] was not unfavourable to a new project for a closer relationship with the Dutch. This was a reversion to Rechteren's "Barrière en Arrière". Instead of garrisoning the frontier fortresses, the Dutch proposed that they should keep Upper Guelderland, fortify Lier and Hal, keeping the land between these towns and the Dutch frontier to themselves, together with an extension of their territories in Flanders to Sas van Ghent. This would enlarge their territories and make them compact: money spent by Dutch troops would return to and circulate in the Republic.[3]

In reporting this scheme, Strafford felt that the gravest objection would be the harm to English commerce, if the Emperor were master of the Spanish Netherlands, without the restraint of the presence of Dutch troops. Strafford had heard that Eugene would be made Governor-General and feared that the Prince, with the true Italian spirit of revenge "...would avenge himself on our commerce".[4]

Sinzendorf assured Strafford that he would be informed of the course of negotiation by Count Maldighem,[5] one of the Deputies sent by the States of Brabant to protest against the Barrier Treaty. The plan was fantastic, since it was not to be expected that the Emperor would cede so much to the Dutch—including the control of Antwerp—to keep them out of the Spanish Netherlands.

In any case, the Emperor was not put to the trouble of a decision. On the 28th of February the Prussian King announced

[1] 3 March. S.P.F.H. 248.
[2] Weber, pp. 357–86.
[3] Strafford to Oxford. Portland MSS.
[4] *Ibid.*
[5] *Ibid.*

his intention of retaining Guelders and of compensating the Prince of Frise for their joint loss of the Principality of Orange, which the French refused to give up. The Dutch Plenipotentiaries were astonished and chagrined: they pointed out vainly that the King of Prussia had no right to keep Guelders in compensation for Orange. They blamed the Ministry for favouring the King, but Strafford replied that the Queen had behaved impartially to her three allies, and that he had always resisted the French claim to Orange.[1]

The Imperial Ministers were at first as indignant as the Dutch, but they were pacified by the proposal that they should be given Roermond and Stevensweert, as communications between the Empire and the Spanish Netherlands. Strafford believed that they would prefer to share Upper Guelders with Prussia rather than cede all to the Dutch,[2] thus showing that the Emperor had not taken the "Barrière en Arrière" seriously.

The arrangements for the Princess des Ursins were once more upset, but Strafford hoped to gain his point by a further division of Upper Guelderland. He proposed that the Emperor should keep Roermond, with the sovereignty of the Province, and that the Dutch in compensation for Guelders should be permitted to share the garrison of Roermond and to have Stevensweert, Fort St Michael and Venloo. If they should agree to this, they should desist from Fort Damme, which they were to have by the second Barrier Treaty. This would be advantageous to England, as the Deputies from Brabant alleged that the possession of Damme would make the Dutch masters of the canal from Ostend to Bruges and Ghent.[3]

Bolingbroke agreed to this proposal[4] and on the 27th of March a conference was held, at which the disposal of Upper Guelderland was finally arranged. A Treaty was concluded on the 2nd of April,[5] by which the Emperor and the Dutch received the towns proposed by Strafford, and the King of Prussia kept the town and district of Guelders, the Circle of Kriekenbeek and

[1] Plenipotentiaries to Bolingbroke, 28 Feb. S.P.F.H. 246.
[2] *Ibid.* [3] 18 March. *Ibid.*
[4] Bolingbroke to Plenipotentiaries, 16 March. S.P.F.H. 248.
[5] Plenipotentiaries to Bolingbroke, 4 April. S.P.F.H. 246.

Kessel, on condition that he renounced his other claims and promised the Dutch free communications on the Maas.[1]

The disposal of Upper Guelderland removed one of the remaining obstacles to peace. The Dutch continued to create difficulties over the Principality for the Princess des Ursins, but were persuaded to include a guarantee of the Principality in their treaty with France. The last difficulty in the way of signature was the provision for the Elector of Bavaria.

Uplifted by his successes with the Dutch, Louis raised his terms for Maximilian Emmanuel. He demanded that the Emperor should compensate the Elector for infringement of the Treaty of Ilbesheim, the treaty by which, in 1704, the Emperor took over Bavaria on the understanding that Maximilian should keep certain revenues. This claim led to the withdrawal of the Emperor from the Congress.[2] Meanwhile Louis insisted that the Elector should retain the sovereignty of those places he still held in the Southern Netherlands. This the Dutch opposed, but, under pressure from England, the difficulty was settled in the following way: on the interchange of ratifications between France and the Republic, the Elector would place in the hands of the Queen an act of cession of the Spanish Netherlands. This renunciation would be given to the Emperor when the Elector's claims were satisfied. Until then, the Elector would remain undisturbed in the possession of Namur, Charleroi and Luxemburg.

The Dutch Treaty[3] with France was signed on the 11th of April, the day on which the English Treaty was also concluded. In the Treaty the tariff of 1664 was dropped, as the Dutch refused to grant the French a reciprocal tariff, that of 1665.

[1] The final settlement was hindered by the Prussian king's refusal to evacuate Erkelenz. The Dutch refused to give him Kriekenbeek and Kessel until this condition was fulfilled, but they were forced to give way on 5 June 1713. Then ensued an endless quarrel between the King and the Republic as to whether the right given to the town of Guelders, of putting tolls on the Maas, would go with the town, or with the Maas fortresses, Venloo, Roermond and Stevensweert, as the tolls were intended for their upkeep. In the end, the Emperor decided in favour of the Dutch. Cf. Rive.

[2] Weber, pp. 370–86. Neither party had adhered strictly to the Treaty, this was the Emperor's ground for refusing compensation.

[3] Terms printed in Gachard, p. 230. The Treaty is in Dumont, vol. VIII.

Each country was in future to impose what duties it pleased. Strafford suspected that the Dutch agreed to this in the hope that Louis would not grant the tariff of 1664 to Britain.[1] The Treaty confirmed the settlement in Upper Guelderland. As to the Barrier, it stipulated that the Spanish Netherlands should be given to the Emperor when the Dutch had received satisfaction. To their Barrier Louis ceded Menin, Tournai and the Tournesis (except Amand and Mortagne), Furnes, Knocke and Ypres, with its dependencies (except Bailleul). Finally, in a separate article, Louis promised, on behalf of Philip, to confirm the advantages of the Treaty of Münster. In return, the Dutch agreed that the French Commissioners should assist at Anglo-Dutch Conferences on the duties in the Spanish Netherlands which the Emperor should be asked to confirm. Till then, all parties should pay on the footing of the arrangements of 1680. The French attempted to secure the same advantages as the Maritime Powers (the tariff of 1680), but to this the Dutch would not agree.

IV

In the disposal of the Spanish Netherlands, the English aimed at security for British Commerce. This could only be achieved by two safeguards, precautions against Dutch competition and arrangement for favourable treatment from the Emperor.

The second Barrier Treaty imposed restrictions on the Dutch: they were to lay no new impositions (Art. IX); the Queen's troops might remain in the Spanish Netherlands until she was satisfied in all her interests (Art. XII); finally the Commissioners of the Maritime Powers were to arrange commercial regulations by which English trade should be put on an equal footing with the Dutch, after the ratification of peace (Art. XIII). As this provision could not be executed at once, the Ministry turned to negotiations with the Emperor.

[1] Plenipotentiaries to Bolingbroke, 11 April. S.P.F.H. 246. The fate of the Anglo-French commercial treaty was other than the Dutch anticipated. Louis did agree to the tariff of 1664, but the Treaty was rejected by Parliament when it met to propose the act in which the Treaty should come into force. Parliament rejected the Treaty for fear that if the Methuen Treaty were overshadowed, Portugal would retaliate by prohibiting English woollens. Further the Portuguese trade left a money balance to England. Hewins, *English Trade and Finance*, p. 141.

Bolingbroke realised the possibilities of gaining commercial privileges from the Emperor, by skilful use of the jealousy between Charles and the Dutch over the Spanish Netherlands. Charles "cannot but be sensible", he wrote[1] "that the manner in which he will have (the Southern Netherlands) depends directly on Her Majesty...and takes the turn of desiring to be reconciled to the Queen, and thereby to procure something more than the empty name of sovereign". Gradually the English inclined to the policy of a separate agreement with the Emperor, behind the back of the Dutch Ministers.

In this Bolingbroke was encouraged by the Emperor's relations with his future subjects, the people of the Spanish Netherlands. The States of Brabant, alarmed at the exactions of the Condominium, sent a deputation to Utrecht in the winter of 1712 to ask for the immediate inauguration of the Emperor.[2] On the 12th of November the Deputies presented a Memorial to the British Plenipotentiaries in which they demanded the inauguration of the Emperor and recalled the promises of Marlborough in May 1706.[3] The Queen replied in a letter assuring them of her protection and support, but nothing was said as to the evacuation of the Provinces by the Maritime Powers.[4]

The next step on the part of the Southern Netherlands was to draw the attention of the Court at Vienna to the danger that the Maritime Powers would establish the tariff of 1680 for ever, by making it a condition of the inauguration of the Emperor.[5] They suggested that the Emperor should divide the Maritime Powers, by pointing out to the English that while they could import only by Ostend to Bruges, the Dutch could use the rivers and canals. Further, while the Dutch could import to Antwerp, Mechlin, Brussels, Ghent, Dendermonde and part of the land of Waes at ordinary rates, the English goods were required to pay "vatghelt".[6]

[1] Bolingbroke to Orrery, 2 Jan. 1713. Foreign Entry Books, 13.

[2] Gachard, p. 221. The Province of Flanders, with the exception of Ghent, refused to join this deputation.

[3] *Ibid.* pp. 222–3.

[4] *Ibid.* p. 225 *note* 2, 7 Jan. 1713.

[5] Huisman, p. 51.

[6] 15 Jan. 1713. S.P.F. Flanders, 62. "Vatghelt" explained by Orrery to

Unfortunately the Emperor did nothing, whether because of his difficulties in the peace negotiations, or from indifference to the grievances of his new subjects. This left the way clear for the Maritime Powers to gain their terms in accordance with the Barrier Treaty.

For the Dutch the situation was complicated by their claims for the upkeep of the Barrier. They demanded not only the tariff of 1680, but also an annual payment of a million florins from the revenues of the Southern Netherlands exclusive of the New Conquests. These territories had formerly yielded six million florins annually, or at the most eight millions, under the extraordinary taxation of Count Bergeyck. In the opinion of Laws, secretary to Lord Orrery at Brussels, the depredations of war, and the expenses of the troops in occupation of the Spanish Netherlands made it impossible to raise more than five million florins per annum.[1] Clearly it would be impossible for the Emperor to appropriate one-fifth of this diminished income for the upkeep of the Barrier.

On account of this difficulty, Lord Orrery proposed to Bolingbroke that the Queen should safeguard her interests by a separate commercial treaty with the Emperor, after which she should remove her troops from the Southern Netherlands to avert risings on the part of the impoverished people "who grow more and more out of humour since the signing of the Treaty of Barrier",[2] leaving the Dutch to extricate themselves from their troubles as well as they could.

Orrery forwarded the project of a commercial treaty. It contained the usual articles concerning debts, lawsuits and contraband, and also important financial provisions.[3] The tariff of 1680 was to be granted with minor alterations (Art. II); "vatghelt" was to be discontinued when the payments for which it was assigned were discharged (Art. III); the malt tax, similarly assigned for payment of forage, should be abandoned

Bolingbroke: "Octrois or grants made to members of the States of Flanders and assigned for certain payments".

[1] Laws to Bolingbroke, 15 Jan. 1713. S.P.F.Fl. 62.

[2] Orrery to Bolingbroke, 6 Feb. S.P.F.Fl. 62.

[3] Project of a commercial treaty between the Queen and the Emperor. *Ibid.*

when the debts on forage were paid off, or at least the tax should be lowered to its former rate, to relieve "the gentlemen of Norfolk and Suffolk" (Art. VI); goods were to pass freely through the Provinces, after having paid duty at Ostend and Nieuwport (Art. VII); no additional duty was to be laid on goods exported from the Provinces, and in the case of goods re-exported within thirty days, the duties of entry were to be refunded (Arts. VIII and X); a sum was to be earmarked from convoy duty for repairs to Ostend (Art. XI); to keep Ostend out of "the hands of those whose views might be prejudicial to the Emperor's trade", the Queen was to be permitted to garrison the town and was to receive certain sums for the expenses of the garrison (Art. XII). Finally, by Article XIII, the activities of the Conference from 1706–13 were to be confirmed to preserve "the honour of the two powers, and to show a resentment... against those who have been most active in opposing their Authority".

"This," wrote Orrery, "or some Treaty of this kind, I think should be stipulated between the Queen and the Emperor, because there are some parts of it that perhaps should not be common to the Dutch, who will have another Treaty of their own, I suppose, with the Emperor on their Barrier."[1]

Meanwhile it became more and more apparent to the English Plenipotentiaries that some time must elapse before the Emperor and the Dutch could settle their difficulties. The Dutch Plenipotentiaries received powers to treat on the 8th of February 1713,[2] and on the 10th of March an important Conference on the Barrier Treaty was held between the Maritime Powers and the Imperialists.[3] Sinzendorf opposed the Dutch claims to the million florins and to garrisons in Damme and Ghent. The Conference drew up a list of "points to be regulated between the States General and the Emperor by the good offices of the Queen". In addition to the points already mentioned there were other difficulties: freedom of worship for those of the Reformed religion in the Barrier towns, the Emperor's confirmation of the financial administration of the Conference, the arrangement for

[1] Orrery to Bolingbroke, 13 April. S.P.F.Fl. 62.
[2] 8 Feb. 1713. Heinsius Archives, 76 A.
[3] Plenipotentiaries to Bolingbroke, 10 March. S.P.F.H. 246.

debts of the Spanish Low Countries, the continuation of the privileges of the Treaty of Münster and the extension of the States' territories in Flanders.

The Imperialists' comments on the second Barrier Treaty were reduced to writing: in Article IV they objected to Ghent, Damme, Perle and Philippe and suggested that Fort St Donas should be razed: in Article VII they required a clause providing that in the appointment of officers, governors, etc., only those should be appointed who were not disagreeable to the Emperor: further they should take an oath of allegiance to the civil authorities in matters of finance, jurisdiction and in ecclesiastical affairs: finally they should promise never to admit foreign troops into the Barrier without the Emperor's permission. To Article VIII, by which the Dutch were permitted to repair and fortify the Barrier, they added the words "at their own expense". They objected to Article IX, which concerned the payment of the million of revenue and they relegated the discussion of Article XII, concerning commerce and the separate article for extension of the limits in Flanders to a future date, not then determined.

On the 28th of March the Dutch went so far as to relinquish Damme and to admit a common garrison in Ghent, but there was no concession on either side as to the million.[1]

Much as Bolingbroke would have preferred to separate England from the Dutch in commercial arrangements, the Emperor's withdrawal from negotiations precluded any such manœuvres. By the end of March, it was obvious that Charles would once more leave the Maritime Powers, and that the Conference would be required to carry on the government of the Spanish Netherlands for a longer period. This necessitated a closer co-operation on the part of the Maritime Powers. Their relations with the Council of State had been unfriendly in the past: they were now to reach a climax, after which the Southern Netherlanders were more fully subjugated to the Conference than ever.

The struggle had begun in March 1711 when Marlborough and Orrery, in conjunction with Van den Bergh and his colleague van Reede, had drawn up a new Regulation defining

[1] Plenipotentiaries to Bolingbroke, 28 March. S.P.F.H. 246.

the relations between the Conference and the Council of State. This Regulation was insufficient in the eyes of Van den Bergh, at whose instigation new provisions were drawn up in October of the same year. This second Regulation aroused the opposition of the Council of State, who refused to sign it. To the disgust of Van den Bergh, Orrery did not insist on their signature, but was content with a declaration that they would observe the new Regulation.[1] No doubt Orrery sided with the Council of State on account of the Dutch restrictions on English trade in the Southern Netherlands, and hoped to gain the support of the inhabitants in defence of English privileges. This view is supported by the change in English policy in December 1712, when Orrery returned, after a year's absence, to Brussels. After the capitulation of the Dutch which led to the second Barrier Treaty, the Maritime Powers were again united and Orrery was instructed to make the Council of State obey the Conference. On the 5th of January 1713 Orrery and Van den Bergh signed a requisition in which the Council was charged with exceeding its powers, by resisting the demands of the Conference. The Council of State replied that they had to consider the interests of the Emperor, an answer which was both ambiguous and disrespectful, according to Orrery. The Ministry was the more indignant, as "for some years past the Queen had employed her authority as a screen for them against...hardships in another Quarter".[2]

Orrery now demanded that the Council of State should not only sign the Regulation of the 29th of October 1711, but also that they should acknowledge their subordination to the Maritime Powers. The Council of State protested and appealed to the Emperor. In this protest they were supported by the States of Brabant.[3] Once more the Emperor was unable to defy the Maritime Powers and ordered his Ambassador to disavow the conduct of his subjects.[4] This left the Council of State at the mercy of the Conference: on the 18th of March Orrery and Van den Bergh demanded that the members of the Council

[1] Gachard, pp. 373–80.
[2] Bolingbroke to Orrery, 2 Jan. F.E.B. 13.
[3] Gachard, p. 386.
[4] *Ibid.* p. 387. Cf. Orrery to Bolingbroke, 20 March. S.P.F.Fl. 62.

should sign the declaration and acknowledge the subjugation to the Conference, or absent themselves from the Council.[1] As the Council of State refused to sign, Orrery and Van den Bergh proceeded, with the help of Clairmont, the only friendly member of the Council, to appoint new members.[2] The protests of the States of Brabant and Flanders and the capitulation of the old Council, at the bidding of Sinzendorf, came too late. The new Council of State remained until the definitive Barrier Treaty of 1715 released the Southern Netherlands from the government of the Conference.[3]

The result of this conflict was to convince Bolingbroke that Orrery must remain in the Southern Netherlands to assist Van den Bergh until the Emperor was inaugurated. To protect English interests, as he wrote to Orrery, "the Government must hobble on as hitherto".[4]

V

The choice of an English Commissioner "to regulate trade to the Spanish Netherlands from Her Majesty's Dominions" fell wisely upon Drummond. Drummond received his commission on the 25th of April.[5] He expressed the hope "that neither the Dutch nor the English could say he was ignorant of his work".[6] He was chosen not only for his qualifications but also because Orrery could not leave Brussels, as his presence was required to keep the Council of State in check.[7] Van den Bergh was appointed Dutch Commissioner and three delegates were sent from the Council of State.[8] The Commissioners assembled at Utrecht, as the Maritime Powers feared to arouse popular feeling by holding the conferences at Brussels.[9] When they met, it was clear that the aims of the Commissioners were very different.

Drummond was to find "how to bring the Dutch to reason,

[1] Orrery to Bolingbroke, 20 March. S.P.F.Fl. 62.
[2] Gachard, p. 392. [3] *Ibid.* p. 401.
[4] Bolingbroke to Orrery, 1 May. F.E.B. 13.
[5] Drummond to Oxford, 25 April. Portland MSS.
[6] *Ibid.*
[7] Orrery to Bolingbroke, 8 May. S.P.F.Fl. 62.
[8] Huisman, p. 55.
[9] Orrery to Bolingbroke, 13 April. S.P.F.Fl. 62.

who have so long used to turn everything to their own advantage in the Spanish Netherlands and to lay the Queen's subjects under Double Duties".[1] To do this it was necessary for him to remove the "comptoirs" between the New Conquests and the Spanish Netherlands.[2] Further, the Ministry did not wish the new Regulation to be seized as an excuse to alter the tariffs.[3]

The additional duties laid by the Dutch on goods going from the Spanish Netherlands to the New Conquests have been detailed in a previous chapter.[4] There were similarly two duties of export on British woollens, fish and East India goods going beyond the Barrier to France, Lorraine and the Empire "for a better market and a greater consumption".[5]

On his arrival at Utrecht Drummond claimed redress for these impositions by Article XIII of the new Barrier Treaty. The Dutch opposed alterations on the ground that the French might demand a like equality; in reality the Dutch designed "to keep matters on the foot they are", wrote Drummond.[6]

Drummond drew up a project for the Provisional Regulation. Before it was agreed upon, he persuaded the Dutch to make two important Resolutions. By the first, the States General promised to remove all "comptoirs" and officers of receipt of customs from betwixt the Spanish Netherlands and the New Conquests, both of export and of import, and to declare "that all the trade of Great Britain, having once paid the duty of Ostend and Nieuwport, should be free from all other duties in and through the Spanish Netherlands and New Conquests". By this means the duties of export and import into the New Conquests, amounting to 8 per cent., were removed.

By the second Resolution, all goods and manufactures of Great Britain passing through the Spanish Netherlands and New Conquests towards France, Germany or any other countries should pay once and for all, duties of import and export, 2½ per cent. of the value, as duty of transit.[7]

[1] Drummond to Oxford, 25 April. Portland MSS.
[2] Huisman, p. 55.
[3] Bolingbroke to Plenipotentiaries, 3 March. S.P.F.H. 248.
[4] Cf. Part II, Chap. 1.
[5] Drummond to Oxford, 8 May. Portland MSS.
[6] Drummond to Oxford, 11 July. Portland MSS.
[7] *Ibid.*

The next step was to arrange the footing on which the duties of export and import should be paid in future. The Dutch were again unwilling to make alterations and resorted to "groundless and unreasonable chicaneries", which Drummond does not retail to the Lord Treasurer. As these artifices failed, they provoked a quarrel between Strafford and Drummond, by reporting to Strafford that Drummond had said that the Plenipotentiaries had no more power over him than the Dutch Plenipotentiaries had over their Commissioners, "an expression not at all becoming in a broken Merchand", wrote the indignant Strafford.[1] The Ministry tactfully made no complaint to Drummond, and the quarrel subsided, although Strafford continued to cherish his resentment.

The Commissioners from Brabant and Flanders arrived to confer upon the million promised by the Barrier Treaty to the Dutch.[2] They complained of the exactions made by Orrery on behalf of English troops in the Southern Netherlands.[3] The Dutch seized this point as another obstacle in the way of the Provisional Regulation. They agreed for once with the Southern Netherlanders that these exactions were a contravention of the Barrier Treaty. Strafford argued that in virtue of the Treaty, the Queen's troops might stay in the Southern Netherlands until commerce was satisfactorily arranged; this meant, in his opinion, that the troops should be kept at the expense of the Southern Netherlands. The Dutch replied that the revenues of the Southern Netherlands should be applied first for civil expenses, then for the million paid to the States General, next for interest on loans and finally what remained should be applied for the maintenance of an equal number of English and Dutch troops. Strafford retorted that preservation was the main object, and that unless the administration was well supported there would be no revenues to pay for anything.[4]

[1] Strafford to Bolingbroke, 17 July. S.P.F.H. 246.

[2] The Commissioners were appointed by the Council of State. It is interesting to notice that the Plenipotentiaries recommended Orrery to exert his influence that "such will be chosen as will be most useful to our trade, those of the side of Ghent and Bruges rather than of Brussels, and interested in making English commerce easy, rather than in the improvement of the finances of the Spanish Low Countries". 3 June 1713. S.P.F.H. 246.

[3] Strafford to Bolingbroke, 21 June. S.P.F.H. 246.

[4] *Ibid.*

After a month, the persuasions of Strafford and Drummond began apparently to have effect. More probably, the fear of an insurrection in the Southern Netherlands prompted this yielding to the Queen: Van den Bergh's report of the behaviour of the Council of State in spring demonstrated the necessity of co-operation with Lord Orrery. This would not be forthcoming if the Provisional Regulation were not signed. On the 19th of July Buys showed Strafford letters which he had written to the Dutch Plenipotentiaries "explaining the reason why they ought to change their conduct and do everything to settle a harmony between the Queen and themselves, or else naturally all things in these countrys must fall into confusion before the time comes to deliver them to the Emperor".[1]

On the 22nd of July Buys, Van der Dussen and Kniphausen informed Strafford that they were ready to sign the Provisional Regulation. In proof of their goodwill, they showed him a Resolution of the States General, "to take off immediately their Comptoirs and to require the Council of State at Brussels to remove them to the frontiers, the States General being content that all ye officers (officials) should belong to the Flemings", with a Dutch controller at their head. They desisted from their demand to have Dutch officials, as Strafford had objected that "any collectors of theirs would be inspectors of our commerce".[2] Further, they suggested that the revenues of the conquered Provinces should be collected in the following way: the Dutch should give up their claim to duties of entry and exit in the conquered Provinces, and should receive instead duties on the manufactures or growth of these countries and on goods entering them for consumption in the Provinces. To avoid confusion, they would take a certain proportion of these duties, and suggested one-third.[3]

These proposals were agreeably received by the English Plenipotentiaries and on the 15th/26th of July the Provisional Regulation was signed and despatched to England for ratification.[4]

[1] Strafford to Bolingbroke, 19 July. The Hague, S.P.F.H. 246.

[2] Strafford to Bolingbroke, 22 July. S.P.F.H. 246.

[3] *Ibid.*

[4] Printed in *Actes et Mémoires concernant la Paix d'Utrecht*, IV, 556. Signed by Bristol and Strafford and by six of the Dutch Plenipotentiaries.

The most important provision, from the English point of view, was Article I, by which trade was to be regulated on the footing of the tariffs for France, Britain and the United Provinces in the year 1680.[1] Then followed the precautions against the Dutch. All goods, whether from Britain or from the United Provinces, should pay a fixed duty of transit, $2\frac{1}{2}$ per cent. *ad valorem* (Art. II). No goods, either British or Dutch, should pay additional duties of entry, or of exit, on going from the Southern Netherlands to the New Conquests (Art. III). Goods going to France or other countries from the Southern Netherlands or from the New Conquests should pay only one duty of exit according to that paid in 1680 (Art. V).[2] The duty of convoy was to be arranged by the Conference at Brussels (Art. VI). All the articles in the Treaty were to be promptly executed by the Conference (Art. VII).

The Provisional Regulation, if it could be adequately executed, would secure British trade in the interim until the Emperor made peace and took over the Southern Netherlands. It was a great triumph to have forced the Dutch to yield, for, as Bolingbroke wrote to Bristol, "it is of some consequence to pin down the Dutch as soon as possible by a formal and positive agreement. We must enforce the execution of it as a subsequent instead of a previous concert with the Council of State and Finance".[3]

[1] In sending the draft of this article to Oxford, Drummond said it ensured "the equality of duties to be paid by both Nations, viz. by the Queen's subjects at Ostend and Nieuwport, not to exceed in any manner what the Dutch pay at or by the Scheldt, Sas or Swyn, and...the duties shall not exceed what was paid in the year 1680, which is the most reasonable and easy foot we ever were on". Drummond to Oxford, 11 July. Portland MSS. These duties were more favourable to the Maritime Powers than to France: nevertheless, the French Commissioners for the present proposed no alterations in the Provisional Regulation. Cf. Bristol to Bolingbroke, 21 July. S.P.F.H. 246.

[2] Cf. Drummond to Oxford, 18 Aug. 1713. Portland MSS. This meant that English woollens arrived in France more cheaply than if they had been sent directly from England to France.

[3] Bolingbroke to Bristol, 23 June. S.P.F.H. 248.

VI

As Orrery was in England, the task of enforcing the Provisional Regulation at Brussels was entrusted to Laws.[1] The re-establishment of the tariff of 1680, the removal of "comptoirs" on the frontier of the Southern Netherlands and New Conquests and the replacement of Dutch officials by those appointed by the Council of State were the points of chief importance to England.

To the Dutch the payment of the million of revenue and the adjustment of the revenues of the New Conquests were of paramount importance. They were reluctant to give up their control of the "comptoirs" until these points had been settled beyond dispute. Thus their first Resolutions contained the proviso that they would remove the "comptoirs" on the frontier of the New Conquests, and put the remaining "comptoirs" in the hands of the Council of State, if they might appoint a Dutch controller, to supervise the new officials, and if they would be assigned one-third of all the revenues of the New Conquests.[2]

The Council of State refused to accept a Dutch controller and offered not one-third but a quarter of the revenues of the New Conquests, although they resolved to accept the Provisional Regulation. A further proof of their recalcitrance in the matter of payments to the Dutch was afforded when it was reported that they were busy with a Memorial to show the impossibility of paying the million assigned on the revenues of the Southern Netherlands.[3]

There appeared no prospect of a settlement between the Dutch and the Council of State, without English intervention. In the meantime the Dutch had not improved their chances of success in winning the support of the Ministry: their representative in the Conference, Van den Bergh, claimed the power to sign the requisitions of the Conference in his name, without even consulting Strafford or Laws, during the absence of Lord

[1] Bolingbroke to Laws, 15 July. F.E.B. 13.

[2] Plenipotentiaries to Bolingbroke, 28 July. S.P.F.H. 246.

[3] Laws to Bolingbroke, 5 and 18 Aug. S.P.F.Fl. 62.

Orrery. "As matters go," wrote the indignant Strafford, "that scandalous fellow governs all alone."[1]

Bolingbroke at once took steps to remedy this defect. Laws was instructed to act jointly with Van den Bergh, as Orrery was not to be replaced. Bolingbroke gave him further instructions to soothe the feelings of the Council of State: he had no wish to stir up the bitterness of the previous March by making fresh definitions of the relations between the Conference and the Council. In his final letter to Laws—for he was about to leave the northern department in charge of Bromley—he reiterated his policy: "We do not think of becoming legislators in the Spanish Netherlands, or forming a new model of Government. It is enough for us to patch and prop up this, that it may last while the Queen has to do with it, which she hopes will be as little a while as possible".[2]

The Dutch, alarmed at the prospect of losing the million, desired a Conference on the subject with Strafford. To propitiate the Ministry, they hinted that they would withdraw their troops from Ostend.[3] They proceeded to denounce Orrery's exactions for "forage and logement" of British troops. Strafford remarked that "he was sorry they had begun with complaints" which he considered trifling. He refused to confer upon the million and demanded that Van den Bergh should be ordered to refrain from signing for the Conference without Laws.[4]

Nevertheless, the grievances of the Dutch moved Strafford. In a second Conference they assured him they had not received one farthing of the million, as the Council of State alleged inability to pay while the Queen demanded 90,000 florins per month for upkeep of her troops. The States pointed out that this was unfair, when they had come to an agreement with the Queen in the second Barrier Treaty: "the States are certainly inexcusable in some things," wrote Strafford,[5] "but in others

[1] Strafford to Bolingbroke, 19 Aug. S.P.F.H. 246.

[2] Bolingbroke to Laws, 26 Aug. F.E.B. 13.

[3] Strafford to Bolingbroke, 25 and 31 July, 26 Aug. S.P.F.H. 246. Ostend was of such importance to British trade that if the Dutch were to evacuate it, the Ministry might comply with their request to garrison Ghent and Bruges.

[4] Strafford to Bolingbroke, 26 Aug. S.P.F.H. 246.

[5] Strafford to Bromley, 9 Sept. S.P.F.H. 246.

(pardon my presumption), they have but too just reason of complaints".

The new secretary, Bromley, replied that the million would be considered when the States permitted Laws to exercise a joint sovereignty in the New Conquests. Her Majesty's friendship, could "never be had without mutual complyance".[1]

A new factor entered into this web of negotiation: at Utrecht the French Commissioner Voultier demanded that France should be granted the commercial concessions which she enjoyed in the Spanish Netherlands in the year 1680.[2] This was in accordance with the Franco-Dutch Treaty, but the Council of State had not been consulted on the matter. The Council had already agreed to favourable terms for the Maritime Powers and they were not prepared to lower their tariff for yet another country, particularly as the duties of entry into France were almost prohibitive. This view earned the sympathy of Laws, who saw that the high duties on goods imported into France would hamper the exportation of British goods from the Southern Netherlands.[3]

With Laws, the Ministry was in agreement, but, fearing to offend the French, they suggested that any opposition must come from the Council of State or from the Dutch, as England could not actively protest.[4]

The Council of State received no help from the Dutch, who were also anxious to propitiate France and to gain the support of England in the matter. To conciliate the Ministry the Dutch again declared their readiness to evacuate Ostend, if the Queen would allow them to occupy Ghent and support their claim to the million.[5] Further, by a Resolution of the 11th of October, they confirmed the establishment of one duty of import and export in the Spanish Low Countries.[6] By the end of November the double duties had altogether ceased and the "comptoirs" on the frontier of the New Conquests were removed.[7]

[1] Bromley to Strafford, 8 Sept. F.E.B. 80.
[2] Drummond to Oxford, 23 Sept. Portland MSS.
[3] Laws to Bromley, 5 Oct. S.P.F.Fl. 62.
[4] Laws to Bromley, 1 Nov. S.P.F.Fl. 62.
[5] Drummond to Oxford, 1 Nov. Portland MSS.
[6] Strafford to Bromley, 18 Oct. S.P.F.H. 246.
[7] Drummond to Oxford, 10 Dec. Portland MSS.

This harmony between the Maritime Powers effectually hampered the Council of State in its resistance to France. The Council heard with irritation that Fraula and Castillon, the Deputies sent to Utrecht to treat on the commercial terms for France, had been stopped at The Hague to confer on the million promised to the Dutch. In their report the Council of State alleged that the sum could be raised, not from the revenues of the Spanish Netherlands, but only by extraordinary voluntary aids from the Provincial Estates, such as were granted for the maintenance of Imperial troops. Such a payment would be difficult for the Dutch to obtain, as they were esteemed "to be the greatest enemies to those countries".[1]

On the 29th of December a stormy Conference was held at The Hague. Strafford was represented by his chaplain, Ayerst, as he was on leave. The Dutch opened the proceedings by requesting Fraula and his colleague to lower the duties on French goods to those paid in the year 1680. The French Commissioner had arrived from Utrecht to complain at the delay in execution of this promise by the Dutch. The Deputies of the Southern Netherlands begged the question by replying that they could not make peace with an enemy of the Emperor. They complained that French duties on goods of the Southern Netherlands would not be correspondingly lowered. The Dutch assured them that if the Council of State would grant the desired tariff, the States General would use their good offices with France for the removal of this grievance.

As to the million, Fraula and Castillon said that it was impossible to raise so large a sum on account of the ravages of war and also because certain revenues still accrued to Maximilian Emmanuel from those towns which he held as yet. The two Deputies grew angry as the Conference proceeded and finally declared that they would never "pay tribute" to the Dutch: the most they would do would be to keep a greater number of their own troops, which the Dutch might employ in defence of their Barrier if they pleased.[2] Ten days later, they left The

[1] Laws to Bromley, 15 Nov. and 25 Dec. S.P.F.Fl. 62, enclosing the Council of State's Report.

[2] Ayerst to Bromley, 29 Dec. S.P.F.H. 246.

Hague without having reached an agreement on the million or the terms of France.[1]

For the present, the question of the French tariff was the more important. The Maritime Powers feared to offend France, while Louis was about to make peace with the Emperor. Van den Bergh was ordered to join with Laws in persuading the Council of State to give way. The Council of State could not resist all three powers without the support of the Emperor which was not forthcoming. On the 20th of January Laws reported that the Council of State had agreed to remove the double duties on French goods, imposed since the French had been driven out by the Allies. Further, the Council agreed to grant to the French the tariff of 1670 and subsequent ordinances up to 1680.[2] Thus by the 24th of January 1714, French grievances were removed.[3]

The Provisional Regulation was now fully executed, with the exception of the continued dispute between the Maritime Powers as to the admission of Laws into the administration of the New Conquests. The provision of securities for the Dutch million livres remained in abeyance, and the desire to obtain adequate payments was to influence the Dutch project of the third Barrier Treaty with the Emperor.

English interests were satisfied: it remained for the Ministry to obtain the Emperor's sanction of the commercial privileges in the Southern Netherlands.

[1] Laws to Bromley, 8 Jan. S.P.F.Fl. 62.
[2] *Ibid.* and Laws to Bolingbroke, 20 Jan. S.P.F.Fl. 62.
[3] Cf. Huisman, p. 58.

CHAPTER VII

The Preliminary Negotiations of the Third Barrier Treaty

I

THE approaching peace between the Emperor and Louis XIV made it apparent that the Barrier Treaty would soon be the subject of negotiations, as the conclusion of peace would not be reached until the Emperor took over the Southern Netherlands from the Maritime Powers.

The anticipation of negotiations with the Emperor made the States General reluctant to take any steps which might offend him, by guaranteeing possessions to the Duke of Savoy or to the Princess des Ursins in their treaty with Spain.[1]

During the negotiations between Charles VI and Louis XIV at Rastadt, a new danger arose. The Maritime Powers feared that the Emperor might exchange the Southern Netherlands for Bavaria. The English were against this as they were apprehensive that commerce might be restricted if the Elector were to take over these Provinces. As a precaution Strafford was instructed to obtain the Emperor's promise never to alienate Ostend and to appropriate a fund from the revenues of the Southern Netherlands for the maintenance of the port.[2]

As a further safeguard Strafford was sent to Brussels in order to uphold the Queen's authority and, if possible, to placate the Regency.[3]

[1] Strafford to Bolingbroke, 30 Aug., S.P.F.H. 246, and Strafford to Bromley, 20 March. S.P.F.H. 249.

[2] Bromley to Strafford, 16 Jan. F.E.B. 80.

[3] The English term for the part of the Condominium in which the people of the Southern Netherlands represented the Emperor. There was a controversy at Brussels between Laws and Van den Bergh as to whether the Dutch should appoint magistrates in the New Conquests alone, or jointly with the Queen. Laws to Bromley, 15 Feb. S.P.F.Fl. 63.

The Queen had been adored in the Southern Netherlands, (was his conclusion[1]) had more care been taken to manage these people, who reproach us the rigour with which we exacted the forage from them for the Queen's troops and those foreigners in her pay. However a little kind and impartial usage will soon make them forget that and bring them entirely to be devoted to the Queen.

This optimism was not justified, although for the moment the Council of State assured Strafford that they were "very sensible of Her Majesty's goodness" and gave him "a Positive Promise before Mr Laws that no change should be made to oblige Her Majesty's subjects to pay more than they did at present".[2]

If we are to believe Laws, the members of the Council of State were flattered by the visit of a person of such "high quality and distinguished character".[3] Doubtless the motive underlying their complaisance was the desire to gain the Queen's support against the Dutch in the forthcoming negotiations, as the Emperor had hitherto paid little attention to their struggles. In a later letter,[4] Laws made a further observation on feeling at Brussels (one which has not been indicated in the work of Gachard). "They are very apprehensive of being governed by the maxims of the Court of Vienna, or any General from thence, to whom they would infinitely prefer the Elector of Bavaria and do not despair of some expedient being found for his returning thither."

II

When Strafford returned to The Hague towards the end of February 1714, he found the Pensionary undecided as to the course he should adopt in negotiating with the Emperor. "They seem to grow every day more and more perplexed in their politics", reported the Ambassador.[5] The question turned on whether the Dutch should bid for the support of Britain against the Emperor, or forgo the aid promised in the second Barrier Treaty and negotiate alone.[6]

[1] Strafford to Oxford, 20 Feb. Portland MSS.
[2] Strafford to Bromley, 2 Feb. S.P.F.H. 249.
[3] Laws to Bromley, 15 Feb. S.P.F.Fl. 63.
[4] To Bromley, 14 May. S.P.F.Fl. 63.
[5] To Bromley, 23 March. S.P.F.H. 249.
[6] Cf. Bussemaker, "De Republiek der Vereenigde Nederlanden en de Keurvorst Koning George I" (*Bijdragen voor vaderl. Geschiedenis verz.*

The Dutch had reason to mistrust the present Ministry in England. Heinsius was again in correspondence with Lord Oxford, who was now on bad terms with Bolingbroke, because he disliked the latter's predominance and mistrusted his dealings with the Pretender. Oxford indicated the probability of the Queen's demise and encouraged Heinsius to resist the Ministry. The result was seen in the Grand Pensionary's refusal to deal with the guarantee of the King of Sicily or to send a Minister to watch the negotiations at Baden until the disposal of the Southern Netherlands had been arranged. "It was plain that the Republic sought their security in the benevolence of the Court of Vienna, while waiting for the change in England: the Dutch believed their natural friends to be the Whigs, the Elector of Hanover and the Emperor."[1]

Strafford was determined that England should mediate between the Republic and the Emperor, in order to protect British trading interests. In April he perceived that Heinsius was equally determined to exclude him from negotiations. Heinsius suggested that the concert of the Queen should be confined to those points only which were included in the second Barrier Treaty. Strafford replied that "several points required extension", before the Queen would give up the Southern Netherlands, particularly those concerning trade. He suggested that before the Queen would leave the Southern Netherlands, the Emperor should sign a definitive treaty of commerce and a convention never to alienate Ostend.[2]

The Pensionary replied that the second Barrier Treaty made no such stipulation, upon which Strafford argued that it was implied in Article XII and pointed out that the Dutch themselves intended to negotiate on points not included in the Treaty,

Blok en Muller, vol. IV, 1900), in which he notes the reluctance of the Dutch to agree to Strafford's points for Anglo-Dutch co-operation. 23 Feb. 1714:

(1) To watch the negotiations at Baden to protect the Protestant interest.
(2) To guarantee the King of Sicily.
(3) The Dutch to conclude peace with Spain.
(4) Joint squadron for the Baltic.
(5) The conclusion of the Barrier Treaty with the Emperor and the evacuation of Ostend by the Dutch.

[1] Bussemaker, *op. cit.* p. 76.

[2] Strafford to Bromley, 6 April. S.P.F.H. 249.

namely their claim to garrison Huy, Liège, Roermond and Venloo.

Heinsius saw clearly that the Ministry wished to prevent a close understanding between the Dutch and the Emperor.[1]

In the meantime, he received reassuring news from Vienna as to the Exchange Project. Bruyninx, the Dutch Ambassador, informed him that "the Emperor himself was more inclined to prefer the Southern Netherlands partly...to keep on good terms with the Dutch and also partly from motives of ambition and affection for the Spaniards, to keep so much of the Spanish Inheritance as is possible". There was one important condition attached to this decision: "there must be no additional burden on the Emperor; with the help of the Dutch, the Southern Netherlands must protect themselves...as no money can be sent from here, as the Spanish Kings have hitherto done".[2]

A week later,[3] Bruyninx had an important Conference with Sinzendorf, who informed him of the instructions to be sent to Heems, the Imperial Minister, at The Hague. The Emperor insisted upon two points: (1) the Southern Netherlands and the New Conquests must be treated as "an inseparable entity", to be preserved in the Emperor's hands; (2) the Southern Netherlands must be delivered up without additional burdens on the Emperor. As to the place for negotiation, the Emperor preferred Vienna, but would substitute Frankfurt, Cologne or Brussels if the States desired.

These points were made by Heems in a Conference at The Hague on the 15th of May. He intimated that the Barrier Treaty of 1713, as part of the Utrecht settlement, could not be recognised by the Emperor, and that accordingly negotiations would proceed without reference to it. Further, the Southern Netherlands belonged "by right" to the Emperor, who would himself keep sufficient troops for their defence, unless the Dutch would accept the terms of the Treaty of Ryswick and

[1] Hetzlar to Bolingbroke, 14 April. S.P.F.H. 251. A correspondent of Bolingbroke informed him that "some people do maliciously intimate that Britain chiefly aims to make the Republic fall out with the Emperor on the subject of the Spanish Low Countries".

[2] Bruyninx to Fagel, 2 April. Heinsius Archives, 56 A.

[3] Bruyninx to Fagel, 28 April. Heinsius Archives, 56 A.

permit the Emperor to appoint the governors in the Barrier towns.[1] This meant a reversion to the old idea of the Barrier of isolated garrisons, Mons, Charleroi, Namur, Luxemburg, Courtrai and Oudenarde. It was plain that the Emperor meant to ignore the events from 1706–14 and to disregard the new conception of the Barrier evolved by the Dutch at the beginning of the century. To him, the Southern Netherlands were to be treated as one of his hereditary Provinces and he refused to look upon them as lands in trust for the security of the Dutch.

The apparent acquiescence of the Dutch in the proposition to negotiate alone alarmed the English Ministry. Strafford pointed out that if, as Drummond suggested, the Queen were to make a private commercial treaty with the Emperor, instead of one in concert with the Dutch, she might be left in the lurch when the Republic had arrived at a settlement with the Emperor.[2] "If they make such a condescension to the Emperor," replied Bromley,[3] "Her Majesty will conclude that they intend to observe no measures with her in the future, Her Majesty's concurrence being certainly necessary in this transaction because of settling the trade in Flanders." Bromley intimated that the cession of the Southern Netherlands must be made jointly by the Maritime Powers and stated that the Queen would refuse to evacuate them until her interests were satisfied. The situation was considered so grave that Bolingbroke wrote an additional letter in the same strain, warning the Dutch that the Queen had resources "if pushed to extremity".[4]

Further news was still less reassuring: Strafford reported that the Dutch made their communications to him unofficially, as they did not wish him to take a formal part in negotiations. He was aware that Heinsius hoped for a change in the Ministry. "I know," he wrote,[5] "some time ago they did not address themselves to us because they were assured of a change...and thought the Whigs would have got the uppermost."

On the 18th of May, Strafford made a vigorous protest

[1] Strafford to Bromley, 15 May. S.P.F.H. 249. Cf. Bussemaker, p. 76.
[2] Strafford to Bromley, 6 April. S.P.F.H. 249.
[3] Bromley to Strafford, 27 April (O.S.). F.E.B. 80.
[4] Bolingbroke to Strafford. *Bol. Cor.* III, 525.
[5] Strafford to Bromley, 30 April/11 May. Portland MSS.

against the attempt to exclude England from negotiations. As to the Emperor's pretended right to the Southern Netherlands without regard to the Barrier Treaty, Strafford argued that

taking the matter from its original, he will find himself consequently obliged to it, being he was certainly a party to the Grand Alliance in which it is stipulated that the Allies should engage to conquer the Spanish Low Countries to serve for a Rampart and Barrier to separate France from the Provinces of the States General and that the Allies should afterwards agree to the manner of settling these countries to that end.

Further, the Emperor had virtually admitted this by allowing Eugene and the troops in the Southern Netherlands to be under the joint administration, by objecting to certain parts of the Townshend Treaty and by holding conferences before the conclusion of the second Treaty. Though by the Treaty of Rastadt the Emperor was not strictly bound to treat with the Queen on the subject, yet the Dutch, by the Barrier Treaty, were bound not to treat without her. Strafford concluded by saying that the Queen would not object to the negotiations taking place at Brussels, but that the Emperor could not first appoint a governor until the Treaty was concluded, as it would give him more power there than that enjoyed by the Conference.[1]

On the 22nd of May, in obedience to instructions,[2] Strafford delivered an ultimatum. If the Dutch did not admit the Ambassador into negotiations the Queen would "take care of her own interests without them". Instructions would be sent to Dunkirk to transfer the English troops there to the garrisons at Nieuwport, Bruges and Ghent, where they would remain until the Queen had come to terms with the Emperor. On this news, the Pensionary showed some signs of relenting and asked if the Ministry would object to their coming to a composition with the Emperor on the terms of the Barrier Treaty. Strafford replied that they would agree and wrote complacently to Bromley that the Queen would be included in negotiations. "I continue still to think", he concluded, "that the way to treat these people is with a mixture of authority and kindness."[3]

[1] Strafford to Bromley, 18 May. S.P.F.H. 249.
[2] Bromley to Strafford, 1 May. F.E.B. 81.
[3] Strafford to Bromley, 22 May. S.P.F.H. 249.

Bromley did not leave the protection of the Queen's interests to Strafford alone. He wrote to Brussels to ask the advice of Laws as to the making of a separate commercial treaty with the Emperor. Laws suggested the revival of the commercial treaty of 1667, with a proviso for the tariff of 1680 and a convention as to Ostend. His only fear was that the people of the Southern Netherlands would demand reciprocal treatment in the reduction of the high duties on the importation of linen into Great Britain.[1]

At The Hague the uncompromising attitude of the Emperor, coupled with the fear of the rupture with the Queen, made Heinsius decide that the best course to adopt would be to placate England by admitting Strafford to the Conferences on the Barrier, and to use the Queen's guarantee to obtain their demands from the Emperor. The pacific party was again in the ascendancy.[2]

The States showed their disposition to friendly relations with the Queen by announcing on the 25th of May that they would insert her name in a letter to the Emperor on the arrangements for negotiations. This was followed by a Resolution promising to join with the Queen in using their "good offices" to obtain the principality for the Princess des Ursins, to guarantee the King of Sicily and to admit Strafford to the Barrier Conferences.[3]

Rumours of the instability of the Ministry again made the States reluctant to put their promised concert with the Queen into execution.[4] With this in mind, they merely communicated their Barrier Project to Strafford, without subjecting it to negotiation with him.[5]

[1] Laws to Bromley, S.P.F.Fl. 63.

[2] Strafford to Bromley, 29 May, S.P.F.H. 249. Strafford had feared the influence of the party who had formerly favoured the maintenance of friendly relations with the Emperor, who had advocated "that it would be the wisest and surest way for the States to give up at once to the Emperor all their pretentions to the Barrier which can only prove of expense and danger to the Republic". The Pensionary disagreed with this view, as he thought the Emperor's threats were made in order to bring them to easier terms. Cf. Strafford to Bromley, 15 May. S.P.F.H. 249.

[3] Strafford to Bromley, 25 May and 22 June. S.P.F.H. 249.

[4] Strafford to Bromley, 26 June. Utrecht, S.P.F.H. 249.

[5] Strafford to Bromley, 6 July, S.P.F.H. 250, enclosing the Project.

This Project consisted of four articles headed "Propositions for an agreement with His Imperial Majesty". The most noteworthy feature of these Propositions was the departure from the newly concluded Barrier Treaty for which the support of the English Ministry might be expected, and the reversion to the Townshend Treaty as the basis of the new Project. This policy demonstrates the dissatisfaction of Heinsius with the Utrecht settlement and his mistrust of England. It was, however, dangerous to abandon the chance of the Ministry's guarantee and to trust to the generosity of the Imperial Court, which had hitherto shown itself disinclined to make sufficient concessions. This change of policy is inexplicable, as the death of the Queen and the return of the Whigs to power were events upon which Heinsius could not calculate. All he achieved was the alienation of the present English Ministry with which he had just been at pains to come to an understanding.

By Article I the States proposed a joint garrison in Roermond and sole garrisons in Menin, Tournai, Mons, Namur, Ghent and the Scheldt Forts of Perle and Marie, "with lodgment, fire and candle", provided according to the arrangement made when the Elector of Bavaria was governor of the Southern Netherlands. Further, the Emperor should cede to the Dutch Venloo, St Michael and Stevensweert and the territories in the Upper Quarter of Guelderland not ceded to the King of Prussia. The Forts of Philippe and Rodenhuisen should be razed and St Donas should be annexed to the Dutch Fort Sluis. As to Huy and Liège, the States would agree to raze the latter if they were allowed to garrison the former.

The Propositions deviate from the Townshend Treaty in the retrenchment of the Barrier against France. The Dutch, as Strafford pointed out in a letter of the 20th of July,[1] "are indifferent to places against France, saying that they were important only when the King of Spain had them". If they belonged to the Emperor, "he had sufficient power of his own to defend them". Accordingly, the Dutch turned their attention to the east, and this Project, by which they should be strengthened

[1] Strafford to Bromley, 20 July. S.P.F.H. 250.

on the Maas, and in Huy, seems to indicate that they were not unaware of the rising power of Prussia.

By Article II, arrangements were proposed for the upkeep of the Barrier. The Dutch should receive over and above the forage provisions, one million livres annually and the revenues of the New Conquests, or an equivalent. Further, the Emperor should give sufficient surety for this amount and should recognise the debts incurred by the Maritime Powers during the administration of these Provinces.

Article III provided for an extension of the limits of Dutch territory in Flanders, a line from Blankenbergh to Damme, and thence to Fort Perle on the Scheldt.[1]

In conjunction with the shrinkage in the number of fortresses on the French frontier, it is clear that as well as the line on the Maas, the Dutch wished to have strong defences on the Scheldt, the Forts of Perle, Marie, St Donas and Sluis and the extension above-mentioned which would give them a large part of the Land of Waes, "the richest part of that Province".[2]

Finally, in Article IV, before the Provisional Government should be given up in favour of the Emperor, and before the withdrawal of the troops of the Maritime Powers, "the trade of the United Provinces shall be established on the foot of the Treaty of Münster and other Treaties made since... and reasonable satisfaction shall be given to Her Britannic Majesty".

This Project, wrote Strafford, was "more calculated for the Private Interest of this State than for the Publick Security".[3] It is true that the States demanded fewer fortresses and the same amount of money, with the extension of their territories in addition. It must, however, be conceded that the Project was for the public security, in that it was strategically well conceived, on the understanding that the Emperor would keep up the strength of the remaining fortresses on the French frontier.

It was not surprising that Heems condemned the Project as "hard, onerous and prejudicial", since the Emperor

[1] Cf. Huisman, p. 68.
[2] Strafford to Bromley, 6 July. S.P.F.H. 250.
[3] *Ibid.*

was expected to keep up more fortresses and to pay the Dutch a relatively larger sum. The weak state of finances of the Imperial Treasury made it impossible for him to accept such a proposal. "The States General," said Heems, "cannot expect that the Emperor will let Terms be imposed on him which will render the possession of his own Patrimony hard, bothersome and inconvenient." All he would offer was a reversion to the Treaty of Ryswick with the addition of Tournai. The three fortresses, Namur, Tournai and Menin were the key fortresses of the passage through the Southern Netherlands to the Dutch Republic and were, in his opinion, sufficient security.[1]

Heems concluded his Memorial with the threat that the Emperor would occupy the Spanish Low Countries with his troops and impose his own terms, if a Resolution were not at once taken as to terms, place and time of negotiation.

This threat was the more serious since the people of the Southern Netherlands hated the continued military occupation to such an extent that they seemed "disposed to facilitate their (the Imperial troops) taking possession in case they meet with any difficulty from the Dutch".[2] This might seem inconsistent with their fear of government by the Emperor,[3] but it should be remembered that the troops of the Maritime Powers were foreign, while Imperial troops would be, at the least, those of their future Sovereign.

III

The irritation with which the Imperial Ministers received the Dutch Project was Strafford's opportunity to insist upon good terms for English commerce in the Southern Netherlands. He wrote a long despatch in cipher to Bromley. He suggested[4] that the Ministry should agree to Frankfurt as the place for the negotiations as it would show deference to the Emperor, and yet be farther from the influence of "any third power" (i.e. France) than Brussels. He took care to explain to Heems that the Emperor had no reason to be apprehensive of the Queen's

[1] Heems' Memorial on the States Project, 13 July. S.P.F.H. 250.
[2] Laws to Bromley, 4 Aug. S.P.F.Fl. 63.
[3] Cf. p. 322.
[4] Strafford to Bromley, 13 July. S.P.F.H. 250.

part in negotiations: her influence could be nothing but advantageous to the Imperialists.

> I have also taken care to have it observed to the Imperial Court (he continued) that according to the Dutch plan (and) their manner of transacting it, the Queen's obligations by her Treaty are so changed that unless she pleases, they can be of no prejudice to the Emperor, but rather an advantage to him in this negotiation since the interest and apparent meaning of the Treaty of Barrier was only to strengthen and assure the States against France.... By their plan, which they have taken upon themselves to make without any previous concert with the Queen, they have departed from all those places which could serve as a Barrier against France.

For this reason the Queen is no longer bound to adhere to the terms of the Treaty with regard to fortresses. As to the million "undoubtedly the Queen's engagements for obtaining the said Revenues must diminish in the same Proportion".

"I own to you," wrote Strafford to Bromley on the 20th of July, "I think the Dutch have given us an handle to redress the false steps made by the late Ministry in their favour." This was the burden of his conversation with Sinzerling, with whom he was on better terms than Heems, characteristically because of the humble connections of the latter.

On the same day[1] Strafford drew up a list of remarks on the Dutch Project and his suggestions for the safeguarding of English interests. Trade and commerce should be on the footing of the time of Charles II, with the tariff of 1680 (Art. I). Ostend should never be alienated (Art. II). The Queen should not use her good offices to obtain Ghent and Fort Perle as they concerned English commerce (Art. III). As the number of fortresses was reduced, the Queen should press only for the revenues of Tournai and Menin from the New Conquests and a proportion of the million, "though in strictness H.M. need not demand any (revenues) since the Dutch so much changed the Treaty" (Art. IV). As the separate article of the Barrier Treaty was construed by the Dutch to mean a large part of the land of Waes, the Queen should confine her guarantee to mean no more than a cannon shot round the places fortified by the Dutch (Art. V).

[1] Strafford to Bromley, 20 July. S.P.F.H. 250.

As to the demand of Huy and Liège and the cession of those parts of Upper Guelders not assigned to the King of Prussia, the Queen should oppose the latter and insist upon an agreement as to the two former with the Emperor (Art. VI).

"For the rest contained in the Barrier Treaty," concluded the remarks, "Her Majesty will help the States unless they treat separately with the Emperor, when she will consider herself at liberty to do the same."

On Article I Strafford had consulted Laws, who considered that "a general stipulation of commerce in Flanders will be better than extending it...(as) a larger extention will only give a handle to the people of the Low Countries to demand redress of several grievances from us..." as well as giving the French and the Dutch the advantage to demand similar advantages, "which we cannot deny them if we make a new Treaty in form".

This suggestion had been opposed by Drummond, who was for making a new treaty, though the former plan was the more adroit. "Drummond", wrote Strafford spitefully, "may perhaps think that receiving a good salary for that (drawing up a treaty), he shall appear to have done little should not a voluminous Treaty be made."[1]

Laws had the advantage over Drummond as he had received a list of the grievances of the people of the Spanish Low Countries. He pointed out that they would demand reciprocal treatment if a new treaty was to be made to the advantage of Britain.[2] He suggested that the Ministry should confine its demands to free sale of English leather at Bruges and the tariff of December 1680, rather than that in force in 1680. On the 6th of August[3] Laws enclosed a list of the exports of the Southern Netherlands on which the inhabitants would demand a reduction on import into Britain. This is given fully in order that the commercial advantages to Britain may be appreciated.

On entry into Britain:

(1) Linen cloths of Brabant and Flanders are taxed 30–80 per cent. beyond their value.

[1] Strafford to Bromley, 20 July. S.P.F.H. 250.
[2] Laws to Bromley, 14 July. S.P.F.Fl. 63.
[3] Laws to Bromley, 6 Aug. S.P.F.Fl. 63.

(2) Common cloths and damasks from 50–150 per cent. beyond their value.

(3) Tickings 25–30 per cent. beyond their value.

(4) "Bombasinnes" 60 per cent. beyond their value.

(5) Velvets, brocades, silks of Antwerp 50 per cent. beyond their value.

(6) Pictures 40 per cent. beyond their value.

As well as these, tapestries, gilt, leathers, ironwares, thread, ribbons, printing paper, images, household stuff and woollens were either prohibited or charged with prohibitive duties.

Further, the merchants of the Southern Netherlands could not trade in England without English partners.

When we consider the advantages given to England by the tariffs of 1680 and December 1680, it is possible to estimate the enormous benefit to the trade of England as judged by the mercantilist principles then in force.

Strafford and Laws were disappointed that no reply came to their advice on which they had written "so amply".[1] The domestic difficulties of the Ministry explain this silence. On the 14th of August[2] the news of the Queen's death was received at The Hague. It was obvious that the accession of George I would mean the return of the Whigs to power. Strafford's counsels no longer seemed of use. Nevertheless, had he but known it, his "Remarks on the Dutch Project" were largely followed by the Whigs during the negotiations at Antwerp.

The immediate result of the Queen's death was the withdrawal of British forces from Ghent, Bruges and Nieuwport. The only forces left in the Southern Netherlands, with the exception of Bavarian regiments in Ghent and in Luxemburg, were those of the States General.[3]

With the recall of Strafford and the formation of a Whig Ministry, it was expected that a new turn would be given to the Barrier negotiations. Strafford returned to England, where, like his predecessor, Lord Townshend, he was impeached; this time the charge was of having betrayed the interests of the Allies, whereas Townshend had been charged with making too great concessions to one of them.

[1] Strafford to Bromley, 24 July. S.P.F.H. 250.

[2] 14 Aug. S.P.F.H. 250.

[3] Gachard, p. 234.

CHAPTER VIII

The Final Settlement

I

During the summer months of 1714, it was decided that the Congress on the Barrier should meet at Antwerp. The Emperor appointed Koenigsegg as Plenipotentiary, a soldier who was more successful in the pursuit of his career than in the conduct of diplomatic negotiations.[1] The Dutch appointed Rechteren, Gueldermalsen, Van der Dussen and Gockinga; Rechteren and Gueldermalsen belonged to the party which was in favour of maintaining good relations with the Emperor.[2]

The accession of George I and the return of the Whigs to power produced a change in the attitude of the Emperor and the Dutch towards the admission of an English Plenipotentiary to the Congress. Both parties were as eager as they had formerly been disinclined to accept English mediation.[3] Nevertheless, the prestige of the new Whig ministry was very different from that its predecessor enjoyed.

> Only with the ending of the '15 Rebellion and the passing of the Septennial Bill was the credit of the New Government secure...until that time indeed, the British position in international diplomacy was pitiful. At the conclusion of a victorious war, her Allies were alienated or withheld their confidence until the dynasty should be securely established...the Empire considered herself betrayed by the Tory Government...Louis XIV took advantage of British weakness to cease the dismantling of Dunkirk, and Spain raised a customs Barrier against British goods.[4]

In these circumstances security was the maxim of George I and his Ministers: to achieve it, they hoped to revive the "Old System" of William III, the Alliance of the Maritime Powers

[1] Huisman, p. 61.
[2] Bussemaker, *op. cit.* pp. 292–3. Cf. *supra*, p. 258.
[3] Michael, *Englische Geschichte im 18ten Jahrhundert*, p. 630.
[4] F. L. Edwards, *James Stanhope and English Foreign Policy*, p. 26.

with the Emperor. The way of approach would be a speedy conclusion of the Barrier Treaty which would reconcile all parties. Once the "Old System" was re-established, Britain would achieve a position commensurate with her gains by the Treaty of Utrecht and similar to that enjoyed during the reign of Queen Anne, when she was leader of the Coalition.[1]

With regard to the Barrier negotiations, the Whigs returned to power with the resolution to be more watchful over English interests in the Southern Netherlands; it was impossible for them to disregard the lessons of the last three years, when they, the natural protectors of the commercial classes, had been unable to refute the accusation that they had sacrificed British commerce in the Treaty. In the second Barrier Treaty and correspondence of Strafford with the Tory Ministry they found safeguards laid down for them. For this reason, the return of the Whigs involved no break in the continuity of commercial policy. They, no less than the Tories, desired to exclude such towns as Ghent and Dendermonde from the Barrier on account of their importance to British trade.

The Dutch did not at first perceive this change: they looked upon the new Ministry as their natural supporters, and hoped, at last, to realise the advantages of the Townshend Treaty. Heinsius naïvely set forth this view in a conversation with Walpole, the secretary at The Hague. He said, wrote Walpole,[2]

> that affairs had lately taken such a happy turn that he could not think that anything taken from that Treaty (of 1713), or from ye circumstance of ye time in which it was imposed upon them, would now be a reason for not granting them what was necessary for their safety... that it seemed very extraordinary that the States having made a fair and honest Barrier Treaty with ye good Ministry of England, and being afterwards compelled by a bad Ministry to a bad Treaty, the good Ministry should now insist upon their accepting of terms forced upon them by a bad one.

The views of the Whigs with regard to the Barrier were of great importance to the Dutch, since circumstances forced them to depend on English influence with the Emperor. The Republic

[1] Michael, p. 639.
[2] Walpole to Townshend, 22 Jan. 1715. S.P.F.H. 252.

had been at the zenith of its fortunes in 1709: now all was changed. Their desertion by the Tory Ministry at Utrecht, their vacillations and their final acceptance of the terms dictated for them by England had lowered the prestige of the Republic. Further, this policy had alienated the Emperor, who was irritated when in the autumn of 1712 they had deserted him to follow the dictates of the Ministry which had made peace at his expense.

The decline of the United Provinces as a first-rate Power was accelerated by exhaustion after a war which had been prolonged beyond the resources of the country. The state of finances which in 1709 was critical had become by 1714 almost intolerable.

Finally, with the removal of the pressure of a war, the defects in the Dutch constitution reasserted themselves: dissensions between parties in the Republic led to delays and vacillations in policy which were responsible for the contemptuous attitude which began to prevail towards the United Provinces.

The accession of George I was hailed in the Republic as the first step to a return to better days.[1] On his way to England, the King spoke at The Hague of his desire to see the Barrier speedily and favourably concluded.[2]

Strafford was under recall and Cadogan was appointed as Ambassador and Plenipotentiary at Antwerp. During the absence of Cadogan, Walpole was appointed to take charge of matters at The Hague.

Cadogan was a staunch Whig who had previously served under Marlborough in the field and also in the administration of the Southern Netherlands. As well as his experience, his friendship with Eugene made him a fit person for the Barrier negotiations. He had, however, faults in temperament which detracted from his fitness for the task. He was of an impetuous and over-sanguine disposition: this led to mistaken judgments during the negotiations, when he over-estimated the willingness of the Emperor and the Dutch to make sacrifices for "the general

[1] Cf. Laws to Bromley, 18 Aug., S.P.F.Fl. 63, on the news of the Queen's death. "Mr van den Bergh seems very sanguine upon this late unhappy accident."

[2] Michael, p. 395. On 6 Sept. George I arrived at The Hague where he conferred with both Heinsius and Heems.

good". The result was that both parties accused him of misrepresentation and obstacles continuously arose just when he had assured the English Ministry that all was settled.

Before the arrival of Cadogan at Antwerp, the Dutch drew up a new Barrier Project which they presented to Koenigsegg on the 9th of October. The Project[1] clearly shows that they counted upon English support, "although they may have raised their demands a little in order to retract if necessary".[2]

The Dutch demanded not only Furnes, Ypres, Menin, Tournai, Namur, Ghent and the Forts of Perle and St Donas, to which the English were pledged by the Treaty of 1713, but also Knocke, Dendermonde, Fort Philippe, Lier and Hal (Art. IV). To balance these additions they withdrew their claims to Mons and Charleroi. This was an advance upon the project of July 1714, in the inclusion of Furnes, Ypres, Knocke, Lier, Hal, Fort Philippe[3] and Dendermonde.

The Project contained other conditions similar to those demanded in July (regulation of troops, repairs of fortifications, securities for trade and for Protestant worship, etc.) including the subsidy article, the demand for a joint garrison at Roermond, the cession of Venloo, Fort St Michael, Stevensweert and the "bailliages et seigneuries" of Upper Guelders not ceded to the King of Prussia (Art. V). To their demand of Huy by the July Project they added a claim to garrison Liège.

It is clear that this Project resembled the Townshend Treaty more closely than any made since its repudiation.

Before turning to its reception by Koenigsegg, it should be noticed that the Emperor no less than the Dutch counted on the support of George I in the negotiations.

George I, in his capacity of Elector, had been one of the most faithful supporters of the House of Hapsburg in the Empire. For past services, his house had been raised to electoral rank in 1697. During the war of the Spanish Succession, he had followed the Emperor when he left the Conferences at Utrecht.

Consequently, when George succeeded to the throne, the

[1] 9 Oct. S.P.F.Fl. 64. Extract printed in Gachard, pp. 240–1.

[2] Bussemaker, *op. cit.* p. 294.

[3] Cf. p. 229. By the July Project Fort Philippe was to be razed.

Emperor entertained the belief that "the most easy method of moderating the high demands of the Dutch will be His Majesty's mediation".[1] "By what I can discover," wrote Laws[2] after an interview with Koenigsegg, "the Imperial Court flatter themselves the King will not think it necessary the Dutch should have so large a Barrier as they demanded first when it was probable that these countries might have been united to the crown of Spain."

Hoffmann spoke in the same vein in London: not only was Charles VI in a stronger position to defend the Southern Netherlands as Emperor, but also he would feel more keenly any limitations placed upon the restricted share of the Spanish inheritance allotted to him; in such case, remarked Hoffmann, "even Townshend himself would not wish to adhere to the terms of his own Treaty".[3] To this Townshend replied that the King's part in the negotiations would be that of an arbitrator between the two powers.

With the Imperial Court in this frame of mind, it was not surprising that Koenigsegg's Project[4] fell far short of that delivered by the Dutch.

The Emperor demanded that the Dutch should deliver up the Southern Netherlands and the New Conquests, which he proposed to defend with 19,000 of his own troops if the States General would contribute 16,000 Dutch troops (Arts. I and II). He offered to the States garrisons in Namur, Tournai, Menin and Furnes—fortresses on the French frontier only—in the other garrisons of the Southern Netherlands he proposed to put his own troops and any troops remaining to the Dutch after the garrisons allocated to them were invested (Arts. IV and V). As to religion, he would permit the Dutch to worship in their own houses, if they would refrain from creating disturbances (Art. VIII). For the upkeep of the Barrier he offered a subsidy of 400,000 crowns[5] annually, payment to begin on the day on

[1] Laws to Townshend, 20 Oct. S.P.F.Fl. 63.

[2] Laws to Bromley, 12 Sept. S.P.F.Fl. 63.

[3] Michael, p. 631.

[4] 9 Oct. S.P.F.Fl. 64. Extract printed Gachard, p. 238.

[5] Cf. p. 381 (Art. 11), the million livres for which the Dutch had asked (cf. p. 329) was equal to 400,000 crowns. The States however demanded the revenues of the New Conquests and forage money as well.

which he was installed in the Southern Netherlands, on condition that the States desisted from the Barrier Treaty of 1713 and from the demand for an additional payment for forage (Art. XIII). As for commerce, the Emperor proposed that conditions should remain upon the present footing until he was installed in his new provinces, when he would appoint Commissioners to treat with the Maritime Powers (Art. XIV).

Liège, Huy, the extension of the limits in Flanders and Upper Guelderland were not mentioned in the Project: presumably the Emperor intended to make no concessions on these points. This was corroborated by the declaration of Koenigsegg on the 12th of October of his master's intention never to alienate any territory. The question of Guelderland he considered irrelevant to the present negotiations.[1]

The discrepancy between the two Projects created difficulties immediately. Neither side would relax upon a single point and conferences were suspended until the arrival of Cadogan.

II

Cadogan arrived at Antwerp on the 5th of November.[2] His instructions were drawn up by Townshend.[3] He was ordered to make Koenigsegg

> sensible that it is much for his master's advantage to be well with the States and to cultivate a strict friendship with them in all cases, and that the Emperor ought not to look on the Barrier as the particular interest of the States only, but as what he himself is equally concerned in, and to lay it down for a maxim, *that neither power singly of itself is able to secure and defend the Netherlands but that the joint efforts of both are necessary for that purpose.*

It is plain that the Whigs were of the opinion that the Southern Netherlands were not to be treated as an hereditary province of Charles VI, but as a trust to be shared with the States for the preservation of the balance of power.

The need for adequate security against France was the greater as the Ministry contemplated a renewal of the war. For this reason, as much as for the benefits of a reconciliation

[1] Gachard, p. 241.
[2] Gachard, p. 243.
[3] S.P.F. Treaty Papers 105. Draft of instructions to Cadogan.

between the Maritime Powers and the Emperor, they desired a speedy conclusion of the Treaty.[1]

Townshend seems to have been unwilling to lay down rules in the instructions as to the concessions to be demanded for the Dutch. In the draft he wrote at first that "We (George I) look upon the Treaty made by our late dear sister as if it were our own engagement", then crossed the passage out and substituted the words "You have our orders to employ your utmost endeavours to obtain for them all that can be thought reasonable and necessary for their security". The English did not wish to increase the number of towns to be garrisoned by the Dutch, either because they realised the difficulty of obtaining them from the Emperor, or because they feared that the addition of other towns would interfere with English commerce. Nevertheless, as they desired that the Barrier should be strong, they were prepared to make up the deficit in another way.

> Whereas (continued the instructions) several strong towns are left out of the Barrier (of 1713) which were intended to fortify it, and which would have rendered it secure and sufficient to oppose the invasion of an Enemy; and whereas in the present situation the best method of supplying the want of towns is to keep up as large a number as possible of standing forces in the several garrisons of the Low Countries, you are therefore, in the best manner you can, to encourage and support all such proposals as shall tend to the increasing the numbers of troops to be kept in the Southern Netherlands.

As to Dendermonde, Cadogan received specific instructions that, as the Dutch "were brought to give it up upon the Renewal of the Treaty in 1713, they cannot reasonably expect it should be granted them". If the Dutch persisted in their demand for this town, Cadogan was to suggest the expedient of demolition.

The instructions further provided that an article should be included in the Treaty by which the Emperor should promise never to alienate the Southern Netherlands. Finally, Cadogan was to arrange the best terms possible for English commerce.

At the first Conference after the arrival of Cadogan, Koenigsegg delivered the Emperor's answer to the October Project of the States General: the Imperial Court saw with displeasure

[1] Michael, p. 633.

that the States had increased instead of modifying their demands of July. Such a proceeding showed no sincere desire to concert matters with the Emperor: on the contrary, it was evident that under the pretext of a Barrier against France, the Dutch wished to extend their domination in the Southern Netherlands. In consequence, the Emperor desired his Plenipotentiary to reject the Project of the 9th of October.

Cadogan attempted to soothe the mortified Deputies by explaining this as meaning that they must obtain fresh instructions. Conferences were adjourned until these should be forthcoming.[1]

In the interim Cadogan persuaded Koenigsegg to sign the new Commercial Treaty simultaneously with the Barrier Treaty, and not to defer commercial negotiations as the Emperor had suggested (Art. XIV, Imperial Project) until after his installation in the Southern Netherlands.[2] This was a concession of importance to both the Maritime Powers, as the Emperor would have been more able to dictate his own terms for the tariffs if he were already in possession of the Provinces.

After this Conference with Koenigsegg, Cadogan perceived that the Austrian would never agree to the Dutch proposal for the extension of territories in Flanders. He suggested, in a letter to Townshend,[3] that a reasonable expedient would be to cede the land within a cannon shot of the Scheldt fortifications occupied by the Dutch, together with rights over sufficient sluices to enable them to flood the country. In this proposal he was merely extending Article V of Strafford's remarks upon the Dutch Project.[4]

Koenigsegg offered to yield Ypres, Knocke and Warneton which, with the addition of Namur, Tournai, Menin and Furnes, the towns already promised to the Dutch, would, in Cadogan's opinion,

> give them such a Barrier from the Scheldt to the sea as all persons who understand the war and know the situation of that part of the country will think as strong as anything of that nature ever was....

[1] Gachard, pp. 243–4.
[2] Cadogan to Townshend, 10 Nov. S.P.F.Fl. 64 (two letters).
[3] Cadogan to Townshend, 10 Nov. S.P.F.Fl. 64.
[4] Cf. p. 331.

They have a line of strong towns at a little distance, and by making inundations in some places...a small army may act on the defensive against a very great one without hazard.[1]

Having persuaded Koenigsegg to make these concessions, Cadogan turned his attention to the Dutch. Here he received cordial approval when he suggested that all parties should agree to exclude the Prussian Envoy from negotiations. The King of Prussia had despatched this Envoy to take part in conferences relating to the Upper Quarter of Guelderland.[2] His exclusion from negotiations was a point in favour of the Dutch, who stood to lose if the King of Prussia should support the Emperor's resolution not to concede any territory in Upper Guelders to the Republic.

Cadogan paid a visit to The Hague not only in order to confer with Heinsius but also to counteract the influence of Châteauneuf, the French Ambassador, who sought to prevent the conclusion of the Treaty by encouraging the States to hold firm to their demands of October.

The States agreed to give way in their demand for Lier and Hal if they were permitted to garrison the Demer line from the Scheldt to the Maas in time of war.

Further, they would "make such concessions as are absolutely necessary" but they insisted on the subsidy of 500,000 crowns with provision for forage[3] and on Dendermonde.[4]

Accordingly, Cadogan drew up an expedient by which the chief difficulties should be settled between the two parties.[5]

1. For the extension of the limits in Flanders, he proposed that the States should be given enough territory to have control of the sluices by which inundations could be made, and the land within a cannon shot of their fortifications.

2. As to Upper Guelders, he proposed a joint garrison in Roermond: Venloo, St Michael and Stevensweert and the lands not ceded to the King of Prussia should be given to the States,

[1] Cadogan to Townshend, 10 and 17 Nov. S.P.F.Fl. 64.
[2] Gachard, p. 245.
[3] Cadogan to Townshend, 17 Nov. S.P.F.Fl. 64.
[4] Cadogan to Townshend, 1 Dec. *Ibid.*
[5] Cadogan to Townshend, 1 and 6 Dec. S.P.F.Fl. 64. Cf. Gachard, p. 246.

on condition that the Catholic Church should preserve the liberties and immunities enjoyed at the time of the death of Charles II.

3. The States should have the right to garrison the Demer line in time of war.

4. The States should receive a yearly subsidy of 500,000 crowns a year without additions for forage. On this point Koenigsegg pledged his good offices with the Emperor, though he was not authorised to make any advance beyond the 400,000 crowns authorised in his Project of October.[1]

5. For Dendermonde Cadogan proposed a joint garrison. This was a concession on the part of the Whigs who had desired the demolition of the town.

On the whole, this Project involved no undue concessions by either party. Gachard criticises it as being much to the advantage of the States General,[2] but this can hardly be maintained as it would force them to modify their demands for the extension of the limits and give up Lier and Hal. Further, they were bitterly opposed to any scheme by which they should lose their claim to the sole command in Dendermonde.

Neither party pledged itself to the acceptance of these points, as they awaited news from Vienna, where Stanhope was engaged in negotiating on the subject.

In the meanwhile, two points of importance were concerted: Koenigsegg agreed to include an article in the Treaty by which the Emperor should promise never to alienate the Southern Netherlands[3] and to increase the number of troops in the Barrier to 40,000, of which the States General should provide 16,000.[4]

A new difficulty arose over the Dutch claim to garrison Liège and Huy. Koenigsegg refused to accede to this demand. Instead, he proposed that the fortifications of the towns should be demolished. Cadogan thought that the States might give way over Huy, if they were permitted to garrison Liège.[5]

[1] Cadogan to Townshend, 6 Dec. S.P.F.Fl. 64.

[2] Gachard, p. 246. [3] Cf. p. 346.

[4] Cadogan to Townshend, 6 Dec. S.P.F.Fl. 64, but the number was later reduced to 35,000.

[5] Cadogan to Townshend, 6 and 9 Dec. S.P.F.Fl. 64.

Meanwhile, two circumstances arose which put the Dutch in a position even less favourable than that they already occupied.

In the first place, Koenigsegg delivered an ultimatum over the question of Imperial troops, which, since the Elector of Bavaria was restored to his electorate, were waiting at Aix-la-Chapelle preparatory to occupying the Southern Netherlands. He informed the States that if they did not evacuate Luxemburg and Limburg, these troops would receive orders to occupy the Southern Netherlands. Despite the fact that this was an infringement of the Treaty of Utrecht, by which the Emperor was not to be installed in the Southern Netherlands until the Dutch had received satisfaction as to their Barrier, the States General were forced to give way. On the 1st of January 1715, Gockinga and Rechteren left for Brussels to effect the evacuation of the two Provinces.[1] The presence of Imperial troops so near at hand made resistance to the Emperor still more difficult.

Secondly, when Stanhope arrived at The Hague on the 6th of January,[2] his account of his mission to Vienna was very different from the expectations of both George I and the States General.

The despatch of Stanhope to Vienna on the 21st of October (O.S.) 1714 was in furtherance of the Ministry's policy of renewing the "Old System".[3] Before he left England, Stanhope had exchanged angry words with d'Iberville, the French Ambassador, over the erection of fortifications at Mardyck (intended to replace Dunkirk, which was demolished by the Treaty of Utrecht). In view of this speech, it was generally believed that Stanhope's mission was to conclude an offensive alliance against France.

The prospect of a renewal of the war alarmed the Dutch. When Stanhope passed through The Hague on his way to Vienna, they asked him to communicate his intentions. Stanhope showed them his instructions which contained no mention of an offensive alliance: he assured them that his mission concerned the conclusion of the Barrier Treaty, in order that the three Powers might conclude an alliance.[4]

Nevertheless, the Ministry secretly hoped to gain the consent

[1] Gachard, p. 248.
[2] Michael, p. 641.
[3] Cf. p. 339.
[4] Michael, p. 636.

of the Emperor to an offensive alliance. The weakness of the Dutch, and their determination to avoid a war at all costs, made England more than ever dependent upon the Emperor. As for the Dutch, "if we do not negotiate for them," wrote Stanhope, "nothing will happen. There is no one among them who dares to take any responsibility".[1]

When Stanhope arrived at Vienna at the end of November 1714, he found the Emperor in an uncertain temper, as Bruyninx, the States' Ambassador, reported to The Hague.[2] Among the Emperor's councillors, there were two parties with extreme opinions as to the fate of the Barrier. One party wished to send troops into the Southern Netherlands before the conclusion of negotiations and then to dictate a settlement. The other, favoured by Eugene, argued that the Southern Netherlands were of little value if the Dutch were to garrison the best fortresses and suggested that the provinces should be exchanged for Bavaria, if the Elector were agreeable.[3]

Stanhope found Eugene "very much incensed against the Dutch":[4] the Prince said he would never counsel the Emperor to accept the Southern Netherlands on the terms they demanded.

In an audience with the Emperor,[5] Stanhope intimated that his master would be displeased if he were to return without having come to an understanding on the Barrier. He begged the Emperor not to take it in bad part that the King was obliged to support the Dutch "as guarantor of a Treaty made to secure his succession". The Emperor assured him that he was aware that "the King could not dispense with his obligations", but he did not offer to facilitate negotiations by making any concessions.

Stanhope was not more successful in his project for an

[1] Michael, p. 636. Stanhope to Townshend, 6 Nov. 1714.

[2] Bruyninx to Fagel, Heinsius Archives, 56 A. "I do not know what to make of this Court at present: they preserve a strange and mysterious bearing: they assemble troops...and seem to apprehend something and...to mistrust everyone, even England. This Emperor seems very overbearing in humour, having perhaps in his sojourn in Spain acquired something of the Spanish manner, which the Spaniards who remain here encourage."

[3] Cf. Michael, p. 638.

[4] Stanhope to Townshend, 24 Nov. S.P.F. Germany (Empire), 32.

[5] Stanhope to Townshend, 5 Dec. *Ibid.*

offensive alliance against France. The Emperor refused to take this step until the Barrier Treaty was concluded. Nor would he agree to Stanhope's next proposal of a guarantee of the Utrecht Settlement. The Englishman was told that if negotiations at Antwerp were speedily concluded, an Imperial Plenipotentiary would be sent to concert matters in London.[1]

To expedite the Barrier negotiations, a second Imperial Project was drawn up which was presented to Stanhope some days before he left Vienna.

1. In the Upper Quarter of Guelderland, the Emperor would permit the States to garrison Venloo, St Michael and Stevensweert: he refused to accede to their demand for the lands not ceded to the King of Prussia.

2. He would permit Dendermonde to be garrisoned by troops belonging to both parties, on the understanding that the States should desist from their demand for Hüy and Liège. As a further concession he would agree to the demolition of the fortifications of the two last.

3. Finally, he offered to the Dutch a subsidy of 500,000 crowns, on the understanding that this should include provision for forage.

These offers made it unlikely that the Barrier Treaty would be speedily concluded. The sole point on which Stanhope was successful was a promise made by the Emperor never to alienate the Southern Netherlands, thus closing the possibilities of an Exchange Project with Bavaria.[2]

> I am fully persuaded (wrote Bruyninx on the 26th of December[3]) that without the consideration of the King, the zeal and strong representations of the English Ministers who have done everything on their side, and the agreeable person of Stanhope, to whom the Emperor has on many occasions shown marks of favour, the negotiations could never have been brought so far.

Nevertheless, Stanhope's report to the Pensionary on the 6th of January awakened bitter resentment. The Dutch had set their hopes on the mediation of George I, and the Emperor's

[1] Michael, pp. 639–40.
[2] Stanhope to Townshend, 22 Dec. S.P.F.G. 32. Cf. p. 343.
[3] Bruyninx to Heinsius, Heinsius Archives, 56 A.

plan involved the renunciation of those points which they had most at heart.[1]

The States General made earnest representations to George I for further assistance through their Ambassador, Van Borselle and through Duivenvoorde, who was sent to London specially for this task.[2]

III

The year 1715 opened unfavourably for George I. At home the Ministry feared a Jacobite invasion. Abroad they had no ally except the Dutch, who were unlikely to lend their troops to England if the Barrier Treaty were not concluded. Still worse, it was rumoured that the Emperor and Louis XIV were in negotiation; whatever the truth in the story, it exerted a powerful influence on English policy.[3]

It was more than ever imperative that the Ministers should win the Emperor to the side of George I. Accordingly it was decided that Cadogan should be sent to Vienna to attempt once more the conclusion of the Barrier negotiations. To effect this it was necessary that the Dutch should be brought to lower their demands. With this intention Townshend instructed Walpole to inform the States[4] that

> however reasonable these articles of the Castle of Huy, the Castles of Ghent and Dendermonde might have been at the time when the first Barrier Treaty was stipulated, and when the affairs of Great Britain and Holland were at the highest Pitch of Prosperity, yet the false turn which has been given them for these last four years has not only overthrown that scheme, but even brought us into such unhappy circumstances as not to leave us masters of such conditions as we ourselves may think reasonable, and the King cannot but wish for the sake of the States as well as his own that this were the only instance wherein the Maritime Powers felt the ill consequence of the late conduct...this is a real state of the case arising from the present circumstance of both Britain and Holland.

At The Hague, the announcement of George I's intention to conciliate the Emperor at the expense of the Barrier was received with very natural resentment. Some of the Regents in the Republic suspected that the desire of George I for Bremen

[1] Michael, p. 641.

[2] Cf. Bussemaker, *op. cit.*

[3] Cf. Michael, p. 643.

[4] 18 Jan. 1715. F.E.B. 81.

and Verden made him anxious to propitiate the Emperor.[1] Eight months later,[2] Duivenvoorde wrote to Heinsius from London of his conviction that "in the Barrier Negotiations this state has been sacrificed to the German Ministers (of George I) who wished to conciliate the Emperor in order to obtain Bremen and Verden".[3]

It is obvious that an understanding with the Emperor would greatly assist George's chances of success, but it must be admitted that the security of George I on the throne was the chief consideration of the Ministry.

Cadogan's instructions[4] were, if possible, to find out whether there were any truth in the rumours of a Franco-Austrian *rapprochement*, and to reiterate the desire of George I to renew the alliance with the Emperor. As to the Barrier, he was to attempt to effect a settlement on the basis of his propositions of December, on the understanding that the Dutch would accept the Project. He was to point out that the addition of the revenues of the New Conquests to those of the Southern Netherlands would make it possible for the Emperor to pay a subsidy of 500,000 crowns, as the revenues of the New Conquests alone were worth more than that sum.

Cadogan was further charged "to make things as easy as possible concerning British Commerce". Matters had not advanced in this direction beyond an assurance from Koenigsegg that his master would favour British trade, to which Townshend replied that "the compliment would be the more acceptable were it not clogged with a condition that is impracticable with

[1] Bussemaker, p. 282.

[2] Duivenvoorde to Heinsius, 27 Aug. 1715. *Ibid.*

[3] There is no evidence in the Foreign State Papers of Holland or the Empire that this was the case. On the other hand, Eugene told Cobham, the English ambassador at Vienna, that "if the king had not succeeded to the crown, they would have seen this (the Barrier) decided in a much shorter manner". 2 Feb. S.P.F.G. 34. Nevertheless Duivenvoorde's stay in England confirmed his belief that the Dutch were sacrificed to the interests of the German ministers. Stanhope and Townshend admitted the justice of the claims of the Republic but did nothing to help them. Duivenvoorde suspected Townshend had been won over by the German Ministers. Michael, p. 651, supports the view that the sacrifice of Dutch interests in Nov. 1714–Jan. 1715 was partly due to the ambitions of George I in the North.

[4] F.E.B. 14.

us, that is to lessen the duties on their manufactures here.... Innovations in these matters are of ill consequence as the late Experiments in our Treaties with France and Spain sufficiently show".[1]

Cadogan paid a visit to The Hague before he left for Vienna. There he received an unofficial visit from three Deputies who came "positively to assure him" that if the Emperor would yield the points in favour of the Republic in the Project, the States would give up Dendermonde and Huy.[2] It was evident that the representations of the English were not without effect in certain sections of the Republic.

From Vienna, Townshend received the news that the Emperor became daily more incensed with the Dutch, especially over the question of religion. Eugene was of the opinion that the best method of negotiation with the Republic was "de leur montrer les dents".

I do not know (continued Cobham, the English ambassador, in the same letter[3]) to what I should attribute the indifference with which they treat the King our Master and the States General, if it is not to the opinion which they insinuate everywhere here that the Dutch are in a bad condition and must subscribe to the conditions which are made for them, and that the King's interest demands...a strict union with the Court. You see, my Lord, by what I say to you, that it is not the time to speak to them about our commerce in the Low Countries.

From this letter it is clear that the Emperor realised that he had the upper hand with the Maritime Powers.

Cadogan arrived on the 22nd of February and was received with marks of personal friendship by the Emperor and Eugene.[4] After many conferences with Eugene and the more tractable Sinzendorf, he pledged himself to make the Dutch withdraw from the demand for a sole garrison in Dendermonde, for Huy and for a forage regulation with the subsidy, if the Emperor would agree to the extension of the limits as proposed by the engineer, De Bauffe (on condition that the Dutch should not

[1] Townshend to Cadogan, 31 Dec. F.E.B. 14.
[2] Cadogan to Townshend, 4 Feb. S.P.F.Fl. 64.
[3] Cobham to Townshend, 6 Feb. S.P.F.G. 32.
[4] Michael, p. 643.

disturb the religion of the inhabitants), and to the cession of Venloo, St Michael and Stevensweert and the seigneurie of Montfort in Upper Guelderland (also on condition that the rights of Catholics should be preserved). In deference to a request from the Emperor, Cadogan promised to withhold Montfort unless he saw that the Dutch would refuse to conclude the Treaty without it.[1]

To the surprise of England, the Emperor accepted these proposals. His compliance sprang from the wish to avoid the suspicion of a secret understanding with France.[2] He declared that he was willing to conclude an alliance with the Maritime Powers: Cadogan suspected that this was dictated by the fear that if he refused, the States General would come under French influence.

"As to the business of commerce," wrote Cadogan, "'tis very little understood here, and all I have been able to obtain by force of my most earnest solicitations is the promise of an order in general terms to Ct Koenigsegg to negotiate with me over this."[3]

On the whole, when Cadogan returned from Vienna, he had been successful in the execution of his instructions. Bruyninx was again satisfied that the Englishman had done his best, except in one particular:

> I must notify you (wrote Bruyninx to Heinsius)[4] that I had never thought things would have been brought so far here: I must add in confidence and secrecy, that during the whole negotiation of the English Ministers at the Court, I have observed that even England would not have gladly seen this state in Dendermonde, and on this point they have not worked with the same earnestness and zeal as they have about the others.

This letter confirms the fact that the Whigs had no wish to include towns of commercial importance in the Barrier.[5] When Cadogan returned to Antwerp, "there was much joy in England over his success, which greatly exceeded English expectations.

[1] Cadogan to Townshend, 10 March. S.P.F.Fl. 64.
[2] Michael, p. 664.
[3] Cadogan to Townshend, 10 March. S.P.F.Fl. 64.
[4] 27 March 1715, Heinsius Archives, 58 A.
[5] Cf. p. 340.

In consequence England placed herself on the side of the Emperor and sought to make the States agree to his proposals".[1]

Opinion in the Republic was divided as to whether the Emperor's terms should be accepted. Although Cadogan had obtained concessions which had surpassed the expectations of Bruyninx, the States General felt they deserved some modification of the Emperor's terms with regard to Liège, Huy, Dendermonde and the subsidy.[2]

The towns of Amsterdam, Rotterdam and Leyden desired that negotiations should at once be concluded with the Emperor.[3] Their compliance was probably dictated by the fact that as the Imperial troops had advanced further into the Southern Netherlands in March,[4] resistance was almost out of the question.

The opposition party, led by Duivenvoorde, hoped to gain more by a last appeal to the King. Cadogan was aware of this and advised Townshend that "it would extremely advance the conclusion of the Treaty if His Majesty's sentiments in relation to it were signified to Mr Duivenvoorde, who flatters himself that he and his friends shall be able to obtain something more for them".[5] This new project was the demand that the king should fulfil the guarantee of the Treaty of 1713, and pay a subsidy which would make up the deficit between that offered by the Emperor and the million livres with the addition of the revenues of the New Conquests promised in 1713.[6]

Townshend replied that no Ministry could possibly ask this of Parliament. Further, as France was a menace to the Maritime Powers, the Barrier Treaty must be speedily concluded.[7]

When George I refused to support their demands, the States could hope for nothing further. If they broke with the Emperor, they would lose the Barrier, the object of their policy since the reign of William III; further, they had no desire to give up the extension of the limits in Flanders, the tariff in the Southern Netherlands and the right to garrison Venloo and Stevensweert,

1 Michael, p. 664.
2 Bussemaker, p. 309.
3 Cadogan to Townshend, 7 May. S.P.F.Fl. 65.
4 Bussemaker, pp. 307–8.
5 Cadogan to Townshend, 27 April. S.P.F.Fl. 65.
6 Cadogan to Townshend, 19 April. S.P.F.Fl. 65.
7 Bussemaker, pp. 309–11.

which the Emperor might cede to the King of Prussia, who was already powerful in the Province: finally they would be without an ally in Europe if they refused to accede to the request of the King and the Emperor.[1]

On the 3rd of May Van der Dussen informed Cadogan that the States would accept the offers which he had brought with him from Vienna,[2] though they would not declare their resolution until the revenues of the Low Countries were satisfactorily arranged and the treaty of commerce was settled.

In matters of commerce, Cadogan decided that to negotiate the new Treaty "would have the same effect as the Physick which killed the Person who in most perfect health took it in order to be better".[3] Accordingly, he persuaded Koenigsegg "to stipulate in an article of the Barrier Treaty that the commerce of Britain, Holland and the Austrian Low Countries shall remain and continue on the foot it is at present till it shall be otherwise settled by a Treaty of Commerce and till ye said Treaty of Commerce shall be settled to ye mutual satisfaction of all parties interested".[4]

This expedient avoided three difficulties which would otherwise have stood in the way of favourable treatment of English commerce.

In the first place, the project of a treaty which had been drawn up by the Commissioners of Trade had met with an unfavourable reception by the Commissioners of the Southern Netherlands who refused to accede to English demands unless given reciprocal treatment on goods of the Southern Netherlands exported to England.[5]

Secondly, the Dutch and the English could not agree upon a project "several of the towns of Holland having interests very opposite to those of His Majesty's subjects".[6] The differences arose from the Dutch desire for a reduction in the duties on butter, meat, coals and wines on going into the Southern

[1] Bussemaker, p. 314.
[2] Cadogan to Townshend, 3 May. S.P.F.Fl. 65.
[3] Cadogan to Townshend, 27 June. S.P.F.Fl. 65.
[4] Cadogan to Townshend, 19 April. S.P.F.Fl. 65.
[5] Enclosed Cadogan to Walpole, 17 May. S.P.F.Fl. 65.
[6] Cadogan to Townshend, 19 April. S.P.F.Fl. 65.

Netherlands, and an increase in the duties on coarse woollens,[1] an export of particular importance to England.

Thirdly, Cadogan feared that if a new commercial treaty were negotiated, French Commissioners would be sent to demand alterations in their tariff with the Southern Netherlands for the benefit of France.[2]

The Commissioners of Trade and Plantations were reluctant to give up their project of a commercial treaty, as it contained an article providing for the reintroduction of the tariff of the 21st of December 1680, which through some misunderstanding had not been restored by the Provisional Regulation. The Provisional Regulation enjoined that all parties should pay according to the duties existing in the year 1680.[3] Laws and Drummond had in vain pointed out that this would mean that British goods would pay according to the less advantageous tariff of 1679, but, for some inexplicable reason,[4] their objections had been overruled.

When Cadogan received the reply of the Commissioners of Trade and Plantations, he sent Leathes to London[5] to explain that in an edict of the 11th of December 1713 the Council of State had rectified the mistake by a declaration that duties should be paid according to the regulations prevailing before the signature of the Provisional Regulation. In practice this amounted to the tariff of December 1680 with a few minor alterations.[6]

Nothing can be a greater mark of the present good state of British trade in the Austrian Netherlands (wrote Cadogan[7]) than that we have supplied seven to eight hundred thousand pounds of goods, in return for which they supply us only with lace and some linnen to a very small value, so that the balance is considerably in our favour

[1] Townshend to Cadogan, 3 June, enclosing a Report of the Commissioners of Trade and Plantations on "Particulars in which the Dutch Project differs from Ours". F.E.B. 14.

[2] Cadogan to Townshend, 19 April. S.P.F.Fl. 65.

[3] Cf. p. 315.

[4] Possibly Strafford made the mistake, as he himself admitted that he had no knowledge of commercial matters.

[5] Cadogan to Townshend, 17 June. Cf. Cadogan to Tilson, 17 June. S.P.F.Fl. 65.

[6] Townshend to Cadogan, 3 June. F.E.B. 14.

[7] To Townshend, 25 May. A Memorial in answer to the queries of the Commissioners of Trade and Plantations. S.P.F.Fl. 65.

at present, and sent into Britain in specie, and therefore the inhabitants of the said Netherlands in general look upon the present state of trade with us to be very prejudicial.

With this the Commissioners of Trade and Plantations were satisfied. Cadogan arranged with Koenigsegg that before the conclusion of the Treaty, the Council of State should sign an edict reducing the duties on Dutch spirits and coarse woollens.[1]

The States General agreed to this expedient for commerce as it was, on the whole, beneficial to Dutch trade and since they, like the Ministry, were anxious to exclude French Commissioners from negotiations.[2]

While the commercial negotiations were in progress, the States General, in accordance with their promise to Cadogan,[3] came to a resolution on the 31st of May to accept the Emperor's terms, although they were "a heavy burden".[4]

To their chagrin, Koenigsegg announced on the 25th of June that the Emperor would cede neither the territory of Montfort in Upper Guelderland, nor the large extension of territories in Flanders necessitated by De Bauffe's plan. Cadogan had considered himself authorised to offer these terms to the States,[5] but the Emperor argued that they must be referred to the arbitration of George I. Koenigsegg was ordered to lay his demands before the King, when it was hoped that they would be settled to the satisfaction of the Emperor.[6]

Koenigsegg and Cadogan arrived in London in July. There the Imperial Minister met with an unexpected firmness on the part of the King. Every effort was made to induce the Emperor to grant Montfort and the extension of the limits. The Ministry feared that if the Dutch were not satisfied in their demands they would refuse to send troops to assist in suppressing the rebellion which had broken out in Scotland.[7]

In response to these representations, the Emperor decided to give way. On the 9th of September[8] Koenigsegg declared to the Dutch Plenipotentiaries that he would agree to the subsidy, the

[1] Cadogan to Tilson, 17 June. Cadogan to Townshend, 20 June. S.P.F.Fl. 65.

[2] Cadogan to Townshend, 25 May. S.P.F.Fl. 65.

[3] Cf. p. 352. [4] Bussemaker, p. 314. [5] Cf. p. 349.

[6] Gachard, p. 262. [7] Michael, p. 647. [8] Gachard, p. 264.

cession of Montfort and the extension of the limits according to Cadogan's plan, on condition that the Treaty should be signed within six weeks. If the Dutch delayed beyond this period, the Emperor would consider his obligations with regard to the Barrier at an end.

A letter from Schaub to Townshend convinced him that the threat was seriously intended. "They are irritated at the Dutch," he wrote on the 9th of October[1], "and think of facts rather than negotiations, and are for rupture, counting on Palatine troops and the hate of the inhabitants of the Southern Netherlands and the bad state of the Dutch. The Emperor thinks his honour engaged and the moderate ministers dare not open their mouths."

As the States were not yet agreed with Koenigsegg on the question of religion, this time limit appeared insufficient. The Ministry determined to intervene on their behalf and Schaub was instructed to demand at Vienna for an extension of the six weeks.[2] Cadogan was sent to support the States at Antwerp where he intimated to Koenigsegg that any attempt to change the system in the Southern Netherlands would be looked upon as an open breach with the Maritime Powers.[3]

Next, the last differences were adjusted between the States and Koenigsegg with the help of Cadogan's mediation. The States agreed to accede to the Emperor's demand that they should guarantee the privileges of the Catholics in Upper Guelderland, if he would grant them freedom of worship and take over the interest on the debts incurred by Charles II to the Republic.[4]

Koenigsegg agreed to this proposal on the 26th of October[5], but refused to concede more to the Protestants in the Southern Netherlands than "to confirm by an article the leaving all things concerning religion in these countries...on the same foot as in the time of Charles II". Cadogan advised the States that it would be impolitic to ask more. The effect of this article would

[1] Schaub to Townshend, 9 Oct. S.P.F.G. 32.
[2] Cf. Michael, p. 646.
[3] Cf. Bussemaker, p. 216.
[4] Cadogan to Townshend, 18 Oct. S.P.F.Fl. 64.
[5] Cadogan to Townshend, 26 Oct. S.P.F.Fl. 64.

be tantamount to religious toleration; although Protestant worship was to be confined to private observance.

The Treaty was signed on the 15th of November by Koenigsegg and the Dutch Plenipotentiaries, and on the 16th by Cadogan. The latter was late in signing because his presence had been required at Brussels to coerce the Council of State into reducing the duties on coarse woollens and distilled spirits in accordance with his agreement with Koenigsegg.[1]

The Treaty[2] contained the following provisions:

After the preamble, in which no mention was made of the Treaty of 1713,[3] Article I provided that the States General should hand over the Southern Netherlands to the Emperor, after the exchange of ratifications.

Article II. The Emperor agreed never to alienate any territory to any member of the French Royal House, nor to anyone who should not succeed to the hereditary possessions of the Hapsburgs in the Empire.

Article III. A force of 35,000 men should be employed in the defence of the Southern Netherlands, of which the Emperor should supply three-fifths.

Article IV. The Emperor promised to allow the States to garrison Namur, Tournai, Menin, Furnes, Warneton, Ypres and Knocke.

Article V provided for a joint garrison in Dendermonde, with a governor appointed by the Emperor, who should take an oath never to act contrary to the interests of the States General.

Articles VII and VIII provided for the appointment of governors and commanders by the States General, with precautions in favour of the Emperor.

Article IX provided for private worship for Protestants in the garrisons of the States General. "As for the inhabitants of the provinces, everything which concerns religion shall remain on the foot on which it was under Charles II."

Articles X, XI, XII, XIII and XV provided for the changing

[1] Cf. p. 354. [2] See Appendix E.

[3] Cf. Michael, p. 649. The Emperor refused to recognise any claim to the Barrier later than 1701.

of troops, fortifications and munitions, Article XIV for the delivery of the posts.

Article XVI provided that if the enemy should attack the provinces through Brabant, the States should be permitted to occupy the towns on the Demer, acting in concert with the Governor of the Low Countries.

Article XVII provided for an extension of the limits in Flanders, including Fort St Donas to the States, while Fort Rodenhuysen should be razed. The Catholic religion should be preserved in the ceded places on the footing it enjoyed during the life of Charles II.

Article XVIII pledged the Emperor to cede Venloo, Fort Michael, Stevensweert and the territory of Montfort, on condition that the immunities and privileges granted to the churches and monasteries and other ecclesiastical rights should be preserved as in the time of Charles II.

By Article XIX the Emperor promised to pay 500,000 crowns yearly to the States General over and above the forage regulation of 1698, the payment to begin on the day of the signature of the Treaty.

By Article XX the Emperor confirmed the administration of the Provisional Government, and by Article XXII he took over the debts of Charles II. Further, he promised to recognise the debts incurred for forage during the administration of the Maritime Powers. In Article XXIV he promised to make arrangements for the liquidation of these debts.

By Article XXVI he promised that the exports and imports on goods of the Maritime Powers should be paid on the present footing until the arrangement of a new commercial Treaty,[1] and confirmed the privileges of the United Provinces according to the Treaty of Münster.

Article XXVII stipulated the demolition of the fortifications of Liège and Huy.

Finally, the King guaranteed the Treaty which was to be ratified within six weeks (Arts. XXVIII, XXIX).

A secret separate article provided for the payment of the subsidy promised to the States General.

[1] Cf. p. 353. This amounted to the tariff of 21 Dec. 1680.

The contrast between the terms of this Treaty and the expectations of the Dutch in 1714 has been brought out in the account of the negotiations at Antwerp. The new Treaty fell short in some respects of even that of 1713, by the omission of Mons, Ghent, Charleroi, the Forts of Philippe and Damme and by the reduction of the subsidy. For this the States were to some extent compensated by the cession of Venloo, St Michael, Stevensweert and the territory of Montfort; further, their commerce was now firmly established on a satisfactory basis. Nevertheless, when the Dutch looked back to the pledges of 1709, the new Treaty could never be anything but a source of disappointment and humiliation.

It was otherwise with George I and his Ministers. In the conclusion of the Treaty they saw with triumph the realisation of their aims of 1714, which had at one time seemed unlikely of fulfilment.

In the first place, they considered they had provided adequate defences for the Southern Netherlands against France.

Secondly, the system seemed to realise their aim of uniting the Emperor and the Dutch more closely by giving neither one side nor the other undue power in the Southern Netherlands.

Thirdly, the Treaty was satisfactory as regards English commerce. The Dutch were not permitted to garrison towns which were of importance to English trade. The Emperor was pledged to maintain the present advantageous state of commerce until a new Treaty was drawn up. This the Maritime Powers intended to postpone indefinitely.

Finally, there seemed no obstacle to the renewal of the alliance between the three Powers which had been hampered by the negotiations at Antwerp.

It remained to be seen how the Treaty would work in practice, and whether the Emperor would observe the limitations put upon his new Provinces.

The controversies over the ratification of the Treaty and the difficulties which emerged before it was fully executed were soon to prove that, with the exception of the commercial advantages, the hopes of the Ministry were ill-founded.

IV

By the 29th Article the signature of the Barrier Treaty was to be ratified within six weeks. The refusal of the Council of State at Brussels to lower the duties on English woollens in accordance with the requisition of the 6th of November 1715 caused the English to withhold their ratification.[1]

This delay gave Châteauneuf, the French Ambassador at The Hague, the opportunity to make trouble between the Maritime Powers. In the hope of making the Dutch abandon the Treaty he proposed that all powers should guarantee the neutrality of the Southern Netherlands in the event of war.[2]

The Ministry was not deceived by this project. Stanhope bade the Dutch remember that the Partition Treaty made after the Peace of Ryswick had not prevented war: "the best way to avoid war is to be not too afraid of one, and to form such a union with the Allies as to let the French see that if they have a mind to fall out with one of us, they will certainly bring all the rest into the quarrel".[3]

Cadogan wrote from Stirling, where he was engaged in the suppression of the Jacobite rebellion, to advise the Ministers not to hold up the ratifications of the Treaty on account of the duty on woollens.[4] Accordingly, the ratifications arrived at The Hague in time to placate the Emperor, who had threatened to take the Southern Netherlands by force if they were not delivered up to him by the 21st of January.[5] With the ratification of the Treaty the Dutch were bound more firmly than ever to the policy of alliance with England and the Barrier system. On the 21st of January 1716 Walpole informed Townshend that all danger of their accepting the neutrality project was over.[6]

George I and his Ministers hoped that all obstacles to the renewal of the "Old System" were now removed. In preparation for a defensive alliance with the Emperor and the

[1] Michael, p. 652.
[2] Dollot, p. 413.
[3] Townshend to Walpole, Jan. 1716. F.E.B. 81.
[4] Michael, p. 653.
[5] Walpole to Townshend, 21 Jan. S.P.F.H. 253.
[6] Weber, *Die Quadrupel Allianz*, p. 11.

States, they concluded a defensive alliance with the Republic to which it was hoped the Emperor would accede. A series of incidents kept the three powers apart for many months.

The Emperor refused to accede to the alliance of the Maritime Powers on the ground that this was beneath his dignity.[1] To remedy this defect negotiations were set on foot for a new defensive alliance between the three Powers. There seemed to be little chance of conclusion since quarrels arose between the Emperor and the States.

It will be recollected that by Article II of the Barrier Treaty the Emperor promised never to alienate the Southern Netherlands, or any part of them. The Dutch now discovered that the Emperor had made a secret Treaty with the Elector Palatine in which he promised to cede Limburg to the latter in reward for his services to the House of Hapsburg. The States opposed this cession as illegal and the quarrel continued until on the death of the Elector his brother agreed to renounce his claim.[2]

Before this quarrel was settled a new dispute arose. The States claimed the right to garrison Bonn by the Treaty of Utrecht. As the Emperor did not recognise the Treaty, the Elector of Cologne expelled the Dutch garrison on the 11th of December 1715. The States appealed to the Emperor for an apology from the Elector and for the demolition of the fortifications of Bonn.[3] The Emperor agreed to the apology but did not insist upon the demolition, whereupon the Dutch refused to evacuate Huy and Liège, which in accordance with the Barrier Treaty were to be demolished. The dispute was not settled until 1717, when the States were forced to evacuate Huy and Liège while the fortifications of Bonn were left almost intact.[4]

The third source of friction between Charles VI and the States arose over the execution of the Barrier Treaty. By the separate article, the subsidy payable to the Dutch was secured

[1] Cf. Michael, pp. 664–6. The Emperor was irritated by the conclusion of a commercial treaty between George I and Philip V which seemed to preclude the possibility of English assistance against Spain.

[2] Michael, p. 665.

[3] Walpole to Townshend, 14 Feb. 1716. S.P.F.H. 253.

[4] Whitworth to Sunderland, 17 Dec. 1717. S.P.F.H. 253.

upon the revenues of Brabant and Flanders; in default of payment the Dutch were promised the right of military execution against the Provinces. This article had been kept secret as it was an infringement of the rights of the Provinces to grant money.[1] When it became known, the Provinces prepared to send two deputations to Vienna to protest against the Barrier Treaty.[2]

The arrival of these deputations caused embarrassment at Vienna,[3] where it was considered that the Deputies "had even passed the limits to which they should have been confined by respect for the Emperor".[4] Nevertheless, instructions were given to the Marquis de Prié, the deputy-governor of the Southern Netherlands, to stop at The Hague on his way to Brussels to discuss the revision of certain points in the Barrier Treaty.[5]

De Prié was a subtle diplomatist, for whom both Schaub and Whitworth entertained a great dislike, since his method of negotiation was "one of unaccountable shuffling".[6] He had a difficult task before him, since the Emperor feared to offend the Dutch at a time when Châteauneuf offered a defensive alliance between France and the Maritime Powers.[7] Fortunately for the Emperor, the English wished to delay negotiations with France until England had recovered her former prestige. Accordingly, they negotiated a defensive alliance with the Emperor which was concluded on the 25th of May (O.S.) 1716. Just as in their former Treaty with the Dutch, a clause provided for the accession of the missing link in the "Old System", but until the disputes as to the Barrier were settled there seemed little chance of success.

De Prié was instructed to seek redress on four points: the safeguards for the Catholic religion in territories ceded to the Republic, securities for the subsidy without military execution, the extension of the limits in Flanders, and finally a project for

[1] Cadogan to Townshend, 5 Nov. 1716. S.P.F.H. 255.
[2] Gachard, p. 451.
[3] Schaub to Tilson, 8 Feb. 1716. S.P.F.G. 34.
[4] Schaub to Tilson, 5 Sept. 1716. S.P.F.G. 34.
[5] Gachard, p. 456.
[6] Whitworth to Sunderland, 15 Feb. 1718. S.P.F.H. 261.
[7] Cf. Michael, pp. 670–1.

a new commercial treaty, a point on which the Maritime Powers were certain to combine against him. De Prié was privately instructed to prevent the Deputies of the Southern Netherlands from taking part in the conferences, as they might embroil the Emperor with the Dutch.[1]

Cadogan (now a Peer in recognition of his services in connection with the Barrier Treaty) was sent from England to take part in the negotiations. Several conferences took place in October 1716, but De Prié left The Hague without having gained one point.[2] Nor was he able to avert the conclusion of the Triple Alliance between France and the Maritime Powers on the 4th of January 1717.[3]

The effect of the Treaty was to make the Dutch more independent of the Emperor and more insistent upon adequate securities for their subsidy. It is possible that the conclusion of the Triple Alliance made the Emperor abandon his project of a commercial treaty, as De Prié never again broached the subject during the negotiations.

"The States complayn extremely of ye ill Treatment they have had from ye Emperor," wrote Leathes,[4] "and therefore resolve to have him tied up in such terms as he can't break." All De Prié's projects for securities for the subsidy were considered insufficient. At length it was agreed that the revenues of the New Conquests and the Customs of the Southern Netherlands should be assigned for this purpose. The Dutch demanded in addition the right to proceed in case of default against the magistrates of the New Conquests and the Receiver General of Finances. De Prié agreed to this with the exception of the Tournesis, as the Emperor could not permit a non-catholic power to proceed against the archbishop of the Tournesis.[5]

Before these questions were settled, two fresh points of dispute emerged. In accordance with the Barrier Treaty, the subsidy

[1] Gachard, p. 475.
[2] Cadogan and Walpole to Townshend, 9 and 20 Oct. S.P.F.H. 254.
[3] Cf. Michael, p. 679.
[4] Leathes to Sunderland, 30 July 1717, S.P.F.H. 256. Leathes was appointed to The Hague in the interim between Walpole and Whitworth.
[5] Gachard, p. 478. Cf. Cadogan and Whitworth to Sunderland, 8 Oct. 1717. S.P.F.H. 258.

should have been paid to the Dutch from the 15th of November 1715, the day on which the Treaty was signed. This had not been done. When they claimed for payment of these arrears the Emperor refused to accede to their request.

The second dispute arose from the Emperor's claim to munitions which the States had appropriated on taking possession of Venloo, St Michael and Stevensweert. In reply the Dutch counterclaimed for debts incurred by Koenigsegg in 1716 for munitions in the Southern Netherlands.

The negotiations extended throughout 1717, without coming to a conclusion. There was no prospect that the States would form a defensive alliance with the Emperor while the Barrier Convention was unconcluded.[1] This was the more serious, since the Whigs intended that the defensive alliance should be the prelude to a more important scheme, in which they wished for the active co-operation of the Dutch.

The departure of the Spanish fleet on the 11th of August 1717, for an unknown destination,[2] seemed to portend war between the Emperor and Spain. The policy of the Regent and George I was to avert war by the conclusion of the so-called Quadruple Alliance which should settle the disputes between Philip V and the Emperor.

In deference to the wishes of the English, who desired to include the Dutch in the projected alliance, the Emperor ordered De Prié to expedite the Barrier Convention.[3] On the 4th of March 1718, De Prié delivered a project for the subsidy in which he assigned 280,000 crowns on the revenues of the New Conquests, and 220,000 crowns on the customs of the Southern Netherlands. As a further security he offered the revenues of Ghent and Bruges, which in six years would be cleared of the debts charged on them since 1710. This grant would be made on condition that the States would agree to make no change in duties of exportation and importation in the Southern Netherlands.

If the Dutch would agree to this article, they might, in cases

[1] Leathes to Tilson, 3 Aug. 1717. S.P.F.H. 256.
[2] Weber, p. 42.
[3] Whitworth to Sunderland, 4 Feb. 1718. S.P.F.H. 261.

of default, proceed against the Receivers General of Finances and the magistrates in the New Conquests.

When the news was received that De Prié was prepared to make these concessions, Stanhope wrote to Whitworth of his joy "that this step of the Court of Vienna comes seasonably to help in our grand affair by taking this ugly rub of the Barrier out of our way".[1]

There were still three points on which the Dutch wished satisfaction before they would sign the Convention.[2] These were the liquidation of debts upon the revenues of the Southern Netherlands, the payment of arrears of the subsidy and the extension of the limits in Flanders.

It was at this moment that Whitworth was authorised to reveal the terms of the projected Quadruple Alliance, without disclosing the secret article by which the powers pledged themselves to action if Spain should refuse to accept the settlement.

The Dutch replied by a Memorial stating their objections to the alliance.[3]

(1) As the Emperor had treated them so ill regarding the Barrier, they saw no reason to engage in matters to his advantage.

(2) Since George I and the Regent had proceeded so far without the States, they might finish their work alone.

(3) Alberoni would never accept the terms offered to Spain and war would inevitably follow.

(4) The unfortunate condition of the Republic would not permit the Dutch to risk the dangers of war.

In an effort to induce the Dutch to change this attitude, Cadogan was sent once more to The Hague in the hope that he would expedite the conclusion of the Barrier Convention. He arrived in May 1718.[4] The States informed him that they would accept the subsidy article if the revenues of Ostend were added to those of Ghent and Bruges. If the subsidy were arranged on this basis, they were prepared to settle the question of arrears

[1] Stanhope to Whitworth, 14 April 1718. F.E.B. 82.
[2] Whitworth to Cadogan, 11 March. S.P.F.H. 262.
[3] Whitworth to Stanhope, 22 April. S.P.F.H. 262.
[4] Gachard, p. 481.

by accepting half the sum the Emperor should have paid since the 15th of November 1715.[1]

De Prié replied that out of deference to the King he would accede to these demands: this was more than the Dutch expected.[2] Nevertheless, they made yet another demand for securities for the payment of the arrears. Cadogan suggested that the revenues of Ostend should be appropriated for this purpose. When this point was settled, the States agreed that the spiritual Estates of Tournai should be exempt from military execution.[3]

On the 26th of July Cadogan made earnest representations to De Prié on the necessity of a speedy conclusion of the Convention, as certain towns in the Republic refused to accept the invitation to join the Quadruple Alliance until the Barrier negotiation was concluded. Cadogan attributed the procrastinations of De Prié to the influence of the Spaniards at Vienna.[4]

Accordingly, St Saphorin, the English Ambassador at Vienna, was instructed to inform the Emperor that though he might despise the assistance of the States, the King desired that he would give way over the Barrier, as the English feared that in the event of war, the Dutch would remain neutral and capture trade in South America.[5]

This representation had the desired effect: on the 28th of October De Prié reported that he had orders to conclude, owing to the regard the Emperor had for the King,[6] and on the 22nd of December, the Convention was signed.[7]

By the first article of the Convention,[8] for Article XVII of the Barrier Treaty an article was substituted which reduced the extension of the limits to about a fifth of what the States should have received by the Treaty, though including the Fort of

[1] Whitworth and Cadogan to Stanhope, 3 June. S.P.F.H. 262.
[2] Second letter of 3 June enclosing De Prié's answer. S.P.F.H. 262.
[3] States' observations enclosed in Whitworth to Tilson, 17 June. S.P.F.H. 262.
[4] Cadogan and Whitworth to Craggs, 26 July and 3 Aug. S.P.F.H. 263.
[5] Craggs to St Saphorin, 11 Sept. S.P.F.G. 39.
[6] Whitworth to Craggs, 28 Oct. S.P.F.H. 264.
[7] Whitworth to Craggs, 22 Dec. S.P.F.H. 264.
[8] Terms printed in Gachard, p. 481.

St Donas. As a safeguard for the Catholic religion, the inhabitants of the ceded territories were promised the immunities granted by Article XVIII of the Barrier Treaty to those of Venloo, Roermond and Stevensweert. The limits of Sas van Ghent were to be extended, and in time of war the States were to have the right to garrison Fort Perle.

Article II: the subsidy of 500,000 crowns or 1,250,000 Dutch florins was to be secured in the following manner: 700,000 florins on the revenues of the New Conquests and the remainder on the duties of importation and exportation collected from the comptoirs of specified towns. These sums were to be paid from the 1st of December 1718. As to arrears from the 15th of November 1715 to the 1st of January 1718, the States were to accept 550,000 florins payable in instalments of 50,000 florins per year. For the first eight months of 1718 they were to receive an annual payment of 55,000 florins, after the liquidation of the first arrears. When this was paid up, the States should receive 120,000 florins in 1720, the amount of arrears for the remaining months of 1718 up to December.

In default of payment, the States might proceed against the Receiver General of Finances, the Receiver General of the New Conquests, the customs bureaux, and also the magistrates and states of the Tournesis (excepting the ecclesiastics). If these stipulations were not adequate, the States might proceed according to Article XIX and the separate article of the Treaty of 1715 against the provinces of Brabant and Flanders.

Articles III and IV provided for the liquidation of debts upon the revenues of the Southern Netherlands.

By Article V the Emperor renounced his claim to the munitions appropriated by the States in St Michael, Venloo and Stevensweert. In return, the States agreed to desist from their claims to Koenigsegg's agreement for munitions of the 30th of January 1716.

In Article VI, the States agreed to deliver up the New Conquests after the exchange of ratification.[1] Finally, the Barrier Treaty and separate article were confirmed (Art. VII)

[1] The States had refused to evacuate the New Conquests until the payment of the subsidy was adequately secured.

and George I undertook to guarantee the whole Settlement (Art. VIII). Ratification was to take place within six weeks (Art. IX).

For the Dutch, this Convention was extremely advantageous. Though they were forced to make concessions as to the limits in Flanders, they now received adequate security for the payment of the subsidy and arrears and ample provision for liquidation of debts upon the revenues of the Southern Netherlands.

It was otherwise with the Emperor, though the concessions in Flanders and the security of the Catholic religion were points of great importance to him. The Convention added to the series of restrictions imposed by the Barrier Treaty, by the appropriation of revenues for payment of the subsidy and arrears, and by the provision for execution against the Receivers General of Finances in case of default. Nor had he succeeded in obtaining a new commercial treaty in return.

Despite the fact that the Convention was to their advantage, the Dutch procrastinated over the exchange of ratifications. Their reason was to provide themselves with an excuse for remaining outside the Quadruple Alliance.[1]

In this policy they were assisted by a fresh dispute with the Emperor. At Venloo, the Dutch troops had molested a Catholic procession. To prevent further disturbances, the governor ordered that in future the priests should carry the sacrament under their gowns when in procession. The Bishop of Roermond complained to the Emperor that this order infringed the immunities promised to Catholics in Upper Guelderland by Article XVIII of the Barrier Treaty. The Emperor refused to ratify the Barrier Convention until the States withdrew this order.

After some delay, the Dutch proposed to arrange matters to the Emperor's satisfaction after the exchange of ratifications.[2] As De Prié still withheld the ratifications the Ministry began to fear that his "refining genius" would lose them the concurrence of the States in the Quadruple Alliance.[3]

[1] Whitworth to Stanhope, 17 March 1719. S.P.F.H. 265.
[2] Whitworth to Tilson, 28 Feb. and 10 March. S.P.F.H. 265.
[3] Whitworth to Stanhope, 18 April. S.P.F.H. 265.

Stanhope again used his influence at Vienna and eventually persuaded the Emperor to despatch an order to De Prié to send the ratifications to London, where they were exchanged with those of the King and the States General at the end of May 1719.[1]

To the irritation of George I and his Ministers, the ratification of the Barrier Convention produced no change in Dutch policy with regard to the Quadruple Alliance: "being in actual possession of all the advantages they are entitled to by the Barrier Treaty", was Cadogan's conclusion,[2] "they believe they have no occasion for anybody's friendship".

V

With the conclusion of the Barrier Convention, the Maritime Powers succeeded in their object of imposing a new system in the defence of the Southern Netherlands. For thirty years the Dutch enjoyed peace in the belief that the new system no longer necessitated a struggle against the power of France.[3]

Upon examination, it will be found that the new system was unworthy of the confidence placed in it by the Maritime Powers.

In the first place, the conception of a Barrier had been evolved on the understanding that the Southern Netherlands would belong to Spain. The Spanish Kings had proved incapable of undertaking their defence alone and had come to rely upon Dutch assistance. The Dutch had conceived the idea of legalising their assistance by defining their powers within a treaty.

When the time came for the conclusion of the Treaty, the system had become obsolete,[4] since the allocation of the Southern Netherlands to the Emperor gave to the Provinces a sovereign strong enough to undertake their defence alone.

The conception of a Barrier was by this time deeply implanted in the policy of the Republic. As they held the Southern Netherlands in conjunction with England, on the understanding that the new sovereign was not to be installed until he had agreed

[1] Gachard, p. 484. [2] Cadogan to Stanhope, 15 July. S.P.F.H. 267.

[3] In accordance with a Franco-Dutch convention, the neutrality of the Southern Netherlands was preserved during the War of the Polish Succession in 1733. The Barrier was thus unattacked till 1745.

[4] Cf. Michael, p. 655.

to their conditions, they were able to impose upon the Emperor terms which militated against his enjoyment of the usual privileges of sovereignty. Dutch troops occupied the strongholds of his new provinces, the best revenues were appropriated for payment of a subsidy for their upkeep and commercial regulations which gave the advantage to the Maritime Powers were preserved.

The result of the Treaty was to weaken instead of to strengthen the Southern Netherlands, as the Emperor felt them to be a burden rather than an acquisition to his patrimony. Consequently, throughout the century, the successive Hapsburgs considered the possibilities of freeing themselves from the Southern Netherlands by an exchange with the Elector of Bavaria, and paid little attention to the defence of their new provinces.

This weakness was intensified by the English policy of making the Emperor and the Dutch mutually dependent in the Southern Netherlands. Bereft of the advantages they had been promised in the Townshend Treaty, the Dutch lost interest in the defence of the Barrier. It is fair to admit that the laxity with which they regarded their obligations was in part due to the general decline of the Republic, consequent on the loss of prestige after the Treaty of Utrecht, to their exhaustion after the series of wars in which they had played a leading part, and to the confusion in their domestic politics.

The defence of the country was further impaired by the hatred of the inhabitants for a system imposed upon them from without. The presence of foreign troops was tantamount to military occupation, although the troops were intended for the defence of the Provinces. This grievance was intensified by the difference of religion between the inhabitants and the Dutch.

Finally, the insistence of the Maritime Powers upon the continuance of commercial tariffs overwhelmingly in their favour further weakened the Provinces by the drain on their resources, as well as by increasing their hatred for the Dutch.

These factors explain the *débâcle* of 1745, when the Barrier system was proved totally inadequate as a protection against France. The ease with which the French captured the Barrier fortresses was a source of surprise and humiliation to the Maritime Powers. The Barrier was re-established after the Treaty of Aix-la-Chapelle, but the confidence in its efficacy was never restored. A series of negotiations, beginning with a revisal of the tariffs in the Southern Netherlands, culminated in the repudiation of the Treaty by the Emperor Joseph II.

In conclusion it must be admitted that the Whigs failed in their object of making the Barrier Treaty a bond between the members of the "Old System". Instead of uniting the Emperor and the Maritime Powers, the constant friction arising out of the Treaty was a contributory feature to the "diplomatic revolution" of 1756. This was the price paid by England for the commercial advantages in the Southern Netherlands. To obtain them, the Maritime Powers were willing to imperil the Barrier system: neither power could afford to let the other make a separate bargain with the Emperor. Their joint exploitation of the Austrian Netherlands proved disastrous politically and strategically, though commercially profitable to themselves.

APPENDICES

APPENDIX A

Marlborough's feelings on the subject of the Patent

(*a*) MARLBOROUGH AND CHARLES

If Marlborough solicited the government of the Netherlands, and there appears to be almost convincing proof of this (cf. Noorden, II, 345), one cannot be surprised at finding him keenly anxious to be able to accept the offer when it was actually made to him. It is clear that in the summer of 1706 when he wrote to Charles and the Emperor that he "could not yet" accept the Patent, he looked forward to a time when, to the already existing desire to accept it, there should be added the possibility of accepting. His letter to Stanhope, referred to on p. 86 *note* 1 shows that he considered that the settlement of the Barrier would afford him the opportunity he longed for. Even in 1708 he still apparently (cf. p. 93 *note* 1) cherished the hope that he would gain his object after the peace. But it would seem that for some reason, which at the present time it is difficult to explain, a change came over his feelings in 1709. On the 2nd of February 1709 Charles wrote offering Marlborough the Patent a third time. Instead of expressions of pleasure on the subject, however, the Duke mentioned in a letter to Godolphin, "the resolution you know I have taken of not accepting the offer of the King of Spain" (Marlborough to Godolphin, 16 April 1709. Coxe Papers). Moreover, he sent his answer to Charles in the form of an autograph letter to Stanhope (cf. Marlborough to Charles, 16 April. Murray), which was of such a nature that Charles, on the 16th of June, replied: "Ce que le Général Stanhope vient de dire de votre part m'a été un sujet de peines et d'inquiétudes. Je veux néanmoins espérer que les considérations que vous voulez bien avoir pour les Hollandais en cette conjoncture viendront bientôt à cesser dans une autre et qu'ensuite vous puissiez avoir le plaisir de jouir de cette petite marque de ma reconnaissance" (Charles to Marlborough, 16 June 1709. Coxe Papers). It was also after this letter from Marlborough to Stanhope that Charles declared to Wratislaw that, as Marlborough had thrice refused the Patent, his hands were no longer tied (see p. 173 *note* 1). Marlborough's next letter to Stanhope (to whom, it may be added, there was no reason for his not speaking the truth) was even more decisive. He wrote: "His M. is very kind on that subject but it is what I think can be no ways consistent with the service of the public, nor does it indeed suit with my own inclinations, *which are rather for a peaceable retirement at home*. However you see I do not absolutely decline it, not knowing yet what Her M. may think proper hereafter to determine in respect to the good of the public, which must be my rule to walk by, whatever my private inclinations may be" (Marlborough to Stanhope, 31 July 1709. Murray). Marlborough's letter to Godolphin on the subject contained the following passage: "I enclose the King of Spain's letter by which you will see that he does not admit entirely of my excusing myself from the acceptance of this government. As I would not make any answer before I have the Queen's leave, so I conjure you as a friend to represent it so to Her M. that my resolutions are such as I cannot accept of this government. *Besides, should I continue in so great a station, it might give my enemies an opportunity for censuring my actions*, which by the Queen's leave I shall endeavour for the rest of my life to avoid by not meddling in any public business but where her personal concern may require it" (Marlborough to Godolphin, 18 July 1709. Coxe Papers).

The Queen's answer was that he might "do as he thought like to be most for his own satisfaction" (Godolphin to Marlborough, 20/31 July 1709. Coxe Papers). I have italicised the two observations that seem to give a possible clue to Marlborough's action. Was it that he had seen, when in England in the spring, that the foundations of the Whig ascendancy were giving way, and that it behoved him not to aggravate Tory hostility to himself by accepting the Patent?—or was it that he was becoming weary of overwork and disappointed as to the prospects of the war, and desirous of settling down quietly at home with the Duchess? The fact that he consented to serve under the Tories until actually dismissed inclines us to the first view.

(*b*) MARLBOROUGH AND VIENNA

It would seem to be the case that the effect of Marlborough's early professions of his desire for the government of the Netherlands were not so easily dispelled at Vienna as at Barcelona. When Charles suggested the appointment of Eugene, instead of Marlborough, the Imperial Court hesitated. Arneth, in his *Life of Prince Eugene*, describes the matter thus: "In Vienna also they were persuaded that he (Eugene) was the only possible stadholder, but, apart from the consideration of losing him, it weighed heavily with them that Marlborough, as they knew, had most unwillingly renounced this post so splendid and lucrative—a point of great importance to him. They also believed that Marlborough, though he had declared the reverse, had always the hope that, after the conclusion of the peace, the obstacles which had hitherto barred the way would be removed and he would reach at last the goal of his secret ambition. The correspondence of the Duke which has since come to light shows how right this view had been". (I do not know to what correspondence Arneth refers.) "They not unjustly feared to arouse jealousy and suspicion of Marlborough by prematurely naming Eugene to the post, as if the Prince had aspired to an office promised to Marlborough" (Protocol of Conference of 1 Oct. 1709).

(c) MARLBOROUGH AND THE DUTCH

In the United Provinces Marlborough's policy was, of course, one of consistent renunciation from the first; but the letter from Pesters to Heinsius (p. 93 *note* 1) shows how little the Dutch trusted these assurances.

APPENDIX B

[EDITOR'S NOTE]

Guelderland

The Province of Guelderland was originally divided into four parts: Veluwe, Zutphen, Nymwegen and Roermond. The latter or Upper Quarter had been reconquered by Spain during the eighty years' war. It was the ambition of the Dutch to have this part of the Province restored to them. During the negotiations of the Peace of Münster they found the Spanish obdurate. On the 13th of April 1647, the States of Holland passed a Resolution declaring that the Upper Quarter should be returned in exchange for an equivalent.[1] In the subsequent negotiations the Republic was so far successful in that this Resolution was embodied in Article LII of the Treaty of Münster, with the provision that should the parties concerned be unable to agree as to the equivalent, the dispute should be referred to a court which was to be appointed for the settlement of this and other problems left unsolved by the Peace of Münster.[2] It was expected that this Tribunal—known as the Chambre Mi-Partie—would meet six months after the conclusion of the Treaty.

Unfortunately for the States General, the Chambre Mi-Partie was neither so speedy in assembling, nor so decisive in settling the problem as the framers of the Treaty had anticipated. It did not

[1] Rive, *Nederland en Pruissen*, chap. I.
[2] Dumont, *Corps Universel*, VI, I, 30 Jan. 1648.

meet until 1658, at Mechlin.[1] As nothing was concluded there with regard to Guelderland, the States preferred to treat at home with the Spanish Ambassador. This was equally inconclusive; the Ambassador excused himself on the ground that he had no orders on the subject. The States were handicapped by their inability to suggest an equivalent. In 1661 an embassy, despatched by the Republic to Madrid, concluded the negotiations of Mechlin with the exception of the Upper Quarter's fate.[2] The question was left unsolved and undiscussed until the eighteenth century.

APPENDIX C

The New Conquests

The New Conquests were afterwards defined at the Treaty of Utrecht as follows:

The Dutch handed back to Louis: Lille, Orchies, Aire, Bethune, St Venant, St Amand and Mortagne.

Louis ceded to the Dutch, in trust for the Emperor, Menin, Tournai and the Tournesis (except St Amand and Mortagne), Furnes and the Furnambacht (Knocke, Loo and Dixmude), Ypres and the five Châtellanies (Roulers, Poperinghe, Warneton, Commines and Wervicq).

These were the New Conquests about which the disputes arose between England and the States over administration (cf. p. 318).

APPENDIX D

Dutch Opposition to English Dictation

Holland 2950 No. 72. Letters to Heinsius regarding peace, 1710–13, 19 Nov. 1711. To Heinsius, unsigned. "Further considerations on the conciliatory advice with regard to the peace negotiations."

...Because if the English Ministers find that this State, even at the beginning, is so afraid of them, that they dare deny them nothing, be it never so unreasonable and injurious, it is to be feared, that in consequence of this they will use our forbearingness to put further disadvantages on us, and our trade in the West Indies, Spain and

[1] Basnage, *Annales des Provinces Unies*, I, 346, 545.

[2] *Ibid.* p. 664. Cf. Aitzema, Boek XLIII, from which Basnage takes his account.

the Mediterranean. On this account there are two extremes to be avoided:

(i) the extremity of refusing everything to Britain,

(ii) the extremity of giving in on all points to Britain...one must find a middle way...keep a good countenance, with the utmost confidence, foresight and moderation and procrastinate to see what Parliament will say on the matter.

...As to the Allies, this State ought to act openly and trustfully and not help to betray and surprise them...may God please to conduct this land and Church through all these dark and troublesome negotiations to the best for all Protestants and Patriots. Amen.

APPENDIX E

The Barrier Treaties

I. Treaty between *Great Britain* and the *States General* relative to the Succession and Barrier. October 1709.[1]

Sa Majesté La Reine de la Grande Bretagne, et les Seigneurs États Généraux des Provinces Unies, ayant considéré combien il importoit au repos, et à la seureté de leurs Royaumes et États, et à la tranquillité publique de maintenir et d'asseurer d'une part la succession à la couronne de la Grande Bretagne, telle qu'elle est présentement établie par les loix du Royaume, et que d'autre part, les dites États Généraux des Provinces Unies, ayent une forte et suffisante barrière contre la France et autres, qui les voudroient surprendre ou attaquer, et Sa Majesté et les dits Seigneurs États Généraux appréhendant, avec juste raison, les troubles et les malheurs, qui pourroient survenir au sujet de cette Succession, s'il se trouvoit un jour quelque personne ou quelque Puissance, qui la révoquât en doute, et que les pais et estatz des dits Seigneurs Estats Généraux, ne fussent pas munis d'une telle barrière. Pour ces dites raisons, La dite Majesté la Reine de la Grande Bretagne, quoy que dans la vigueur de son âge, et jouissant d'une parfaite santé, que Dieu luy conserve longues années, par un effet de sa prudence et de sa piété ordinaire, a jugé à propos, d'entrer avec les Seigneurs États Généraux des Provinces Unies, dans une alliance et confoedération particulière, dont la principale fin, et l'unique but, seront le repos et la tranquillité publique, et de prévenir par des mesures prises à tems, tous les événemens, qui pourroient exciter un jour de nouvelles guerres; C'est dans cette

[1] Public Record Office. State Papers Foreign. Treaties (Holland). S.P. 108/343.

veuë, que Sa Majesté Britannique a donné son plein pouvoir, pour convenir de quelques articles d'un traitté additionnel aux traittéz et alliances, qu'elle a déjà avec les Seigneurs États Généraux des Provinces Unies, à Son Ambassadeur Extraordinaire et Plénipotentiaire, Le Sieur Charles Vicomte de Townshend, Baron de Lyn-Regis, Conseiller du Conseil privé de Sa Majesté Britannique, Capitaine des Gardes Hallebardiers de Sa dite Majesté, et son Lieutenant dans la Comté de Nortfolk; et les Seigneurs États Généraux des Provinces Unies, aux Sieurs Jean de Welderen, Seigneur de Valburgh, Grand Baillif de la Basse Betuive, du Corps de la Noblesse de la Province de Guelre; Fredrik Baron de Reede, Seigneur de Lier, St Antoine et Fer Lee, de L'Ordre de la Noblesse de la Province de Hollande et Westfrise; Antoine Heinsius, Conseiller Pensionnaire de la Province de Hollande et Westfrise, Garde du Grand Sceau et Surintendant des fiefs de la même Province; Corneille van Gheel, Seigneur de Spanbroek, Bulkesteyn &c[a], Gedeon Hoeuft, Chanoine du Chapitre de l'Église de St Pierre à Utregt, et Conseiller éleu dans les États de la Province d'Utregt; Hessel van Sminia, Secrétaire de la Chambre des Comptes de la Province de Frise; Ernst d'Ittersum, Seigneur d'Osterhof du Corps de la Noblesse de la Province d'Overyssel, et Wicher Wichers, Sénateur de la ville de Groningue, tous Députéz à l'assemblée des dits Seigneurs Étatz Généraux de la part respectivement des Provinces de Guelre, de Hollande et Westfrise, de Zeelande, d'Utregt, de Frise, d'Overyssel et de Groningue et Ommelandes, lesquels en vertu de leurs plein pouvoirs, sont convenus des articles suivans.

1

Les traittéz de paix, d'amitié, d'alliance et de confoedération, entre Sa Majesté Britannique et les États Généraux des Provinces Unies, seront approuvéz et confirméz par le présent traitté, et demeureront dans leur première force et vigueur, comme s'ilz y étoient inséréz de mot à mot.

2

La succession à la Couronne d'Angleterre ayant été réglée par un acte du Parlement, passé la douzjème année du règne de feu Sa Majesté le Roy Guillaume Trois, dont le titre est, Acte pour la plus ample limitation de la Couronne, et pour la plus grande seureté des droits et des libertéz des sujets: et nouvellement en la sixjème année du règne de Sa Majesté la Reine à présent régnante, cette même succession ayant encore été établie et affermie, par un autre Acte, fait pour la plus grande Seureté de la Personne et du Gouvernement de Sa Majesté, et de la Succession à la Couronne de la Grande

Bretagne &c[a] dans la ligne de la Sérénissime maison de Hanover, et en la personne de la Princesse Sophie, et de ses héritiers, successeurs et descendants, males et femelles, néz et à naître. Et aucune Puissance n'ayant droict de s'opposer aux loix faites sur ce sujet, par la Couronne et le Parlement de la Grande Bretagne; s'il arrivoit néanmoins, sous quelque prétexte, ou par quelque cause que ce peut être, que quelque personne ou quelque puissance ou État, prétendît révoquer en doute l'établissement, que le Parlement a fait de la dite succession, dans la Sérénissime maison de Hanover, de s'opposer à la dite succession, d'aider ou de favoriser ceux qui s'y opposeroient, soit directement ou indirectement, par une guerre ouverte, ou en fomentant des séditions et des conspirations, contre celle ou celuy, en faveur de qui la Couronne de la Grande Bretagne seroit ouverte, conformément aux actes susdits. Les États Généraux des Provinces Unies s'engagent et promettent d'assister et de maintenir dans la dite succession, celle ou celuy, à qui elle appartiendra, en vertu des dits actes du Parlement, de les aider à en prendre possession, s'ilz ne l'avoient déjà prise, et de s'opposer à ceux qui voudront les troubler dans la prise de possession ou dans la possession actuelle de la dite succession.

3

Sa dite Majesté et les États Généraux, en conséquence du cinquième article de l'alliance conclue entre l'Empereur, le feu Roy de la Grande Bretagne, et les Seigneurs États Généraux le 7 Septembre 1701 employeront toutes leurs forces, pour recouvrer le reste des Pais Bas Espagnolz.

4

Et deplus, on taschera de conquérir autant d'autres villes et forts, qu'il se pourra, afin qu'ilz puissent servir de barrière et de seureté aux dits Seigneurs États.

5

Et comme suivant le neufjème article de la dite alliance, on doit convenir entre autres choses, comment et de quelle manière l'État sera mis en seureté, par le moyen de cette barrière, la Reine de la Grande Bretagne fera ses efforts, pour procurer, que dans le traitté de paix, il puisse estre convenu que tous les Pais Bas Espagnolz, et ce que l'on pourroit en outre trouver nécessaire, soit à l'égard des villes et places conquises ou non conquises, serviront de barrière à l'État.

6

Qu'à cette fin Leurs Hautes Puissances pourront mettre et avoir garnison, la changer, augmenter et diminuer, comme ilz le jugeront à propos, dans les places suivantes: à Scavoir Nieuport, Furnes avec le Fort de Knocke; Yperen, Menin, La ville et la citadelle de Lisle; Tournay et sa Citadelle; Condé; Valenciennes; et les places qu'on pourra conquérir encore sur la France; Maubeuge; Charleroy; Namur et sa Citadelle; Lière; Halé à fortifier; Les Forts de La Perle; Philippe; Damme; Le Château de Gand; et Dendermonde; Le Fort de St Donas étant attaché aux fortifications de l'Écluse, et y étant entièrement incorporé, demeurera et sera cédé en propriété à L'État. Le Fort de Rodenhuysen en deçà de Gand sera razé.

7

Les dits Seigneurs États Généraux pourront aussi mettre, en cas d'attaque apparente, ou de guerre, autant de troupes, qu'ilz jugeront nécessaire, dans toutes les villes, places et forts des Pais Bas Espagnolz, où la raison de guerre le demandera.

8

Et pourront aussi envoyer dans les villes, forts et places, où ilz auront leurs garnisons, sans aucun empêchemente, et sans payer aucuns droits, des vivres, munitions de guerre, armes et artillerie, des matériaux pour les fortifications, et tout ce que pour les dites garnisons et fortifications sera trouvé convenable et nécessaire.

9

Les dits Seigneurs Estats Généraux pourront aussi mettre dans les villes, forts et places de leur barrière mentionnés dans l'article six cy dessus où ilz auront leurs garnisons, tels Gouverneurs, et Commandants, majors et autres officiers, qu'ilz trouveront à propos, lesquels ne seront sujets à aucuns autres ordres, qui regardent la seureté des dites places et le militaire, quels qu'ilz soient et de qui ilz puissent venir, que seulement et privativement à ceux de Leurs Hautes Puissances, sans préjudice pourtant aux droits et libertéz tant Ecclésiastiques, que Politiques du Roy Charles Trois.

10

Qu'en outre les dits Seigneurs États pourront fortifier les dites villes, places, et forts qui en dépendent, et en réparer les fortifications, de la manière qu'ilz le jugeront nécessaire, et de plus faire tout ce qui sera utile pour leur défense.

11

On laissera aux Seigneurs Estats Généraux tous les revenus des villes, places, Châtellenies et leurs dépendances, qu'ilz auront pour leur barrière, de la France, desquelles la Couroñe d'Espagne n'estoit pas en possession, au tems de la mort du feu Roy Charles Second:

et outre cela, on fixera un million de livres, à payer cent milles écus chaque trois mois, des revenus les plus clairs des Pais Bas Espagnolz, dont le dit Roi estoit alors en possession, pour servir l'un et l'autre à l'entretien des garnisons de l'Estat, et pour fournir aux fortifications, comme aussi aux magasins et autres dépenses nécessaire, dans les villes et places susdites; Et afin que les frays à supporter, puissent être trouvéz des dits revenus, on taschera d'étendre les dépendances et châtelenies susmentionnées, autant qu'on pourra, et spécialement de stipuler avec la Châtelenie d'Ypre, celle de Cassel, et le bois de Niépe, et avec la Châtelenie de Lisle, la gouvernance de Douay, l'une et l'autre y ayant esté attachées avant la présente guerre.

12

Qu'aucune ville, fort, place ou pais des Pais Bas Espagnolz, ne pourra être cédé, transporté ou donné, ou eschevir à la Couronne de France, ou à quelqu'un de la ligne Françoise, soit en vertu d'aucun don, vente, eschange, convention matrimonielle, haerédité, succession par testament ou abintestas, de quelque titre que ce puisse estre, ni de quelque autre manière que ce soit, être mise au pouvoir ou sous l'authorité du Roy Très Chrétien, ou de quelqu'un de la ligne Françoise.

13

Et comme les dits Seigneurs États Généraux, en conséquence de l'article neuf de la dite alliance, doivent faire une Convention, ou un traitté avec le Roy Charles Trois, pour mettre l'État en Seureté, par le moyen de la dite barrière, la Reine de la Grande Bretagne concurrera par ses devoirs, afin que tout ce que dessus, touchant la barrière de l'État soit inséré dans le susdit traitté ou convention, et que Sa dite Majesté continuera ces devoirs jusqu'à ce que la susdite convention entre l'Estat et le dit Roy Charles Trois soit conclue, conformément à ce qui est dit cy-dessus, et que sa majesté garantira le dit traitté ou Convention.

14

Et afin que les dits Seigneurs Estatz jouissent dès à présent, autant qu'il est possible d'une barrière aux Paix Bas Espagnolz, il leur sera permis de mettre leurs garnisons, dans les villes déjà occupées, et qui pourront l'estre encore, avant que la paix soit faite, et mise en exécution. Et cependant le Roy Charles Trois, ne pourra entrer en possession des dits Pais Bas Espagnolz, ni entout ni enpartie; et pendant ce tems-là, la Reine aidera Leurs Hautes Puissances à les y maintenir dans la jouissance des revenus, et à trouver le million de livres par an, cy dessus mentionnéz.

15

Et comme Leurs Hautes Puissances ont stipulé par le traitté de Munster Article quatorze, que la rivière de l'Escaut, comme aussi les canaux du Sas, Swyn et autres bouches de mer y aboutissans, seroient tenues closes du côté de cet État.

Et article quinze, que les navires et denrées entrants et sortants des havres de Flandres seroient et demeureroient chargées de toutes telles impositions et autres charges, qui se lèvent sur les denrées, allants et venants au long de l'Escaut et autres canaux susmentionnéz.

La reine de la Grande Bretagne promet, et s'engage, que Leurs Hautes Puissances ne seront jamais inquiétées dans leur droit et possession à cet égard, directement ni indirectement; mais qu'elles continueront d'en jouir pleinement, comme aussi qu'au préjudice du dit traitté, le commerce ne sera pas rendu plus aisé par les ports de mer, que par la dite rivière, canaux et bouches de mer, du costé de l'Estat des Provinces Unies, ni directement, ni indirectement.

Et puis que par le même traitté de Munster article seize et dixsept, Sa Majesté le Roy d'Espagne s'est obligé de traitter les sujets de Leurs Hautes Puissances, si favorablement, que les sujets de la Grande Bretagne, et des villes Anséatiques, qui étoient alors les nations les plus favorablement traittées. Sa Majesté Britannique et Leurs Hautes Puissances promettent aussi, de faire en sorte, que les sujets de la Grande Bretagne et de Leurs Hautes Puissances, seront traittéz dans les Pais Bas Espagnolz, aussi bien que dans toute l'Espagne, royaumes et estats en dépendants, également et tant les uns que les autres, si favorablement que les nations les plus favorisées.

16

La dite Reine et les Estats Généraux s'obligent à donner par mer et par terre les secours et assistances nécessaires, pour maintenir par la force Sa dite Majesté dans la paisible possession de ses royaumes, et la Sérénissime maison de Hanover dans la dite succession, telle qu'elle est établie par les actes du Parlement cy dessus mentionnéz, et pour maintenir les dits Estatz Généraux dans la possession de la dite barrière.

17

Après les ratifications de ce traitté, on fera une convention particulière des conditions, auxquelles la dite Reine, et les dits Seignrs Etats Généraux s'engageront de fournir les secours, que l'on jugera nécessaire, tant par mer que par terre.

18

Si Sa Majesté Britannique ou les États Généraux des Provinces Unies étoient attaquéz de qui que ce peut être, à cause de cette convention, ilz s'assisteront mutuellement l'un l'autre de toutes leurs forces, et ilz se rendront garands de l'exécution de la dite convention.

19

Seront invitéz et admis dans le présent traité, le plutost qu'il pourra, tous les Roys, Princes et États, qui voudront y entrer, particulièrement Sa majesté Impériale; les Roys d'Espagne et de Prusse, et l'Électeur de Hanover; et il sera permis à Sa Majesté Britannique, et aux États Généraux des Provinces Unies, et à chacun d'eux en particulier, de requérir et inviter ceux qu'ilz jugeront à propos de requérir et inviter, d'entrer dans ce traitté, et d'estre garands de son exécution.

20

Et comme le tems a fait connoistre l'omission qui s'est faite dans le traitté signé à Ryswick l'an 1697 entre l'Angleterre et la France, au sujet du droit de la succession d'Angleterre, dans la persoñe de Sa Majesté la Reine de la Grande Bretagne à présent régnante et que faute d'avoir étably dans ce traitté, ce droit incontestable de Sa Majesté, la France a refusé de la reconnoistre pour Reine de la Grande Bretagne, après la mort du feu Roy Guillaume Trois de Glor: mém^{e}. Sa Majesté la Reine de la Grande Bretagne, et les Seign^{rs} États Généraux des Provinces Unies, conviennent, et s'obligent aussy de n'entrer dans aucune négociation, ni traité de paix avec la France, avant que le titre de Sa Majesté à la couronne de la Grande Bretagne, comme aussy le droit de la succession de la Sérénissime maison de Hanover à la susdite Couronne, telle qu'elle est réglée et établie par les susdits actes du Parlement, ne soit pleinement reconnu par la France, comme praeliminaire, et que la France n'aye en même tems promis, l'éloignement hors de ses étatz, de la personne qui praetend estre Roy de la Grande Bretagne. Et que l'on n'entrera dans aucune négociation, ni discussion formelle des articles du dit traitté de paix, sinon que conjointement et en même tems avec La dite Reine, ou avec ses ministres.

21

Sa Majesté Britannique et les Seigneurs Estatz Généraux des Provinces Unies, ratifieront et confirmeront tout ce qui est contenu dans le présent traitté, dans l'espace de quatre semaines à compter, du jour de la signature. En foy de quoy les sous signéz Ambassadeur

Extraordinaire et Plénipotentiaire de Sa Majesté Britannique et Députéz des Seigneurs États Généraux, ont signé le présent traitté, et y ont apposé le cachet de leurs armes. A la Haye le vingt neufjème d'Octobre L'an mil sept cent neuf.

Townshend

J. v. Welderen
F. B. van Reede
A. Heinsius
G. Hoeuft
H. Sminia
E. v. Ittersum
W. Wichers

Article Séparé.

Comme dans les Articles Praeliminaires, signés ici à la Haye le Vingt et huitième may mil sept cent et neuff, par les Plénipotentiaires de Sa Majesté Impériale, de Sa Majesté la Reine de la Grande Bretagne, et des Seigneurs États Généraux des Provinces Unies, il est stipulé entre autres choses que les Seigneurs Étatz Généraux auront en toute propriété et souveraineté le Haut Quartier de Gueldres selon le cinquant deuxième Article du traitté de Munster de l'an mil six cent quarante huict; comme aussy que les garnisons, qui se trouvent, ou se trouveront cy après de la part des Seigneurs États Généraux dans la ville de Huy, la Citadelle de Liège et dans la ville de Bonne, y resteront jusques à ce qu'on en soit convenu autrement avec Sa Majesté Impériale et l'Empire. Et comme la barrière sur la quelle on est convenu aujourd'huy dans le traité principal pour la garantie mutuelle entre Sa Majesté Britannique et les Seigneurs États Généraux, ne peut donner aux Provinces Unies la seureté pour la quelle est établie, sans qu'elle soit bien serrée d'un bout jusques à l'autre, et que la communication en soit bien liée ensemble, à quoy le Haut Quartier de Guelres, et les garnisons dans la Citadelle de Liège, Huy et Bonne sont absolument nécessaires; l'expérience ayant fait voir par trois fois, que la France ayant voulu attaquer les Provinces Unies, s'est servie des endroits susmentionnéz, pour venir à elles, et pour pénétrer dans les dites Provinces. Que de plus à l'égard de l'équivalent, moyennant le quel le Haut Quartier de Guelres, doit estre cédé aux Provinces Unies, suivant l'article Cinquante-deux du traitté de Munster susmentionné, Sa Majesté le Roy Charles Troisième sera beaucoup plus gratifié et avantagé en d'autres endroits, que cet équivalent ne peut importer: Ainsi pour faire avoir aux Seigneurs États Généraux le Haut Quartier de Guelres en toute propriété et souveraineté, et pour que le dit Haut Quartier soit cédé de cette manière aux Seigneurs États Généraux, dans la convention ou le traitté, qu'ilz doivent faire avec Sa Majesté le Roy Charles Troisième suivant l'article Treizième du traitté conclu aujourd'huy; comme aussi pour que leurs garnisons dans la Citadelle de Liège, dans celle de Huy, et dans Bonne, y restent, jusque à ce qu'on en soit convenu autrement avec Sa Majesté Impériale et l'Empire, Sa Majesté la Reine de la Grande Bretagne s'engage et promet, par cet Article séparé, qui aura la même force, que s'il estoit inséré dans le traitté principal, de faire pour tout cela les mêmes efforts, qu'Elle s'est engagée de faire, pour leur faire obtenir la barrière dans les Pais Bas Espagnols.

En foy de quoy les sousignés Ambassadeur extraordinaire et Plénipotentiaire de Sa Majesté Britannique, et Députéz des Seigneurs Estats Généraux ont signé le présent Article Séparé, et y ont apposé le cachet de leurs Armes, à la Haye le vingt et neufième d'Octobre l'an mil sept cent et neuff.

Townshend

W. v. Welderen
F. B. van Reede
A. Heinsius
G. Hoeuft
H. Sminia
W. Ittersum
W. Wichers

Deuxième Article Séparé.

Comme les Seigneurs Estats Généraux ont représenté, que dans la Flandre les limites entre la Flandre Espagnole, et celle de l'État, sont réglés de telle manière, que le terrain de l'État y est extrêmement étroit, de sorte qu'en quelques endroits, le territoire de la Flandre Espagnole s'étend jusques aux fortifications et sous le canon des places, villes et forts de l'Estat, dont il arrive plusieurs inconvéniens, ainsy qu'on en a veu un exemple, peu avant le commencement de la présente guerre, quand on a voulu bâtir un fort sous le canon du Zas de Gand, sous prétexte que c'estoit sur le territoire d'Espagne; et comme pour éviter ces sortes d'inconvéniens et autres, il est nécessaire, que le terrain de l'Estat aux confins de la Flandre soit élargi, et que par là les places, villes et forts soient mis plus à couvert, Sa Majesté Britannique, entrant dans les justes motifs des dits Seigneurs Estats Généraux à cet égard, promet et s'engage, par cet article séparé, que dans la convention que les dits Seigneurs Estats Généraux doivent faire, avec sa Majesté le Roy Charles trois, Elle les aydera, à ce qu'il soit convenu, que par la cession aux dits Seigneurs Estats Généraux de la propriété d'une étendue de terrain nécessaire à obvier à des pareils et autres inconvéniens, leur limites en Flandre soient élargis plus convenablement à leur seureté et ceux de la Flandre Espagnole plus éloignés de leurs villes, places et forts, pour que ceux-cy ne soient plus si exposés. En foy de quoy les sousignés Ambassadeur extraordinaire et Plénipotentiaire de Sa Majesté Britannique, et Députés des Seigneurs Estats Généraux ont signé le présent article séparé, et y ont apposé le cachet de leurs armes. A la Haye le vingt neufième d'Octobre l'an mil sept cent neuf.

Townshend

F. B. van Reede
A. Heinsius
G. Hoeuft
H. Sminia
W. Ittersum.

II. Treaty between *Great Britain* and the *States General*. January 1713.[1]

Quandoquidem in Tractatu, qui super Successione ad Coronam Magnae Britanniae, atq; obice sive Repagulo, vulgò Barriere, Unitarum Belgii Provinciarum 29° die Octobris anno 1709, inter Serenissimam ac Potentissimam Principem, Dominam Annam, Magnae Britanniae, Franciae & Hiberniae Reginam, Fidei Defensorem &c. et Celsos ac Praepotentes Dominos, Ordines Generales Foederati Belgii conclusus fuit, complures Articuli Clausulaeq; contineantur qui ampliorem Explicationem desiderant, quiq;, nisi emendationes aliquae ex aequo adhibeantur jam nunc damnosi, et proinde ex iis, quae hinc olim sequi poterint, commodis rationibusq; Subditorum dictae Suae Regiae Majestatis periculum allaturi videantur; aliiq; porro extent, qui, posteaquam Tractatus supradictus initus est, diutius nec necessarii neq; apti sunt; Cumq; Articulo 17 praememorati Tractatus provisum fuerit, ut Conventio quaedam speciatim fieret de conditionibus, quibus praefata Regia Sua Majestas Dominiq; Ordines Generales promitterent sponderentq; sese subministraturos auxilia, quorum usus foret, ad Fidejussiones, vulgo Garantias, mutuo praestandas; quoe quidem Conventio haudquaquam facta est; Antedicta Regia Sua Majestas Magnae Britanniae, et Domini Ordines Generales Foederati Belgii serió perpendentes quanti intersit ut nihil imperfectum, nihil obscurum restaret in Tractatu, qui utriq; Nationi permagni adeo momenti est, quodq; nulla ineunda sit Pactio quae Subditis alterutrius Partis gravis esse videatur, in Foedere, cujus scopus propositumq; fuerit, ut amicitiae vincula arctius utrinq; adstringerentur, et de mutuá

[1] P.R.O. State Papers Foreign. Treaties (Holland). S.P. 108/346.

securitate melius efficaciusq praecautum esset, ê re fore existimauerunt novum Tractatum conficere, caeteris Tractatibus Foederibusq qui inter Ipsos nunc vigent addendum; atq eum deniq in Finem Regia Sua Majestas Magnae Britanniae Mandatis suis atq authoritate sufficienti instruxit Reverendum admodum in Christo Patrem, Johannem, Episcopum Bristoliensem, Privati Angliae Sigilli Custodem, Regiae Majestati a Consiliis Intimis, Decanum Windesoriensem et Nobilissimi Ordinis Periscelidis Registrarium, ut et Nobilissimum Illustrissimum atq Excellentissmum Dominum D^m.num. Thomam Comitem de Strafford, Vice Comitem Wentworth de Wentworth, Woodhouse, et de Stainborough, Baronem de Raby,[1] Regiae Suae Majestati a Consiliis Intimis, Ejusdemq Legatum Extraordinarium et Plenipotentiarium ad Celsos et Praepotentes Dominos, Ordines Generales Uniti Belgii Regiae Suae Majestatis Dimarchorum Legionis vulgó Regiment, Tribunum, et Exercituum Regiorum Locum-tenentem Generalem, Primarium Admiralitatis Magnae Britanniae et Hiberniae Dominum Com̃issarium, ut et Nobilissimi Ordinis Periscelidis Equitem, Ambos, ad Pacem Generalem hac in Urbe Trajectinâ conficiendam, a parte Regiae Suae Majestatis Plenipotentiarios; Domini vero Ordines Generales a sua parte Mandatis atq authoritate sufficienti muniverunt Dominos Jacobum de Randwyk, Toparcham in Rossem &c. Burggravium Imperii et Praesidem Civitatis Neomagensis; Wilhelmum Buys, Civitatis Amstelodamensis Consiliarium & Syndicum; Brunonem Van-der-Dussen, Consularem et Senatorem, ut et Consiliarium et Syndicum Civitatis Goudanae, Concilii, quod Agro Schielandiae prae est, Assessorem, et Agri Crimpensis Dijk-Gravium; Fredericum Adrianum Baronem de Rheede, Toparchum in Renswoude, Emmiuk-huysen, Moerkerken &c: Praesidem Ordinis Nobilium Provinciae Ultrajectinae; Sicconem de Goslinga, Ditionis Franequeranae in Frisia Grietmannum, et Universitatis Franequeranae Curatorem; et Carolum Ferdinandum Comitem de Inhuysen et de Kniphuysen, Toparchum in Vredewold &c: in Consessu dictorem Ordinum Generalium ex Provinciis Gelriae, Hollandiae et West Frisiae, Ultrajecti, Frisiae et Groningae atq Omlandorum Deputatos, ac eorundem ad Pacis Conventum, qui in hac Urbe Trajecti ad Rhenum habetur, Plenipotentiarios. Qui quidem Ministri Plenariis Potestatibus instructi munitiq, vi earundem, in articulos subsequentes convenerunt.

[1] "de Newmarch, et de Oversley" crossed out.

1

Tractatus ille vulgo de Successione et de Obice, sive Barriere, nominatus qui 29° die Mensis Oct^{ris} Anno D^{mni} 1709 Hagae Comitum, inter Serenissimam Reginam Magnae Britanniae et Dominos Ordines Generales Uniti Belgii conclusus fuit una cum duobus Articulis Separatis eodem die signatis nullius abhinc vigoris virtutisve esse censebitur; dictusq Tractatus articuliq duo praefati rescinduntur jam, irritiq declarantur eodem modo ac si nunquam facti aut ratihabiti fuissent omnes autem alii Pacis, Amicitiae, Unionis, Confoederationisq Tractatus inter praememoratam Regiam Suam Majestatem et Dominos Ordines Generales conclusi, hisce comprobantur confirmanturq, atq eandem vim virtutemq obtinere debent ac si in praesenti hoc Tractatu inserti fuissent.

2

Cum Lege quadam in Parliamento Angliae lata anno 12° Regni nuperi Serenissimi Regis Gulielmi 3^{ii} cui titulus est *An Act for the Further Limitation of the Crown & better securing the Rights & Libertys of the Subject*, Latine, *Actam de alteriori Coronae Limitatione, et meliori securitate Jurium Libertatumq Subditorum*, sancitum declaratumq fuerit, quod post obitum praedicti Regis Reginaeq jam regnantis, Quae tum Princeps Anna Daniae vocabatur, et deficiente Prole ex Reginâ, atq etiam ex Rege supramemoratis oriundâ, Corona Regalisq Gubernatio Angliae, Franciae, atq Hiberniae, et Ditionum eo spectantium deveniret pertineretq ad excellentissimam Principem Sophiam, electricem, et Ducissam viduam Hanoveranam, et ad Haeredes Ejus Protestantes; Cumq ex eo tempore, in pluribus cum Angliae, tum Scotiae Parliamentis, statutum fuerit, ut Successio ad Monarchiam Regni Uniti Magnae Britanniae et Ditionum eo spectantium post dictae Serenissimae Reginae obitum, et sobole ab Eadem deficiente, deveniret pertineretq ad Excellentissimam Principem Sophiam, Haeredeisq Ipsius Protestantes; utq Pontificii omnes atq Ji Eaeve qui cum Pontificiis Matrimonium contraherent, excluderentur a Coronâ Magnae Britanniae, et Ditionum eo spectantium; atq in perpetuum Haereditatem, Possessionem, vel Usufructum earundem habendi incapaces redderentur. Quae quidem Provisio, diversis Parliamenti Actis constituta super Successione antedicta, postea stabilita firmataq fuit Lege quadam in Parliamento Magnae Britanniae latâ Anno sexto Reginae nunc regnantis, cui Titulus est *An Act for the Security of Her Majesty's Person & Government, & of the Succession to the Crown of Great Britain in the Protestant Line*; Latine, *Actam de Securitate Personae et Gubernationis Regiae Sua Majestatis, Successionisq ad Coronam Magnae*

Britanniae in Stirpe Protestantium: Cumq; nulla Potestas extranea neq; Persona ulla quaecumq; jus habeat revocandi in dubium Provisionem aliquam a Parliamento Magnae Britanniae factam, aut sese eidem opponendi quoad Devolutionem Limitationem, Haereditatemve Coronae ejusdem Regiae; Sin autem contigerit ut Potestas aliqua extranea vel Status seu Persona Personaeve quaecunq;, sub specie qualibetcunq;, directé vel indirecté, bello aperto vel Conspiratione proditoriâ, seu vi perfidâ sese opponere vellent Juri Successionis Haeredum Majestatis Suae Regiae, de corpore suo natorum, post Ipsius obitum, vel deficientibus ejusmodi Haeredibus Juri Successionis praedictae Excellentissimae Principis Sophiae aut Haeredum Ejus quorumcunq;, ad quos dicta Successio tum spectaverit secundum Leges et Statuta Magnae Britanniae; Domini Ordines Generalis Foederatarum Belgii Provinciarum promittunt ac spondent, sese omni prorsus tempore, vivente Serenissimâ Reginâ antememoratâ, Ipsi opitulaturos ad propugnandum Jus Successionis ad Coronam Regiam Magnae Britanniae prout per Leges et Statuta ejusdem Regni stabilita determinataq; est; et post obitum antedictae Serenissimae Reginae sese opem laturos Haeredibus ejus de corpore suo natis, iisve deficientibus Serenissimae Principi Sophiae supra memoratae, aut talibus Ipsius Haeredibus ad quos, ut praefatum est, Successio ad Coronam Regiam Magnae Britanniae post obitum Serenissimae Reginae nunc regnantis legitimé spectaverit, ut veniant in ejusdem Possessionem, eandemq; conservent; Obstituros autem, Personae cuilibetcunq; quae Possessioni Coronae antedictae ejusq; conservationi impedimentum aliquod afferre voluerit, secundum ejusmodi Requisitiones atq; ad ea tempora, eoq; modo, ac eâ virium proportione terrâ Mariq; sicuti articulo 14° hujusce Tractatus explicatius dictam est.

3

Quandoquidem Articulo 5° Foederis inter Serenissimum Romanorum Imperatorem Leopoldum, Serenissimam Regem Magnae Britanniae, Gulielmum 3.um, Gloriosae utrumq; Memoriae, et Dominos Ordines Generales Foederati Belgii Hagae Comitum die 7° Septembris anno 1701 confecti cautum provisumq; fuerit ut dicti Foederati omnes nervos intendant, quo recuperent Provincias Hispano-Belgicas ut sint obex et Repagulum; vulgó Barriere, Galliam a Belgio Foederato removens et separans pro securitate Dominorum Ordinum Generalium, quemadmodum ab omni tempore inservierunt, donec Rex Christianissimus eas Milite suo occupavit; Conventum jam concordatumq; est, ut Regia Sua Majestas Magnae Britanniae omni ope atq; opera enitatur in Tractatu Pacis ineundo non solum ut Provinciae Hispano-Belgicae verum Urbes oppidaq; alia, quae opus esse videantur, seu bello partae, sive nondum captae sint, formando ordinum Generalium Repagulo, sive Barriere, inserviant.

4

Tum itaq; in finem pactum constitutumq; est ut Domini Ordines Generales Praesidia collocare, conservare, augere, sive diminuere possint, prout Ipsis visum erit in Locis sequentibus, Scil^{t}. Furnis, Fortalitio Kenoque dicto, Ipris, Menatiaco seu Menin, in Urbe et Arce Fornacensi, Montibus, Caroloregio, in Urbe et Arce Namurcanâ, in Arce Gandovensi, in Fortalitiis la Perle, Philippe et Damme appellatis, Fortalitii S^{ti}. Donati, munitionibus Clusensibus penitus annexi, Proprietas Ordinibus Generalibus concedetur et Fortalitium Rodenhuysen nominatum eis Gandavum diruetur.

5

Sin autem evenerit ut dicti Domini Ordines Generales bello reapse implicati fuerint contra Galliam, aut aperté patuerit Galliam Ipsos aggressuram esse; eo casu Iisdem licitum erit talem Copiarum numerum, quem é re sua esse judicaverint, in eas urbes, oppida, et Fortalitia Provinciarum Hispano-Belgicarum mittere, quas belli ratio et necessitas postulaverint.

6

Licitum porro Ipsis erit in Urbes, Oppida et Fortalitia ubi Praesidia habuerint, commeatum, apparatus bellicos, arma, Tormenta grandiora, Munitionum construendarum materiam, quodcunq; deniq; Praesidiis supradictis et munitionibus idoneum aut necessarium fuerit, sine impedimento, et absq; omni vectigali seu Portorio subvehere.

7

Altememorati etiam Domini Ordines Generales in Urbibus, oppidis et Fortalitiis Articulo 4° recensitis, ubi Praesidia habuerint, tales Gubernatores, Praefectos, Majores, aliosq; officiarios constituere possint prout Ipsis visum erit; adeo ut nullius omnino imperio quoad securitatem locorum supradictorum et Leges sive consuetudines militares subjiciantur, praeter solos unicosq; Ordines Generales, salvis tamen usq; Juribus et Libertatibus cum Ecclesiasticis tum Policitis Serenissimi Imperatoris Caroli Sexti.

8

Licitum insuper erit praefatis Dominis Ordinibus Generalibus dictas Urbes et Fortalitia eodem pertinentia munire, munitionesq; reficere, eo modo quem necessarium esse duxerint atq; adeo ea omnia facere, quae eorundem defensioni conducere posse videantur.

9

Conventum vero cum sit quod Provinciarum Hispano-Belgicarum proprium et supremum Dominium ad Caesaream suam Majestatem pertineat tam earum quae a nupero Hispaniarum Rege Carolo secundo tempore mortis suae possessae fuerant, quam earum quae in ejus possessionem non venerant, quaeq; a Gallia Pacis futurae Transactione cedi contigerit. Necesse itaq; est ut stipulatio fiat, atq; adeo hisce pactum concordatumq; est, ut omnes Reditus (praeter eos, quibus opus erit ad sustinendam Gubernationem civilem) Urbium, Oppidorum, Castellaniarum, Locorumq; ab iis dependentium, quae praesenti hoc Tractatu Repaguli sive Barriere pars fieri debent; quaeq; ad nuperum Hispaniarum Regem Carolum Secundum tempore mortis suae nequaquam pertinebant, in posterum ad Dominos Ordines Generales attinere censebuntur, atq; ab iisdem colligentur in usum sustentationemq; Militum Praesidiariorum, et ad sumptus munitionum, Apothecarum, sive Armamentariorum, aliarumq; rerum suppeditandos. Sub eâ autem speciatim conditione ne Ordines Generales virtute hujus Articuli, vel quocunq; alio nomine, Potestatem sibi unquam sumant, nova Vectigalia in Locis praedictis imponendi, vel antiqua augendi diminuendive. Conventum porro conclusumq; est sub eâdem conditione, haudquaquam vero aliter, ut ad Impensas supramemoratas subministrandas decies centena millia Florenorum quotannis, sive centum millia Imperialium tertio quoq; mense, Dominis Ordinibus Generalibus numerentur, ex certissimis optimisq; proventibus earum partium Provinciarum Hispano-Belgicarum, quae a dicto nupero Hispaniarum Rege tempore mortis suae possessae fuerant.

10

Nulla Urbs, Oppidum, Fortalitium sive Territorium in Provinciis Hispano-Belgicis cedi, transferri, donari aut devenire potest ad Coronam Gallicam vel ad quemquam ex Stirpe Gallicâ, sive id fiat virtute Doni alicujus, seu venditionis, commutationis, Conventionis Matrimonialis, Haereditatis, Successionis ex Testamento, vel ab Intestato, neq;, quocunq; demum titulo, vel quocunq; sit modo, ulla pars ex praedictis Provinciis Potestati authoritative Regis Christianissimi aut Cujusquam ex stirpe Gallica unquam Subjici potest.

11

Quandoquidem vero articulo 9° Foederis supradicte septimo die Septembris anno 1701 facti, constitutum est ut, tempore quo Transactio vel Pax fiet, Foederati inter se convenient praeter alias res de modo quo Domini ordines Generales per obicem antedictum, vulgó Barriere, securi reddantur, Regia Sua Majestas Magnae

Britanniae vi hujusce Pactionis promittit, sese omnem operam collaturam, ut Caesaream suam Majestatem perducat ad ineundum cum Dominis Ordinibus Generalibus Tractatũ iis omnibus, quae superius de obice sive Barriere concordata sunt, consentaneum; Dictaq; Sua Regia Majestas promittit insuper Se studio omni et officiis continuò enisuram, donec Tractatus antememoratus conclusus fuerit, eidemq; confecto Fidejussionem suam sive Garantiam daturam esse.

12

Quandoquidem verò suprema authoritas in Provinciis Hispano-Belgiciis, ex quo ab hoste eas recuperari contigerit, in Regia Sua Majestate Magnae Britanniae et in Dominis Ordinibus Generalibus collocata fuerit, copiaeq; dictae Regiae suae Majestatis et Dominorum Ordinum Generalium maximam partem Urbium, Oppidorum, Fortalitiorumq; ad eas pertinentium, jam nunc Praesidiis occupent, conventum hisce concordatumq; est quod neq; Provinciarum antememoratarum Gubernatio mutabitur, neq; de quapiam ex Urbibus, Oppidis aut Fortalitiis praefatis Militis Praesidiarii deducentur donec Commercia Utilitatesq; Subditorum Magnae Britanniae ad mentem Regiae Suae Majestatis, atq; ibidem Commercia et Utilitates Subditorum Unitarum Belgii Provinciarum ad mentem Dominorum Ordinum Generalium accommodatae fuerint, atq; obex, sive Barriere, Dominorum Ordinum Generalium modo supra designato constitutus fuerit et firmatus.

13

Cum vero usu compertum sit summé necessarium esse, non solúm omnem obstructionem Interruptionemq; aut alia quaecunq; gravamina praevenire, quae Commercio Britannico oriri possint, ex eo quod jus Praesidii Dominis Ordinibus Generalibus in tot Locis, quae fluviis et canalibus imposita sunt, atq; in aliis Provinciarum Hispano-Belgicarum partibus conceditur, verum etiam omnes Fraudes et Collusiones praescindere quae factitari queant ex abusu Privilegii, sive Immunitatis articulo 6° Hujus Tractatus iisdem concessae, pactum conventumq; est ut Subditi Serenissimae Reginae Magnae Britanniae in posterum, tam belli quam pacis tempore, in omnibus locis Provinciarum Hispano Belgicarum, atq; obiciis, sive Barriere, dictis ordinibus Generalibus cedendis, Privilegiis, exemptionibus, Libertatibus, Facilitatibusq; universis, quoad Commercia tam quae Importationem, quam quae Exportationem spectant, fruantur (quibus)[1] unquam olim gavisi sunt, aut gaudere debuerunt; Ut omnibus porro Privilegiis, Exemptionibus, Libertatibus, et Facilitatibus perfruantur, quae Subditis Dominorum Ordinum Generalium in Provinciis Hispano Belgicis et in locis ad

[1] Cf. text of ratification.

obicem sive Barriere, attinentibus, vel jam concesse fuerint, vel unquam in posterum concedantur, eo quidem modo, ut nulli omnino officiario sive civili sive militari, Mercimoniorum, ad dictos Magnae Britanniae Subditos pertinentium, transitum impedire vel tardare unquam permittatur; Spondentibus praefatis Ordinibus Generalibus Sese graves poenas, quantum in Iis situm erit, Illi Illisve irrogaturos qui menti hujusce articuli quovismodo in contrarium egisse coarguantur. Antedicti Ordines Generales sese porro obstringunt mandata sedulo et efficaciter daturos, eademq; stricte observari curaturos, ne commeatus, apparatuum bellicorum &c: quorum in dicto articulo 6° mentio facta est, subvehendorum nomine fraudes ullae committantur, quoad vectigalia rebus Mercatoriis imposita, quae quidem res mercatoriae in Navigiis iisdem aliisve vehiculis una cum dicto commeatu, apparatibus bellicis &c: nec onerabuntur unquam neq; transportabuntur; Quó tamen leges et conditiones singulae instituantur quae generali huic articulo melius et plenius observando necessariae esse queant; Hisce insuper conclusum est, ut Comissarii abutraq; parte nominentur, qui Bruxellis intra 15 dierum spatium a Ratihabitione hujus Tractatûs convenient ad statuendum et praefiniendum inter Se et cum Comissariis Caesareae Suae Majestatis, se quos Ipsa a sua parte nominare voluerit, omnes res rationesq; quae ad Commercia in Provinciis Hispano Belgicis et in locis ad obicem, sive Barriere, pertinentibus spectant, secundum verum sensum mentemq; explicatissimam hujus articuli.

14

Quó veró Fidejussiones, sive Garantiae, vi hujus Tractatûs mutuó susceptae melius certiusq; executioni mandentur, pactum conventumq; est, ut Serenissima Regina Magnae Britanniae, ejusq; Haeredes vel Successores, Requisitione facta à parte Dominorum Ordinum Generalium, et non aliter, auxilia interius expressa subministrabunt ad praestandam obicis, sive Barriere, Fidejussionem, vulgó Garantiam; Similiterq; Domini Ordines Generales, Requisitione factâ ex parte Regiae Suae Majestatis, aut, post obitum Ipsius, Haeredis proximi ex Illâ nati, aut, Eo Jisve deficientibus, successoris proximi Protestantis qui titulum ad Coronam tunc temporis habuerit, virtute Actorum Statutorumq; Magnae Britanniae, et non aliter, auxilia inferius designata subministrabunt, ad praestandam Ipsorum Fidejussionem sive Garantiam, super Successione ad Coronam Magnae Britanniae Pactum ulterius conventumq; est, ut, casu existente, quo Partium contrahentium alterutra requisita fuerit modo supradicto, auxilia quae subministranda erunt secundum proportiones insequentes mittentur; Scil^t. Serenissima Regina Magnae Britanniae, Ejus Haeredes et Successiones, in auxilium Dominorum ordinum Generalium decies mille Pedites mittent, et vicissim Domini Ordines

Generales, in auxilium Regiae Suae Majestatis, Ejus Haeredum Successorumq;, sexies mille Peditis mittent[1] armis bene instructos sub ejusmodi Praefectis aliisq; Officiâriis, et in tales Legiones, vulgo Regimenta, atq; Cohortes distributos, prout Regiae Majestati suae ejusq; Haeredibus et Successoribus, si Ipsa Ipsive auxilium miserint, visum erit; Et quemadmodum Domini Ordines Generales opportunum esse duxerint si ab Ipsis auxilia submittenda fuerint. Tenebitur etiam Pars alterutra viginti Naves Bellicas expedire probé rebus omnibus ornatas munitasq;, atq; auxilia antedicta impensis Partis, quae ea miserit, alentur, instruenturq; in opem et usum Partis quae eadem requisiverit. Sin autem acciderit ut periculum adeo repentinum immineat ut nihil temporis reliqui sit officiosis Intercessionibus adhibendis, adeoq; magnum, ut majorem Copiarum Naviumq; bellicarum numerum postulet, tenebitur tum Pars utravis ab alterâ requisita auxiliorum vim adaugere, Pacem cum Aggressore dirimere, Copiasq; suas omnes terrâ mariq; cum Copiis Partis Bello impetitae conjungere.

15

Conventum porro est ut omnes Reges, Principes, Statusq; qui huic Tractatui accedere cupiant eó invitentur admittanturq;, isto tamen modo, ut dicta Invitatio atq; admissio junctim, et non separatim, a Serenissimâ Reginâ Magnae Britanniae et a Dominis Ordinibus Generalibus proficiscantur.

16

Regia Sua Majestas Magnae Britanniae et Domini Ordines Generales omnia et singula, quae in praesenti Tractatu continentur, confirmabunt ratihabebuntq; intra Spatium quatuor Hebdomadûm a die subscriptiones, vel citius, si fieri poterit;

In quorum fidem, supramemorati Plenipotentiarii, commutatis, hinc inde, Plenipotentiarum suarum Tabulis, Hunc Tractatum Manu Quisq; suâ signarunt, et Sigillis suis confirmaverunt Ultrajecti die $\frac{\text{decimo nono}}{\text{trigesimo}}$ Mensis Januarii, anni a Christo nato millesimi septingentesimi $\frac{\text{duodecimi}}{\text{decimi tertii}}$.

John Bristol, C.P.S.
Strafford

J. v. Randwyk
Willem Buys
B. v. Dussen
F. A. Baron van Reede
Vryh.r tot Renswoude
S. v. Goslinga
Graaf van Kniphuysen.

[1] Inserted in margin.

Articulus Separatus.

Quandoquidem Domini Ordines Generales Uniti Belgii proposuerunt, quod Ditionum Suarum limites in Flandriâ tam arctē et tam incongrué constituti, ut nonnullis in locis territorium alterius Flandriae ad ipsa ibidem Dominorum Ordinum Fortalitia pertingat, unde plurima oriuntur incommoda, uti et ex eo patuit quod sub initium belli praesentis evenit, quum Fortalité constructio sub ipsis munimentis loci, vulgo Sas de Gend appellati, tentata fuit, eo nempe praetextu quod illud in alterius Domini territorio fieret, et cum proinde ad ejusmodi aliaq, incommoda evitanda necessarium sit ut territorium Dominorum Ordinum ibidem ita protendatur, ut loca urbes et Fortalitia eâ in parte ditionum suarum satis in tuto sint; Regia Sua Majestas Magnae Britanniae, ista rationum momenta probans, per hunc Articulum Separatum, qui ejusdem ac Tractatus hodie conclusus, vigoris erit, promittit spondetq,, sese in pactis Caesaream suam Majestatem inter et Dominos Ordines Generales ineundis, operam et officia collaturam esse, quó per Caesaream suam Majestatem Dominis Ordinibus Generalibus talis territorii Flandrici pars in proprietatem perpetuam quae praedictis aliisq, incommodis evitandis, et limitatibus ibidem apte amplificandis, meliusq, constituendis omnino sufficiat.

In quorum Fidem suprammemorati Plenipotentiarii commutatis hinc inde Plenipotentiarum suarum Tabulis, hunc Articulum manu quisq, sua signarunt et sigillis suis confirmaverunt, Ultrajecti: Die $\frac{\text{decimo nono}}{\text{trigesime}}$ Mensis Januarii Anni a Christo nato millesimi septengentesimi $\frac{\text{duodecimi}}{\text{decimi tertii}}$.

John Bristol, C.P.S., etc. *J. v. Randwyk, etc.*

III. Barrier Treaty between *Great Britain*, the *Emperor* and the *States General*. November 1715.[1]

Comme il a pleu au Tout Puissant de rendre depuis quelque tems La Paix à L'Europe, et que rien n'est plus désirable, et nécessaire que de rétablir et assurer par tout, autant que se peut, la Sûreté, et la tranquillité commune, et publique, et que Leurs Hautes Puissances, Les Seigneurs États Généraux des Provinces Unies, se sont engagées de remettre Les Pays-bas à Sa Majesté Impériale et Catholique

[1] Public Record Office. State Papers Foreign. Treaties (Germany, Empire). S.P. 108/137.

Charles VI: Selon qu'il a été stipulé, et arrêté par le Traité fait à La Haye le Sept de Septembre Mille Sept Cent et un, entre Sa Majesté Impériale Léopold de glorieuse mémoire, Sa Majesté Britannique Guillaume III. aussi de glorieuse Mémoire, et les dits États Généraux, que les dites Puissances conviendroient ensemble, sur ce qui regarderoit leurs Intérêts réciproques, particulièrement, par rapport à la manière dont on pourroit établir la Sûreté des Pays-bas, pour servir de Barrière à La Grande Bretagne, et aux Provinces Unies, et par rapport au Commerce des Habitants des dits Pays-bas, de la Grande Bretagne, et de ceux des Provinces Unies, et qu'à présent Sa Majesté Impériale et Catholique Charles VI. à qui les dits Pays-bas seront remis par ce Traité, Sa Majesté Britannique George tous deux aujourdhuy régnants, et tous deux Héritiers et Successeurs Légitimes des dits Empereur et Roy, et Les Seigneurs États Généraux des Provinces Unies agissants en cela par les mêmes principes d'amitié, et dans la même intention de procurer et d'établir la dite sureté mutuelle, et d'affermir de plus en plus une étroite union, ont nommé, commis, et établi pour cette fin pour Leurs Ministres Plénipotentiaires, scavoir Sa Majesté Impériale et Catholique, Le Sieur Joseph Lothaire Comte de Koenigsegg, son Chambellan, Conseiller de Guerre, et Lieutenant Général de ses Armées, Sa Majesté Britannique Le Sieur Guillaume Cadogan Écuyer, Son Envoyé Extraordinaire auprès de Leurs Hautes Puissances Les Seigneurs États Généraux des Provinces Unies, Député au Parlement de la Grande Bretagne, Maître de la Garderobe Lieutenant Général de ses Armées, et Colonel du Second Régiment de ses gardes, et Les États Généraux Les Sieurs Bruno Van der Dussen, Ancien Bourguemaître, Sénateur et Conseiller Pensionnaire de la Ville de Gouda, Assesseur au Conseil des Heemrades, de Scheeland, Dykgraaf de Crimpenerwaard: Adolphe Henry Comte de Rechteren, Seigneur de Almelo, et de Urieseveen et C[a]. Président des Seigneurs États de la Province d'Overyssel, Drossard du Quartier de Zalland: Scato de Goslinga, Sénateur de la Ville de Groningue: Et Adrien de Borssele, Seigneur de Gueldermalsen et C[a]. Sénateur de la Ville de Flessingue, Les trois premiers Députés à L'Assemblée des Seigneurs États Généraux de la part des Provinces d'Hollande, et Westfrise, d'Overyssel, et de Groningue, et Ommelanden et le quatrième Député au Conseil d'État des Provinces Unies, Les quels étant assemblés dans la Ville d'Anvers qui d'un commun consentement avoit été nommée pour le lieu du Congrès, et ayant échangé Leurs Pleinpouvoirs dont les Copies sont insérées à la fin de ce Traité, après plusieurs Conférences, sont convenus pour et au nom de Sa Majesté Impériale, et Catholique, de Sa Majesté Britannique, et des Seigneurs États Généraux de la manière comme il s'en suit.

Article 1er.

Les États Généraux des Provinces Unies remettront à Sa Majesté Impériale et Catholique en vertu de la Grande Alliance de l'année Mille sept Cent et un, et des Engagements dans les quels Ils sont entrés du depuis immédiatement après l'échange des Ratifications du présent Traité, toutes les Provinces et Villes des Pays-bas, et Dépendances, tant celles qui ont été possédées par le Feu Roy d'Espagne Charles IId. de Glorieuse Mémoire, que celles qui viennent d'être cédées par Feue Sa Majesté Le Roy très Chrétien aussi de glorieuse mémoire; Les quelles Provinces et Villes ensemble tant celles que l'on remettra par ce présent Traité que Celles qui ont déjà été remises, ne seront désormais, et ne composeront, en tout ou en partie, qu'un Seul et indivisible, inaliénable, et incommutable Domaine qui sera inséparable des États de la Maison d'Autriche en Allemagne, pour enjouir Sa Majesté Impériale et Catholique, ses successeurs et Héritiers en pleine, irrévocable Souveraineté, et Propriété, sçavoir à l'égard des premières Provinces comme en a joui, ou d'en jouir le feu Roy Charles IId. de Glorieuse Mémoire conformément au Traité de Riswick, et à l'égard des autres Provinces de la manière, et aux conditions qu'elles ont été cédées, et remises aux dits Seigneurs États Généraux par le Feu Roy très Chrétien de glorieuse mémoire, en faveur de la très Auguste Maison d'Autriche, et sans autre charges, ou Hypothécations, constituées de la part des États Généraux, et à leur profit.

Article 2d.

Sa Majesté Impériale et Catholique promet et s'engage qu'aucune Province, Ville, Place, Forteresse ou Territoire des dits Pays-bas ne pourra être cédé, transféré, donné, ou écheoir à la Couronne de France, ni à aucun Prince, ou Princesse de la maison et Lignée de France, ni autre qui ne sera pas Successeur, Héritier, et Possesseur des États de la Maison d'Autriche en Allemagne, soit par donation, vente, échange, contract de Mariage, hérédité, succession Testamentaire ou ab Intestato, ni sous quelque autre Titre ou prétexte que ce puisse être, de sorte qu'aucune Province, Ville, Place, Forteresse, ni Territoire des dits Pays-bas ne pourra jamais être soumis à aucun autre Prince qu'aux seuls successeurs des dits États de la Maison d'Autriche, à la réserve de ce qui déjà a été cédé au Roy de Prusse et de ce qui sera cédé par le présent Traité aux dits Seigneurs États Généraux.

Article 3e.

Comme la sûreté des Pays-bas Autrichiens dépendra principalement du nombre des Troupes qu'on pourra avoir dans les dits Pays, et dans les Places qui formeront la Barrière qui a été promise aux Seigneurs États Généraux par la Grande Alliance; Sa Majesté Impériale et Catholique, et Leurs Hautes Puissances sont convenus d'y entretenir chacun à leurs propres fraix toujours un Corps de Trente mille, à Trente cinq mille hommes des quels Sa Majesté Impériale et Catholique donnera trois cinquièmes, et Les États Généraux deux Cinquièmes, bien entendu que si sa Majesté Impériale et Catholique diminue son Contingent, Il sera au pouvoir des dits États Généraux, de diminuer le Leur, à proportion, et lorsqu'il y aura apparence de Guerre ou d'attaque, on augmentera le dit Corps jusques à quarante mille hommes suivant la même proportion, et en Cas de Guerre effective, on Conviendra ultérieurement des Forces qui se Trouveront nécessaires.

La Répartition des dites Troupes en tems de Paix, pour autant qu'elle concerne les Places commises à la garde des Troupes de Leurs Hautes Puissances sera faite par Elles seules, et la répartition du reste par Le Gouverneur Général des Pays-bas en se donnant part réciproquement des dispositions qu'ils auront faites.

Article 4e.

Sa Majesté Impériale et Catholique accorde aux États Généraux Garnison privative de Leurs Troupes dans les Villes, et Châteaux de Namur, et de Tournay, et dans les Villes de Menin, Furnes, Warneton, Ypres, et le Fort de Knoque, et s'engagent Les États Généraux de ne pas emploier dans Les dites Places des Troupes qui bienqu'à leur solde pourroient être d'un Prince, ou d'une Nation qui soit en guerre, ou suspecte d'être dans des Engagements contraires aux Intérêts de Sa Majesté Impériale et Catholique.

Article 5e.

On est convenu qu'il y aura dans la Ville de Dendermonde Garnison Commune, qui sera composée pour le présent d'un Bataillon de Troupes Impériales, et d'un Bataillon de celles des États Généraux, et que si dans La suitte il pourroit être nécessaire d'augmenter la dite Garnison, cette Augmentation se fera également des Troupes de part et d'autre, et de commun concert. Le Gouverneur sera mis de La part de L'Empereur le quel aussi bien que Les subalternes, prêteront serment aux États Généraux de ne jamais rien faire, ni permettre dans la dite Ville, qui puisse être préjudiciable à Leur Service par rapport à la Conservation de la Ville et de La Garnison, et il sera obligé par le dit serment de donner libre passage à Leurs Troupes, toutes et quante fois qu'ils le souhaitteront, pourveu qu'il en soit requis préalablement, et que ce ne soit que pour un nombre modique à La fois: Le tout selon le Formulaire dont on est Convenu, et qui sera inséré à La fin de ce Traité.

Article 6e.

Sa Majesté Impériale et Catholique consent aussi que dans les Places cy dessus accordées aux États Généraux pour y tenir Leurs Garnisons privatives, Ils y puissent mettre tels Gouverneurs, Commandants, et autres Officiers, qui composent L'État Major qu'Ils jugeront à propos, à condition qu'ils ne seront pas à charge de Sa Majesté Impériale et Catholique, ny aux Villes et Provinces, si ce n'est pour Le Logement convenable, et les Émoluments provenant des Fortifications, et que ce ne soient pas des personnes qui pourroient être désagréables ou suspectes à Sa dite Majesté, pour des raisons particulières à alléguer.

Article 7e.

Les quels Gouverneurs, Commandants, et Officiers seront entièrement, et privativement dépendants et soumis aux seuls ordres, et à la seule Judicature des États Généraux pour tout ce qui regarde la défense, garde, sûreté, et toute autre affaire militaire de Leurs Places, mais seront obligés les dits Gouverneurs aussi bien que Leurs Subalternes à prêter serment à Sa Majesté Impériale, et Catholique, de garder les dites Places fidèlement à la Souveraineté de la Maison d'Autriche, et de ne se point ingérer dans aucune autre affaire, selon le Formulaire dont on est convenu, et qui est inséré à La fin de ce Traité.

Article 8e.

Les Généraux se rendront réciproquement tant dans les Villes où il y aura Garnison de Sa Majesté Impériale et Catholique, que dans celles qui sont confiées à la garde des Troupes de Leurs Hautes Puissances, les honneurs accoutumés selon leur caractère, et la manière de chaque service, et au cas que Le Gouverneur Général des Pays-bas vînt dans les Places commises à la garde des Troupes des États Généraux, on lui rendra les honneurs qu'il est accoutumé de recevoir dans les Places des Garnisons de Sa Majesté Impériale et Catholique, et pourra mêmes y donner la parole, Le tout sans préjudice de L'Article Sixième.

Et les Gouverneurs, et en leur absence les Commandants donneront part au dit Gouverneur Général des dispositions par eux faites, pour la sûreté et garde des Places confiées à leurs soins, et ils auront des égards convenables pour les changements que le dit Gouverneur Général pourroit juger y devoir être faits.

Article 9e..

Sa Majesté Impériale et Catholique accorde l'exercice de la Religion aux Troupes des États Généraux par tout où elles se trouveront en Garnison, mais çela dans des endroits particuliers convenables et proportionnés au nombre de la garnison, que Les Magistrats assigneront et entretiendront dans Chaque Ville et Place où il n'y en a pas déjà d'assignés, et aux quels endroits on ne pourra donner aucune marque extérieure d'Église, et on enjoindra sévèrement de part et d'autre aux Officiers Politiques et militaires, comme aussi aux Ecclésiastiques et à tous autres qu'il appartient, d'empêcher toute occasion de scandale et de Contestation qui pourroit naître sur le sujet de la Religion, Et quand il naîtra quelque dispute ou difficulté, on les applanira à l'aimable de part et d'autre. Et quant à La Religion par rapport aux Habitants des Pays-bas Autrichiens, Toutes choses resteront, et demeureront sur le même pied qu'elles étoient pendant le Règne du Roy Charles IId. de glorieuse mémoire.

Article 10e.

Toutes les Munitions de guerre, Artillerie, Armes des États Généraux, comme aussi les matériaux pour les Fortifications, les grains en tems de disette, Les vivres pour mettre en magazin, lorsqu'il y aura apparence de guerre et de plus les draps, et fournitures pour l'habillement des soldats que l'on vérifiera devoir être emploiés à cet usage passeront librement, et sans paier aucuns Droits, ou Péages, au moyen des Passeports qui seront demandés et accordés sur la spécification signée, à condition néanmoins qu'au premier Burreau de Sa Majesté Impériale et Catholique, où les dites Provisions, matériaux, Armes, et montures entreront, qu'à l'Endroit où elles devront être déchargées, les batteaux et autres Voitures pourront être duement visités, pour empêcher qu'on n'y mêle d'autres marchandises et pour éviter toute Fraude et abus, contre Les quels Il sera toujours libre de prendre telles précautions que La suitte du tems, et L'expérience feront juger nécessaires sans qu'il sera permis aux Gouverneurs et Leurs Subalternes d'empêcher en quoy que ce soit l'effet de cet Article.

Article 11e.

Les États Généraux pourront changer Leurs Garnisons, et les dispositions des Troupes dans les Villes, et Places commises à Leur Garde privative, selon qu'ils le trouveront à propos, sans qu'on puisse empêcher ou arrêter le passage des Troupes qu'Ils y enverront de tems à autre, ou Celles qu'Ils en tireront sous quelque prétexte que ce puisse être, pourront mems les dites Troupes quand le cas le requéreroit passer par toutes les Villes de Braband et de Flandre, et par tout le plat pays, faire des ponts, tant sur le Canal entre Bruges and Gandt, que sur tous les autres Canaux, et sur toutes les Rivières qu'elles trouveront dans leurs routes, à condition néanmoins que ce seront des Troupes d'un Prince, ou d'une Nation non en guerre avec Sa Majesté Impériale et Catholique ni suspecte d'aucun engagement ou Liaison contraire à ses Intérêts, comme il est dit cy-dessus en L'Article quatrième, et que préalablement il en sera donné connoissance et réquisition faite au Gouverneur Général des Pays-bas, avec le quel on réglera les routes et les autres besoins par quelcun qui en aura la commission de Leurs Hautes Puissances.

On observera le Règlement fait par Les États Généraux sur le passage des Troupes comme il est observé dans Leur propre Pays.

Et les États Généraux tâcheront de faire les dits changements de garnison, ainsi que les dispositions nécessaires pour cela de la manière qu'elles soient le moins qu'il se pourra à charge et incommodité des habitants.

Article 12e.

Comme La Sûreté commune demande en tems de guerre, ou dans un éminent[1] danger de guerre que Les États Généraux envoient leurs Troupes dans les Places qui se trouveront le plus exposées au péril d'être attaquées, ou d'être surprises, Il est convenu entre Sa Majesté Impériale et Catholique et Les États Généraux que Leurs Troupes seront receues dans les dites Places autant qu'il sera nécessaire pour Leur défense, quand le cas viendra évidemment à exister, bien entendu que cela se fasse d'accord, et de concert avec le Gouverneur Général des Pays-bas.

Article 13e.

Les États Généraux pourront à leurs fraix et dépens faire fortifier les susdites Villes et Places soit par de nouveaux Ouvrages, ou en faisant réparer les vieux, les entretenir, et généralement pourvoir à tout ce qu'Ils trouveront nécessaire, pour la Sûreté et défense des

[1] Mistake for "imminent"; cf. text of ratification.

dites Villes et Places, à la réserve qu'Ils ne pourront pas faire construire de nouvelles Fortifications, sans en avoir donné connoissance préalable au Gouverneur Général des Pays-bas, et avoir entendu son avis et ses considérations là dessus, et sans qu'on pourra les porter à la charge de L'Empereur, ou du Pays, qu'avec consentement de Sa Majesté.

Article 14e.

Pour La Sûreté de communication entre les Provinces Unies, et les Villes et Places de la Barrière, Sa Majesté Impériale et Catholique aura soin de faire en sorte que les Lettres et Messagers, tant ordinaires qu'Extraordinaires pourront passer librement pour aller et venir dans les Villes et Places de la Barrière, et par celles des autres Pays, à condition que les dits Messagers ne se chargeront pas des Lettres ou des Paquets des Marchands, ou autres particuliers, les quels tant pour Les Places de la Barrière, que pour toute autre part, devront être remis aux Bureaux des Postes de Sa Majesté Impériale et Catholique.

Article 15e.

Pour ce qui regarde l'Artillerie, Magazins, et Provisions de guerre que Leurs Hautes Puissances ont dans les Villes et Places qu'elles remettent à Sa Majesté Impériale et Catholique, Il leur sera permis de les faire transporter sans aucun empêchement, et sans paier aucuns Droits, ou Péages, tant celles qu'Elles y ont fait conduire Elles-mêmes, que L'Artillerie marquée de leurs armes, perdue dans la dernière guerre, et leur appartenantes d'ailleurs, qu'Elles auront trouvé dans les dites Places; A moins que Sa Majesté Impériale et Catholique, ne souhaitte de prendre la dite Artillerie et Munitions de guerre pour son compte, et ne convienne du prix avec Leurs Hautes Puissances avant la reddition des Places; Et quant à L'Artillerie et Munitions qui sont présentement dans Les Places commises à la garde des Troupes des États Généraux, elles seront laissées à leur garde et Direction, suivant les Inventaires qui en seront dressés, et signés de part et d'autre avant l'échange des Ratifications du présent Traité, sans qu'il sera permis de les faire transporter ailleurs, que d'un commun consentement; Et restera la propriété à Sa Majesté Impériale et Catholique pour autant qu'il s'en est trouvé dans les dites Places, au tems de leur cession ou reddition.

Article 16e.

En cas que les Provinces des Pays-bas Autrichiens fussent attaqués, et qu'il arrivât (ce qu'à Dieu ne plaise) que Les Armées des Ennemis entrassent dans le Brabant, pour y agir, et faire le siège de quelques Places dans la dite Province, ou de quelcune de Celles qui en font la Barrière, Il sera permis à Leurs Hautes Puissances de faire occuper, et prendre poste par Leurs Troupes, dans les Villes, et Endroits sur le Demer, depuis L'Escault jusques à la Meuse; Comme aussi d'y faire des retranchements, des Lignes, et des Inondations pour empêcher les progrès ultérieurs des Ennemis, autant que la raison de guerre le pourra demander, pourveu que le tout se fasse de concert avec le Gouverneur Général des Pays-bas.

Article 17e.

Comme il conste par l'expérience de la guerre passée que pour mettre en sûreté les Frontières des États Généraux en Flandre, Il falloit y laisser plusieurs Corps de Troupes si considérables, que L'Armée se trouvoit beaucoup affoiblie par là. Pour prévenir cet Inconvénient, et pour mieux assurer les dites Frontières à l'avenir Sa Majesté Impériale et Catholique cède aux États Généraux, tels Forts, et autant de Territoire de la Flandre Autrichienne Limitrose de Leurs dites Frontières qu'on aura besoin pour faire les Inondations nécessaires, et pour les bien couvrir depuis L'Escault Jusques à la mer dans les endroits où elles ne sont pas déjà suffisamment assurées, et où elles ne scavroient l'être par des inondations sur les seules Terres déjà appartenantes aux États Généraux. Pour cette fin Sa Majesté Impériale et Catholique agrée et approuve que pour L'avenir les Limites des États Généraux en Flandre, commenceront à la mer entre Blankenberg, et Heyst, à l'endroit où il n'y a point de Dunes, moyennant qu'ils n'y feront pas bâtir, ny ne permettront pas qu'on bâtisse des Villages ou des maisons auprès du dit Poste, ny ne souffriront point aucun établissement de Pêcheurs ou d'y faire des Écluses à la mer.

Et promettent de plus Leurs Hautes Puissances que si Elles trouvent bon de faire construire quelques Fortifications à la tête de Leurs nouvelles Limites Elles auront soin de ne pas diminuer la force de la Digne et nonseulement se chargeront des Fraix extraordinaires qui pourroient être causés à l'occasion des dites Fortifications mais mêmes dédommageront les Habitants de la Flandre Autrichienne de toutes les portes qu'ils pourroient souffrir au cas que la Mer vint à faire des inondations par les Fortifications susdites.

On tirera du Poste susnommé une Ligne droite sur le Goteweegje, d'où la Ligne continuera vers Heyst: De Heyst elle ira sur le Driehoek, et Sivarte Sluys, De là sur le Fort de St Donas le quel Sa Majesté Impériale et Catholique cède en propriété, et souveraineté à Leurs Hautes Puissances (moyennant que les portes des Écluses au dit Fort seront et resteront ôtées en tems de Paix) et cède pareillement le Terrain situé au Nord de la Ligne cy dessus marquée.

Du Fort de St Donas les nouvelles Limites des États Généraux s'étendront jusques au Fort de St Job, d'où on regagnera les Anciennes près de la Ville de Middelbourg, Les quelles Limites on suivra le long du Zydlingo-dyk, jusques à l'endroit où Le Eeckeloosewatergang, et Le Waterloop se rencontrent à une Écluse.

En suite de quoy on suivra le Graaf Jansdyk, jusques au Village de Bouchoute (aux Intéressés des Écluses du quel on permet de Les remettre où elles ont été cy devant) et du dit Bouchoute on continuera La Ligne droite pour regagner les Anciennes Limites des États Généraux.

Sa Majesté Impériale et Catholique cède aussi en pleine et entière souveraineté aux États Généraux le Territoire situé au Nord de La dite Ligne.

Et comme pour Leur entière Sûreté, Il est nécessaire que L'Inondation soit continuée de Bouchoute jusques au Canal du Sas de Gandt, Le long de Graaf Jansdyk il sera permis en tems de guerre à Leurs Hautes Puissances d'occuper, et faire fortifier toutes les Écluses qui se trouveront dans le Graaf Jansdyk et Zydlingsdyk.

A l'égard de la Ville de Sas de Gand, Les Limites seront étendues jusques à la distance de deux mille pas Géométriques, pourveu qu'il n'y aie point de Villages compris dans cette étendue.

Et pour La Conservation du bas Escault, et la communication entre la Brabandt, et la Flandre des États Généraux, Sa Majesté Impériale et Catholique cède en pleine et entière propriété, et souveraineté aux États Généraux Le Village et Polder de Doel, comme aussi les Polders de St Anne et Ketenisse.

Et comme en tems de guerre il sera besoin pour plus de sûreté, de former des inondations par les Écluses entre les Forts de la Marie et de La Perle, Sa Majesté Impériale et Catholique remettra aussitôt que La Barrière sera attaquée, ou la guerre commencée, La Garde du Fort de Perle, à Leurs Hautes Puissances, et celle des Écluses. Bien entendu que la guerre venant à cesser, Elles remettront ces écluses, et le dit Fort de Perle, à Sa Majesté Impériale et Catholique, comme aussi celles qu'Elles auront occupées dans le Graaf Jansdyk et Zydlingsdyk. Les États Généraux ne pourront faire aucune inondation en tems de paix, et se croiant obligés d'en former en tems de guerre, Ils en donneront connoissance préalable au Gouverneur Général des Pays-bas, et en concerteront avec Les Généraux, Commandants les Armées au Pays-bas. Promettant de plus que si à l'occasion de la cession de quelques Écluses (dont les Habitans de la Flandre Autrichienne conserveront le libre usage en tems de paix) Ils vinssent à souffrir quelque dommage, ou préjudice, tant par les

Commandants, que par d'autres Officiers Militaires, que non seulement, Les États Généraux y remédieront incessamment, mais aussi qu'ils dédommageront Les Intéressés.

Et puisque par cette nouvelle situation des Limites, il faudra changer les Bureaux pour prévenir les fraudes, En quoy Sa Majesté Impériale et Catholique et Leurs Hautes Puissances sont également intéressées, On conviendra des Lieux pour l'établissement des dits Burreaux, et des précautions ultérieures, qu'on jugera convenir de prendre.

Il est de plus stipulé par cet Article qu'une juste évaluation sera faite avant la Ratification du présent Traité, des revenus que le Souveraineté des Terres qui se Trouveront cédées à Leurs Hautes Puissances par cet Article, comme aussi de ce que le Souverain a profité par le renouvellement des Octroys, sur le pied qu'ils ont été accordés depuis trente ans en deçà, a être déduits et défalqués, sur le subside annuel de Cinq cent mille Écus.

Et la Religion Catholique Romaine sera conservée et maintenue dans les Lieux cy dessus cédés, en tout sur le pied qu'elle y est exercée actuellement, et qu'elle l'a été du tems du Roy Charles II[d] de glorieuse mémoire, et seront de mêmes conservés et maintenus tous les Privilèges des habitans.

Le Fort de Roden Huysen sera rasé, et les différents touchant le Canal de Bruges seront remis à la décision d'Arbitres neutres, à choisir de part et d'autre; Bien entendu que par la Cession du Fort de St Donas, ceux de la Ville de L'Écluse n'auront pas plus de droit sur le dit Canal, qu'avant cette Cession.

Article 18[e]

Sa Majesté Impériale et Catholique, cède à Leurs Hautes Puissances Les États Généraux à perpétuité en pleine souveraineté, et Propriété dans le haut Quartier de Gueldre, la Ville de Venlo avec sa Banlieue, et le Fort de St Michel; de plus le Fort de Stevenswaert avec son Territoire ou Banlieue, comme aussi autant de Terrain qu'il faudra pour augmenter leurs Fortifications en de çà de La Meuse, et promet Sa dite Majesté, de ne faire jamais bâtir, ou permettre qu'un autre bâtisse aucune Fortification de quelque nom que ce soit, à la distance d'une demi Lieue de la dite Forteresse.

Sa Majesté Impériale et Catholique cède de plus aux États Généraux, L'Ammanie de Monfort, consistant (à l'exception des Villages de Swalmt et Elmt qu'elle se réserve) dans les petites Villes de Neustadt, et d'Echt, avec les Villages Suivants, sçavoir, Ohe, et Laeck, Roosteren, Braght, Besel, Belfen, Vlodorp, Postert, Berg, Lin, et Montfort, pour être possédés par les dits États Généraux, de la manière que les a possédés, et en a joui Sa Majesté Le Roy Charles II^{d} de glorieuse mémoire, avec les Préfectures, Burgs, Fiefs, Terres, Fonds, Cens, Rentes, Revenus, Péages, de quelque nature qu'ils soient, subsides, Contributions, et Collectes, Droits Féodaux, Domaniaux, et autres quelconques appartenants aux dits Lieux cédés cy dessus; Le tout pourtant sans préjudice, et sauf touts les Droits qui pourront compéter à Sa Majesté Le Roy de Prusse; Et ce nonobstant toutes Exceptions, Prétensions, ou Contradictions, faites ou à faire, pour troubler les États Généraux dans la paisible posession des Lieux cédés par le présent Article; tous Pactes, Conventions, ou Dispositions contraires au présent Article, étant censés nuls, et de nulle valeur. Bien entendu que cette Cession se fait avec cette Clause expresse, que Les Status, Anciennes Coutumes, et généralement touts les Privilèges Civils, et Ecclésiastiques, tant à l'égard des Magistrats, et des particuliers, que des Églises, Convents, Monastères, Écoles, Séminaires, Hospitaux, et autres Lieux Publics, avec toutes Leurs Appartenances, et Dépendances, de même que le Droit Diocésin de L'Évêque de Ruremonde, et généralement tout ce qui regarde les Droits, Libertés, Immunités, fonctions, usages, Cérémonies, et L'Exercice de La Religion Catholique seront conservés, et subsisteront sans y apporter changement, ou innovation, ny directement, ny indirectement, dans tous Les Lieux cy dessus cédés, de la manière que du tems du Roy Charles II^{d} de glorieuse mémoire, et selon qu'on l'expliquera de part et d'autre plus amplement, en cas qu'il arrive quelque dispute sur ce sujet; Et ne pourront être données les Charges de Majestrature, et telles autres de Police, qu'à des personnes qui soient de la Religion Catholique.

Le droit de Collation de Bénéfices qui a été jusques icy au souverain appartiendra doresenavant à L'Évêque de Ruremonde, à Condition que les dits Bénéfices ne pourront être données qu'à des personnes qui ne seront pas désagréables aux États Généraux, pour des raisons particulières à alléguer.

Il est aussi stipulé, que Les États Généraux, ne prétendront pas d'avoir acquis par la Cession de la Ville d'Echt aucun Droit de Judicature, ou d'Appel par rapport au Chapitre de Thorn, ou autres Terres de L'Empire, et il sera libre à Sa Majesté Impériale et Catholique de nommer tel endroit qu'il conviendra pour la dite Judicature ou Appel.

Et puisque Les Habitans de la partie du Haut Quartier qui vient d'être cédée ne pourront plus porter Leurs procès en cas d'appel à la Cour de Ruremonde, Il sera libre à Leurs Hautes Puissances d'établir une Cour d'appel pour Leurs Sujets, dans tel Lieu de la Province qu'Elles trouveront convenir.

On est convenu de plus, que les Droits d'entrée et de sortie, qui se lèvent tout le long de La Meuse, ne pourront être haussés, ny baissés, en tout, ou en partie, que d'un commun Consentement, des quels Droits Sa Majesté Impériale et Catholique tirera à son profit, ceux qui se Lèvent à Ruremonde et à Navagne, et Les Seigneurs États Généraux ceux qui se Lèvent à Venlo; Et comme les dits Droits sur La Meuse en Général, comme aussi ceux sur L'Excault subsidiairement sont affectés au Payement de deux rentes distinctes sçavoir une de quatre vingt mille et une de vingt mille florins par an, en vertu de la transaction passée et conclué le vingt sixième de Décembre, Mille Six Cent quatre vingt et sept, avec feue Sa Majesté de la Grande Bretagne, Guillaume IIIe. On est convenu que Leurs Hautes Puissances, à cause de la Cession susmentionée, subviendront à Sa Majesté Impériale et Catholique dans le Payement des dittes Rentes, et autres dettes, qui pourront y être hypothéquées annuellement, et à proportion du produit des Droits d'entrée et de sortie qu'Elles recevront le tout suivant Les Constitutions mêmes des dites rentes.

Et quant aux debtes et charges contractées et constituées sur la Généralité du Haut Quartier,[1] Les États Généraux, concourront dans le Payement d'iceux pour leur quote part selon la Proposition[2] portée par le Matricule de tout le dit haut Quartier. Touts les Documents et papiers qui concernent le haut Quartier de Gueldre resteront comme cy devant dans les Archives à Ruremonde; Mais on est convenu qu'il en sera formé un Inventaire ou Regître à l'intervention des Commissaires de Sa Majesté Impériale et Catholique, de sa Majesté Prussienne, et des Seigneurs États Généraux, et Copie authentique sera donnée du dit Inventaire à Chacune des trois Puissances, pour avoir toujours libre accès à tous les papiers et Documents dont Elles pourroient avoir besoin pour la partie qu'Elles possedènt dans le dit haut Quartier de Gueldre, et dont Copie Authentique leur sera délivrée à La première réquisition.

Article 19e.

En considération des grands fraix, et Dépenses extraordinaires aux quelles Les États Généraux sont indispensablement obligés, tant pour entretenir le grand nombre de Troupes qu'Ils se sont engagés par le présent Traité, de tenir dans les Villes cy dessus nommées, que pour subvenir aux grosses charges absolument nécessaires pour L'Entretien et Réparation des Fortifications des dites Places, et pour les pourvoir de munitions de guerre et de bouche, Sa Majesté Impériale et Catholique s'engage et promet de faire paier annuelle-

[1] "de Gueldre" omitted; cf. text of ratification.
[2] "proportion" omitted; cf. text of ratification.

ment aux États Généraux la somme de Cinq Cent mille écus, ou douze Cent cinquante mille Florins monnoye d'Hollande par dessus le convenu de la partie du Haut Quartier de Gueldre cédée en propriété par Sa Majesté Impériale et Catholique aux États Généraux par le dix huitième Article du présent Traité; Comme aussi par dessus les Fraix pour le Logement des Troupes selon le Règlement fait en l'année Mille six cent quatre vingt et dix huict de la manière que l'on en conviendra en détail; La quelle somme de cinq cent mille Écus, ou douze cent cinquante mille florins monnoye d'Hollande, sera assurée et hypothéquée par cet Article généralement sur touts les revenus des Pays-bas Autrichiens, y compris les Pays cédés par la France, et spécialement sur les Revenus les plus clairs et liquides des Provinces de Brabant, et de Flandre et sur ceux du Pays, Villes, Châtellenies, et Dépendances cédées par la France, selon qu'on est convenu plus spécifiquement par un Article séparé, tant pour L'Hypothèque que pour les moiens et termes de les percevoir; Et commencera le dit Payement du subside de Cinq cent mille écus, ou douze cent cinquante mille Florins monnoye d'Hollande du jour de la signature du présent Traité, sur quoy seront déduites au prorata du tems, les Revenus des Villes, Châtellenies, et dépendances cédées par la France, écheus depuis le dit Jour jusques au jour que les dits Pays-bas seront remis à Sa Majesté Impériale et Catholique pour autant que Les États Généraux les auront receus.

Article 20e.

Sa Majesté Impériale et Catholique confirme et ratifie par cet Article les Capitulations accordées aux Provinces et Villes des Pays-bas cy devant appellés Espagnols du tems de leur réduction sous l'obéissance de Sa dite Majesté ainsi que l'administration Générale du dit Pays y exercée par la Grande Bretagne et Les États Généraux des Provinces Unies, ayans représenté le Légitime Souverain par Leurs Ministres qui ont résidé à Brusselles, et par le Conseil d'État commis au Gouvernement Général des dits Pays-bas; En suitte du pouvoir et des Instructions qui lui ont été faites de la part des deux Puissances, tant en matière de Régale, de Justice, de Police, que de Financer, comme aussi L'Administration particulière des États des Provinces, des Collèges, des Villes, et des Communautés au Plat-pays, de mêmes que des Cours Souveraines de Justice, et autres Cours, et Juges subalternes, les quels Actes de Police, Régale Justice, et Finances, subsisteront et sortiront leur plein et entier effect, selon la teneur des dits Actes, et des Sentences rendues; Le tout de la même manière comme s'ils avoient été faits par le Souverain Légitime du Pays, et sous son Gouvernement.

Article 21e.

Tout ce qui est compris dans L'Article précédent sera aussi observé, ratifié, et maintenu de la part de Sa Majesté Impériale et Catholique à l'égard de haut Quartier de Gueldre et des Pays conquis sur la France (dont le Roy Charles IId. de glorieuse mémoire, n'étoit pas en possession à son décès) pour toutes les Dispositions faites au nom et de la part des États Généraux des Provinces Unies.

Et pour ce qui est des Bénéfices et Dignités Ecclésiastiques, ceux qui en ont été pourveus et qui se trouvent en possession ne pourront être dépossédés, et ceux qui ne sont pas encore en possession y seront admis, sans qu'on puisse s'y opposer, que par les voyes et dans l'ordre de La Justice, selon les Loix et Coutumes du Pays.

Article 22e.

Sa Majesté Impériale et Catholique reconnoit et promet de satisfaire les obligations, qui ont été passées de la part de Sa Majesté Catholique Charles II de glorieuse mémoire, pour les Levées d'argent que Leurs Hautes Puissances ont fait négotier pour Sa dite Majesté dont la Liste est jointe au bas de cet Article; Et comme on n'a point encore remis aux États Généraux les obligations des États des Pays-bas Espagnols pour la somme de deux cent mille florins par an, à fournir par eux pour le payement des Intérêts et pour remboursement d'un Capital de quatorze cent mille florins Levés à Intérest en l'an mille six Cent quatre vingt et dix huict pour être employés aux nécessités des Frontières des dits Pays-bas Espagnols, et de quatre années d'Intérest portant la somme de deux cent vingt quatre mille florins dont le dit Capital de quatorze cent mille Florins est augmentée, les quelles obligations le dit Roy Charles IId. de glorieuse mémoire avoit promis de faire tenir, sans que cela s'est fait, Sa Majesté Impériale et Catholique promet par cette de faire passer les obligations par Les États des Provinces du dit Pays-bas et de les faire délivrer incessamment après aux dits États Généraux conformément à la Teneur de la dite Obligation de Sa Majesté Catholique du trentième de May Mille six cent quatre vingt et dix huict, à la première Convocation des États, ou au plus tard dans le terme de deux mois après L'Échange des Ratifications de ce Traité.

(Here follows a memorandum of the debts of His Majesty Charles II amounting to 8,396,000 f.)

Article 23e.

Pareillement Sa Majesté Impériale et Catholique reconnoît, approuve, et confirme toutes les Levées d'argent (dont la Liste est jointe au bas de cet Article) qu'on a été obligé de faire pour le Payement de plusieurs nécessités indispensables pour la Conservation des Pays bas Espagnols, et pour L'Entretien des Troupes de Sa Majesté Impériale et Catholique, pendant le Gouvernement Provisionnel de la Grande Bretagne, et des États Généraux des Provinces Unies, et fait par Leurs Hautes Puissances de concert avec Sa Majesté de la Grande Bretagne. Promettant Sa Majesté Impériale et Catholique d'y satisfaire, et de faire deuement enrégîtrer les dites Négociations dans les Chambres des Finances, et des Comptes, et d'en faire délivrer Acte en forme à Leurs Hautes Puissances, et de faire payer le Capital et les Intérêts hors des Fonds et Hypothèques tant principales que subsidiaires affectées pour cette fin: Sans que Sa Majesté Impériale et Catholique pourra apporter si ce n'est de l'aveu des États Généraux aucun changement à la Direction ou à L'Administration des Hypothèques sur les quelles les Négociations ont été faites, mais qu'Elle les laissera à Leurs Hautes Puissances conformément à la teneur des obligations, et si ces fonds n'étoient point suffisants, ce qu'il y manquera sera supplée par Les États des Provinces des dits Pays-bas Autrichiens.

(Here follows a memorandum of the debts incurred by the Provisional Government of Her Majesty Queen of Great Britain and their Highnesses the States General in the Low Countries amounting to 4,618,975 f.)

Faisant les susdites Levées ensemble la somme de quatre millions six cent dix huict mille neuf cent Cinquante cinq Florins, L'Employ de la quelle aussi bien que de la somme de Cinq Cent Cinquante mille Florins que les Receveurs des Droits d'entrée et de sortie en Flandre ont fourni en Lettres de change aux États Généraux en l'an mille sept Cent et dix, de cent mille Florins qu'ils ont receu du Receveur des Médianates, et de Cent cinq mille florins, salvo errore calculi, qu'ils ont receu de la Troisième Chambre du Conseil de Flandre, a été vérifié au Ministre Plénipotentiaire de Sa Majesté Impériale et Catholique de la manière que cela est expliqué plus particulièrement par sa Déclaration mise au bas de L'État des Négotiations et argent fourni, et de L'Employ des dits deniers signé ce même jour.

Article 24e.

On procédera aussitôt que faire se pourra à la Liquidation du Payement fait des Intérêts et du Capital des Emprunts mentionnés dans les deux Articles précédents dans la quelle Liquidation ne sera porté à la charge de Leurs Hautes Puissances que tout ce qui se trouvera payé effectivement et réellement, en vertu des dites obligations et sans que de la part de Sa Majesté Impériale et Catholique on pourra faire contre le Payement des dits Intérêts quelque difficulté ou Prétension de rabats ou Diminution à cause de non possession des Hypothèques, Confiscation en tems de guerre, dépravation des Hypothèques, à cause de diminution de Droits d'entrée et sortie ou autre cause ou prétexte quelconque.

Et sans qu'à cause de cette Liquidation on pourra de la part de Sa Majesté Impériale et Catholique discontinuer le Payement pour le recouvrement des Intérêts, et Termes de remboursement, dans lequel il sera continué conformément aux Conditions portées par les obligations Jusques à ce qu'il constera que tous les Emprunts et Intérêts diseux seront entièrement acquittés et remboursés, après quoy Les Hypothèques seront deuement déchargées et restituées.

Article 25e.

De plus sont ratifiés et confirmés par le présent Article touts les Contracts pour le pain, chariots, et Fourrages des Troupes Impériales et Palatines, faits par les Ministre des deux Puissances à Bruselles ou par le Conseil d'État, commis au Gouvernement des Pays-bas, sur la réquisition des dits Ministres et sont pareillement confirmés et ratifiés touts les Payemens déjà faits à ce sujet, par le Conseil des Finances, et les ordres donnés par le dit Conseil pour assigner le restant de ce qui est deu pour les dits pain, Fourrages, et Chariots sur les Droits d'exérescence des quatre Espèces, Ensuitte des Réquisitions du Conseil d'État, sans que les dits Droits d'exérescence puissent être divertés à d'autres usages sous quelque prétexte que ce puisse être, avant que les Entrepreneurs qui ont livré les dits pain, Fourage, et Chariots soient entièrement satisfaits selon la teneur de leurs Contracts, En suitte des Réquisitions des Ministres des deux Puissances, et des ordres du Conseil d'État, et de celui des Finances.

Article 26e.

Pour ce qui regarde le Commerce, on est Convenu que Les Navires, marchandises, et Denrées, venant de la Grande Bretagne, et des Provinces Unies, et entrant dans les Pays-bas Autrichiens, de même que les Navires, marchandises, et Denrées sortant des dits Pays-bas vers la Grande Bretagne, et les Provinces Unies ne payeront les Droits d'entrée, et de sortie, que sur le même pied qu'on les Lève à présent, et particulièrement tels qu'ils ont été réglés avant la signature du présent Traité, selon la réquisition faite au Conseil d'État à Brusselles par les Ministres des deux Puissances en datte du sixième de Novembre, et qu'ainsi le tout restera, continuera, et subsistera généralement sur le dit pied, sans qu'on y puisse faire aucun changement, innovation, Diminution, ou augmentation sous quelque prétexte que ce puisse être jusqu'à ce que Sa Majesté Impériale et Catholique, Sa Majesté Britannique, et Les Seigneurs États Généraux en conviendront autrement par un Traité de Commerce à faire le plustôt qu'il se pourra, demeurant au reste le Commerce, et tout ce qui en dépend, entre Les Sujets de Sa Majesté Impériale et Catholique dans les Pays-bas Autrichiens, et Ceux des Provinces Unies en tout, et en partie, sur le pied établi; et de la manière portée par les Articles du Traité fait à Munster le trentième Janvier, Mille six cent quarante huict entre Sa Majesté le Roy Philippe Quatrième de glorieuse mémoire et les dits Seigneurs États Généraux, concernant le Commerce, les quels Articles viennent d'être confirmés par le présent Article.

Article 27e.

Que les Fortifications, et tous les Ouvrages de la Citadelle de Liège de même que celles du Château d'Huy aussi avec touts les Forts et ouvrages seront rasés, et démolis, sans qu'ils puissent être jamais rebâtis ou rétablis; Bien entendu que la dite démolition se fera aux Dépens des États et du Pays de Liège, à qui les Matériaux resteront pour être vendus, et transportés ailleurs. Le tout aux ordres et sous la Direction des États Généraux qui enverront pour cette fin des personnes capables pour avoir la Direction des dites Démolitions aux quelles on commencera de travailler immédiatement après la Signature du présent Traité et que l'on achevera en dedans trois mois, ou plustôt s'il se peut, et que Cependant les Garnisons des États Généraux ne sortiront des dites Places avant que la Démolition ne soit achevée.

Article 28e.

Et pour plus grande sûreté, et Exécution du présent Traité promet, et s'engage Sa Majesté Britannique de la confirmer, et de le garantir dans touts ses points et Articles, comme Elle le confirme, et le garantit par celui cy.

Article 29^e

Le présent Traité sera ratifié et approuvé par Sa Majesté Impériale et Catholique, par Sa Majesté Britannique, et par Les Seigneurs États Généraux des Provinces Unies, et les Lettres de Ratification seront délivrées dans le terme de six semaines, ou plustôt si faire se peut à compter du jour de La signature.

En foy de quoy nous Ministres Plénipotentiaires de Sa Majesté Impériale et Catholique, de Sa Majesté Britannique, et des Seigneurs États Généraux en vertu de nos Pouvoirs respectifs avons les dits noms signé ces Présentes de nos seings ordinaires, et à Icelles fait apposer les Cachets de nos Armes. Fait à Anvers ce quinze de Novembre Mille sept Cents quinze.

J. L. C. de Koenigsegg
Wm. Cadogan

B. v. Dussen
Le Comte de Rechteren
S. L. Gockinga
Adr. M. de Borsselle
Sigr. v. Geldermalsen.

(Here follows "Declaration des Droits d'entrée et sortie qui se lèvent aux Pays-bas Autrichiens à l'esgard de la Grande Bretagne et des Provinces Unies".)

Article Séparé

Comme dans l'Article dix neufième du Traitté de la Barrière pour Les États Généraux des Provinces Unies dans les Pais-bas Autrichiennes conclu ce jourdhuy, quinzième de Novembre, Mille sept Cent et Quinze entre Sa Majesté Impériale et Catholique, Sa Majesté Britannique et les dits Seigneurs États Généraux, on est convenu de s'expliquer plus spécifiquement par un Article séparé au Sujet des Hypothèques et des moyens de percevoir le subside y mentionné. Sa Majesté Impériale et Catholique, pour assurer et faciliter d'autant plus le payement du dit Subside de cinq cens mille Écus ou douze Cens cinquante mille florins monnoye D'Hollande par An, accordé et stipulé par le dit Article, assigné spécialement sur les Pais, les Villes, Châtellenies et Dépendances, cédées par la France, annuellement la somme de six Cens et dix mille Florins monnoye D'Hollande selon la Répartition suivante, a sçavoir.

Sur la Ville de Tournai cinquante cinq mille florins. Sur la Châtellenie de Tournai, dit le Tournesis, vingt cinq mille florins. Sur la Ville et Verge de Menin Quatre vingts dix Mille florins, Et sur la Partie de la Flandre occidentale qui a été cédée par la France à répartir sur les Villes, Châtellenies et Dépendances, suivant le

Transport de Flandre Quatre cens Quarante mille florins. Et le Restant sur les subsides de la Province de Braband un tiers faisant la somme de deux cens treize mille, trois Cens, trente et trois et un tiers florins et sur ceux de la Province de Flandre deux tiers, faisant la somme de quatre Cens vingt et six mille, six Cens Soixante six et deux tiers florins, faisant les dites somes respectives ensemble la susdites somme Totale de cinq cens mille Écus, ou douze Cens cinquante mille florins, monnoye D'Hollande.

La Portion de la Province de Braband est assignée sur le Contingent des sept Quartiers D'Anvers et des autres Districts de Braband dans les subsides de cette Province. Et la Portion de la Province de Flandre sur le Contingent du Pais de Waas y compris Beveren du Pais D'Oudenbourg, du France de Bruges, du Pais D'Alost et de la Ville et Pais de Dendermonde dans le subside de cette Province.

Et pour assurer d'autant plus de Payement régulier des susdites sommes respectives Sa Majesté Impériale et Catholique promet et s'engage Que le Payement se fera de trois en trois mois à commencer du jour de la Signature du Présent Traitté, à payer à l'écheance du terme, et au défaut du dit Payement à la fin des dits trois mois.

Ordonne Sa Majesté Impériale et Catholique dès à présent et par ce Traitté aux États des Provinces et Départemens et les Receveurs des subsides, tant Ordinaires Qu'extraordinaires de même que ceux de ses droits et Domaines, hors desquels le payement se doit faire conformément à la Répartition cy dessus Qu'en vertu de cet Article et sur une Copie d'iceluy, ils auront à payer incessamment à chaque écheance et sans délay au Receveur Général des dits États Généraux ou à ses Ordres les sommes cy dessus marquées et sans attendre autre Ordre ou Assignation, ce présent Article leur devant servir D'Ordre et D'Assignation dès à présent et pour lors.

Et le dit Payement leur sera passé en Compte à la Charge de Sa Majesté Impériale et Catholique, comme s'il avoit été fait à elle même.

Faute de Quoy, ou bien, en cas que les dits États n'accordassent pas avec la promptitude nécessaire les Subsides pourront les États Généraux procéder aux moyens de Contrainte et d'exécution et même par voye de fait contre les Receveurs, États et Domaines des dites Provinces et Départemens, les quels Sa Majesté Impériale et Catholique, y soumet en vertu de cet Article, le tout sans préjudice du Droit de Leurs Hautes Puissances sur les autres Revenus du Souverain par dessus le subside des Provinces, comme sont les Droits d'entrée et de sortie, Impôts, Tailles, Péages et autres Domaines.

De plus on est convenu, que le payement du dit subside, ne pourra être Retardé, moins refusé, sous prétexte de Compensation,

Liquidations ou autres Prétentions de quelque nom ou nature qu'elles puissent être.

Et aura cet Article Séparé la même Force que le dit Traité de la Barrière et tout comme s'il y étoit inséré de mot à mot, et sera ratifié dans le même tems que ce Traité.

En foy de quoy nous Ministres, Plénipotentiaires de Sa Majesté Impériale et Catholique, de Sa Majesté Britannique et Des Seigneurs États Généraux, avons signé le présent Article, et y avons fait apposer Les Cachets de Nos Armes à Anvers ce Quinzième de Novembre Mille sept Cens et Quinze.

J. L. C. de Koenigsegg
Wm. Cadogan

B. v. Dussen
Le Comte de Rechteren
S. L. Gockinga
Adr. M. de Borsselle
Sigr. v. Geldermalsen.

BIBLIOGRAPHY

SOURCES

I. ENGLISH SOURCES IN MSS.

Public Record Office. State Papers Foreign, Holland, Flanders, Germany (Empire), Foreign Entry Books and Treaty Papers.

Journal of the Commissioners of Trade and Plantations.

British Museum.

Strafford Papers (chiefly copies of correspondence in the P.R.O., but important for the year 1712, Add. MSS. 22205).

Stepney Papers.

Coxe Papers.

Blenheim Archives. Marlborough Papers, 1705–10.

II. PRINTED ENGLISH SOURCES

British Diplomatic Instructions, France, ed. Wickham Legge, 1925.

Correspondence of Bolingbroke, ed. Parke. London, 1798 (requires to be supplemented by letters in S.P. Foreign, Holland, at P.R.O.).

Hardwicke State Papers, 1778.

Royal Historical Manuscripts Commission, Appendices III, IV and V, Harley Papers.

Marlborough's Despatches, ed. Sir John Murray, 1845.

Correspondence Diplomatique entre Marlborough, Heinsius et Hop, ed. Vreede, 1850.

Wentworth Papers, ed. Cartwright, 1883.

III. DUTCH SOURCES IN MSS.

Rijksarchief, *The Hague*.

Legatie Archief (official documents on foreign policy).

Heinsius Archives (much more valuable than official documents).

Archives of the States of Holland.

Gouda. Notes on the Assembly of the States of Holland 1709–13 (Memoranda kept by one of the Deputies from Gouda, important in giving comments of the Deputies before the States of Holland came to a Resolution).

Gemeente-Archief, *Amsterdam*.

General Archives.

Resolutions of the town of Amsterdam.

British Museum.

Add. MSS. 20985, Buys Papers, a collection of papers relating to the Treaty of Utrecht.

IV. TREATIES

Dumont, *Corps Universel Diplomatique du Droit des Hommes*, 1726–31.
Actes et Mémoires concernant la Paix d'Utrecht.
A general Collection of Treaties from 1642 to the end of the Reign of Queen Anne.

V. PAMPHLETS

In the British Museum.

A letter to the Examiner concerning the Barrier Treaty, 1713.
The Barrier Treaty Vindicated, 1712. Stephen Poyntz. F. Hare, *Works*, Vol. IV.
The Dutch Barrier Our's, 1712.
Some Remarks on the Barrier Treaty. Swift, 1711.

In the Koninklijke Bibliotheek, The Hague.

Een dialogue tusschen een Vlaminck en Hollander over het Werck van de Barriere, 1715.

VI. ADDITIONAL PRINTED SOURCES

Recueil des Instructions données aux Ambassadeurs et Ministres de France, ed. Sorel, 1884, etc. Paris, Autriche, Hollande.
Archiv für Oest. Geschichtsquellen, vol. XVI, 1856. Correspondenz zwischen Carl VI und Wratislaw.

GENERAL WORKS

SEVENTEENTH AND EIGHTEENTH CENTURIES

Aitzema, *Saken van Staet en oorlogh in en omtrent de vereenigte Nederlanden*, 1621–68.
Basnage, *Annales des Provinces Unies*, 1719–26.
Colbert, Jean, Marquis de Torcy, *Mémoires*, ed. Michaud et Poujoulet, 1850.
—— *Journal Inédit, pendant les années* 1709–11, ed. Masson. Paris, 1884.
Goslinga, *Mémoires*, 1857.
Lamberty, *Mémoires pour servir à l'histoire du XVIIIe siècle* (14 vols.), 1735–40.
Swift, *History of the Last Four Years of Queen Anne*, 1758.
—— *Journal to Stella*, ed. Bohn.
De la Torre, *Mémoires et Négociations Secrètes de diverses Cours de l'Europe*. The Hague, 1721–5.
Wagner, *Historia Josephi.*
Wagenaar, *Vaderlandsche historie*, 1749–59.

NINETEENTH AND TWENTIETH CENTURIES

Arneth, A. R. von, *Prinz Eugen*, 1858. Eugen's *Feldzüge*, 1876.

Blok, *History of the Dutch People*. London, 1912. Translated by Ruth Putnam.

Bussemaker, "De Republiek der vereenigde Nederlanden in haar staatkundige Betrekkingen gedurende de eerste Jaren na den Vrede van Utrecht". *Gids*, July, 1899.

—— "De Republiek der Vereenigde Nederlanden en de Keurvorst koning George I". *Bijdragen voor vaderl. Geschiedenis*, vol. IV, 1900, p. 263.

Campbell, *Lives of the Chancellors*.

Chance, J. R., *George I and the Northern War*. London, 1909.

Coxe, *Life of Marlborough*. London, 1818–19.

Dollot, *Les Origines de la neutralité de la Belgique et le système de la Barrière*. Paris, 1902.

Edwards, *James Stanhope and British Foreign Policy*. London, 1925.

Elzinga, *Het Voorspel van den Oorlog van* 1672. Haarlem, 1926.

Gachard, *Histoire de la Belgique au Commencement du* 18*e siècle*, 1882.

—— *Documents Inédits concernant l'Histoire de la Belgique*.

Geyl, P., "Nederland's Staatkunde in de Spaansche Successieoorlog". (*Mededeelingen der Koninklijke Akademie van Wetenschappen*, Afdeeling Letterkunde Deel 68, Serie B, No. 6.)

Hewins, *English Trade and Finance*, 1892.

Hubert, *Garnisons de la Barrière*.

Huisman, *La Belgique Commerciale*. Bruxelles, 1902.

Klopp, *Der Fall des Hauses Stuart*. Vienna, 1875–88.

Landau, *Geschichte Kaiser Karls VI als König von Spanien*. Stuttgart, 1889.

Legrelle, *La diplomatie française et la Succession d'Espagne*, 1888–92.

Mahon, *History of the War of the Spanish Succession*, 1832.

Michael, *Englische Geschichte im* 18*ten Jahrhundert*. Berlin-Leipzig, 1921.

Noorden, von, *Europäische Geschichte im* 18*ten Jahrhundert*, 1870–82.

Pirenne, *Histoire de la Belgique*. Bruxelles, 1900, etc.

Rahlenbeek, *Histoire du Système de la Barrière*.

Reginald, H., "Gispert Cupar's Diary". *Revue Historique*, 1876.

Rive, *Nederland en Pruisen*.

Salomon, *Geschichte des letzten Ministeriums königin Annas von England*, 1899.

Weber, O., *Der Friede von Utrecht*. Gotha, 1891.

—— *Die Quadrupel Allianz*. Vienna, 1887.

Willequet, "Histoire du Système de la Barrière". (*Annales des Universités de la Belgique*, vol. VI, 1848.)